"The balance of biblical a............., ..., ...g ....tra-tions, and life-changing applications make this commentary a must-have addition to the library of every pastor and everyone else who wants to understand and apply the Gospel of John."

Stephen Davey, Th.M., D.D., senior pastor, Colonial Baptist Church, Cary, North Carolina; president, Shepherds Theological Seminary, Cary, North Carolina

"Matt and Joshua provide an excellent resource on John's Gospel. With a clear outline of content, a concise purpose for writing, and a faithful handling of the text as it points to Jesus, the authors give the reader a valuable resource for study and preaching. They herald a clear message to remind the reader, 'The gospel is the good news that you no longer have to wander about in the darkness and despair of sin, but you can enjoy the light of righteousness through Jesus Christ' (p. 27). I commend this commentary as it will prove beneficial for many, for years to come."

Lane Harrison, D.Min., lead pastor, LifePoint Church, Ozark, Missouri

"The Gospel of John has no shortage of commentaries, raising the obvious question: what sets this one apart from all the others? The unique contribution of Matt Carter's work is rooted in his personal profile. Carter is both a highly successful church planter and long-tenured pastor who has built and led a large church through text-driven preaching. A church holding forth the truth in the heart of one of the most socially liberal cities in the country. A church that has multiplied itself many times over through planting new churches in their own city and in some of the most difficult countries on the planet. As a trustworthy, twenty-first-century pastor-theologian, Carter has not only produced a commentary, but a sermon and bible study starter for preachers and teachers seeking to accurately interpret and prophetically apply the Word of God to this radically changing culture."

Nathan Lino, senior pastor, Northeast Houston Baptist Church; president, Southern Baptists of Texas Convention

"This commentary on John is incredibly practical. Written from a pastor's heart, it provides both deep theological insight and practical application. Both ministers of the gospel and people in the pew need this work!"

Jerry McCorkle, executive director, SpreadTruth Ministries, Bloomington, Illinois

"As a pastor for more than twenty-one years, I appreciate a commentary that stands on solid scholarship while at the same time fitting comfortably in the pulpit. Any pastor, teacher, or small group leader will be able to open this book and find a Christ-centered resource at their fingertips which will enhance their preaching or teaching ministry. In fact, any believer reading this Christ-centered exposition will find themselves learning more about the Lord Jesus Christ and His place in Scripture. The Christ-Centered Exposition Commentary series seeks to exalt Jesus. This volume succeeds in meeting that goal!"

Eric Peacock, D.Min., senior pastor, Westchester Baptist Church, High Point, North Carolina

"As the church navigates an age of profound confusion and doubt, the Gospel of John serves as an immoveable anchor. This commentary is an invaluable tool for believers in understanding and applying God's Word to our lives as we combat the litany of competing worldviews that surround us. This work remains faithful to the timeless truth of Scripture while challenging contemporary issues in a thoughtful manner. Believers will be well-served by using this book to supplement their efforts to delight in God's Word and to live by faith in Jesus, the Savior of the world."

Kevin Peck, lead pastor, The Austin Stone Community Church, Austin, Texas

"John said the purpose of his Gospel was 'so that you may believe that Jesus is the Christ, the Son of God, and that by believing you may have life in his name' (20:31, ESV). This volume is a literary GPS in helping us arrive at that place. Carter and Wredberg wed exegetical integrity with sermonic beauty, and they combine historical accuracy with contemporary relevance, all to show us Jesus. Pastors, teachers, and all who love the Bible and its Christ will be helped greatly by this work."

Jim Shaddix, Ph.D., D.Min., W. A. Criswell Professor of Expository Preaching, Southeastern Baptist Theological Seminary, Wake Forest, North Carolina

"Josh and Matt have given us a gospel-fueled treatment of John. You will discover, as I have, that this volume exposes areas you thought you had conquered. Worship your way through this exposition by these two Christ–Centered Ninjas."

Kyle Shearin, D.Min., pastor of preaching and vision, Faith Family Church, Oak Grove, Kentucy

CHRIST-CENTERED
Exposition

AUTHORS Matt Carter and Josh Wredberg

SERIES EDITORS David Platt, Daniel L. Akin, and Tony Merida

CHRIST-CENTERED

Exposition

EXALTING JESUS IN

JOHN

HOLMAN®

REFERENCE

BRENTWOOD, TENNESSEE

B&H Publishing Group
Brentwood, Tennessee
All rights reserved.

ISBN: 978-0-8054-9654-3

Dewey Decimal Classification: 220.7
Subject Heading: BIBLE. O.T. JOHN—
COMMENTARIES\JESUS CHRIST

Printed in the United States of America

8 9 10 11 12 • 27 26 25 24 23

SERIES DEDICATION

Dedicated to Adrian Rogers and John Piper. They have taught us to love the gospel of Jesus Christ, to preach the Bible as the inerrant Word of God, to pastor the church for which our Savior died, and to have a passion to see all nations gladly worship the Lamb.

—David Platt, Tony Merida, and Danny Akin
March 2013

AUTHORS' DEDICATIONS

For my son John Daniel,

I cannot express in words how thankful I am to God for placing you in my life. Your kindness, leadership, intelligence, and love for Jesus are a daily inspiration to me. I love you with all my heart.

—Matt

For Cari,

Your love is shown in the way you lay down your life daily for our family. I cannot adequately express my affection and gratitude for you. I love you, Dear.

—Josh

TABLE OF CONTENTS

John

ACKNOWLEDGMENTS

I, Matt, would like to thank Danny Akin for believing in me enough to ask me to be a part of this project; Jim Shaddix, Tony Merida, and Charles Harvey for the countless hours spent with me during the research phase of this project; Stephen Crawford, Halim Suh, Brice Johnson, and Travis Whitehead for your editing and contributions to the final work; Chris Osborne for teaching me to love and preach God's Word; and lastly, Jesus, the subject of this commentary and the reason we labor, write, and preach.

I, Josh, would like to thank my brothers, Chris, Jason, and Justin, for walking the path of Christ with me; my parents, Dave and Sandy, for teaching me who Jesus is from the second I was born; both Redeemer and Calvary, who patiently listened as I labored with them through this Gospel; Erin Judd for deciphering my scribbles and protecting my schedule; and finally, my sons, Jack, Max, and Caed, who graciously put up with their father's failure to live like Jesus. May you see the beauty of Jesus even through my brokenness.

SERIES INTRODUCTION

Augustine said, "Where Scripture speaks, God speaks." The editors of the Christ-Centered Exposition Commentary series believe that where God speaks, the pastor must speak. God speaks through his written Word. We must speak from that Word. We believe the Bible is God breathed, authoritative, inerrant, sufficient, understandable, necessary, and timeless. We also affirm that the Bible is a Christ-centered book; that is, it contains a unified story of redemptive history of which Jesus is the hero. Because of this Christ-centered trajectory that runs from Genesis 1 through Revelation 22, we believe the Bible has a corresponding global-missions thrust. From beginning to end, we see God's mission as one of making worshipers of Christ from every tribe and tongue worked out through this redemptive drama in Scripture. To that end we must preach the Word.

In addition to these distinct convictions, the Christ-Centered Exposition Commentary series has some distinguishing characteristics. First, this series seeks to display exegetical accuracy. What the Bible says is what we want to say. While not every volume in the series will be a verse-by-verse commentary, we nevertheless desire to handle the text carefully and explain it rightly. Those who teach and preach bear the heavy responsibility of saying what God has said in his Word and declaring what God has done in Christ. We desire to handle God's Word faithfully, knowing that we must give an account for how we have fulfilled this holy calling (Jas 3:1).

Second, the Christ-Centered Exposition Commentary series has pastors in view. While we hope others will read this series, such as parents, teachers, small-group leaders, and student ministers, we desire to provide a commentary busy pastors will use for weekly preparation of biblically faithful and gospel-saturated sermons. This series is not academic in nature. Our aim is to present a readable and pastoral style of commentaries. We believe this aim will serve the church of the Lord Jesus Christ.

Third, we want the Christ-Centered Exposition Commentary series to be known for the inclusion of helpful illustrations and theologically driven applications. Many commentaries offer no help in illustrations, and few offer any kind of help in application. Often those that do offer illustrative material and application unfortunately give little serious attention to the text. While giving ourselves primarily to explanation, we also hope to serve readers by providing inspiring and illuminating illustrations coupled with timely and timeless application.

Finally, as the name suggests, the editors seek to exalt Jesus from every book of the Bible. In saying this, we are not commending wild allegory or fanciful typology. We certainly believe we must be constrained to the meaning intended by the divine Author himself, the Holy Spirit of God. However, we also believe the Bible has a messianic focus, and our hope is that the individual authors will exalt Christ from particular texts. Luke 24:25-27,44-47 and John 5:39,46 inform both our hermeneutics and our homiletics. Not every author will do this the same way or have the same degree of Christ-centered emphasis. That is fine with us. We believe faithful exposition that is Christ centered is not monolithic. We do believe, however, that we must read the whole Bible as Christian Scripture. Therefore, our aim is both to honor the historical particularity of each biblical passage and to highlight its intrinsic connection to the Redeemer.

The editors are indebted to the contributors of each volume. The reader will detect a unique style from each writer, and we celebrate these unique gifts and traits. While distinctive in their approaches, the authors share a common characteristic in that they are pastoral theologians. They love the church, and they regularly preach and teach God's Word to God's people. Further, many of these contributors are younger voices. We think these new, fresh voices can serve the church well, especially among a rising generation that has the task of proclaiming the Word of Christ and the Christ of the Word to the lost world.

We hope and pray this series will serve the body of Christ well in these ways until our Savior returns in glory. If it does, we will have succeeded in our assignment.

David Platt
Daniel L. Akin
Tony Merida
Series Editors
February 2013

John

Introduction: The Purpose of the Gospel of John

JOHN 20:30-31

NTRD.

Ex.)

Every semester on the first day of class I would sit in my seat with a feeling of dread. The professor would walk us through the syllabus as I desperately hoped not to hear the dreaded words *term paper*. When I had to write term papers, I distinctly remember my professors making a big deal about the thesis statement. The thesis statement gives the purpose of the paper. It's the point of the paper—what you're arguing for or attempting to prove. Everything in the paper is supposed to support the thesis statement. The Gospel of John is no different. The Gospel writer gives us a clear and distinct thesis in John 20:30-31:

> *Jesus performed many other signs in the presence of his disciples that are not written in this book. But these are written so that you may believe that Jesus is the Messiah, the Son of God, and that by believing you may have life in his name.*

We can summarize John's thesis in one word: *believe*. He says, "I've written this book, including these particular accounts, so that you might believe." John witnessed nearly three years of stories, sermons, and conversations, but he didn't include them all. He selected certain ones— the ones that would help us believe.

CULTURAL

x.)

The current religious culture in America loves to talk about *belief* and *believing*. Those spiritual buzzwords are often used generically and end up devoid of meaning. Contemporary spirituality trumpets not belief in an object or a person but rather a *belief in belief*. It goes something like this: "It doesn't matter *who* you believe or *what* you believe. All that matters is *that* you believe." There's a belief in belief.

For twenty-five years the high priest of this philosophy in the United States was Oprah Winfrey. She didn't care *what* you believed; she just wanted you *to* believe. She was convinced that if you believed something, your life would improve. A few years ago she had an atheist on her show. The atheist described the sense of wonder she experienced when she stood at the edge of the ocean. Here was Oprah's response: "Well, I don't call you an atheist then. . . . I think if you *believe in the awe and the*

3

wonder and mystery then that is what god is. . . . It's not a bearded guy in the sky" (cited in Stedman, "Oprah"). Oprah was peddling a brand of spirituality that revolved around believing in belief. As long as a person has faith, he or she is fine. She ignores the object of faith.

John's Gospel doesn't call us to believe in belief or to put our faith in faith. His teaching on belief is much deeper and more robust and infinitely more life giving than any modern, pop-culture philosophy. In the course of twenty-one chapters, the Gospel writer will answer three questions:

- What do we need to believe?
- What does it mean to believe?
- Why do we need to believe?

Question 1: What Do We Need to Believe?

We need to believe that Jesus is the Christ and that Jesus is the Son of God (v. 31). What does it mean that **Jesus is the Christ**? *Christ* is not Jesus's last name. People would have identified him as Jesus of Nazareth or Jesus the carpenter's son. *Christ* is a title, and John tells us early on in his Gospel what it means. In chapter 1 he records an encounter between two brothers, Andrew and Simon Peter. Andrew has just seen Jesus and runs to find Simon. He tells his brother, "'We have found the Messiah' (which is translated 'the Christ')" (1:41).

Christ is a title synonymous with "Messiah," and *Messiah* is a term with roots in the Old Testament. The Old Testament focuses on one called "Messiah" whom God would send. By the time Jesus came on the scene, the nation of Israel had been waiting for centuries for the Messiah to come. As we walk through the Gospel of John, we'll see this expectant climate Jesus entered. He came to a people who were waiting for the Christ.

When John identifies Jesus as the Christ, he's not saying a person just needs to acknowledge that Jesus is the one called "Messiah" but that one must believe that Jesus is the one who will fulfill all of the promises God made to his people. The promises of God tie the entire Old Testament together, and they all center on a person. The Old Testament is not a collection of stories but rather one story. It's a single story of God creating man, man rebelling against God, and God sending his Son to reconcile man back to God. John is saying, "You must believe Jesus is that person. Jesus is the promise keeper. All of God's promises come true in him." What are some of those promises of God fulfilled in Christ?

(margin note: GEN 3:15, LORD EVANGELION)

- The first promise is found in Genesis 3. Mankind has just sinned against God, and Adam and Eve are learning about the consequences of their sin. In the midst of their punishment, God promises to send a son, born from the seed of a woman, who would fix everything that sin had broken.

(margin note: PS. 2:2, "HIS ANOINTED" or "MESSIAH")

- In Psalm 2 we find a promise that the Christ will end all injustice and rebellion. Kings and leaders oppress people and make a mockery of justice, but the Christ will come to put an end to their reign. He will judge them for their wickedness, and only those who run to him will find mercy.

(margin note: ISA. 53:5)

- In Isaiah 53 we find the promise of a Suffering Servant. God's servant, the Christ, will be perfectly righteous. He will be the only person who never sins. But he will be punished and killed. He will willingly offer his perfect life as the payment for our sins. He takes the guilty's punishment so the guilty can be declared innocent.

(margin note: DAN 7: 9-14, "SON OF MAN")

- The prophet Daniel records a vision of God ruling in heaven (ch. 7). In his vision one who looks like a man comes before God, and God gives him a kingdom that never ends. His eternal kingdom is also universal—it includes people from every tribe, tongue, and nation.

So when John says we need to believe that Jesus is the Christ, he's making a sweeping statement. We need to believe Jesus is the one who will fix all that's been broken, the one who will end tyranny and oppression, the one who will reign forever as King and Lord, and the one who gave his life so we who are guilty can be forgiven and reconciled back to God.

(We also need to believe that Jesus is the **Son of God.**) John not only makes the claim that Jesus is the promised Messiah but also that Jesus is God. Only someone divine could do all that God promised in the Old Testament. Only someone divine could be trusted with the absolute power and authority promised to the Messiah. Only someone divine could be the perfect sacrifice and payment for the sin of the world. If Jesus were not divine, then he could not be the fulfillment of all the promises God made.

II. Question 2: What Does It Mean to Believe?

We use the word *believe* in numerous ways. Someone asks, "Is the weather supposed to be nice out today?" We answer, "I believe it's supposed to warm up." We really mean, "I think" or "I may have heard" or "I have no idea, but it would certainly be nice." In school we're taught certain facts about history and physics, so we believe those facts. In that sense *believe* means we hold it to be true but have no real attachment to it. If someone shows us different evidence, we are willing to change our minds. The kind of belief to which John calls us looks much different from these two types of belief.

The word *believe* translates the Greek word *pisteuō*, which means "to trust" or "to put one's faith *into* something or someone." To believe in Jesus as the Christ and the Son of God requires more than mere intellectual adherence to a set of facts about the life of Christ. It requires *trusting* one's whole self *into* who Christ said he was and what he was sent to accomplish.

Imagine you are on a hike through a beautiful mountain pass, approaching the edge of a cliff that drops a thousand feet to the canyon floor. The only way to continue is to walk across a bridge from one side of the cliff to the other. It's one thing to say, "I believe the bridge can hold my weight as I walk across this great chasm." It's something altogether different to actually start walking across the bridge. The former is a kind of belief based on intellectual adherence to a possible outcome. The latter is placing one's *trust in* the bridge. John did not write his Gospel just so we could know facts about Jesus's life. He wrote his Gospel so we would know facts about who Jesus is and what he was sent to do and in response trust in him completely.

III. Question 3: Why Do We Need to Believe?

One of the dominant themes of John's Gospel is our need for life, and it's always connected to the person and work of Jesus Christ.

> *In him was* life, *and that* life *was the light of men.* (1:4; emphasis added)

> *For God loved the world in this way: He gave his one and only Son, so that everyone who believes in him will not perish but have eternal* life. (3:16; emphasis added)

Truly I tell you, anyone who hears my word and believes him who sent me has eternal life *and will not come under judgment but has passed from death to* life. (5:24; emphasis added)

I am the resurrection and the life. *The one who believes in me, even if he dies, will* live. *Everyone who* lives *and believes in me will never die.* (11:25-26; emphasis added)

I am the way, the truth, and the life. (14:6; emphasis added)

The life we need—spiritual, eternal life, delivered from the judgment of hell—comes through belief in Jesus Christ (20:31). But life does not come to us like a UPS package. It's not a transaction in which we believe in Jesus, then he hands us our life at the front door and walks away. The life he gives us is life "in him."

(Ex)   Life in Christ can be illustrated by adoption. When a child is adopted, the significance is not a piece of paper he can place in a file folder. The real meaning of adoption is that he is brought into relationship with a family that is now his own. His existence is tied up with these new family members. They sleep in the same house. They sit and eat meals together. They exchange gifts at Christmas. They cry together when Grandma dies. They pass the flu to one another. Adoption is not an exchange; it's a new relationship. It's the beginning of a new life. Life in Christ is not an exchange; it's being drawn into an eternal relationship with Jesus Christ. He illustrated it for his disciples by comparing their relationship to a vine with branches. The branch doesn't get a one-time injection of life from the vine. It gets daily nourishment from its connection to the vine, and if something were to sever the branch from the vine, the branch would die. When we truly believe, we truly begin to live.

(Ex)   (ABERCOMBIE STORE) **Conclusion**

I was walking through the mall one day when I entered a store and something strange caught my eye. I couldn't figure out what it was. I stopped and looked around and realized it was something about the mannequin by the window. I walked a little closer, trying to figure out what didn't fit, when the mannequin looked at me. Then the mannequin blinked. It wasn't a mannequin; it was a model. The store paid some models to stand in the window and display their clothes.

Models and mannequins are similar in many ways. You find them in the same place. You see them wearing the same clothes. You notice them working the same job. Despite all the similarities, there's one major, all-important difference. Models are alive; mannequins aren't. The most expensive mannequin still falls infinitely short of the worst model in one category—life.

The Gospel of John reveals that the most moral, religious, pious person is no more alive than a mannequin in the store window. Though imperfect and struggling with sin, the one who believes on Jesus and commits to following him has been given life. The wrath of God has been removed, the relationship with God reconciled, and eternal life with God guaranteed.

Reflect and Discuss

1. Why did John write his Gospel?
2. What two things does John want you to believe about Jesus?
3. What is the result of believing that Jesus is the Christ, the Son of God?
4. When John says we need to believe that Jesus is the Christ, what is he saying we need to believe?
5. What are some common "spiritual" beliefs the world holds? How are these different from belief in Jesus?
6. What does it mean to believe in Jesus?
7. What is John asking his readers to believe *about* Jesus and what he has done and will do?
8. Name some of the promises God has fulfilled in Christ.
9. How can belief bring life through Jesus?
10. How has belief in Jesus changed your life?

Introducing Jesus

JOHN 1:1-5

Main Idea: Jesus is God, born to deliver mankind from death and darkness.

I. **Who Is Jesus (1:1-3)?**
II. **Why Did Jesus Come to Earth (1:4-5)?**

(Ex)

*T*ime magazine once asked "Who Was Jesus?" on their cover. They went on to ask more questions in the article:

> How is Jesus to be understood? Did he stride out of the wilderness 2,000 years ago to preach a gentle message of peace and brotherhood? Or did he perhaps advocate some form of revolution? When did he realize his mission would end with death upon a cross? Did he view himself as the promised Messiah? Did he understand himself to be both God and man? (Ostling, "Who Was Jesus?")

These are important questions to ask and to answer. We live in a culture increasingly spiritual yet hesitant to commit to saying there is one absolute truth. To many in modern society, Jesus was a philosopher. Others view him as a good man with important things to say. Still others view Jesus as just another prophet who came to point us to God. This is why the first words of the Gospel of John are so vitally important. They answer the questions, Who is Jesus, and why did he come to earth?

I. Who Is Jesus?

JOHN 1:1-3

The clear testimony of the Holy Scriptures is that Jesus of Nazareth was more than a good man or wise rabbi; Jesus Christ is God. In verse 1 Jesus is given the unique title, "the Word." Words are powerful. Anyone who thinks words are painless never went through middle school. Our own experiences and the testimony of history teach us the power of words. During World War II, Winston Churchill said these words: *(Ex)*

Let us therefore brace ourselves to our duties, and so bear
ourselves that if the British Empire and its Commonwealth last
for a thousand years, men will still say, "This was their Finest
Hour."[1]

His words rallied England and emboldened the citizens to stay the
course and stand strong against their enemy.

As powerful as Churchill's words were, they are no match for the
power of the word of God. "The heavens were made by the *word* of the
LORD, and all the stars, by the breath of his mouth" (Ps 33:6; emphasis
added). "Then God *said*, 'Let there be light,' and there was light" (Gen
1:3; emphasis added). "He sent his *word* and healed them; he rescued
them from the Pit" (Ps 107:20; emphasis added). Creation and salvation
both came through the word of God.

God reveals his power and will through his word. There is no greater
revelation of the character and nature of the Father than through the
person of Jesus.

- Jesus reveals God's mind.
- Jesus expresses God's will.
- Jesus displays God's perfections.
- Jesus exposes God's heart. (Pink, *John*, 21)

The Gospel of John begins with a phrase that sounds familiar. The
first three words of this book echo the first three words of the Bible.
Genesis 1:1 opens, "*In the beginning* God created the heavens and the
earth" (emphasis added). John is connecting Jesus Christ with creation,
claiming Jesus existed *before* creation. Jesus existed before the world
began, before there was time. If we were to hit the rewind button on
history, we could take it back to the very beginning, when God created
the world out of nothing, and Jesus was there. In fact, we could go back
before God began creation, and Jesus would have existed with him. This
was the testimony of Jesus himself: "Now, Father, glorify me in your
presence with that glory I had with you *before the world existed*" (John 17:5;
emphasis added). Genesis 1:1 contains no hint of the creation of God,
and here in John 1:1 there is no hint of the creation of Jesus. This is
what sets Jesus apart from so-called gods—gods made by human hands
and invented by human minds—Jesus has always existed.

---

[1] House of Commons, June 18, 1940 following the collapse of France.

Jesus shares his nature and being with God—"the Word was God."
He is of the same character and quality as God (v. 1). Everything that
can be said about God can be said about Jesus Christ. We call this the
Trinity—the understanding that there is one God but that the one God
exists as three persons: God the Father, Jesus the Son, and the Holy
Spirit. In verse 1 we find a precisely worded statement about Jesus that
leads us to only one conclusion: Jesus Christ is God.

This phrase proves critical in distinguishing the Christian faith from
other expressions of religion. When Jehovah's Witnesses meet to discuss
their religion, they pick up a translation of Scripture called *The New
World Translation*. If you opened that book, turned it to the Gospel of
John, found verse 1, and looked at the last phrase, you would read, "and
the Word was a god." Does that small change matter? Does a simple little
monosyllable make any difference? By adding that little word *a,* they are
making a statement that Jesus is something *less than fully God.* He may be
a god in some sense. He may be one of many "gods," but he is not the
true God. From the beginning of his Gospel, John argues that Christ is
not one of many gods but is God himself. John MacArthur writes,

> Confusion about the deity of Christ is inexcusable, because the
> biblical teaching regarding it is clear and unmistakable. Jesus
> Christ is the preexistent Word, who enjoys full face-to-face
> communion and divine life with the Father, and is Himself
> God. (*John 1–11,* 20)

As God, Jesus was not only present at creation, but he also was active
in creation. He created "all things" (v. 3). John chose the specific term
all things and used it to focus on each individual thing Jesus created.
John could have phrased it in such a way that our eyes were drawn to the
whole universe collectively—sort of like throwing open the warehouse
and simply saying, "He made all of this." However, John chose a
word that looks at each created thing individually. Like opening the
warehouse and taking us around on a tour and saying, "Look at this
here. Check out that detail there." Jesus Christ made everything from
the largest whale to the smallest amoeba. From the sunflower seed to
the redwood tree, from the beautiful sunset to the tiny lightning bug,
Jesus Christ designed and created all of it (cf. Col 1:16). One day Jesus
will be worshiped in heaven with the words, "Our Lord and God, you are
worthy to receive glory and honor and power, because you have created
all things, and by your will they exist and were created" (Rev 4:11).

II . Why Did Jesus Come to Earth?

JOHN 1:4-5

Can you imagine someone asking the apostle John, "If this Jewish carpenter from Nazareth is really God, then why is he here? Why is he walking around as a man? What's the point of all this?" John provides two
grand and glorious answers: life and light (vv. 4-5).

Without Jesus we are dead in our sin (Eph 2:1-3). What's it mean
to be dead in sin? *Death is fundamentally separation.* At death the spiritual
part of man—his soul—is separated from the physical part of man—his
body. We feel this separation when we attend a funeral or a wake. We walk
into the room, greet the family who are mourning over the separation
that has taken place between them and the one they love, and then we
walk to the front of the room and look into the coffin. In that coffin
we see a shell. Though the body is still with us, the person—the part of
that person that really makes her who she is, the part you can't see—is
no longer there. It's gone. Her soul has been separated from her body,
and all that remains is a decaying, worn-out husk with a bad makeup job.

If physical death is the separation of the soul from the body, then
spiritual death is the separation of the soul from God. Physical death pictures the
far more terrifying and sobering reality of spiritual death. Sin separates
us from God! Right here and right now, our sin separates us from the
sinless God of the universe. That separation is made permanent after
physical death, when God, the just Judge, will punish sin with eternal
separation from him in the horrors of hell.

Jesus came to give us life—to reconcile us with God, changing both
our present condition and our future destination. How do you receive
spiritual life? By placing your faith and trust in Jesus Christ (John 11:25).
He will reconcile you with his Father. You will no longer be separated
from God and cut off as an enemy but welcomed as a son or daughter.
Your future is life forever in the glorious kingdom of God. Jesus Christ
takes God's judgment on your sin, and his victory over death and the
grave become yours. Do you know what a Christian is?

- A Christian is someone who was dead in sin but now has
  received life.
- A Christian is someone who was cut off from God but has now
  been reconciled.
- A Christian is someone who was a spiritual corpse but now has
  the life of God flowing through him or her.

- A Christian is someone who was dead to God but has now been made alive by and for him.

Why did Jesus come to earth? Jesus came to call people from death to life—to a living, vibrant relationship with God—through faith in him. Those who believe he makes alive and gathers into a living community that bears the fruit of his life flowing through them. Together we demonstrate and declare his life.

Jesus brought life to the spiritually dead and light to the spiritually darkened (v. 5). Though a different metaphor it pictures the same truth. We have a great need we cannot meet. We need to be rescued from the domain of darkness, and we're powerless to do anything about it. Jesus came to earth because only he could meet that need. We could never come to know what God desires and expects from us unless Jesus revealed it. We would be staggering about in the darkness of our own opinions if Jesus had not brought the light of God's revelation. Hundreds of years before Jesus came, his coming was predicted with these words: "The people walking in darkness have seen a *great light*; a *light* has dawned on those living in the land of darkness" (Isa 9:2; emphasis added). When Jesus came, he said, "I am the *light* of the world. Anyone who follows me will never walk in the darkness but will have the *light* of life" (John 8:12; emphasis added).

The gospel is the good news that you no longer have to wander about in the darkness and despair of sin, but you can enjoy the light of righteousness through Jesus Christ. John is not suggesting we need more religion. Jesus came into a very religious world—a world where the religious leaders had memorized lengthy portions of the Bible. Yet these men were in the darkness of sin. They stumbled about, attempting to please God through their own self-righteousness. Jesus offers light and life.

Throughout John's Gospel we find an ongoing struggle between light and darkness. Jesus, the light of the world, is opposing and being opposed by those who are in darkness. Near the end of the Gospel, we discover how Jesus was betrayed by one of his own friends. He was arrested by the Roman soldiers and brought to trial. Before, during, and after his trial, he received cruel beatings, his back whipped so many times the blood flowed freely. To make the mockery worse, he was dressed in a purple robe, and a crown of thorns was brutally smashed into his scalp. A cross was thrown on his back, and he was forced to carry it up to a hill called Golgotha where he would be hung to die like a common criminal. After having his hands and feet nailed to the cross, his cross was lifted into place and there he died, despised by those he came to save. His corpse was taken down from the cross and placed in a cold, dark tomb.

If we were to stop reading after chapter 19, we could say to John, "John, you're wrong. Jesus was not God. He did not bring life. We're all doomed to death and darkness." But there's a chapter 20, and there we read about the most wonderful event to ever take place on this earth—the resurrection. After his death on the cross, Jesus did not stay buried because he is the life, and the life could not remain dead. He arose, conquering forever the sting of death and hell.

John describes this wonderful scene—this amazing resurrection—with this simple phrase: "That light shines in the darkness, and yet the darkness did not overcome it" (1:5). Look at these two verbs. John says "that light *shines*." *Shines* is in the present tense. He's saying, "The light is *still shining* in the darkness." Now look at the next phrase: "The darkness *did not overcome* it." Here John uses a verb that signifies a completed action: The darkness has done everything it could: it schemed and plotted, but it ran out of ideas. No matter what the darkness does, the light will still shine; it will not be overcome. What an awesome truth! Jesus Christ is still shining in this dark world. The light can still be seen.

Reflect and Discuss

1. Who is Jesus?
2. Why are God's words powerful? What Scriptures show the power of God's Word?
3. Why does John call Jesus "the Word"? What does this title tell us about Jesus?
4. What does John want us to believe about Jesus from this passage?
5. Describe the connection between Genesis 1:1 and John 1:1. How does this connection show a distinction between Jesus and creation?
6. Why did Jesus come to earth?
7. What would the world look like if Jesus had not brought the light of the gospel?
8. What does it mean to be a Christian? What changes have taken place in your life as a result?
9. What is the good news of the gospel? If someone took an inventory of your life, what would they think is your good news?
10. Are there moments in your life when you feel overwhelmed by anxiety, fear, or isolation? How does the picture of Jesus as a light shining in the darkness speak to you in those circumstances?

A Witness, a Testimony, and a Decision

JOHN 1:6-13

Main Idea: God sent John the Baptist to tell us we need to make a life-defining decision about Jesus Christ.

I.   John's Call to Make a Decision about Jesus (1:6-10)
II. The People's Decision to Reject Jesus (1:11)
III. The Result of Receiving Jesus (1:12)
IV. Understanding the Decision to Receive Jesus (1:13)

Dietrich Bonhoeffer, one of the great Christian thinkers of the twentieth century, was born in Germany in 1904 and was coming of age as a scholar, teacher, and pastor when Hitler rose to power. Early on he recognized the great evil of the Nazi ruler. Bonhoeffer struggled with the role a Christian should play in a country being led into a path of destruction by a government whose cruelty seemed endless. At the height of World War II, Bonhoeffer joined a resistance movement, and he was arrested for helping a group of Jews escape to Switzerland. Later he was implicated in a plot to assassinate Adolf Hitler. After two years in various prisons and concentration camps, he was marched down a flight of steps and, with a handful of other resistance members, executed. His execution took place just four weeks before the fall of the Nazi regime.

While in prison Bonhoeffer wrote letters to his family and close friends. One particularly sobering letter described his decision to join the resistance. He understood that even if they were successful, his life would never be the same—this *one decision would define him*. Can you imagine realizing that one decision would define your life? As we continue to study John, we learn that each one of us faces such a life-defining moment.

John's Call to Make a Decision about Jesus

JOHN 1:6-10

The text turns our attention for a moment from Jesus to a man called John the Baptist. God sent John to tell us about an important decision we need to make (vv. 6-8). John the Baptist is a new character in this Gospel, but he is not the author of this Gospel. The author of this Gospel—the apostle John—never refers to himself by name in this book. Every time we read the name John, it refers to John the Baptist. He appears on the scene to relay a message from God about Jesus, and it contains the call for a decision: What will you do with Jesus? John did not design the message; he was sent on a mission by God to deliver it. That's why John is given the title *witness*. John is called to the witness stand and asked for specific information. We sit like the jury, needing to *make a decision* with the information. We must decide how we will respond to his testimony.

John is on the stand to share his testimony about the light. How many people have you ever told about light? Imagine giving someone a tour of your home. How many times did you have to say after turning on a light switch, "You probably didn't notice it, but let me point out that there's now light in this room." They did not need to be told about the light. They could see it. Why did John need to tell people about the light? A. W. Pink answers:

> When the sun is shining in all its beauty, who are the ones unconscious of the fact? Who need to be told it is shining? The blind! How tragic, then, when we read that God sent John to "bear witness of the light." How pathetic that there should be any need for this! How solemn the statement that men have to be told "the light" is now in their midst. What a revelation of man's fallen condition. (*John*, 26)

Jesus came as the light, but the world was blind and could not see it. The one who *created* the world was *in* the world, yet the world did not recognize him (vv. 9-12).

- Jesus made our eyes, yet we refused to *see his glory*.
- Jesus made our ears, yet we refused to *listen to his words*.
- Jesus made our heads, yet we refused to *bow before him*.

John illustrates what a proper witness of Jesus Christ does. John is not the light himself, but what he can do is *reflect* the light of Christ. In chapter 5 (v. 35) Jesus calls John "a burning and shining lamp." John's life pointed others to the true light and burned as a testimony to the transforming power of Jesus Christ. God sent John into the world to tell us we need to make a life-defining decision about Jesus Christ.

The People's Decision to Reject Jesus
JOHN 1:11

Jesus was not just ignored by the world in general. He came to his own people, and they did not receive him. God had chosen a special people for himself—the Jews. He had made a covenant with them and promised a Messiah who would come and deliver them from their sins. When Jesus arrived, they were seeking their Messiah, but they rejected him, the one promised and sent by God.

Even in the Jews' rejection of Jesus, God was at work. God used it to usher in the salvation of the Gentiles. But the truth remains that the rejection of Jesus—whether it was the Jews two thousand years ago or you today—leaves a person in sin without a Savior. No one else can bring you salvation. No other light can pierce the darkness of your sin. Don't turn your back on him, hoping your own good works will be enough—they won't.

Jesus was rejected for the most part, but some turned and received him (v. 12). They had been lost in darkness, but they embraced the light. The only way some were able to receive him was by *believing* in his name. This is the key term in the Gospel of John, a term we find nearly one hundred times throughout the book. If we're to receive Jesus Christ, we must completely rely on him.

The Result of Receiving Jesus
JOHN 1:12

When we receive Jesus by believing in him, we become "children of God" (v. 12). We, who were dead in our trespasses and sin, are now brought into the family of God. Because of Jesus, we who deserve death are now made to share in God's inheritance as his children. We don't deserve this. We could never say, "I have given myself the right to be called a child of God." Only Jesus can do it. He has the authority to declare that sinners, God haters like us, are now fully accepted children of the Father. Do you see now how this one decision to receive Christ completely defines our lives? Our lives are radically altered by our position in the family of God.

- We don't need to fear the future because we are going to the Father's house (John 14).

- We can stop worrying about whether our needs on this earth will be met because our Father gives good gifts to his children (Matt 7).
- We don't need to be anxious about our 401k because we recognize that our inheritance is not in earthly banks but in the heavenly realm (Col 1).
- Our hope, our expectation, is not in this world. Someday, as children of the King, we will "shine like the sun in [our] Father's kingdom" (Matt 13:43).

God sent John the Baptist to witness about Jesus. His witness forces each person to consider, Will I reject Jesus or will I receive him? What will I do with Jesus?

Understanding the Decision to Receive Jesus
JOHN 1:13

If we are all lost in darkness, enjoying the perverse pleasures of sin, content to rebel against God, how do some believe? Verse 13 explains *why* some receive Jesus. Behind every decision a person makes to turn and receive Jesus stands the decision of God to give that person new life. We can only be saved through the direct intervention of God. Apart from his choice of us, we would never choose him.

Before we dive into the final phrase, "but of God," which pulsates with the profound truth of God's sovereignty, we should note three wrong reasons people think God saves them.

First, some think God saves people because of their racial or ethnic *background* ("not of natural descent"). This understanding pervaded Judaism in Christ's day. There was a widespread belief that a person would be saved simply because Jewish blood flowed through his veins.

Second, some think God saves people because of their *sincerity.* The phrase "will of the flesh" pictures a man and a woman coming together with great passion to conceive a child. No matter how sincere or passionate you are about spiritual things, you will only be saved if God draws you to himself.

Third, some think God saves people because of their *effort.* The phrase "will of man" could be translated "will of the husband." A husband and his wife can carefully plan to have a child, and their planning may pay off in nine months, but no man can plan his way into the family of God. No amount of work or human effort will bring a person spiritual life.

People will only experience the new birth if God chooses to regenerate them. Upholding every decision to believe is the foundation of God's sovereign grace. James also attributes our new life to God's choice: "*By his own choice*, he gave us birth by the word of truth" (Jas 1:18; emphasis added).

Many people don't like this teaching because it detracts from man's efforts. That's exactly the point! The truth that God chooses sinners and those sinners simply respond (not the other way around) elevates God and humbles us. And humility is *exactly* what we need. Everything that has happened to a Christian for good, especially his salvation, is directly attributable to the work of God in him. Nothing in him merited salvation. Even when he exercised faith, he did so because God gave him that gift (Eph 2:8-9).

Conclusion

Shannon Brown, a good friend of mine, found himself in China on Mother's Day, 2006. He and his wife were there to pick up the newest member of their family—a ten-month-old girl who had been abandoned the day after she was born. A few months before they went overseas to meet her and bring her home, he had written about their decision to adopt:

> I think within a nanosecond of deciding to adopt we knew what our daughter's name would be. In fact, I don't really ever recall discussing it that much. Perhaps it's because of why we chose to adopt. Our driving motivation was to rescue a little girl and give her a family with hope for the future.
>
> This helpless little girl who lives on the other side of the earth will receive all of the benefits of being my child. I will clothe her and feed her. She will take on my name and receive my deepest affection. She will be the object of my love. My energies will be directed towards helping, instructing and training her to be happy, with a secure knowledge that I will never leave her. I will pour out my heart to introduce her to the Savior of the world who can take away all her sins and give her eternal security.
>
> Of course, all of this is done as we completely depend on God and his strength.
>
> Where would we be without the love of God? Where would we be without him revealing himself to us in Scripture? Where

would we be without him divinely sacrificing his own Son and seeking us out to rescue us?

So for us, and what this adoption is a reflection of, we only had one name to choose from . . . Grace. (Used by permission)

Is there a better word than *grace* to describe the adoption of this little girl? She could do nothing to become part of this family. No desire on her part would have connected her with this man and woman who would become mommy and daddy. Her adoption into this loving family was the result of someone outside of herself choosing to love her, to receive her, and to give her the right to be called their child. Someone had to do for her what she could not do for herself. That's grace, and that's exactly what happened to us who have believed on the name of Jesus. Like this little girl, we were helpless and hopeless until someone did for us what we could not do for ourselves. God chose to love us. He received us to himself, and he gave us the right to be called his children. This is grace.

Reflect and Discuss

1. What are some major decisions that have shaped your life?
2. Why was it necessary for John the Baptist to be sent to bear witness to the light?
3. How are you bearing witness to the light of Jesus?
4. In what ways did the world not recognize Jesus?
5. When was the first time you were called to make a decision about Jesus? What was your response?
6. How was the Jews' decision to reject Jesus a part of God's redemptive plan for the world?
7. How is your life radically altered through becoming a child of God?
8. What are three wrong reasons people think God saves them?
9. What is grace? How is it different from mercy (not receiving a punishment you deserve)?
10. How can God's movement to save those he chooses by his own will be a truth worth celebrating?

The Story Continues

JOHN 1:14-18

Main Idea: The coming of Jesus Christ is not the beginning of the gospel story but its next chapter.

I. **The Gospel Embodied in Jesus (1:14a)**
   A. If Jesus did not become a man, he could not be tempted.
   B. If Jesus did not become a man, he could not be an example.
   C. If Jesus did not become a man, he could not die.
II. **The Gospel Explained in Jesus (1:14b-18)**
   A. Jesus and the tabernacle
   B. Jesus and the glory of God
   C. Jesus and the prophets
   D. Jesus and the law
   E. Jesus and the Father

Do you find the Old Testament confusing—just a bunch of people with strange names doing strange things in strange places? Written more than two thousand years ago in a dialect no one speaks anymore, it can feel irrelevant to our lives. Imagine living in John's day as a devout Jew. As you hear John talk about Jesus, it raises a few questions in your mind: Did God start his entire plan of salvation over? How does the coming of Jesus fit into God's plan? What am I supposed to do with everything I've learned and been taught from the Scriptures up to this point?

These are important questions for us to consider. Is the coming of Jesus Christ the start of God's new plan to save people? How does it connect to what was written before? The coming of Jesus Christ is not the beginning of the gospel story but the next chapter. The Old Testament and the New Testament are not two different books about two different subjects. They are two parts of the same story. Mark Dever labeled the Old Testament "Promises Made" and the New Testament "Promises Kept" (*Message of the Old Testament* and *Message of the New Testament*). All of these promises—the ones *made* in the OT and *kept* in the NT—are part of what we call the good news of the gospel.

The good news that God would provide a way for sinners to be reconciled to himself was first proclaimed in the garden of Eden. When mankind sinned, God promised the seed of a woman would be born who would bring victory over sin and its awful effects. The rest of the Old Testament traces the promised seed of God, all the while reminding us of God's grace and his plan to bring salvation. The gospel story did not begin with the birth of Jesus. The gospel story began long before. As John wraps up this prologue to his Gospel, we see a wonderful picture of the gospel in the person of Jesus—in him we see the gospel *embodied* and *explained*.

The Gospel Embodied in Jesus
JOHN 1:14A

Few statements in Scripture are as profound as the first statement of verse 14: "The Word became flesh." The Word is the preexistent, divine Creator of the universe. The Word is the uncreated Son of God. To say the Word became flesh is amazing! How could God become a man?

- Some have suggested the Word (Jesus Christ) came to dwell *in* a man. He did not himself *become* a man. But John says, "The Word *became* flesh."
- Others have said Jesus Christ just *appeared* like a man. He didn't actually take on human form and become a man. He must have been an apparition because it's impossible for God who is Spirit to take on bodily form. While it's difficult for us to understand *how* this could happen, we can understand *what* John writes— "The Word became *flesh*."
- Still others have suggested God simply *chose* a man and made him his Son. But this ignores what John wrote earlier. The same one who became flesh (v. 14) is also the one who was in the beginning with God, who was with God, and who was God (v. 1).

In a small manger in Bethlehem the eternal Son of God *became* a man. We can hold to this truth—called the incarnation—even if we cannot comprehend all it means. We can affirm that Jesus has always existed (v. 1, he *was* in the beginning) and that there was a definite point in human history when he was born as a baby (v. 14, he *became* flesh). Jesus is both fully God and fully human. Anyone who denies either the full deity *or* full humanity of Jesus Christ is a false teacher (1 John 4:1-2).

Affirming the full humanity of Jesus in no way diminishes his deity. The apostle Paul affirms this reality in the book of Colossians: "For the entire fullness of God's nature dwells bodily in Christ" (2:9).

Why would the eternal, preexistent God become this baby cradled in the arms of a peasant woman?

If Jesus Did Not Become a Man, He Could Not Be Tempted

Apart from his human nature, Jesus could not have experienced temptation. The incarnation provides us with an advocate before the Father's throne who knows *exactly* what we're going through and *exactly* how it feels. God became man so he could sympathize with our weakness and so he could assure us that victory over sin and temptation is possible through his strength.

If Jesus Did Not Become a Man, He Could Not Be an Example

Do you remember when WWJD was popular? Bracelets, T-shirts, bumper stickers, pretty much every trinket you could think of was being sold with those four letters. Those letters, of course, stood for *What Would Jesus Do?* Maybe you got a little annoyed with the marketing, but we should ask what Jesus would do. Because Jesus became a man, we can know how he would respond.

If Jesus Did Not Become a Man, He Could Not Die

We should never look at Bethlehem without seeing Calvary. We should never contemplate the incarnation without our thoughts drifting to the crucifixion. J. I. Packer reminds us,

> The crucial significance of the cradle at Bethlehem lies in its place in the sequence of steps down that led the Son of God to the cross of Calvary, and we do not understand it till we see it in this context . . . the taking of manhood by the Son is set before us in a way which shows us how we should ever view it—not simply as a marvel of nature, but rather as a wonder of grace. (*Knowing God*, 58–59)

The incarnation is amazing because of *why* God became man: so he could die for our sin. He renounced the glory due him, becoming poor, so that through his poverty we might become rich.

The Gospel Explained in Jesus
JOHN 1:14B-18

The gospel *is* presented in the Old Testament. From the seed of the woman in Genesis 3 through the exodus from Egypt, from the story of Ruth and Boaz to the words of the prophet Isaiah, the good news of God's salvation was repeatedly made clear. However, Jesus revealed the ultimate embodiment of the gospel. We see this fuller revelation of the gospel when we examine the relationship between Jesus and five Old Testament truths.

Jesus and the Tabernacle

In verse 14 John uses an interesting word—the word translated "dwelt." He only uses it one other time (7:2), when he's referring to the Festival of Shelters (or Booths or Tabernacles). This word *dwelt* could be translated "pitched his tent" and would instantly remind anyone familiar with the Old Testament of the tabernacle. The tabernacle was instituted by God as the place where he would dwell in the midst of the people of Israel. It was the forerunner of the temple; it was a tent that went before the children of Israel as they made their way to the promised land. Within the tabernacle was the most holy place, where God came to meet man. Just as God came to meet man in the tabernacle, he came to meet man in the person of Jesus. Worship for the Jews centered on the tabernacle and then the temple, but once Jesus came, *he* became the center of worship. Only through Jesus could man be brought to God.

Jesus and the Glory of God

One could not think of the tabernacle in the OT without being reminded of the glory of God. As Israel marched through the wilderness on the way to the promised land, the glory of the Lord appearing like a cloud went with them, regularly descending on the tabernacle. In the Old Testament the glory of the Lord was the "visible manifestation of the excellence of God's character" (Grudem, *Systematic Theology*, 221). In other words, the glory of God was *the greatness of God seen visibly*. When Jews looked at the tabernacle, they would see a partial and incomplete picture of the glory of God (this visible display of his goodness, greatness, and holiness) emanating from it. John's point in verse 14 is that when Jesus came to earth as a man to dwell with men, the glory of God was seen in its fullness.

The truthfulness of God to keep his promises and the grace of God to rescue his people found their ultimate expression when God sent Jesus. John could say in effect, "Our fathers experienced the grace and faithfulness of God, but if you want an even greater demonstration of it, look to Jesus."

Jesus and the Prophets

Jesus is superior to John the Baptist because Jesus was before him, even though John the Baptist was born six months before Jesus (Luke 1). John the Baptist is saying Jesus is the eternally existing God. John was considered the last of the OT prophets. Like Isaiah, Jeremiah, and others before him, John's role was to prepare the people for the coming Messiah. The only difference was that he had the opportunity to point to Jesus physically and say in effect, "There he is. There is the one we've been telling you about." Sending Jesus was not a new plan of God. John the Baptist continued in the long line of messengers, testifying to the promise of God and declaring the gospel.

Jesus and the Law

There is no other source of grace but in Christ, where we find an inexhaustible supply (vv. 16-17). The focus here is more than just that we receive grace from Christ; it's that this grace is fuller or more complete than what God had provided before Christ. The giving of the law *was* a matter of grace. God has always desired his people to respond to him in faith and, as a result of that faith, to live in obedience to his word. However, because of the Israelites' lack of faith and their disobedience, God gave them the law as a means of protection. The law was able to show them the sinfulness of their actions (Rom 7:13), but the law was never intended to save the Jews. The purpose of the law was not to draw people to itself, for it had no grace to offer. The law itself was not an instrument of grace. Rather, God would give grace through Jesus to those who violated his law (Gal 3:13).

The grace of the law was that it pointed people to Jesus, but how much more grace was given when Jesus came! The grace of God was seen in the law everywhere the shadow of Jesus Christ fell, whether in the Passover or in the temple sacrifices. But when Jesus came, the shadows no longer mattered; the light of Jesus Christ revealed completely what the shadows had revealed in part.

Jesus and the Father

In Jesus Christ the Father is revealed in a way and a depth previously unknown. In verse 18 the word translated "revealed" is rare—only used six times in Scripture—and carries the idea that the whole story has now been told. Jesus came to share the whole story of God and his perfect plan of redemption. This is not a new story, but in Jesus this wonderful story of grace is perfectly and fully explained.

Conclusion

The first eighteen verses of this Gospel remind us that the promises beginning in the book of Genesis and continuing through the entire Old Testament are finally realized in Jesus Christ. He is the promised Messiah. He's the answer to man's need for a Savior. This man is far *more* than a man; he is God *become* man. These eighteen verses introduce us to the Word, to Jesus Christ, but they also introduce us to God's grace in human form. Only through Jesus could the great gulf between utterly undeserving man and a completely holy God be bridged.

- The gospel story is a rescue story, and Jesus is the rescuer.
- The gospel story is a promise, and Jesus is the fulfillment.
- The gospel story is all about Jesus Christ and the grace he has made available to all.

You may be familiar with John Newton's song "Amazing Grace," but are you familiar with *why* he wrote it? Newton wrote a lot of songs for his church, and a member of his church named William Cowper often helped him. Cowper was a fantastic poet who wrote such songs as "There Is a Fountain Filled with Blood" and "God Moves in Mysterious Ways." Yet Cowper battled his entire life with darkness, depression, and self-condemnation. The song "Amazing Grace" was written by Newton for a New Year's Day service in 1773. Newton always wrote his hymns with the needs of his congregation in mind.

> On January 1, 1773 there was one individual who was desperately in need of understanding the message that God's grace can save the worst of wretches. This was William Cowper whose depression was spiraling downward in a vortex of madness that led to his attempted suicide a few hours later. Central to Cowper's madness was a deep-rooted fear that God had rejected him despite his faith. Newton . . . had tried hard

to persuade Cowper that God's grace is universal and never withheld from a believer. . . . Could Newton have hoped that the words of Amazing Grace . . . might relieve Cowper's fear and spiritual blindness, leading him out of the dangers and snares . . . toward the security of God's grace? (Aitken, *John Newton*, 229)

It was Cowper's struggle with doubt, anxiety, and guilt that motivated these particular words from Newton:

> Through many dangers, toils and snares,
> we have already come.
> 'Twas Grace that brought us safe thus far,
> and Grace will lead us home.

Never forget the grace that flows freely from Jesus Christ. If God was willing to send his Son to be born as a man and to die as a criminal for you, do you think he'll ever withhold his grace from you? If your faith is in Jesus Christ, then from him abundant, overflowing, amazing grace is being poured out. God's grace is sufficient. Never lose sight. Never lose hope. His grace will lead you home.

Reflect and Discuss

1. What are we to believe about Jesus from this passage?
2. How does Jesus show unity between the Old and New Testaments?
3. What are some incorrect understandings of "the Word became flesh"?
4. Why did God choose to lower himself and become a man born as the baby of a peasant woman?
5. How is the gospel presented in the Old Testament?
6. How was God's giving the law in the Old Testament an act of grace? How is that grace made full in Jesus?
7. How does Jesus reveal God's character, excellence, and glory?
8. What about God's character revealed in Jesus is most striking to you?
9. In what way is the gospel a present hope in your life today?
10. When you think of Jesus, do you think of him as a revelation of God's character? Explain your answer.

A Messenger of Hope

JOHN 1:19-34

Main Idea: John the Baptist points us to the one who can fulfill our greatest hopes and satisfy our deepest longings.

I. **John's Identity (1:19-28)**
II. **John's Message (1:29-34)**
    A. The Lamb provides a sacrifice.
    B. The Lamb provides a substitute.
    C. The Lamb provides satisfaction.

In *The Lion, the Witch and the Wardrobe*, we're first introduced to the world of Narnia, a once beautiful world that has grown cold and dark. The four Pevensie children come through a magical wardrobe to a snow-covered forest in Narnia where they learn that it's been winter for over a hundred years. Evil reigns. Hope is dead. But with the arrival of these children, things begin to change. The inhabitants of Narnia slowly begin to hope again. An ancient Narnian prophecy said before deliverance would come, two Sons of Adam and two Daughters of Eve would appear. These children were messengers of hope. But the hopes of the citizens of Narnia are not in the children; their hopes are in someone else, a lion named Aslan. The children hear an old Narnian rhyme:

> Wrong will be right, when Aslan comes in sight,
> At the sound of his roar, sorrows will be no more,
> When he bares his teeth, winter meets its death,
> And when he shakes his mane, we shall have spring again.
> (Lewis, *The Lion, the Witch and the Wardrobe*, 74–75)

The Pevensie children brought hope not in themselves but in the one who would follow their coming and bring deliverance. In John 1 we meet a man who brought a message of hope—hope not found in himself but in someone else. John the Baptist points us to the one who can fulfill our greatest hopes and satisfy our deepest longings.

⊥. John's Identity

JOHN 1:19-28

The religious leaders of Israel sent a group of priests out to interrogate John the Baptist. They ask five questions, and the first four questions have the goal of determining John the Baptist's identity. Their first question is pretty general. They're fishing for information. They ask him who he is, and he lets them know he's not the promised Messiah.

Next they ask John if he's Elijah. That seems like an odd question since Elijah was an Old Testament prophet, dead for hundreds of years. But John shared some striking similarities with Elijah. Matthew describes John's appearance like this: "Now John had a camel-hair garment with a leather belt around his waist" (Matt 3:4). This is similar to what Elijah looked like: "A hairy man with a leather belt around his waist" (2 Kgs 1:8). Their similarities were more than skin deep. They were both prophets of God who preached openly against sin, particularly in the lives of those who were supposed to be leading God's people, and they both called people to repent of their sin.

Next they ask John, "Are you the Prophet?" Notice they don't ask him if he's *a* prophet. They ask him if he's *the* Prophet. They had in mind the prophecy of Moses: "The LORD your God will raise up for you a prophet like me from among your own brothers. You must listen to him" (Deut 18:15). These Jewish leaders had missed the point of this prophecy. Asking John if he was the Messiah and then asking him if he was the Prophet was redundant. They should have understood the Prophet *was* the Messiah. Peter (Acts 3) and then Stephen (Acts 7) both condemned the religious leaders because they not only *missed* the Prophet, but they *killed* him when they crucified Jesus Christ.

They've learned their lesson. This time they simply ask John who he is. His answer is to allude to Isaiah 40:3: "I am a voice of one crying out in the wilderness." The context of Isaiah 40 is the return of Jewish exiles. Because of the sin of his people, God sent Babylon to destroy Judah and to take the people captive. But in Isaiah 40 he is promising to deliver them from their slavery. This voice is crying that a road needs to be made for the exiles to return home. Steep grades needed to be leveled. Potholes needed to be filled. Everything is to be made smooth because God is going to deliver his people. This voice is in essence crying, ("Prepare yourself for God's salvation.") John's role, as the voice, was to prepare God's people for the salvation that would come through Jesus Christ. John called people to repent, turn from their sin, and believe on Jesus as their Savior.

✳ They respond with another question: "Why then do you baptize if you aren't the Messiah, or Elijah, or the Prophet?" He's already answered, but they weren't listening. His role was to prepare the people of Israel for the salvation coming in Jesus Christ. His baptism was a visible sign of repentance. It was an opportunity to testify publicly they were turning from their sin and waiting in faith for the promised Messiah. His authority to baptize was simply an extension of his role as the voice crying to the people to prepare for Jesus's coming.

Throughout this conversation John's humility stands out, particularly in contrast to the religious leaders. The tone of their questions is condescending and arrogant, but John's response is humble. They ask him by what right he baptizes, and he simply points them to Christ. If I had been John, I would have probably said something like, "I'll tell you who I am: I'm the last of the Old Testament prophets. My birth was declared to my father by an angel. The Holy Spirit empowered me for this mission when I was still in the womb. The Son of God called me the greatest man ever to walk the face of the earth [Matt 11:11]. That's who I am! Who are you?"

Instead John points the conversation to Jesus. When they ask who he is, he tells them who he's *not*. "I am not the Messiah." John wants to make sure no one confuses him with Jesus. He doesn't draw attention to himself but directs it to Jesus. When they ask him what right he has to baptize, he doesn't defend himself. He points to Jesus, and when he points to Jesus, he says in essence, "I'm not the one you need to know about. I'm a lowly servant—unworthy even to buckle Christ's sandal. He's the one you need to know."

In high school I was in the school play. Along with a female classmate, I had the responsibility of opening the play. We would come out on stage and begin the play with a dialogue. After a minute or two, the curtain was supposed to open and a scene would start. One of the nights I stood on stage in front of the curtain, saying my lines, waiting for the curtain to open, and nothing happened. There we stood, nothing to say or do, just hoping and praying the curtain operator would pull back the curtain. I don't know how long it took. It seemed like hours, but eventually the curtain was pulled back, and people could see what they came to see. Christians are a bit like curtain operators. We're not the main event.

Our job is to pull back the curtain and direct everyone's attention to Jesus Christ.

✸ The great goal of the church is to point the world to Jesus Christ. We gather on Sundays to worship him and learn about him, but then we go out to share him with others. Just over one hundred years after the apostle John died, Tertullian wrote about the spreading influence of believers:

> We are but of yesterday, and we have filled every place among you—cities, islands, fortresses, towns, marketplaces . . . tribes, companies, palace, senate, forum—we have left nothing to you but the temple of your gods. (Cited in Boice, *John*, 1:101)

Let that be true about Christianity today, that we go out from our places of worship and spread out through our cities and the surrounding communities, pointing everyone to Jesus Christ. I would love to write in twenty years, "We have filled every place among you—cities, counties, schools, rec leagues, restaurants, software companies, engineering firms, grocery stores, post offices, gyms—we have left nothing to you but a few empty buildings that used to house pagan religions."

John the Baptist is described over and over as a witness. Is that a fitting description for you? I wonder if we could better identify with one comedian who claimed to be a "Jehovah's Bystander." "They asked me to be a witness," he said, "but I didn't want to get involved" (Davey, *When Heaven Came Down*, 17). Are you a bystander sitting on the sidelines watching the show, or are you participating?

II John's Message
JOHN 1:29-34

John gives his eyewitness account of the Spirit descending on Jesus. From the other Gospels we understand it took place at Jesus's baptism. First, God himself had given John a message: "The one you see the Spirit descending and resting on—he is the one who baptizes with the Holy Spirit" (v. 33). Second, John witnesses this event (v. 32). He had known Jesus but had not realized Jesus was the one sent from God (v. 31). However, when he saw the Holy Spirit descend on Jesus, it became clear. Third, the Spirit rested on Jesus. The word *rest* is used in both verses 32 and 33. In the Old Testament, when the Holy Spirit came on a person to empower him for a specific task, it was temporary. Yet the Spirit remained permanently on Jesus. When John saw the Spirit descend and remain on Jesus, he recognized the fulfillment of the promise of God to send the Messiah. John testifies to the deity of Jesus Christ in verse 34: "I have seen and testified that this is the Son of God." He does not hesitate, waver, or doubt. John is clear: Jesus Christ is God.

John begins his message with a remarkable statement, "Here is the *Lamb* of God, who takes away the sin of the world!" (v. 29; emphasis added). What does it mean that Jesus is the Lamb?

The Lamb Provides a Sacrifice

This account took place just days before the annual Passover celebration (2:13). The focus of the Passover celebration was the sacrifice of a lamb, which served as a reminder of God's deliverance of Israel from captivity in Egypt. Exodus 12 records the first Passover, when God commanded each family to choose a lamb, kill it, and wipe its blood on the doorposts of their home. God was going to send death to every home except for those with blood on the doorposts. Those homes would be *passed over.* As the Jews congregated in Jerusalem each year to remember this work of God, each family would bring a lamb to the temple to be sacrificed on the altar.

However, lambs were not just sacrificed at Passover. Every day two lambs were killed at the temple, one in the morning and one in the evening. John the Baptist's father was a priest who served at the temple. John would have been familiar with the sacrifices offered there. His father would have returned each day with blood-stained clothes from the slain lambs. Why must lambs be slaughtered every day? Their death was necessary because of sin: blood must be shed for sin to be forgiven (Heb 9:22). These lambs pointed to the one who would be sent from God to shed his blood one time so sin could be forgiven *forever* (Heb 7:27). Jesus was the Lamb sent by God to offer his life as a sacrifice. He was the one of whom Isaiah wrote, "He was oppressed and afflicted, yet he did not open his mouth. Like a *lamb* led to the slaughter and like a *sheep* silent before her shearers, he did not open his mouth" (Isa 53:7; emphasis added).

The Lamb Provides a Substitute

Who was responsible for bringing a lamb as a sacrifice for sin? The sinner. But who brought this Lamb to be sacrificed? God did. Was there sin in God that needed to be covered? No, God was offering his Lamb as a *substitute*. We should pay the price for our own sin, but God provided a way of escape. He sent a Lamb who could perfectly and completely pay the penalty for our sin. Jesus, the Lamb of God, died in our place for our sin. He's the only one whose death was sufficient to pay the penalty for our sin. He is not simply *a* lamb of God. He's *the* Lamb of God. Only through Jesus can we find forgiveness for our sin.

Did you notice that the religious leaders didn't ask John if he was the Lamb of God? They asked him if he was the Messiah or a famous prophet, but not the Lamb. I wonder if it's because they were looking for something other than a lamb. They were hoping for a prophet or a king but not a lamb. They hoped the promised one would come and liberate them from the tyranny of the Romans, but they didn't realize they needed liberation from the tyranny of sin. I wonder if they didn't ask about the Lamb because they had no sense of their own sin. They were right to expect a king—Jesus will reign over all the earth—but they didn't pay close attention to the prophets. Before the King would ascend the throne, he must first lie down on the altar. Before he would come as a conquering leader, he must first come as a crucified Lamb. All the religious leaders were interested in was seeing the Lion of Judah, and he did come, but he came first as the Lamb of God.

John Piper writes,

> The Lion of Judah conquered because he was willing to act the part of a lamb. He came into Jerusalem on Palm Sunday like a king on the way to a throne, and he went out of Jerusalem on Good Friday like a lamb on the way to the slaughter. He drove out the robbers from the Temple like a lion devouring its prey. And then at the end of the week he gave his majestic neck to the knife, and they slaughtered the Lion of Judah like a sacrificial lamb. (*Seeing and Savoring*, 30)

In Revelation 5 we briefly glimpse the worship of Jesus in heaven, and we hear that the "Lion from the tribe of Judah . . . has conquered" (v. 5). But then our eyes look up and we see not a Lion but a Lamb, standing yet looking as if he had been slaughtered. Bowing all around him are people singing, "Worthy is the Lamb who was slaughtered" (v. 12). Jesus conquered sin, death, and hell by sacrificing himself as our substitute. He was a Lamb offered by God for our sin.

The Lamb Provides Satisfaction

The sacrifice of Jesus fully satisfies the demands of justice. Our sin demands a punishment, but the death of Jesus fulfills the punishment that justice demands. God is a gracious and kind God, but he is also just and holy. Because of his justice, we (as vile, filthy, unholy sinners) cannot come into his presence. Beyond that, his holiness demands his just wrath be poured out on sin. As sinners, we are objects of God's wrath, awaiting a day when God's full fury will be poured out on us—a day when we will experience the punishment our sin demands (Rom 2:5).

However, Jesus, the Lamb of God, offered his life on our behalf, and in so doing he took God's wrath upon himself. "How much more then, since we have now been declared righteous by his blood, will we be saved through him from wrath" (Rom 5:9). The great joy of the gospel is that I don't have to pay for my sin; Jesus paid for it. I don't have to endure the wrath of God; God's wrath was poured out on Jesus. Jesus came to take away the sin of the world, to completely satisfy the justice of God. Our sin can no longer be held against us.

Conclusion

John's message was a message of hope. We have no other hope than to flee to Christ, and we need no other hope. Through the sacrifice of Jesus our sin has been forever removed. Our guilt no longer remains. We are free from the power and the penalty of sin.

In the climax of *The Lion, the Witch and the Wardrobe*, Aslan, the great Lion, marches to the Stone Table and is murdered by the White Witch. The two Pevensie girls, Lucy and Susan, cry themselves to sleep at the dead lion's feet, feeling hopeless as the evil witch's army marches to make war on Narnia. At that moment something happens:

> The rising of the sun had made everything look so different—
> all colors and shadows were changed—that for a moment
> they didn't see the important thing. Then they did. The Stone
> Table was broken into two pieces by a great crack that ran
> down it from end to end; and there was no Aslan.
>
> "Oh, oh, oh!" cried the two girls, rushing back to the
> Table.
>
> "Oh, it's *too* bad," sobbed Lucy; "they might have left the
> body alone."

"Who's done it?" cried Susan. "What does it mean? Is it more magic?"

"Yes!" said a great voice behind their backs. "It is more magic." They looked round. There, shining in the sunrise, larger than they had seen him before, shaking his mane . . . stood Aslan himself. (Lewis, *The Lion*, 158–59)

After their initial shock had worn off, Susan asked Aslan what it meant.

"It means," said Aslan, "that though the Witch knew the Deep Magic, there is a magic deeper still which she did not know. Her knowledge goes back only to the dawn of time. But if she could have looked a little further back, into the stillness and the darkness before Time dawned, she would have read there a different incantation. She would have known that when a willing victim who had committed no treachery was killed in a traitor's stead, the Table would crack and Death itself would start working backward." (Ibid., 159–60)

Jesus, the Lion from the tribe of Judah, offered himself as the sacrificial Lamb so traitors would be forgiven, justice would be satisfied, and death would be broken. Worthy is the Lamb who was slain!

Reflect and Discuss

1. What is John's message of hope?
2. How and why does John reference Isaiah 40?
3. Are you pointing other people's attention to Jesus as you go about your daily life? What opportunities exist for you to tell people about Jesus?
4. What would it look like if the gospel radically took root in your neighborhood and city?
5. Would "witness" be a fitting description for you?
6. Why does the Holy Spirit remain permanently on Jesus?
7. What does it mean that Jesus is the Lamb of God?
8. What role do lambs hold in Old Testament sacrifice? What difference is there between those lambs and *the* Lamb of God?
9. Are there circumstances in your life that cause you to want Jesus to be something other than what he is? What are they?
10. How can the message that Jesus came to die as the Lamb of God be a message of hope?

Come and See

JOHN 1:35-51

Main Idea: Four simple, ordinary men whose lives have been transformed offer compelling endorsements of Jesus.

I. John the Baptist Endorses Jesus to the Crowd (1:35-36).
II. Andrew Endorses Jesus to His Brother (1:37-42).
III. Philip Endorses Jesus to His Friend (1:43-46).
IV. Nathanael Endorses Jesus as the Son of God (1:46-51).
V. Application
    A.   Christians are chosen by Jesus to follow him.
    B.   Christians are being transformed by Jesus.
    C.   Christians are calling others to Jesus.

A number of years ago I developed seasonal allergies. I was miserable. I remember describing my misery to a friend at church, and he called his wife over to the table where we were sitting and explained to her what I said. Now, as he was explaining to her what I was going through, I noticed she seemed fine. Her eyes weren't red and puffy like mine were. She wasn't hacking and sniffling every few seconds. Without hesitation she took a small bottle of pills out of her purse and said, "I used to have really bad allergies like you do, but this medicine has made me feel much better." I went to my doctor first thing the next morning and asked him for some of those pills.

Unlike the million-dollar athlete endorsing an inexpensive car he'll never drive, her endorsement meant something. We respond to the endorsements of regular people like you and me when we hear them talk about something that changed their lives. In John 1 four men offer compelling endorsements of Jesus Christ. They're not celebrities. They're not paid spokesmen. They're simple, ordinary men whose lives have been transformed by Jesus Christ.

John the Baptist Endorses Jesus to the Crowd
JOHN 1:35-36

John the Baptist believed what he said. His purpose was to prepare men and women for the coming of Jesus. So when Jesus came, John willingly passed his disciples on to Jesus. If someone really believes what he says, he will continue to say it even when it requires sacrifice on his part. A lot of preachers stand up in pulpits around the globe and say it's all about Jesus, but when it comes time to let a few people leave to spread the message of Jesus in other places, the truth comes out. The message from the preachers' lips is contradicted by the message of their lives. "Go out," some may say, "but don't actually leave my church." "Give your lives," others might prompt, "but don't actually stop giving in the offering."

In church we're often asked, "Are you willing to go?" Maybe we also need to ask, "Are you willing to let go? Am I?" It could be a close friend, a child, an accountability partner, a mentor, or a grandchild. Are we more concerned about keeping people here or sending them out? Are we more concerned about assembling a crowd or spreading the good news of Jesus? One author wrote,

> John provides a genuine model of what it means to be a minister or servant of God. The human tendency is to make a name for ourselves and to attach our names to other people, institutions, and things so that people will remember us. To minimize oneself in order for Jesus to become the focus of attention is the designated function of an ideal witness. (Borchert, *John 1–11*, 141)

John's endorsement rings true because he willingly gave up everything, particularly his influence and authority, to testify to the reality of who Jesus was.

Andrew Endorses Jesus to His Brother
JOHN 1:37-42

Andrew has "found the Messiah" (v. 41). What a discovery! The word translated "found" implies someone was diligently searching for something and then joyously discovers it. "The kingdom of heaven is like treasure, buried in a field, that a man *found* [same word] and reburied.

Then in his joy he goes and sells everything he has and buys that field" (Matt 13:44; emphasis added). In another parable we're told of a man who has a hundred sheep, but one is missing. So he leaves the ninety-nine and searches diligently for the one. "And if he *finds* [same word] it, truly I tell you, he rejoices over that sheep more than over the ninety-nine that did not go astray" (Matt 18:13; emphasis added). With the intensity of a shepherd looking for his lost sheep and the joy of a man who discovered a great treasure, Andrew endorses Jesus Christ to his brother. "We found him—the one we have been searching for, the one we've been waiting for." Why could Andrew say with such great force and conviction they had found the Messiah?

Apparently Andrew was a disciple of John the Baptist (vv. 35-37). One day he and another disciple of John the Baptist are standing around listening to him teach when he directs their attention to Jesus and says, "Look, there's the Lamb of God." As faithful disciples of John, they decide to follow Jesus. Jesus sees them following, stops, and asks them directly, "What are you looking for?" (v. 38). What are you seeking? Is there something I can help you find? They ask Jesus about his lodging. The question demonstrates their desire to go with Jesus. It implies, "We want to follow you, to talk with you, to learn more about you—where are you headed?" Jesus responds, "Come and you'll see" (v. 39). They arrive where he is staying "about 4:00 in the afternoon," and they talk. What a conversation that must have been! We don't know what Jesus told them, but we see the impact the conversation made. Andrew runs quickly from that place to find his brother and makes a clear endorsement of Jesus Christ.

Philip Endorses Jesus to His Friend
JOHN 1:43-46

John the Baptist called Jesus the Lamb of God. Andrew understood Jesus was the Messiah. Philip calls Jesus the fulfillment of the Old Testament promises. Jesus is the one to whom all of the Law and Prophets—another way of saying the entire Hebrew Scriptures—testified. I wonder if Philip understood just how accurate his statement was. Later in the Gospel, Jesus (while talking to those who opposed him) made a similar statement (5:39-40). The Old Testament Scriptures are all about Jesus. What a profound endorsement of Jesus Christ!

Nathanael Endorses Jesus as the Son of God
JOHN 1:46-51

Nathanael understood the Messiah was coming and was the Son of God. As soon as he understood Jesus was the Messiah, he then testified that Jesus was God's Son—his Son who had the right and authority to rule over all nations. When Philip introduced Jesus to Nathanael, he called him "the son of Joseph" (v. 45). Nathanael's eventual response was that Jesus's father was not a Jewish carpenter; his Father was the God of the universe (v. 49). How did Nathanael arrive at the conclusion this unknown carpenter was the Son of God?

Nathanael's first response to hearing about Jesus (v. 46) is not positive. He says, "Can anything good come out of Nazareth?" Nowhere in the Old Testament does it say the Messiah would be from Nazareth. In fact, Nazareth is never mentioned in the OT. We now understand Jesus wasn't born in Nazareth but in Bethlehem, which was identified by the prophets as the place of the Messiah's birth. However, Nathanael only knew where Jesus grew up.

In response to his doubt, Philip brings him to Jesus. When Nathanael meets Jesus, his heart is instantly exposed. Jesus looks *into* him and says, "Here truly is an Israelite in whom there is no deceit."

Jesus was right, but Nathanael, still not ready to believe, challenges him: "How do you know me?"

"When you were under the fig tree, I saw you," Jesus responds. Jesus's omniscience strikes Nathanael powerfully. When Jesus revealed something to Nathanael there was no way he could have known—about Nathanael under the fig tree—then Nathanael knew Jesus could see into his soul. Jesus saw both the outside and the inside of Nathanael. Even when we're not aware of it, Jesus sees us. Even when we don't see God, he is there, fully aware of all that's happening. He knows not only what's happening on the outside, but he also sees your heart.

It's difficult to reject Nathanael's endorsement of Jesus since his first response is disbelief. Nathanael wasn't looking to get caught up in something. He knew the Scriptures, and they said nothing of Nazareth. But when Jesus confronted him and looked directly into his heart, Nathanael could do nothing less than exclaim, "You are the Son of God; you are the King of Israel!" The Gospel of John is bracketed by accounts of unbelief melting into belief: Nathanael, here in chapter 1, and Thomas, in chapter 20. Both men were inclined to disbelieve, but an encounter with Jesus won their faith.

This account ends with a fascinating statement. Jesus said to Nathanael, "You will see greater things than this. . . . Truly I tell you, you will see heaven opened and the angels of God ascending and descending on the Son of Man" (vv. 50-51). Jesus was preparing Nathanael for what was coming down the road, but he was preparing more than just Nathanael. In verse 51 when he says, "You will see," that's plural. You *all* will see. What will they see? In Genesis 28 Jacob falls asleep and has a dream. In this dream he sees a ladder that extends from heaven to earth. Angels are using this ladder to move between the two. Above the ladder stood the Lord God. Jesus is the ladder to God. He is the only way into God's presence. He promises Nathanael he will recognize that Jesus alone can bring a person into God's presence.

We've seen Jesus called the son of Joseph and the Son of God. This passage ends with Jesus claiming one more title—the Son of Man. Jesus is taking this title from Daniel 7:13, a passage that clearly speaks of the Messiah. He's confirming to these disciples they're correct. Their endorsements are true. He is the one promised and sent by God.

Application

The first words of Jesus in the Gospel of John are found in verse 38: "What are you looking for?" This is the **question** that confronts each of us. What are you looking for? What are you seeking in life?

- These two disciples could have been looking for *assurance* that they were OK before God—that their effort and sincerity were sufficient to please him.
- They could have been seeking for authority, *position*, and prominence in the company of a powerful leader.
- They could have been looking for the *excitement* that would come through a new political leader, who would lead a rebellion against the establishment.
- They could have been hoping for an *escape* from the drudgery of boring, purposeless lives.
- They could have been seeking personal *affirmation*—someone to say, "You're OK."
- They could have been looking for a mystical, religious *experience*—some new feeling they'd never experienced.

Jesus asks us the same question: What are you looking for? Acceptance? Position? Influence? Excitement? Escape? Love? Security? Experience? Approval? After the question comes the **invitation**. John points to Jesus and tells his disciples, "Look" (v. 36). Jesus says to these same disciples, "Come and you'll see" (v. 39). Philip invited his friend to come to Christ with the words, "Come and see" (v. 46). Jesus made a promise to his disciples: "You will see" (v. 50). Jesus invites us to come and see what we really need. We all seek something. Jesus invites us to come and to discover in him all we'll ever need. Only Jesus Christ can fill the emptiness inside us. These endorsements of Jesus hold important lessons on what it means to be a Christian.

Christians Are Chosen by Jesus to Follow Him

Five times in this passage we read the word *found*. In verse 41 Andrew *found* his brother and said to him, "We have *found* the Messiah." In verse 43 Jesus *found* Philip. In verse 45 Philip *found* Nathanael and said to him, "We have *found* [him]." This raises an interesting question: Who really finds whom? As the great church father Augustine wrote, "We could not even have begun to seek for God unless He already found us" (quoted in Barclay, *Gospel of John*, 101). We'll see this truth in greater detail later in the Gospel when Jesus says to his disciples, "You did not choose me, but I chose you" (15:16). What did Jesus choose them to do? He chose them to follow him. Three times in this passage we see the word *follow* (vv. 37,38,40), plus "Follow me" is the simple command Jesus gave Philip (v. 43). One mark of a true disciple is following Jesus.

Christians Are Being Transformed by Jesus

When Jesus meets Simon (v. 42), he changes his name to Peter. He gives him a new name—a divinely appointed nickname. Nicknames are usually based on a past event or some defining characteristic. A sportswriter in Michigan watched a high school basketball player do spectacular things with a basketball, and the world was introduced to "Magic" Johnson. Mary I, Queen of England, became "Bloody Mary" by burning more than three hundred religious dissenters at the stake. But when God changes a name, it's often a prophetic nickname. It's a way for him to declare his intent for this person. Abram's name was changed to Abraham because he *would be* the father of many nations (Gen 17:5). Jesus is declaring his intention to transform Simon into Peter—literally, into "the rock." Peter is nothing like a rock. He's emotionally unstable.

He's impulsive. His moods travel by way of roller coaster. Yet Jesus lets Simon know he "will be" (future tense) transformed into a rock. And it happens! We don't turn to the book of 1 Simon, do we? We turn to the book of 1 Peter, and there we read the words of a man whose life has been completely transformed. This is what Jesus does to every true disciple. In the words of D. A. Carson, Jesus "so calls them that he makes them what he calls them to be" (*John*, 156).

Christians Are Calling Others to Jesus

Though Jesus was the one who chose these men, he used his disciples to testify about him—to call others to him. Andrew's first response (v. 41) was to go tell his brother about Jesus. In fact, Andrew is only mentioned three times in this Gospel (6:8; 12:22), and each time he's bringing someone to Jesus. Philip's first response (v. 45), like Andrew's, is to immediately go find a friend to bring to Jesus.

One summer I was trained as a lifeguard. In our training we spent a significant amount of time learning first aid and CPR. We knew there was a strong possibility that at some point in the summer we would scan the water and see a person frantically trying to swim. We were prepared to leap from a seat, dive in the water, swim to him, bring him back to shore, and begin medical treatment immediately. As a lifeguard, when you saw a person begin to struggle, you didn't sit there in your chair and wonder if he would make fun of your swimming stroke or if he'd reject your attempt to save him. No, you saw his helpless condition, and you did something immediately. All around us are men and women drowning in their own sin. They are frantically waving, hoping for someone to notice them and help them. How often do we sit in our shaded chairs and refuse to help them because we're concerned about what they might say or how they might respond? People are dying. Will we get out of our chairs and help them? Andrew did. Philip did. And they started with those closest to them—a brother and a close friend.

Reflect and Discuss

1. Have you ever shared your story of coming to follow Jesus with anyone?
2. Why are personal stories of salvation and change so powerful?
3. Describe what the men who meet Jesus at the end of John 1 have in common.

4. How does Philip's example inform the way you might share the gospel with skeptics?
5. How will Nathanael see greater things than a display of Jesus's omniscience?
6. What claim does Jesus make by calling himself the Son of Man?
7. What are you seeking most in life? How does Jesus answer the desires of your heart?
8. Are there areas in your life where you are not following in obedience to Jesus?
9. What obstacles keep you from sharing Jesus with others?
10. How does Jesus's divine initiative in finding disciples encourage you to tell others about him?

The Power, Passion, and Promise of Jesus

JOHN 2

Main Idea: Jesus's own example and testimony are presented as evidence he is the Christ.

I. **The Power of Jesus (2:1-12)**
   A. Jesus has the power to transform water into wine.
   B. Jesus has the power to transform people's lives.
II. **The Passion of Jesus (2:13-17)**
III. **The Promise of Jesus (2:18-22)**
IV. **Application**
   A. Remember the resurrection.
   B. Recognize Jesus throughout the Old Testament.
   C. Realize his power to transform.

What we believe matters. If we believe the economy is struggling, we choose not to invest extra money in retirement. If we believe our children's education is important, we hold off buying a new boat and instead save extra money for their future. If we believe spending time with our children is vital, we turn down the job that takes us away from home. If we believe a college degree matters, we say no to the party in order to study and pass the class. What you believe is important, but how did you come to believe it? The apostle John understands how important it is to believe on Jesus, so he lays out a detailed analysis of Jesus's life. He presents evidence Jesus is uniquely trustworthy. In chapter 1 John presented four men who made bold and convincing endorsements of Jesus, and in chapter 2 John spotlights Jesus's own example and testimony as proof he is the Christ.

The Power of Jesus

JOHN 2:1-12

Jesus and his disciples are invited to a wedding. Jesus's mother, Mary, seems to be involved in the wedding, so it may be that of a family member or family friend. They arrive and something terrible happens: the hosts run out of wine. Running out of wine is a big deal. It's the groom's responsibility to provide fitting hospitality to all of the guests. To run out of wine is insulting to everyone who's there. No one can run to the grocery store and pick up some more beverages. They're stuck—out of luck.

Mary walks over and fills Jesus in on the situation: "They don't have any wine" (v. 3). Mary isn't sharing the latest gossip with Jesus. She wants him to do something about it. He responds, "What does that have to do with you and me, woman?" (v. 4). If you or I called our mother "woman," it would be disrespectful, but in that culture this title was not mean, rude, or disrespectful. In fact, it's the same way Jesus addresses Mary when he's dying on the cross: "When Jesus saw his mother and the disciple he loved standing there, he said to his mother, 'Woman, here is your son'" (John 19:26). In that context Jesus called Mary "woman" while caring for his mother. He made sure she would be cared for after his death.

This title is not disrespectful, but it does demonstrate less attachment than another title might. Jesus could say, "Mother," but he doesn't. Mary has to learn to approach Jesus like everyone else—as a sinner in need of a Savior. Their relationship has fundamentally changed now that Jesus is embarking on his public ministry. No matter who you are, there's only one way to come to Jesus: as a sinner in need of help.

You could translate Jesus's question this way: "Why do you involve me?" He did not come to earth to do what man wanted. Throughout the Gospel of John, Jesus demonstrates a single-minded focus to accomplish his Father's will (4:34; 17:4). He did not come to obey mankind—even his mother—but God. He did obey his mother. He never sinned. But Jesus did not leave heaven to please men. Otherwise he never would have offered his life as a sacrifice for sin. If he responded to what men desired from him, he would have filled bellies, healed diseases, and overthrown Rome, and then all humanity would have died and gone to hell.

Jesus tells her, "My hour has not yet come" (v. 4). As we travel through the Gospel of John, the "hour" Jesus refers to guides our journey. In chapter 7 John adds this note: "Then they tried to seize him. Yet no one laid a hand on him because his hour had not yet come" (7:30). We find a similar statement in chapter 8. At the end of chapter 12, after Jesus has made his final, triumphal entry into Jerusalem and he is preparing to lay his life down as the perfect Passover lamb, he says to his disciples, "The hour has come for the Son of Man to be glorified" (12:23). The *hour* is the time of his suffering and death. The *hour* is the pinnacle of human history, when the perfect Son of God became sin for us so that we might be made righteous. The *hour* is the reason Jesus came to earth. He came to offer his life on the cross for our sin. He was born for the hour. He was born to die. If you combine this statement about his "hour" with an understanding of his purpose to do his Father's will, you'll see early on that Jesus came for a greater and grander purpose than even his mother or disciples realized at the time.

In spite of his mild rebuke, Mary is confident Jesus could and would do something (v. 5). She demonstrated faith—a willingness to leave it in his hands, confident that whatever he said and did was best. Wow, was she right! He makes the servants fill six large, stone water jars (each of which held between twenty and thirty gallons) to the brim (vv. 6-7). This was no trick by a cunning magician; there was no room left to slip something into the jars. Clear water was pulled from the well, poured into each pitcher until it reached the top, and when water was scooped from the pot, it was no longer water but wine. No hocus-pocus. No waving the hands. Without any outward sign Jesus is able to transform one substance into another.

Why does this account give the purpose of the water jars (v. 6)? Is it more impressive to turn water into wine if it's in jars used for purification? The inclusion of this detail shows us that the rituals associated with the old covenant are giving way to something far greater. The shadow found in the law has been replaced by the substance. Now that Jesus is here, things have changed. The water of ceremony has been replaced with something far better. External purification has given way to internal cleansing.

The servants take the wine to the headwaiter, and he's startled (v. 10). Apparently, the tradition was to use the best wine first, but the wine Jesus creates is far superior to what they had before. Even the quality of the wine testifies to the extraordinary nature of what Jesus did. It's so good that those who know what happened can draw no other conclusion than that it's miraculous. The point of this story is to reveal the power of Jesus. We see that power revealed in two ways.

Jesus Has the Power to Transform Water into Wine

If I invited you to my house, showed you a bottle of water, and asked you to transform it into something else, an entirely different beverage, and you had to do it instantaneously without touching the water or even the bottle, could you do it? Of course not. Neither can I. What does that mean? It means there's something different about Jesus. He can do it.

What are we going to do with this story about Jesus? We have two choices. Choice one: say it's not true. The Bible can't be trusted. The story is a fairy tale, and all who believe it are foolish. Choice two: realize the uniqueness of Jesus. He did something miraculous. How can he do this? The Bible says he can do it because he is the Creator.

Jesus Has the Power to Transform People's Lives

This story ends with an editorial comment by John (v. 11). There are three key words in verse 11: *signs, glory,* and *believe.* D. A. Carson writes about **signs**:

> John prefers the simple word "signs": Jesus's miracles are never simply naked displays of power, still less neat conjuring tricks to impress the masses, but signs, significant displays of power that point beyond themselves to the deeper realities that could be perceived with the eyes of faith. (*John,* 175)

The **glory** of Jesus is made visible in this act. By performing this miracle, Jesus clearly shows one of his divine attributes. His disciples saw his divine power on display, and they **believed**. The point of this account is not that Jesus can meet needs. The point is that Jesus is uniquely the Son of God here to do God's work, and we need to believe him.

The power of Jesus to transform water into wine is amazing, but the power to transform a rebellious sinner into a saint is even more remarkable. In this passage we begin to see this transformation take place in the lives of his disciples as they're trusting in him and their faith in him grows. They hear the testimony of John the Baptist and begin to believe. The works and words of Jesus convince them even further, and as they trust in him, they are transformed from lowly fisherman to bold witnesses of his unmatched power.

The Passion of Jesus
JOHN 2:13-17

Much of the Gospel of John revolves around the Passover festivals in Jerusalem. John wants to make sure we never lose sight of who Jesus was and why Jesus came. Jesus is not the main character in an interesting story. He's more than a wise teacher. Jesus came to earth because of Passover—to fulfill, once and for all, God's promise of a spotless Lamb who will take away the sins of the world (1:36).

Passover is an important time in Israel. In Jesus's day every adult male living within fifteen miles of Jerusalem is required to attend the Passover. If he's over the age of nineteen, he has to pay a temple tax. Many Jews from much farther away will make a pilgrimage to Jerusalem at Passover to participate in the celebration. When they arrive, their first destination is the temple, to pay the tax and then to offer a sacrifice in worship to God. However, when Jesus arrives, the temple doesn't look like a place of worship; it looks like a place of business. Inside the temple he finds men selling animals to be sacrificed and offering to change foreign currency for currency acceptable to pay the tax. Jesus fashions a whip and expels all of these businessmen and their livestock. The money changers have their coins spilled and their tables overthrown, and those who are selling doves are ordered to get themselves and their birds out of the temple.

Jesus is angry. How can Jesus be angry? If God is love, how can Jesus—who is God—get angry? Genuine love is compatible with anger. In fact, genuine love is sometimes demonstrated by anger. At times anger proves love is authentic. Let me give you an example: a friend of mine is passionate about ending modern-day slavery and human trafficking. He writes and speaks about it. He's visited Washington to meet with politicians. He has traveled to foreign countries to learn more about stopping it. He's worked hard to bring it to people's attention. I don't doubt his commitment to ending trafficking. I don't doubt his love for those in slavery. But I would doubt a claim that he never got angry about it. I know his love for the abused is real because he gets angry when he sees the abuse.

I could declare my undying affection for my wife, but if you saw me sit back and yawn while someone hurt her, would you believe I loved her? My love for her would be manifested by the anger I displayed at what was harming her. "Spineless love is hardly love" (Borchert, *John 1–11*, 164). Jesus's love for his Father fuels his anger at the temple's corruption. Jesus doesn't lose his temper. He's not out of control. He doesn't fly off the handle. But he is angry. He's in control of his emotions and can articulate why he's angry, and he displays his anger without sinning.

Jesus is angry because the Jews have desecrated his Father's house (v. 16). When the first temple was dedicated to God, the builder, King

Solomon, called it "an exalted temple for [him], a place for [God's] dwelling forever" (1 Kgs 8:13). At that dedication, "the glory of the LORD filled the temple" (1 Kgs 8:11). God isn't confined to the temple, but the temple is a special place where he would meet men. In this house men would come to worship him, and sacrifices were offered to him. This house was built to display his glory. But the sounds of confession have been replaced with the sounds of commerce. Gone are silent prayers to God. They have been exchanged for the angry chorus of men haggling over the price of bulls and sheep. The cooing of doves and the stink of manure now occupy the place that used to be reserved for men to humble themselves and worship God. Jesus levels a charge, but the charge is not unethical practices. They have twisted the purpose of the temple. Jesus is denouncing impure worship. The holiness and gravity of worship have been lost. People have forgotten why they come to the temple in the first place.

In another place Jesus calls them thieves, but here the focus is not on their exorbitant prices. It's not on *how* they're doing business. The focus is on *where* they're doing business. How dare they take the place of worship and turn it into a marketplace? They've set up shop in the outer court of the temple, the court of the Gentiles. Their lust for money is interfering with the Gentiles' coming to worship the one true God. They've trivialized the worship of God. When an unbeliever entered the temple and saw the commerce, he would assume the God of Israel is a prop used to extort people's money. Jesus is angry because his Father's house is being corrupted. Worship is being perverted. Kent Hughes wrote, "The way we worship reveals what we think about God" (*John*, 70). Jesus thought correctly about God. He perfectly understood the holiness, power, and authority of God. That is why he was so passionate about God's house.

In John 2:16 Jesus says, "*My* Father's house," not "*Our* Father's house." This choice of words implies the men doing this are not children of God. If you come to worship God each week and all you think about is yourself—how you can profit from religion, what you like or dislike, what you want or don't want, and what bothers you or satisfies you—then you may not be a child of God. God's people are in awe of him. God's people worship him. Coming to God in faith requires turning from self-worship to true worship. If each Sunday is a narcissistic activity of self-worship, then you are walking in the footsteps of the temple merchants.

When Jesus calls God his Father, he's stressing his unique authority to protect God's house. He's highlighting his exclusive place as the eternal Son of God—not a child of God by spiritual birth like us but forever the Son of God (1:14). At the end of this account in chapter 2, we find an editorial comment: "And his disciples remembered that it is written: Zeal for your house will consume me" (2:17). Jesus's actions caused his disciples to remember Psalm 69:9: "Because zeal for your house has consumed me, and the insults of those who insult you have fallen on me." Psalm 69 is a psalm of David. David is crying out in despair because of those who oppose him. A major source of the problems between him and his opponents is their failure to understand David's commitment to the temple. The promised Messiah would come as a son of David who was greater than David. Just as David was consumed with zeal for the temple, so too would the greater David—the Messiah, Jesus Christ. Jesus's anger at the abuse of the temple not only demonstrated his commitment to the Father, but it also demonstrated that he was the promised Messiah, sent by God.

The Promise of Jesus
JOHN 2:18-22

The Jewish leaders confront Jesus and ask him for a sign (v. 18). They want to know what right he has to do this. It's a demand for Jesus to justify himself. They desire an explanation—proof Jesus has the authority to drive people out of the temple. Their question ignores whether Jesus is just in doing it. They don't do any self-examination. The first response should have been to ask, Was this necessary? Their question does reveal that even Jesus's enemies recognize something unique about him. If you were in charge of the temple, wouldn't you want Jesus to be prosecuted? If your money-changing table was overturned or your cattle were driven out, wouldn't you hope to see Jesus hauled off to jail? You would unless there was something special about him, unless there might be a reason he's justified in doing this. The religious leaders understand Jesus is different—he's not some crazy radical. There's an inherent authority in what he does.

In verse 19 Jesus offers them a sign: "Destroy this temple, and I will raise it up in three days." It took forty-six years to build the temple, and Jesus says he'll rebuild it in three days. If they want a sign of his authority, they'll have to knock down the temple and see if he'll rebuild it in three days. In essence Jesus says, "How bad do you want a sign? Knock it down, and I'll rebuild it." But the Jewish religious leaders have already missed the sign. His disciples see it. The sign of his authority is the zeal he has for his Father's house. Just as David had great zeal for the temple, the second David would be even more zealous. Jesus comes into their midst, he fulfills the words that David prophesied about the Messiah, yet they're too concerned with other interests to see and understand who he is and what he has done.

John's third and final editorial comment (vv. 21-22) explains the greater significance of Jesus's words. Jesus is actually referring to his body. We can make at least two connections between the temple and Jesus's body. First, the temple is where God meets man. Jesus is God, and through him God has come to man in a new and unique way—a way far greater than in the temple. Second, the temple was where sacrifices were offered for sin. Jesus is the ultimate sacrifice, the sacrifice offered once and for all for the sins of the whole world. But the sign was not that his body was the temple. The sign was that after the Jewish leaders had torn down his body, he would raise it up in three days. The resurrection of Jesus Christ is the ultimate sign of his authority. If he has authority over death, then he has authority over the temple. His disciples don't immediately understand what he's saying. John says they don't make the connection until after his resurrection (v. 22). After his death and before his resurrection, his disciples are terrified. They lock themselves in an upper room (20:19), hopeless and defeated. Then the resurrected Jesus appears to them, and everything changes in an instant. They connect all that he had said before. They realize Jesus has been planning and preparing them all along.

Hearing about God's anger at sin could lead a person to despair, but the next part of the passage tells us about Jesus's death and resurrection. If people refuse to turn from self-worship, then they should despair. God's white-hot anger will be turned on them when they stand before him one day. But Jesus died—his body was torn down—and he rose again so they might find joy and hope in him. His death turned God's anger away, and if they believe in him, God will pardon them and give them life. The resurrection of Jesus assures us that God loves to make beauty out of brokenness. That's good news for broken people.

Application

Those who have trusted in Jesus Christ need to keep trusting him, even in difficult times. Satan knows the powerlessness of a doubting believer, and he attempts to plant seeds of doubt and uncertainty in our minds and hearts. John Bunyan, an English pastor from the 1600s, understood the struggle, even as a Christian, to gain victory over doubt. In his classic allegory on the Christian life, *Pilgrim's Progress,* Bunyan personifies this struggle when

> Christian and his traveling companion, Hopeful, are captured by the Giant Despair. They are taken to the Doubting Castle, where they are thrown into a dungeon cell. Christian and his companion are beaten mercilessly by the Giant Despair. One morning they are taken out of their cell and shown the bones of other pilgrims, out in the castle yard, who never escaped Doubting Castle. Christian and Hopeful refuse to give up, however, and one night, Christian remembers a way to escape. He is able to unlock their cell door and the outer gate as well, and they run for their lives. These pilgrims will escape the Doubting Castle and the Giant Despair, not by some show of force or some innate determination, but by a key called Promise. (Cited in Davey, *The Hush of Heaven,* 23–24)

What we need to conquer doubt is not a show of force or strength but a reminder of what we believe and more importantly in whom we believe. The promise that unlocked the gates of Doubting Castle was nothing more than the testimony of Jesus Christ found in the Scriptures. When you doubt, do three things.

Remember the Resurrection

The resurrection is our hope. It's the promise that turns our faith from *in vain* to *invaluable.* When seeds of doubt begin to take root, remember the promise Jesus made that he would conquer death and the grave and then read the testimony of Scripture that clearly proclaims, "He has risen, just as he said" (Matt 28:6).

Recognize Jesus throughout the Old Testament

One of the most significant keys of promise that helps gain victory over doubt is to see Jesus Christ in the Old Testament. I don't know why God changes hearts this way, but I've seen profound growth in people's understanding, appreciation, and confidence in the gospel as they've studied the Old Testament. Reading through the Old Testament and observing how clearly it testifies of Jesus Christ, how perfectly he fulfills every prophecy and illuminates every shadow, is like an espresso shot of faith. It makes me say, "Wow, God so perfectly planned and prepared my redemption from the beginning; how could I do anything less than believe in Jesus with all my heart?"

Realize His Power to Transform

Jesus can transform water into wine and sinners into saints. Jesus can transform you. He can transform your struggles, your dreams, your failures, your hopes, and your brokenness. He can transform you from the inside out.

Reflect and Discuss

1. How do we know Jesus is the Son of God?
2. How do beliefs affect your decision making?
3. What does the way Jesus addresses his mother tell us about our relationship to him?
4. What does Jesus mean when he says, "My hour has not yet come"?
5. Why does John include the detail about the purpose of the water jars in verse 6?
6. What does the wedding miracle reveal about Jesus's power?
7. How can Jesus be angry? Isn't anger sinful? Explain.
8. How should Jesus's anger with the vendors in the temple caution us in the way we enter into worship?
9. How can Jesus be speaking of his body when referring to the temple?
10. What would you tell someone who is in despair after hearing that God is angry toward sin?

Religious Credentials

JOHN 3:1-13

Main Idea: The only credential that guarantees entrance to heaven is the new birth.

I.   Nicodemus's Religious Credentials (3:1-2)
II. Religious Credentials Are Insufficient to Save (3:3).
III. The New Birth Is the Only Sufficient Credential (3:4-13).

What credentials gain a person entrance into heaven? Every man, woman, and child will stand before the God of heaven to be judged. Some will be sent to hell: a place of eternal torment. Some will be given entrance to heaven: a place of eternal joy. What credentials is God looking for? In chapter 3 Jesus gives a clear—and for many people, surprising—answer.

Before we examine the answer, we must consider the context, found at the end of chapter 2 (vv. 23-25). This short paragraph serves as a transition between the previous account—of Jesus in Jerusalem during the Passover celebration—and the accounts that follow. The next few chapters are filled with conversations. Jesus speaks with a religious leader, a promiscuous woman, a government official, and a lame man. In each conversation Jesus looks into their souls. Some believe and follow him, but many only listen to him because they want him to perform miracles. Jesus's first extended conversation in John's Gospel centers on what credentials are required to get into heaven. The first couple of verses introduce us to Nicodemus and show us his remarkable religious credentials.

Nicodemus's Religious Credentials

JOHN 3:1-2

Nicodemus is very **serious about religion**. He is a Pharisee. This is the second mention of Pharisees in the book (cf. 1:24), but it's the first encounter between Jesus and a Pharisee. The main thing to understand about Pharisees is their zeal to obey God's law. They were serious about obeying every command God had laid out in the Old Testament.

Judaism teaches that the Old Testament has 613 commandments—248 dos and 365 don'ts. The Pharisees were a religious group of around six thousand men committed to obeying every single command. When one became a Pharisee, he pledged in front of three witnesses to uphold every detail of the law for the rest of his life (Barclay, *John*, 1:140). In fact, they were so committed to obeying each command they developed additional commands based on the original 613 commandments to ensure they didn't mistakenly violate the originals.

Here are a few examples. One of the original commands was to keep the Sabbath day holy. To keep it holy one must avoid working on the Sabbath. The Pharisees spent time figuring out what constitutes work. Is tying a knot on the Sabbath work? Yes and no. Tying a rope to a bucket to draw water from a well is work. A lady tying a knot in her clothing on the Sabbath is not work. So, if you need water on the Sabbath, you can have a lady tie a knot in her clothes around the handle of the bucket and lower it. That's acceptable (Barclay, *John*, 2:142). Jeremiah 17:21 commands the Israelites not to bear a burden on the Sabbath. What constitutes a burden? Here are some of the questions the Pharisees asked (ibid., 143): Is moving a chair closer to the table work? If a woman picks up a broach to pin it on, is it work? Can a man wear dentures on the Sabbath? Are these burdens that violate the law?

The Pharisees wrote these laws and commands because they were serious about religion. They were zealous to obey. They wanted to make sure they followed every last letter of God's law. If you had a Pharisee for a kid, you would have been thrilled. You hit the jackpot. He would be serious about obedience.

Nicodemus is serious about religion, and as a result, he's **morally upstanding**. There will be no scandal where Nicodemus is concerned. His closet is free from skeletons. If you ask him a question and he responds, you can believe him. The law says, "Don't bear false witness," so Nicodemus will tell you the truth. Teachers can leave him alone in a class while taking a test, and he won't cheat. The law says, "Don't steal," so the other students' answers are safe around him.

Nicodemus is also a **powerful leader**. He's called a "ruler of the Jews" (John 3:1). Most likely Nicodemus is a member of the Sanhedrin. If you were to combine the United States Senate with the Supreme Court, you would have the Sanhedrin. Seventy men, led by the high priest, serve as the governing body of the nation, and Nicodemus is one of them. Later in the Gospel of John, Nicodemus argues a point in front of the Sanhedrin. He's clearly a man with authority and influence.

With these credentials, we might expect Nicodemus to be arrogant or haughty, but when he speaks to Jesus, he is **kind and respectful**. In verse 2 he addresses Jesus as, "Rabbi." *Rabbi* means "teacher" and is a title of respect. It's a title Nicodemus would have been called by regularly. By calling Jesus "Rabbi," he greets Jesus as an equal.

Finally, in verse 10 Jesus refers to Nicodemus as "a teacher of Israel." In the Greek, Nicodemus is literally *the* teacher of Israel—he is **extremely knowledgeable**. You don't become one of the voices, if not *the* preeminent religious voice, in Israel without having an amazing grasp of the Old Testament. Nicodemus certainly has lengthy portions of the Old Testament memorized. He's an expert in the 613 commandments, plus the additional commandments that explicated the original ones. Other religious leaders would have sought Nicodemus for advice.

If Nicodemus were around today, here's what you would think: *Man, I wish we had hired him instead of our pastor. He's got much better credentials. He's more serious about keeping the law. He's made far fewer mistakes. He's more humble. He knows the Bible better. He comes from a more prominent position. He's everything a church would look for in a pastor and more.*

Religious Credentials Are Insufficient to Save
JOHN 3:3

Jesus looks at Nicodemus and says in effect, "Your religious credentials aren't good enough to get you to heaven. The only way you get to heaven is through rebirth" (v. 3). Try to picture Nicodemus's face at this news. There would be no hiding the look of shock and amazement. "What do you mean? With all I've done, how could I be excluded from God's kingdom?" Jesus is swinging a sledgehammer and shattering the foundation Nicodemus stands on. Nicodemus has lived his entire life assuming his religious credentials guarantee him a place in God's kingdom, and now Jesus essentially says, "Sorry, Nicodemus, you're wrong. You aren't good enough to get in."

Jesus says something similar in the Gospel of Matthew. He tells the people, "Unless your righteousness *surpasses* that of the scribes and Pharisees, you will never get into the kingdom of heaven" (Matt 5:20; emphasis added). Surpasses that of those devout people? Exceeds?

That's impossible! Exactly. Entrance to heaven is out of reach, even for the most moral, upstanding, law-keeping person you know.

The New Birth Is the Only Sufficient Credential
JOHN 3:4-13

Only one thing gains a person entrance to heaven, and that's being born again. Jesus uses the word *unless*. The new birth is the exclusive way to enter heaven. Nicodemus takes it literally: "How does that work? What do you mean? It sounds impossible" (v. 4). But Jesus is not referring to a physical birth (vv. 5-6).

Jesus is flipping Nicodemus's theology upside down. Nicodemus thought entering God's kingdom had everything to do with physical birth. If a person was born a Jew, he would automatically have a spot in God's kingdom. He would only be *kept out* if he were blasphemous or extremely wicked (Carson, *John*, 189). But Jesus says the opposite. No matter who a person is, he is automatically kept out of God's kingdom by his sin. He would only be *let in* if he were born again.

If being born again isn't a physical birth, then what is it? Jesus says it's a spiritual birth. The Spirit of God makes a person alive and new from the inside. The new birth happens when God's Spirit animates the human spirit, making a person alive to the things of God. *It's the total transformation of a person from the inside out.* Nicodemus and the Pharisees had studied the Old Testament, but they missed what God said. God said following external laws would never be enough for a person to enter his kingdom. What a person needed was an internal transformation. God made this promise in the Old Testament:

> *I will also sprinkle clean water on you, and you will be clean. I will cleanse you from all your impurities and all your idols. I will give you a new heart and put a new spirit within you; I will remove your heart of stone and give you a heart of flesh. I will place my Spirit within you and cause you to follow my statutes and carefully observe my ordinances.* (Ezek 36:25-27)

In spite of all of his learning, Nicodemus had missed it. He was so focused on cleaning the outside and keeping external laws that he missed what God said. In essence God said, "You need to be clean on the inside—washed with *water*. You need your heart to come alive by my *Spirit*. Then, and only then, will you be able to obey me." The Pharisees thought God wanted radical external conformity, and they missed the promise of radical internal transformation. God said, "I don't want you to clean yourself up. I want to make you brand-new."

We often think God is after a clean outside. "If I just get things in order—get a haircut, start making better choices, avoid sin, go to church, look nice—then God will be pleased." God is not interested in your personal remodeling project. He wants to remake and reshape you from the inside. We struggle to understand this because we don't understand how bad we are. We think we're pretty good. Like Nicodemus, we think our religious credentials will stand up to God's examination. We don't understand God's requirement: perfection. After Jesus said your righteousness must exceed the Pharisees' righteousness to enter heaven, he went on to say, "Be perfect, therefore, as your heavenly Father is perfect" (Matt 5:48). But you can't be perfect! In fact, we're all far from perfect, so we need more than a little touch-up. We need to be made new. Our radical corruption from sin demands a radical redemption from God: we need a brand-new birth.

Nicodemus is floored by this news, but Jesus explains how this new birth happens (John 3:7-8). The new birth is a sovereign work of the Spirit of God, which is unmistakably evident in a person's life. Jesus uses the wind to illustrate the Spirit's work. He says that "the wind blows where it pleases," and so does the Spirit. In other words, *you can't do anything* to make yourself come alive spiritually. You may be able to clean up the outside, but you can't remake the inside. What must happen for you to enter God's kingdom is something you are unable to do.

You can't do anything to enter God's kingdom. You can't keep enough rules. You can't give enough money. You can't attend enough services. You can't memorize enough verses. You didn't do anything to be born physically, and you can't do anything to be born spiritually. The only way you can be born again is for the Spirit of God to do it all. If you're not a Christian, you won't become one by work or effort or ability or sacrifice, but you can pray for God to send his Spirit like the wind and blow through your dead heart and make you alive. If you are a Christian, you didn't become one because you're particularly lovable, smart, or talented. You're a Christian because the Spirit of God blew where he wished, and he wished to blow inside your soul. He swept through your heart and brought you to life; he made you alive to God. R. C. Sproul wrote,

> If you have in your heart today any affection for Christ at all,
> it is because God the Holy Spirit in his sweetness, in his power,

in his mercy, and in his grace has been to the cemetery of your soul and has raised you from the dead. (*John*, 40)

The new birth is a sovereign work of God's Spirit, and it is an evident work of God's Spirit. We may not know where the wind is coming from, where it's going, or why it's blowing, but we know when it's there. I drove by a stretch of road where a tornado had hit. I wasn't there when the tornado came. I don't remember hearing about the tornado in the news. But I knew a tornado had gone through there because along both sides of the interstate I saw uprooted and snapped trees—unmistakable evidence of a mighty wind. When the Spirit of God blows life into a person's soul, there will be unmistakable evidence. The first piece of evidence is that the person will believe in Jesus. That's what Jesus tells Nicodemus (vv. 9-13).

If you've been born again, you will believe what Jesus says. You will understand he came from heaven to be born as a man, and you will place your faith in him. The single, unmistakable sign of the new birth is faith in Jesus. It's not respect for Jesus or a good opinion of Jesus—Nicodemus had both of those. It's wholehearted faith in Jesus. It's believing every word he says and committing everything to him. When the Spirit blows, we don't find toppled trees; we discover toppled doubts. The Spirit uproots the forest of skepticism and self-reliance that grows in our hearts and plants seeds of faith.

Conclusion

At one point Chuck Colson was one of the most hated men in America. He was part of the Nixon White House and was sent to prison for his role in the Watergate scandal. When he got out of prison, he wrote a book called *Born Again*. In the book he claimed to have had his life radically transformed by Jesus Christ. People were skeptical. Eventually their skepticism faded as they watched Colson devote his life to teaching the Bible in prisons around the world.

It doesn't matter if you're morally blameless like Nicodemus or morally compromised like Chuck Colson. You may think you're really good, or you may think you're really bad. No matter who you are, when you stand before the God of heaven, the only thing that will matter is whether the Spirit of God has transformed you from the inside out.

What Nicodemus thought was a title of honor—I'm a Pharisee, a member of the Sanhedrin, the teacher of Israel—was actually a stumbling block keeping him from God. What's keeping you from being born again? Someday you'll stand before him, and he'll ask to see your credentials. You can't bluff him. You can't trick him. You can't impress him. All that matters is whether he's transformed you from the inside out—whether he's made you new.

Reflect and Discuss

1. Who were the Pharisees, and what did they do?
2. What do we know about Nicodemus from this passage?
3. How is Nicodemus's interaction with Jesus different from the way other Pharisees interacted with Jesus?
4. What are we to believe about Jesus from this passage?
5. How is the central message of this passage good news for you today?
6. What does it mean to be born again?
7. How does the need to be born again show the folly of the Pharisees' extreme focus on obedience?
8. Is it hard for you to believe that God desires an internal transformation in your life rather than external conformity?
9. What evidence will exist in the life of a person who has been born again?
10. Why are Jesus's words to Nicodemus a message of hope to sinners?

The God Who Loves

JOHN 3:14-21

Main Idea: God is not a ruthless old man but a kind, loving Father.

I.   **The Reality of God's Love (3:14-16)**
II. **The Reason Jesus Came (3:17)**
III. **The Result of Belief (3:18)**
IV. **The Response of Man (3:19-21)**

Time magazine asked a number of people how they pictured God. Here was one response: God is "a lot like he was explained to us as children. As an older man, who is just and who can get angry at us. I know this isn't the true picture, but it's the only one I've got" (Elson, "Toward a Hidden God"). This response is pretty common, particularly for those who've grown up in religion. God is the unhappy, white-bearded father figure who "gets angry at us."

These verses provide a close look at the heart of God and reveal he's not a ruthless old man. He's a gracious and kind God—a God who loves. These verses also follow Jesus's conversation with Nicodemus. We're not entirely sure where the conversation with Nicodemus ends and teaching of the disciples begins. Jesus has just said he came from heaven (v. 13), and that leads him to talk about who God is, what God is like, and what God has planned for humanity.

The Reality of God's Love
JOHN 3:14-16

John 3:16 may be the most famous, most well-known, and most loved verse in the Bible. If a person knows just one verse, it's most likely this verse. It's the first verse children learn. But this verse begins with a word that's easy to overlook. It's the little word *for*. It shows us verse 16 connects to verses 14-15. Jesus says he "must be lifted up" in death. Why would Jesus, the Son of God, need to be publicly executed? Verse 16 is the answer. The death of Jesus was necessary because God loved us. The death of Jesus Christ—the horrible crucifixion of the Son of God—is a direct result of the love of God for you and me. God's love is chiefly displayed through the death of Jesus Christ.

The third word in John 3:16, the way most of us memorized it, is the word *so*, which can be understood two different ways. It could mean God really, really loves us—he *so* loves us. Like when you ask a child how big something is and she stretches out her arms and says, "It was *so* big." It could thus reveal the **intensity** of God's love. Or it could refer to the **demonstration** of God's love. That's why the CSB translates it "in this way." That's how it's used here. It doesn't diminish the intensity of God's love for us, but it shows us his love was demonstrated in a real and tangible way. "For God loved the world *in this way: He gave . . .*" (emphasis added). The proof of God's love is that he acted on it.

How do we know someone loves us? They say three magic words: "I love you." These words make your heart explode inside you the first time someone whispers them in your ear. But those words are not the only reason we know someone loves us. In fact, they're probably not the main reason we know we're loved. We've had conversations around our dinner table about love. I remember one time my wife asked our boys how they knew I loved them. Now, I tell them I love them every day, but when they were asked, none of them said, "Because he says so." Without fail, they answered with something I've done, generally involving time or money: "He plays video games with me," or, "He bought me a lightsaber." It's always the *demonstration* of my love that assures them I love them. We can be confident God loves us not simply because we hear the words "I love you" but because we see the demonstration of his love. We see the sacrifice of something far more precious than time or money. The gift of love that God gave was his only Son.

Notice the deliberate choice of words. God "gave" his only Son. In the next verse we find God sent his Son (v. 17). While both are true, this first one reminds us of God's sacrifice. He offered something dear to him, something he cared about. He's not like the boy who giftwraps the toys he no longer plays with as a birthday present for his little brother. God's love is displayed in this amazing gift. God doesn't require us to pay something to purchase it or do something to earn it. Salvation is free, but it's not cheap. This gift costs us nothing, but it cost the Son of God his life. God willingly gave his Son for you.

God gave this gift as a demonstration of his love, and his love was displayed to the entire world. His love for the world is remarkable not because the world is so *big* but because the world is so *bad*. We did not deserve his love. We did not earn it. We were rebels against God, yet God still gave us the gift of his Son (Rom 5:8). John 3:16 is not about our loveliness but about God's love. The text does not say God loves us (present tense) *now* that we have been made his children. It says God loved us (past tense) *before* we were saved. God is the one who acts first in salvation. God is the one who loves first. The apostle John would later write, "We love because he first loved us" (1 John 4:19).

God's righteousness was on display at the cross. His holiness and hatred for sin were seen in the severity of the punishment. When Jesus took upon himself the punishment our sin demanded, he testified to the world that God is absolutely and unquestionably righteous. Let us never doubt the love of God. You were not on the cross; God's own Son hung there. You did not pay that terrible price; Jesus did.

The Reason Jesus Came
JOHN 3:17

God's purpose in sending his Son was not to condemn the world (v. 17). The Jews were looking for a religious leader, a king to condemn the Romans and liberate the Jews from oppression. But that's not why Jesus came. He did not need to come to earth to condemn mankind. We were condemned already (v. 18). That's clear throughout human history. Man first sinned in the garden of Eden. Adam and Eve foolishly stepped out from under God's perfect and wise rule, deciding they knew what was best. The result was condemnation. They were not only expelled from God's presence and from life in the garden, but they were placed under a sentence of death. From that point forward, human history is a series of funerals.

> You are going to die. Take a moment to let that sink in. You are going to *die*. One morning the sun will rise and you won't see it. Birds will greet the dawn and you won't hear them. Friends and family will gather to celebrate your life, and after you're buried they'll return to the church for ham and scalloped potatoes. Soon your job and favorite chair and spot on the team will be filled by someone else. The rest of the world may pause to remember—it will give you a moment of silence if you were rich or well known—but then it will carry on as it did before you arrived. (Wittmer, *The Last Enemy*, 13)

We needed something we could not supply ourselves. No amount of human ingenuity or human cunning would ever bring salvation. We love to make a big deal about mankind's accomplishments. "Look how far man has come. Look what we can do." But are we any closer to solving our greatest dilemma, our need for salvation from sin and death? We could no more save ourselves than a baby could birth himself. That's what Jesus told Nicodemus just a few verses earlier. We were drowning in a sea of sin, and we needed someone to come to our rescue. God sent his Son *into the world*. No mere man could ever save us from death. God had to send Someone unique into the world. One who was both God and man. Jesus came so that you "will not perish" but have "eternal life." In this context *to perish* is used in contrast with *eternal life* and refers to eternal perishing. It's the same word Jesus used in, "Don't fear those who kill the body but are not able to kill the soul; rather, fear him who is able to *destroy* both soul and body in hell" (Matt 10:28; emphasis added).

Each man and woman who rejects Jesus Christ will spend eternity in hell. Hell is not a joke or a party. Hell is a real place. Hell is a lake of fire that burns forever. Hell is a place of eternal conscious torment (Matt 13:42; 25:41; Mark 9:48; Luke 16:19-31; Rev 14:11). Hell is a place where the punishment for sinning against an infinitely holy God is infinitely experienced by sinners. We can place our faith in Jesus Christ and his sacrifice for our sin and enjoy eternal life in our Father's house, or we can reject the truth and eternally suffer in hell as a result of our sin. The difference between eternal death and eternal life is believing on Jesus. We've already seen this word translated *believe* eleven times in the Gospel of John. To *believe* means we must acknowledge the claims of Jesus, yield our allegiance to him, and place our trust in him as the only hope of salvation from sin and death.

In John 3:14 Jesus uses an interesting Old Testament illustration to explain his purpose for coming. After God delivers his people from the land of Egypt, they begin to complain. In Numbers 21:5 they say in essence, "We have no food, no water—the food you gave us is awful. Did you bring us out here to die?" God responds to their complaining by sending poisonous snakes to bite the people. Their bite brings death. After the people repent, God commands Moses to craft the image of a snake and mount it on a pole. Those who look at the pole will live; the serpent's bite won't kill them. There's only one hope for the Israelites who have venom coursing through their veins. They could try something else, but it wouldn't work. Their only hope was the bronze serpent lifted up. Our only hope is the Son of God lifted up. For the Israelites life and death hung in the balance, but for us eternal life and eternal death hang in the balance.

John 3:17 ends with two important words: "through him." Only through Jesus Christ can we be saved. No one else—not Mohammed, not Allah, not the government, not yourself—no one but Jesus can save you from your sin.

The Result of Belief
JOHN 3:18

Whoever believes in Jesus is not condemned. To *condemn* means "to judge a person to be guilty and liable to punishment" (Louw and Nida, *Lexicon*, 56.30). We are no longer guilty. Our sin has been removed, and nothing can be held against us. Jesus did for us what we could not possibly do for ourselves. We could stand before God and proclaim our innocence until blue in the face, but it wouldn't matter. We're *not* innocent. Each one of us has sinned. God says, "For *all* have sinned" (Rom 3:23; emphasis added). Each one of us stands already marked for death. But when we place our faith in Jesus alone to save us, our sin and guilt are washed away, and we're declared innocent.

The righteous demands of the law are fulfilled, and we are free from the law of sin and death. The curse of sin no longer remains on us. We're not condemned, and we cannot be condemned. If God has declared us innocent, who has the right to charge us with sin (Rom 8:34)? Jesus—the one who paid our penalty—is now standing at God's right hand, and no one is going to be able to tell God we still need to pay for our sin. Not a chance. Jesus paid it all. Nothing is left to pay. There's no double jeopardy. The punishment for our sin has been poured out on Jesus Christ, and we will never have to pay it.

In John 3:18 the phrase "is not condemned" is in the present tense, which means our condemnation has already been removed. It doesn't just anticipate a final day when God removes the guilt from us and does not cast us into eternal punishment. It says, "Right now, right here, you are free from condemnation." It's easy for a Christian to feel the weight of sin and guilt and condemn himself. When he does so, he forgets the power of the cross. We've already been freed from sin's guilt. Sin is no longer our master. We shouldn't wallow in the guilt of our sin.

Unfortunately, verse 18 has a second half: "Anyone who does not believe is already condemned." We know sin has consequences. Whenever we hear the gruesome account of a murder, our first thought is that whoever did it needs to pay. We demand justice. All sin, including our own sin, regardless of the size, bears a penalty of death. "For the wages of sin is death" (Rom 6:23). Your sin makes you guilty before God, and someday you will stand before holy God and experience his awful and terrifying judgment. If you have not believed on Jesus Christ, if you have not turned to him as your only Lord and Savior, then your condemnation has not been removed.

Most of us think we're OK because we're decent people. We look around and compare ourselves to the worst people we can find, and we feel pretty good. But pride and self-sufficiency often get in the way of admitting the real problem and addressing the real need. Every man, woman, and child is a sinner in need of a Savior. God is our Creator, and he deserves our trust and honor, but we have disrespected him. Scorning the infinite God is an infinitely serious offense, deserving infinite punishment.

The Response of Man
JOHN 3:19-21

Words like *condemnation* and *judgment* could make you doubt God is loving, but these verses make it clear: condemnation is a result of the refusal to accept God's gift. People will face the consequences of their sin not because God's gift of Jesus is insufficient but because they refuse to turn from their sin and trust in Jesus to save them from sin's penalty. If you reject Jesus Christ, you have no one to blame but yourself. People are condemned to hell not because of something faulty in God's gift of Jesus. He is perfect. He is sufficient. He alone can meet the needs of sinful man. When people reject his gift, it reveals the condition of their hearts. It reveals hearts blinded by sin. The fault lies in the sinner, not the Savior.

The message of the Bible is a simple message about God's love and mercy, about man's sin and need, and about the rescue that's found in Jesus Christ. In simple words Sally Lloyd-Jones captures the love of God demonstrated in the death of his Son:

"So you're a king, are you?" the Roman soldiers jeered. "Then you'll need a crown and a robe."

They gave Jesus a crown made out of thorns. And put a purple robe on Him. And pretended to bow down to Him. "Your Majesty!" they said.

Then they whipped Him. And spat on Him. They didn't understand that this was the Prince of Life, the King of heaven and earth, who had come to rescue them.

The soldiers made him a sign—"Our King" and nailed it to a wooden cross.

They walked up a hill outside the city. Jesus carried the cross on His back. Jesus had never done anything wrong. But they were going to kill Him the way criminals were killed.

They nailed Jesus to the cross.

"Father, forgive them," Jesus gasped. "They don't understand what they're doing."

"You say you've come to rescue us!" people shouted. "But you can't even rescue yourself!"

But they were wrong. Jesus could have rescued Himself. A legion of angels would have flown to His side—if He'd called.

"If you were really the Son of God, you could just climb down off that cross!" they said.

And of course they were right. Jesus could have just climbed down. Actually, He could have just said a word and made it all stop. Like when He healed that little girl. And stilled the storm. And fed five thousand people.

But Jesus stayed.

You see, they didn't understand. It wasn't the nails that kept Jesus there. It was love. (*The Jesus Storybook Bible*, 302–6)

Reflect and Discuss

1. What are we to believe about Jesus from this passage?
2. How would you describe God to someone who has never heard of him?
3. Why is the word "for" at the beginning of John 3:16 so important?
4. How is the death of Jesus a direct result of God's love for us?
5. What reasons do you have for confidence in God's love?
6. In what ways might John 3:16 change how you view and respond to sin in your own life?
7. How has the gift of Jesus changed both your life and your eternity?

8. How do those who place their faith in Jesus mirror the Israelites afflicted by snakes in the wilderness?
9. What does *condemned* mean? What does it mean not to be condemned?
10. Do you feel no condemnation through Christ? How can you remind yourself and other believers that there is no condemnation for those in Christ?

Pointing to Jesus

JOHN 3:22-30

Main Idea: John the Baptist tells his followers that his ministry is all about pointing other people to Jesus.

I. **John the Baptist's Perspective on Ministry (3:27)**
II. **John the Baptist's Pattern of Ministry (3:28)**
III. **John the Baptist's Pleasure in Ministry (3:29)**
IV. **John the Baptist's Purpose in Ministry (3:30)**

The first YMCA was started in London in 1844 in response to the working and living conditions in London at that time. It was a rough place to live, and many of the young men who came there for work were living in awful conditions. A farmer-turned-shopkeeper named George Williams saw the need, and he along with eleven friends founded the YMCA. The acronym stands for Young Men's Christian Association. The YMCA was to be a place for spiritual refuge—Bible studies and prayer times—to help the young men who had moved to London for work.

When I was in the early stages of planting a church, we needed to find a building to meet for our services. One of the places we looked into was a new YMCA. We walked in to talk with the person in charge about the possibility of renting the YMCA out on Sunday mornings for a church service. He told us, "I don't think we're able to do anything with churches or religious organizations." Here's how I wanted to respond: "So you're telling me the Young Men's *Christian* Association can't be associated with Christians?" This organization founded to minister to young men in the name of Christ had forgotten why it started. It had drifted from its purpose. This happens a lot. It can happen to us. The ministry of John the Baptist provides a fresh reminder of the purpose of all Christian ministry.

In John 3 we're deposited into the middle of a brewing conflict (vv. 22-26). Two charismatic leaders have emerged, and people are flocking to hear both of them. The disciples of one of them start to grow a little frustrated. "Why's Jesus getting all of the attention? Why are people following him?" So they bring these questions to their leader.

John's answer is a bit surprising. Here he has a captive audience devoted to following him. He has the perfect opportunity to declare why he's the man. But he doesn't. When John the Baptist is asked about the popularity of Jesus, he tells his followers that his ministry is all about pointing other people to Jesus.

We're dropped dead center into a "dispute." The ESV translates it "a discussion" (v. 25). That's the phrase married couples use that really means "argument," and that's what it means here. Apparently a Jewish man brought up the subject of purification with some disciples of John the Baptist. Something in this conversation triggered frustration over what was happening.

John the Baptist is the well-known, well-liked, popular spiritual leader in Israel. He's the wild man who dresses crazily, eats weird things, and speaks with remarkable power. John is a spiritual attraction. People flock from all over to hear him preach and then to be baptized by him. Now someone is beginning to steal John's thunder. Jesus and his disciples are attracting attention. John's disciples feel people are being forced to make a choice between Jesus and John, and it doesn't sit well with them. After all, they've given their time, effort, and affection to John the Baptist. So they come to him and make a pointed statement—a statement with an implied question. They want to know what he thinks about those who are going to Jesus.

This section of Scripture is built around a contrast between John the Baptist and Jesus. One clue to this contrast is the use of the title "Rabbi" (v. 26). Throughout the Gospel of John, Jesus is called Rabbi. Already in this chapter we've seen it used for Jesus (v. 2), and all the other seven times in the book it's used to address Jesus. The apostle John is including this detail to help us understand how to navigate this particular passage. We're supposed to read this statement not as a question about baptism but about authority. John the Baptist's disciples are wondering who has the authority. Who should men be following?

They've already made up their minds. To them it's clear that men are to be following John, and Jesus is an imposter. You can hear the resentment toward Jesus in their statement: "The one you testified about, and who was with you across the Jordan" (v. 26). They remembered the encounter between Jesus and John. John publicly testified Jesus was the Messiah. Despite hearing what John said, they missed the significance. John's role was to bear witness about Jesus. Once he did that, it was natural for people to then follow Jesus based on John's testimony.

However, in their minds John is still the superior leader. Jesus owes everything to John, and yet he's stealing John's followers. Their concern for John drips from this statement: "Everyone is going to him" (v. 26). That's not true. In verse 23 we read that people are still coming to John to be baptized. But to John's followers the shift in attention feels like a great tragedy. John is losing his popularity and momentum to someone else.

This is one of the typical attacks of Satan that is especially effective. He convinces us to criticize others who are faithfully doing God's work. We see the crowds going elsewhere, and we get jealous. Envy and division were a massive problem for the Corinthian church. The apostle Paul wrote to them,

> *Now I urge you, brothers and sisters, in the name of our Lord Jesus Christ, that all of you agree in what you say, that there be no divisions among you, and that you be united with the same understanding and the same conviction. For it has been reported to me about you, my brothers and sisters, by members of Chloe's people, that there is rivalry among you. What I am saying is this: One of you says, "I belong to Paul," or "I belong to Apollos," or "I belong to Cephas," or "I belong to Christ." Is Christ divided?* (1 Cor 1:10-13)

Christians in Corinth started to rally around a person instead of Christ. Some chose Paul; others Apollos; still more Peter; and then the really spiritual ones looked down their noses at everyone else and said, "Well, I follow Christ." Paul asks a great question: "If you're all following Christ, how can you be on different sides? Unless there's more than one Christ, you shouldn't be split up." The remedy for the ills of the Corinthian church was to focus back on Jesus Christ. Jesus should be the focus, not earthly leaders.

John the Baptist answers the implied question from his disciples similarly. They want to know who should be followed. In essence he says to his disciples, "Don't follow me instead of Jesus. Follow Jesus." Ministry is about pointing other people to Jesus. If we miss that, we miss it all. If we surrender that, we've lost.

John the Baptist's Perspective on Ministry
JOHN 3:27

John understands God is sovereign. Everything good that happens to John is the result of God's grace in his life. As people flocked to John, crowding around him, listening to him preach, it would've been natural for him to think, *Wow, I've got it together. You know, I'm really good at this.* Maybe he'd look at the scribes and say to himself, *Those guys wasted all of that time in seminary. Ha! I didn't need any special training. I've got the tools to do it on my own.* But he didn't. He understood the divine origin of every success he had. He says, "No one can receive anything unless it has been given to him from heaven." We can do nothing good or successful apart from the kindness of God. God brought every person who listened to John preach. God brought every person whom he baptized.

When the apostle Paul was dealing with the jealousy and division in the Corinthian church, he said something remarkably similar:

> *The purpose is that none of you will be arrogant, favoring one person over another. For who makes you so superior? What do you have that you didn't receive? If, in fact, you did receive it, why do you boast as if you hadn't received it?* (1 Cor 4:6-7)

Everything good you've received, whether it's financial prosperity, physical abilities, or ministry success, comes from heaven. It's a gift from God. For John to grow frustrated, angry, or unhappy with God for taking people away from his ministry would be to act as if it was because of himself that people came. His perspective was that God is in control. God brought these people to him, and if God takes them elsewhere, that's God's decision.

The good hand of God is the reason for any success in ministry. Big buildings, growing budgets, and increased attendance don't measure the success of a ministry. The results are not ours, they're God's, and he has the authority to do with us what he desires. Jesus said to his disciples, "I will build my church" (Matt 16:18). Ministry drift happens when we lose that perspective—when ministry becomes focused on our success, our accomplishments, our victories, and our crowds. But it's not about us. It's about God and what he's doing. Ministry is about pointing people to Jesus, not gathering people to us.

John the Baptist's Pattern of Ministry
JOHN 3:28

John reminds his unhappy disciples he is not the Messiah. His role is to come "ahead of" the Messiah. He emphasizes Jesus. It's not important who John is. The only thing that matters is that people know Jesus. The reason God so powerfully used John the Baptist was because John recognized his own, inherent nothingness compared to Jesus. Martin Luther, the sixteenth-century reformer, once said, "God created the world out of nothing. When I realize that I am nothing, perhaps God can create something out of me too!" (cited in Davey, *Nehemiah*, 1). God doesn't need me to accomplish his plan. He can do it without my help, supervision, or permission. Only when I realize that can he use me.

John's role was significant. He wasn't a nobody. Jesus said about John the Baptist, "Truly I tell you, among those born of women no one greater than John the Baptist has appeared" (Matt 11:11). However, John knew his role was to point others to Jesus. He was not the story. He just needed to *share* the story. John's consuming desire was to tell others about Jesus Christ. What an impact a group of believers could make in a community if each one was consumed with a passion to spread the message of Jesus Christ! If each said, like John, "It's not about me. It's about Jesus. I'm just here to point you to him."

John the Baptist's Pleasure in Ministry
JOHN 3:29

John compares Jesus to a bridegroom and himself to the groom's friend—the best man. His role was to prepare the wedding festivities and to make sure the wedding went smoothly. The best man's job was to make sure the bride was there and the wedding could begin. Once the groom showed up, his job was complete. He did what was asked of him. What best man after fulfilling his responsibility is going to get angry because the groom showed up and married the bride? John's point to his disciples is that Jesus is the groom, and he has come to marry his bride. John doesn't matter anymore. John doesn't want people to ignore the groom and focus on him. His joy comes from watching the bride and groom come together.

I don't think John's choice of illustration was random. Throughout the New Testament we see this same imagery applied to Jesus and the church. Paul writes to a local church, "I have promised you in marriage to one husband—to present a pure virgin to Christ" (2 Cor 11:2). The church is the bride, and Jesus is the groom. The apostle John was given a glimpse of the wedding, which will take place at the end of time: "Let us be glad, rejoice, and give him glory, because the marriage of the Lamb has come, and his bride has prepared herself" (Rev 19:7). Each

Sunday worship service is a preview of that wedding, and the bride of Christ—the church—comes before the groom to renew and recite the engagement covenant that has been made. He loves us in spite of our unfaithfulness, our spots, and our failures. We come to worship each week desperate to look upon the face of the groom, to see the one who loves us with an eternal love.

John's pleasure did not come from popularity. It was not affected by influence. His pleasure was seeing the bridegroom appear. His joy was complete in the coming of Christ—not just because his mission was successful but because Jesus was there! In a real way John was both the bridegroom's friend and part of the bride. John's pleasure came not only because the "wedding" was successful—because he'd done his job—but because the one whom he needed as a Savior for his sins had come. The one he was longing for and hoping for, the promised Savior, was present. John's sin would be paid for by Jesus.

John the Baptist's Purpose in Ministry
JOHN 3:30

John's purpose was not to achieve fame or recognition. His purpose was to bring glory to Jesus Christ. He lived so the fame of Jesus might increase. Neither personal ambition nor a growing estimation in the eyes of other men motivated John. In fact, when John had the opportunity, he encouraged his disciples to follow Jesus. Not only in this passage but earlier in chapter 1, he sent Andrew and another disciple after Jesus.

Ministry drift happens when we stop thinking about Jesus and start worrying about ourselves. When we evaluate everything based on what we like and dislike, we've lost our purpose. Next time you're tempted to complain, ask this question: Am I complaining because the glory of Jesus is decreasing, or is it about me? Jesus must increase, but it will only happen as we—our wants, desires, and likes—decrease.

I spent one summer in the mountains of Wyoming. The camp I was at was up on a mountain, a solid twenty-five minutes from the closest small town. When the sun went down, the moon and stars began to light up the sky. There were no city lights for them to compete with—no haze or smog—just cool, clear mountain air. As night deepened, the intensity of the stars and the moon grew. I was amazed at how bright they were. We would lie out under the stars and enjoy the wonders of the night sky. But every morning the sun would come up, and the stars and moon, as bright as they were, would start to fade. When the sun appeared, the stars were unnecessary. John the Baptist was a star, but when the Son came, the star faded. "It's OK," John declared in essence. "Follow Jesus; he's here now."

Reflect and Discuss

1. How is the title "Rabbi" used to contrast John the Baptist and Jesus?
2. Are you too jealous to let Jesus take priority over certain things in your life—jobs, children, school, or relationships? In what ways is Jesus better?
3. Describe God's power.
4. Do you believe God's power is sufficient to do all that he wills?
5. Do you believe God's power is sufficient to change your heart, desires, and passions?
6. Would you say you have a consuming desire to tell others about Jesus?
7. How is a wedding a picture of Christ and the church?
8. Think back to a recent frustration in life and ask yourself, Why am I complaining?
9. How does John the Baptist's example of ministry affect your understanding of evangelism and discipleship?
10. What does this passage show is the ultimate purpose of ministry?

Follow Him, Boys

JOHN 3:31-36

Main Idea: John provides his disciples three reasons to follow Jesus as the Christ.

I. **The Supremacy of Christ (3:31)**
II. **The Testimony of Christ (3:32-34)**
III. **The Authority of Christ (3:35-36)**

An old Disney movie called *Follow Me, Boys* was released in 1966, and the plot is pretty simple. The main character, a musician called Lem Siddons, decides to settle down in the small town of Hickory. His plan is to become a famous lawyer and make a difference. Not long after moving to town, he attends a town meeting where a certain single lady catches his eye. In an effort to impress her, he volunteers to start a Boy Scout troop. Over time he invests more and more energy in the troop, and he impacts dozens of young men. He realizes at the end (after winning the woman's affection, of course) that he made a greater impact investing in the boys than he would have by getting rich. *Follow Me, Boys* shows the impact one person can have on the lives of others. By choosing to follow this man, these boys learned what it took to become a man. Following the right leader changed their lives.

The previous verses record a conversation between John the Baptist and his disciples. They were concerned everyone was following Jesus instead of John. John made clear his ministry was intended to point people to Jesus. In other words, John wasn't saying, "Follow me, boys." He was saying, "Follow him, boys. Follow him." As chapter 3 comes to a conclusion, we find three reasons to follow Jesus.

The Supremacy of Christ
JOHN 3:31

Jesus is not from here. He may have been born in a stable in Bethlehem, but he existed long before. John the Baptist makes a contrast between himself and Jesus. John the Baptist is "from the earth," meaning he was born of a human father and mother and came into existence as a human baby. His origin is earthly. Therefore, he belongs to the earth. He's a normal, ordinary human. Jesus is not from the earth but "from heaven." His origin is not terrestrial but eternal. He has always existed. Therefore, he is "above all."

Jesus is supreme. Nothing and no one is greater than Jesus. He has authority over all things. Everything has been put under his rule and control. Consider the majestic redwood trees, some standing more than three hundred feet in the air, or soaring mountain peaks, reaching five and a half miles into the sky. Jesus is greater. Picture the crashing ocean waves or gigantic solar systems. Jesus is greater. Think about Nobel Prize winners or heads of state. Jesus is greater. Jesus is above all. He is supreme over all creation.

Has your life ever felt out of sync? You get up in the morning and feel unmotivated. You get home and you're too tired to think. You feel like you're jogging in quicksand. In spite of the energy you're putting out, you're just not going anywhere. Your relationships are stalled, and a type of blasé monotony has crept into your soul. We often feel that way when we're out of sync with Jesus. All of creation exists to serve Jesus Christ. Every atom in the universe was created to fulfill his purpose. Whenever our lives don't line up under Jesus, we're out of sync with this world. It's like riding a multispeed bike for the first time. You go to switch the gears, and there are a few anxious moments in which you're between gears. The bike lurches slightly, the pedals aren't spinning right, your heart is in your throat, and then all of a sudden the new gear engages and everything works smoothly. Jesus is supreme over all things, including your life. When you follow him, you're in gear with God's world, but when you try to go your own way, all you're doing is spinning your wheels.

The supremacy of Jesus is easy to state, but it's not so easy to accept. The Gospels are filled with examples of people rejecting Jesus. These same people would claim to obey God, yet they rejected the one God sent. Every time the Bible states that Jesus came from heaven, it exposes the hypocrisy of the religious establishment. How can anyone be obeying God if he doesn't listen to the one who came from God, the one God sent? The more often they heard about Jesus's origin—he was in heaven from the beginning—the more foolish and silly their excuses for not obeying him looked.

For example, in John 9 Jesus heals a man born blind. The Pharisees come out to investigate. At first they dispute the claim that he had been blind. They try to make him out as a fraud. Until his parents show up: "He was born blind," they say (v. 20). The Pharisees question the blind man again, hoping to get him to denounce Jesus. Since they're asking all of these questions, the man innocently asks them in verse 27, "Why do you want to hear it again? You don't want to become his disciples too, do you?" They respond, "You're that man's disciple, but we're Moses's disciples. We know that God has spoken to Moses. But this man—we don't know where he's from" (v. 29). Here's the gist of their claim: "If we knew Jesus came from God, we would recognize his supremacy, that he is over all. But we do not know where he came from." The man Jesus had just healed makes this amazing statement to the religious leaders:

> *This is an amazing thing! . . . You don't know where he is from, and yet he opened my eyes. We know that God doesn't listen to sinners, but if anyone is God-fearing and does his will, he listens to him. Throughout history no one has ever heard of someone opening the eyes of a person born blind. If this man were not from God, he wouldn't be able to do anything.* (9:30-33)

With all Jesus has said and done, it's ridiculous to think he's from the earth. He must be from heaven. It was clear to a blind man, and it should be clear to us. Jesus came from God. Jesus is God himself, and therefore Jesus is supreme.

The Testimony of Christ
JOHN 3:32-34

In the children's game of Telephone, someone on one end of a line of kids comes up with a phrase and whispers it in the ear of the child next to him. He is not allowed to repeat it. That child then turns and whispers it in the next person's ear, and so on until it reaches the last person. The last person in line stands up and tells everyone what he or she heard. After that the person who started shares the original phrase. It's always funny how much distortion the phrase undergoes as it passes from person to person. When something is relayed over and over, you should be skeptical about how accurate it is. That's why when someone shares something with us, we want to know how they know. If they saw it or heard it, we're more likely to believe them than if it came secondhand. Everything Jesus said about God was firsthand knowledge (vv. 32-34). He didn't need to rely on someone else's information. He saw and experienced everything he spoke about.

Let's think about how this works. Do you want to know about heaven—God's home? A lot of people are interested. In fact, people are so interested they buy a book by a four-year-old child who claims to have visited heaven. Do you know who really knows what heaven is like? Jesus. He's been there. In fact, he made heaven and lived there for some time; he lives there today. We can trust what Jesus says about life and death, heaven and hell, God and man because everything he says comes from God himself, as Jesus repeatedly reminded people (8:26; 15:15).

Despite the fact Jesus's testimony is clear and firsthand, it's most often rejected (v. 32). Only a small minority receives his testimony (v. 33). However, those who do believe show their confidence that what God says is true. They affirm, literally "set their seal," that God is honest and trustworthy (v. 33). To *set a seal* is to press a unique emblem into hot wax. You do this over the flap of a scroll or envelope so that if anyone opens it the seal is broken. When a person receives a letter from you, if the seal on the envelope is unbroken and the seal is your seal, he knows that what's inside came directly from you. When a person believes the testimony of Jesus, he says, "Through Jesus I have heard God, and I testify this message is authentic. It's not a forgery. I believe the words of Jesus are the words of God." The opposite is also true—to reject the testimony of Jesus is to reject God himself. If you reject Jesus, you are calling the God of the universe a fraud.

Jesus did not come to deliver his own message but to speak the words of God (v. 34). Jesus came as the ultimate prophet. Prophets in the Old Testament spoke God's word and were given God's Spirit with the right amount of power for just enough time to fulfill their tasks, but Jesus was given "the Spirit without measure." Jesus is absolutely trustworthy. The safest thing to believe in the entire universe is the testimony of Jesus.

The Authority of Christ
JOHN 3:35-36

God has given everything into Jesus's hands. Jesus has authority over life and death, forgiveness and punishment, salvation and condemnation. Jesus has the power and authority to give eternal life. But he only does so to those who believe in him. Notice that the word *believes* (v. 36) is not in contrast with *does not believe* but with *rejects*. An essential element of believing Jesus is accepting his word and obeying him. You can't divorce obedience from belief. To believe you must obey what Jesus has commanded. What we believe and how we live are intertwined. Like strands woven together to make a rope, belief and obedience are woven together in salvation. The New Testament teaches that if you don't turn from your sin to obey Jesus, then you haven't put your faith in him.

> *So the word of God spread, the disciples in Jerusalem increased greatly in number, and a large group of priests became* obedient to the faith. (Acts 6:7; emphasis added)

> *Through him we have received grace and apostleship to bring about the* obedience of faith *for the sake of his name among all the Gentiles.* (Rom 1:5; emphasis added)

> . . . *but now revealed and made known through the prophetic Scriptures, according to the command of the eternal God to advance the* obedience of faith *among all the Gentiles.* (Rom 16:26; emphasis added)

> *This will take place at the revelation of the Lord Jesus from heaven with his powerful angels, when he takes vengeance with flaming fire on those who don't know God and on those who don't* obey the gospel *of our Lord Jesus.* (2 Thess 1:7-8; emphasis added)

> *After he was perfected, he became the source of eternal salvation for all who* obey him. (Heb 5:9; emphasis added)

> *For the time has come for judgment to begin with God's household, and if it begins with us, what will the outcome be for those who* disobey the gospel *of God?* (1 Pet 4:17; emphasis added)

True belief in Jesus is always accompanied by obedience to his Word. When we place our faith in Jesus as Savior, we're putting ourselves under his authority as Lord. You can't accept half of Jesus. You can't say, "Jesus, I'd like you to rescue me from death, but I don't want to follow you." It's a package deal. You either embrace Jesus as your Lord *and* Savior, or the wrath of God remains on you. Real faith always brings the real fruit of obedience. Faith always bears fruit.

I've seen too many parents who say, "I know my child is a Christian." "How do you know?" I ask. "I remember when she prayed and asked

Jesus into her heart." "Where is she now?" I ask. "Well, she doesn't go to church. She doesn't obey God. She lives for money or sex or the weekend. She demonstrates zero fruit of conversion. But I know she's saved." Now, I understand why we *want* to think that, but that thinking doesn't come from the Bible. Whoever believes, obeys. If they don't obey, then they never believed. All they did was profess.

Those who hold on to their sin and refuse to follow Jesus are condemned already (John 3:18), and "the wrath of God remains on" them (v. 36). From the moment we're born as sinners, as rebels against God, the wrath of God—the awesome and fearful justice of God on our sin—is placed on us. By rejecting Jesus as Lord and Savior, by refusing to submit to his authority, we ensure that his wrath remains on us for the day of judgment. But those who believe are granted eternal life. Jesus gives us a gift that cannot be matched. Eternal life has a *future perspective*. After our bodies perish, we will live forever in heaven with Jesus and the Father. But eternal life also has a *present perspective*. Eternal life refers to a certain quality of life. John says those who don't believe "will not see life"—they won't experience or enjoy life. The life Jesus gives us makes a difference now. We're made alive in him immediately. We can experience and enjoy true, spiritual life right now.

In the next chapter Jesus describes the life he offers as a fountain of water that springs up inside us and never runs dry. In chapter 6 Jesus gives the bread of life so that we will never hunger. In chapter 8 he gives us the light of life so that we won't stumble in the darkness. In chapter 10 he promises we will have life and have it abundantly. If you're a Christian, you should have a different quality of life now than you had before following Jesus. I don't mean luxury cars, yachts, and hot tubs. Those don't matter. What does matter is an attitude and perspective on life that only comes from an intimate relationship with the life giver.

Do you realize Jesus created laughter? If you're following him, laughter should be a part of your life. Jesus created adventure and beauty, everything from sunsets to sailboats; his people should not be bored. We're told in Scripture that God rejoices over us with singing (Zeph 3:17). He loves us and enjoys us so much that he can't keep from singing about us. Since that's true, how do you explain all the people in church with their arms folded across their chests who look like they ate some bad guacamole? God thinks you're special enough to sing over, but you don't think he's special enough to sing about? Christians should be the most exuberant, excited, joyful people on the block. After all, we have an intimate relationship with the Creator of exuberance, excitement, and joy. We are partners with the infinitely happy God, whose Spirit has taken up residence inside us. Our joy at being alive to God should be contagious! We should be like bottles of Pepsi that have just been shaken—ready to burst, unable to contain what's going on inside.

Believing in Jesus should make a difference now, not just on the day of judgment. When we choose to follow Jesus, we instantly become partakers of his life, and we can for the first time live as God created us to live in joyful communion with him. We can experience in Jesus the satisfaction that's impossible apart from him. We can be in sync with God and his world. Like starving men, we can run to Jesus and be satisfied forever. For the first time, we can have confidence not in ourselves but in the one who has been given all things by his Father. We don't need to worry because we are *in Christ*. We're no longer dominated by the darkness of sin. We can live in the light of Jesus Christ—abundant life to the glory of God!

In AD 354 one of the great Christian leaders was born. Augustine, bishop of Hippo, has influenced believers for the last sixteen hundred years. You might be surprised to hear the conversion story of this noteworthy Christian leader. Here's how he describes his life as a young adult:

> As I grew to manhood, I was inflamed with desire . . . for hell's pleasures.
>
> I went to Carthage, where I found myself in the midst of a hissing cauldron of lust.
>
> I was willing to steal, and steal I did, although I was not compelled by any lack.
>
> I was at the top of the school of rhetoric. I was pleased with my superior status and swollen with conceit . . . it was my ambition to be a good speaker, for the unhallowed and inane purpose of gratifying human vanity. (Cited in Piper, *Legacy*, 47)

Sin dominated Augustine. Lust and sensual pleasure held him captive. Though by all outward accounts he had everything together, his soul was empty and unsatisfied. In his heart he was dead. But one day God opened Augustine's eyes to his own sin and disobedience, and Augustine turned from his sin and followed Jesus—he rejected his disobedience and called out to Jesus to save him. Here's how he described the moment:

How sweet it was for me to be rid of those fruitless joys which
I had once feared to lose! You drove them from me, you who
are the true, sovereign joy. You drove them from me and took
their place . . . O Lord my God, my Light, my Wealth, my
Salvation. (Ibid., 57)

Listen to Augustine and to John the Baptist before him. Don't try to find
joy yourself, but come to Jesus. Don't follow your own empty desires, but
turn and follow the one who can make you alive! Follow Jesus.

Reflect and Discuss

1. Why should we follow Jesus?
2. How is Jesus "above all"? Why is this good news?
3. Why is the supremacy of Jesus easy to state but difficult to accept?
4. What does it mean to approve or "set a seal"? How does a person set
   a seal that God is true?
5. How does the difference between Old Testament prophets and
   Jesus give us assurance of his words?
6. Why is Jesus's authority good news that we should believe?
7. What is the connection between "believe" and "reject" in verse 36?
8. What always accompanies true belief in Jesus? What does this mean
   is at the foundational level of disobedience?
9. How does eternal life give us both a future *and* a present perspective?
10. How does your belief in Jesus make a difference in your daily life?

Everyone, Everywhere

JOHN 4:1-16

Main Idea: A comparison between Nicodemus and the woman at the well reveals two opposite people in opposite situations who both need Jesus.

I. **Everyone, Everywhere Needs Jesus.**
II. **Application**
    A. The need for Jesus is universal.
    B. The need for Jesus is personal.

It's fascinating to become immersed in a culture completely different from your own. When I went on a trip to Mexico, I was amazed at the differences between Mexico and the United States. They spoke a different language, and all I could say was, "*No comprendo Español.*" They ate different food, which was nothing like Taco Bell's. Their schedule was different; I quickly got used to the hour-long siesta in the middle of the afternoon. Spending time immersed in Mexican culture helped me understand the differences in culture from one country to the next.

Despite the differences one thing is always the same, no matter where you travel: *you always discover sin.* No matter where you look or how far you go, you find men and women who are sinners in need of Jesus Christ. For instance, in 2008 in Mexico, more than thirteen thousand people were murdered. In the United States it was more than sixteen thousand. That same year in Mexico, more than two hundred thousand adults were incarcerated. In the United States it was ten times as many. We could search the globe, investigating every nook and cranny on planet Earth, and everywhere we found people we would find sin. We can't escape sin because sin travels with us. It's woven into the core of our hearts.

In John 4 salvation spreads beyond the borders of Israel. In the previous chapter we eavesdropped on a conversation between Jesus and Nicodemus in which Jesus showed Nicodemus his need for a Savior. Now we'll study Jesus's encounter with a Samaritan woman. These are two different people from two different cultures with one common need. Just as the great religious leader Nicodemus needed Jesus, so too did this foreign woman.

Everyone Everywhere Needs Jesus

Jesus has been ministering publicly in and around Jerusalem and has decided it's time to head back to Galilee. He leaves Jerusalem, the center of Jewish worship, and heads to Samaria, a foreign land. These six verses are the setting for the spread of salvation to non-Jews (vv. 1-6). Jesus leaves the adoring crowds in Jerusalem to go rescue a needy woman.

Jesus and his disciples are taking a long and taxing trip from Judea to Galilee and decide in the heat of the day to stop and rest. The disciples head into town to pick up some food while Jesus rests by the well. He's not there long when a woman approaches the well to draw water. Jesus turns to her and asks for a drink.

She answers, "How is it that you, a Jew, ask for a drink from me, *a Samaritan woman?*" (v. 9; emphasis added). This verse is the key to understanding this passage. In addition, the placement of this account right after the account of Nicodemus in chapter 3 is important. When you compare the two individuals—Nicodemus and this woman at the well—you discover two opposite people in opposite situations who both desperately need the same thing: Jesus. Everyone, everywhere needs Jesus. Rich or poor, religious or secular, Republican, Democrat, or Independent, African, Asian, or American. Consider three striking differences between these two.

Their gender. This culture considered men more important than women. It was unusual for a man even to speak to a woman. When the disciples got back from their visit to town, "they were amazed that he was talking with a woman" (v. 27). Religious conversation between two men was great, but it was inappropriate between a man and a woman.

Their status. Nicodemus was respected. He was a Pharisee, which means he would have claimed obedience to every one of God's laws and more. Pharisees were known for their morality and concern for keeping every command, no matter how small. For instance, they would strain a drink before taking a sip, just in case a gnat had gotten in their cup and died. They didn't want the dead gnat to make them unclean.

This woman did not share Nicodemus's commitment to keeping the rules. Later in this conversation with Jesus, he asks her about her husband. Apparently she'd tried marriage and failed. So she tried it again and failed four more times. Having five divorces on her record, she went a different route: cohabitation.

While any conversation with Nicodemus would have been an honor, it would have been socially unacceptable to talk with the sinful Samaritan woman, but that didn't stop Jesus. In fact, Jesus was criticized repeatedly for his interaction with sinners (Mark 2:15-16).

Their nationality. He was a Jew and she was a Samaritan, and Jews and Samaritans didn't get along. I read a fascinating book on the assassination of Abraham Lincoln and the twelve-day manhunt for his assassin. I was amazed to read of the deep hatred the two sides of the nation had for each other, epitomized in the person of John Wilkes Booth. After killing Lincoln, Booth wrote about it in his diary:

> Our country owed all her troubles to him [Lincoln], and God
> simply made me the instrument of his punishment . . . and
> yet for striking down a greater tyrant than they ever knew I
> am looked upon as a common cutthroat. (Swanson, *Manhunt,*
> 389–90)

Many shared his contempt. Some families still hold an annual celebration on April 15 to commemorate the assassination of Lincoln and to honor Booth.

This same type of contempt marked the relationship between Jews and Samaritans. We get a taste of their deep-seated animosity in verse 9: "For Jews do not associate with Samaritans." A footnote in the NIV provides an alternate translation of this same phrase: "[Jews] do not use dishes Samaritans have used." The surprise on the part of the woman was not just that Jesus was talking to her—a woman, a sinner, and a Samaritan—but that he wanted to drink from a vessel a Samaritan had taken a drink from. The hatred of the Jews for the Samaritans was so strong they considered themselves unclean for even touching, much less drinking from the same cup as, a Samaritan.

The roots of this contempt were hundreds of years old. The nation of Israel had divided into two separate kingdoms, the northern and southern. In 722 BC the Assyrians captured the northern kingdom, whose capitol was Samaria. In the book of Kings, we read of the decision by the Assyrians to deport many of the Israelites from the northern kingdom, particularly from its capital Samaria. Many Assyrian and other foreigners settled in Samaria and intermarried with the remaining Jews. The result of these marriages was not only blended *nationalities* but also blended *worship.* The region of the northern kingdom, now known as Samaria, was a place that worshiped the true God along with false idols. Because of the mixed marriages and corrupt religion, the Jews from the southern kingdom treated the Samaritans with disgust. For centuries the contempt between Jews and Samaritans had grown.

Jesus had every reason not to talk with this woman, but just as he did with Nicodemus, he begins a conversation with her that penetrates to the root of the issue. He understands her heart. He understands her condition, and she doesn't. Jesus reached out to the moral Pharisee and the immoral Samaritan. Both of them were in desperate need of salvation from sin—a salvation that could only come through Jesus.

We see this same pattern in a famous story Jesus told about two brothers (Luke 15). One brother—the younger one—was like the Samaritan woman. He selfishly left his family to go party with his friends. He lived a lifestyle of drunkenness and immorality. He was a rebel, looking for love in all the wrong places. The older brother was moral and religious like Nicodemus. He had a high opinion of himself. He was arrogant (though that was probably hidden under the guise of humility). He was self-righteous and blind to his own sin. He looked down on other people, especially his younger brother. Though he kept all the rules and lived morally, he was miserable and unhappy. Both brothers—just like the Samaritan woman and the Jewish leader—desperately needed Jesus to rescue them.

Everyone, everywhere needs Jesus. The moral can't be saved by their morality; they can only be saved by Jesus. Also, the immoral are never too immoral to find salvation in Jesus.

Application

The Need for Jesus Is Universal

An Israelite needs Jesus and so does a Gentile. Everyone, everywhere needs him. The gospel of Jesus Christ is a universal message. No matter who a person is, no matter what language he speaks, no matter where he calls home, every person needs Jesus. How does this story end? After Jesus dies and rises again, he sends his disciples to every nation, and they go. For two thousand years Christians have followed Jesus's example and taken his message around the globe. First throughout the Roman Empire, then down into Africa and throughout Europe. After that Christian missionaries went east to India and China and west to the

New World. I write this today as a testimony that the need for Jesus is universal. I'm a long way geographically from a well in Samaria, yet I'm in the same place spiritually as that sinful woman.

The spread of the message of Jesus will eventually culminate when people from every tribe, tongue, and nation gather around the throne of Jesus to worship and enjoy him forever (Rev 5). Someone from every people group on the planet will be in heaven.

This reality should fuel our missionary zeal. We should pray for the nations. We should give sacrificially to see the gospel spread. What better way to use your money than to partner in the spread of the gospel around the world? That investment will outlive a boat or beach house any day. We also should go—whether for a week or a lifetime—to be a part of the global plan of King Jesus.

The Need for Jesus Is Personal

Jesus could have appeared on Samaritan television to spread the message. He could have written a book and placed it in every bookstore in Samaria. He could have held a huge evangelistic crusade in Samaria's capital city. But he didn't. He went out of his way to find this one woman and show her her greatest need. He came to her personally.

Jesus is after your heart. He's after your worship. He's after your joy. He loves you and wants to make you whole. Whether you're religious or an atheist, moral or immoral, an outcast or an insider, you need Jesus personally.

We often act as if the gospel can best be shared through big programs and events. We think it can be a large-scale, automated, impersonal process. God always works personally, and he sends us to individual people to tell them about Jesus. Jesus went to an everyday place—a well—and found a woman who needed him, and he told her the good news. Where's your well? Maybe you need to go to the cafeteria at work and talk with someone. Maybe you need to lean over the fence in your backyard. Maybe you need to sit by someone at a sports practice this week. The gospel isn't spread group to group but person to person. Every person you see shares the same need for Jesus. Jesus used this one conversation to change this woman's life. Then she went into town and started telling others. What might God do if we would each engage the people around us personally?

Reflect and Discuss

1. What trait do Nicodemus and the woman at the well share?
2. What does this passage reveal about the character of Jesus?
3. Why is it so shocking for Jesus to speak with the woman at the well?
4. Why does Jesus speak to the woman at the well?
5. Do you believe everyone, everywhere needs Jesus? How is this reflected in your life?
6. Have you ever thought your sin is not as bad as other people's sin? How does this passage refute that belief?
7. Why is the fact that Jesus spoke to the woman at the well good news for us?
8. Do you ever seek out certain types of people to serve while ignoring others?
9. Imagine what it will look like for someone from every people group on the planet to be in heaven. How might this image fuel your missionary zeal?
10. Are there places where you know people who are far from Jesus gather? How might you start a conversation with one of these people? What will you say about Jesus and why his gospel is good news?

Thirsty?

JOHN 4:7-18

Main Idea: Only Jesus can quench our spiritual thirst.

I. **Jesus Exposes Her Spiritual Thirst (4:7-10).**
II. **Jesus Offers Her Living Water (4:10-13).**
III. **Jesus Promises Her Lasting Satisfaction (4:14-18).**

I had been in China one summer for just over a week, and I had been thirsty for just over a week, craving something ice cold but constantly getting either lukewarm or hot beverages when we went to a missionary's home for lunch. We sat down at the table, and my friend brought a two-liter of Pepsi to the table. He had placed it in the freezer that morning. It came to the table perfectly chilled. As I sat there, enjoying that glass of ice-cold Pepsi, I realized how thirsty I had been. For over a week my thirst had been building, and when I finally drank something refreshing, the depth of my thirst became clear.

In John 4 Jesus is engaged in conversation with a woman. The conversation takes place around a well and centers on thirst. Jesus uses an extended metaphor about water and thirst to make a point: all of us are thirsty, and only he can quench our thirst.

Jesus Exposes Her Spiritual Thirst
JOHN 4:7-10

Jesus uses a common, everyday illustration to help her understand a spiritual reality. He asks her for a drink, to which she responds with shock. Now, in verse 10, he transitions this conversation to the spiritual. He tells her he can give her "living water." She doesn't understand him; she thinks Jesus is still talking about physical water. She essentially says, "How in the world are you going to get water from a deep well without a bucket? Where is this 'living water' you claim to have?"

Jesus focuses on one particular question she buried right in the middle of her comments: "Where do you get this 'living water'?" This is what she needs to know. However, before he answers her question about *where* the living water can be found, he first wants her to understand her *need* for this living water. Jesus points to the well and reminds her that anyone who drinks that water grows thirsty again, but the living water will quench someone's thirst forever. Every man and woman is thirsty. We each thirst for something. Jesus offers water that will forever quench our thirst. Some attempt to quench their thirst through buying stuff. They hope accumulating more possessions or the right possessions will satisfy them. Whenever they grow restless, they run to the store, pull out the plastic, and buy something, anything, to distract them for a little while longer. Others attempt to quench their thirst through food or drink. Whenever they begin to long for something more significant in life, they eat. They look for comfort and solace in a fancy dinner or a bag of Oreos. They attempt to silence their spiritual thirst by quenching their physical thirst with another beer, glass of wine, or Diet Coke.

In Ecclesiastes King Solomon writes about his attempt to quench his thirst. In chapter 2 he lists all of the things he did to silence the internal craving for something that would satisfy. He tried laughing, consuming good food and drink, building great houses and gardens, accumulating gold and silver, acquiring slaves, building a harem of concubines to fulfill all of his sexual fantasies, and becoming famous for his knowledge and wisdom—he tried it all, and here is what he found:

> *All that my eyes desired, I did not deny them. I did not refuse myself any pleasure, for I took pleasure in all my struggles. This was my reward for all my struggles. When I considered all that I had accomplished and what I had labored to achieve, I found everything to be futile and a pursuit of the wind. There was nothing to be gained under the sun.* (Eccl 2:10-11)

In John 4, Jesus cuts to the heart of this woman's search for happiness. He tells her to go get her husband (v. 16). "I don't have a husband," she says. "You're right," Jesus replies in essence. "You have had five and a boyfriend." She was attempting to quench her thirst through relationships. She was moving from one bad relationship to another and from one bed to another. But like a traveler in the desert, her thirst was never quenched. Because of our sin each one of us, like this woman, is thirsting for something—some experience, some person, some position—that will satisfy. Yet everything we turn to leaves us empty and longing for more. It doesn't make a difference who we are. We could say, "Sure. Of course she was searching for something. Look at her! She's a wreck." But in the last chapter we looked at Nicodemus. Why do you think Nicodemus came to Jesus? Was it because he had everything figured out? Was it so he could shed light on some theological issue Jesus misunderstood? No. He came because he was thirsty. For years he had attempted to satisfy his thirst by keeping rules and studying theology and helping people, but it wasn't enough. It could never be enough. Nothing he did could ever ultimately satisfy.

Jesus Offers Her Living Water
JOHN 4:10-13

The woman asks Jesus, "So where do you get this 'living water'?" (v. 11). Her question is one each person asks at some point: "Where can I find that which satisfies?" I know you've asked it, whether you've verbalized it or not. Your life is a pursuit of something to satisfy your thirst. Whether you're a homemaker or a vice president, a mechanic or an engineer, you make decisions you hope will, over the long term, bring you satisfaction.

We find the living water by coming to Christ and asking him (v. 10). Only through him will we discover the satisfaction we look for so desperately in other things. The only remedy for our parched souls is the living water freely dispensed by Jesus. Later, Jesus repeats this invitation (v. 14). The solution is that simple. We must abandon our attempts to find satisfaction on our own and turn to Jesus for lasting satisfaction. The more I think about it, the more I'm persuaded it's too simple for many people. We're convinced we can do it ourselves. We think if we're ever going to be happy and satisfied, it'll happen because we've climbed the ladder and done the work on our own. Ultimately we think we've got to find our satisfaction in our own effort because we know best what we need and we're the best ones to supply it. A lot of us are like the man who came to Jesus one day, asking, "Good teacher, what must I do to inherit eternal life?" (Luke 18:18). We want to *do* something for it; we want to earn it. We don't want to admit or acknowledge that we're unable by ourselves ever to be fulfilled. We don't want to concede that we need help. We'd rather go through life filling our jar with water that doesn't satisfy than turn to Jesus and ask him for the water that actually quenches our thirst.

The promise of living water is written throughout the pages of the Bible, and with it we find the result of rejecting the living water—the barrenness of seeking satisfaction apart from God. We see it when the prophet Jeremiah spoke God's words to the people of Israel: "For my people have committed a double evil: They have abandoned me, the fountain of living water, and dug cisterns for themselves—cracked cisterns that cannot hold water" (Jer 2:13). The chosen people of God had the fountain of living water open and available to them. Their thirst could be quenched, their souls satisfied by God! Yet tragically they abandoned God. They turned from the all-satisfying source of life and strength and attempted to find satisfaction elsewhere. Instead of drinking freely from the fountain of life God offered, they took out their hammers and chisels and started carving out little bowls and digging wells. Yet every time they poured water into their handcrafted vessels, it leaked out.

They thought, *I know what's best. I know how to be happy. I want to do it my way.* They sought satisfaction in something other than God. This is the essence of sin: *pursuing satisfaction in something other than God.* Sin is not fundamentally a failure to check certain moral boxes. We think sin is primarily about the actions we do and don't do: "Sin is when I lie, curse, steal, or get angry." But I sin any time I pursue satisfaction in something other than God. That's certainly revealed in lying, cursing, and stealing, but it's also seen in pride, self-reliance, and apathy. Any time we pursue satisfaction in something other than God, we commit idolatry. We're placing that thing on the altar of our hearts, and giving ourselves to it, hoping it will do for us what only God can do.

God is not opposed to your pursuit of happiness and satisfaction. He made you to pursue genuine happiness, joy, and satisfaction in the one person who can truly offer it. He designed you to find true delight in him. In fact, the imagery of living water is full of promise and reward. Consider this promise from the perspective of a people living in a dry and dusty land, where drought would be devastating, where a lack of water meant a lack of food. Clean, pure, abundant, flowing water was a wonderful picture of promise and security. Jesus makes clear to the Samaritan woman that joy and satisfaction can only be found in him.

Jeremiah had warned the people about their sin. He rebuked them for turning from God and attempting to find satisfaction and joy outside of a relationship with him. Another prophet, Isaiah, told the people about the promised Messiah (Isa 11). The one God was sending to redeem the people from their sin, this Messiah, is Jesus Christ. The following chapter, Isaiah 12, is a song the redeemed will sing. "You will joyfully draw water from the springs of salvation" (Isa 12:3). Coming to God in salvation is pictured as a free and open source of water. Every need is met. Our deep, spiritual thirst is finally and fully quenched in Christ.

Jesus Promises Her Lasting Satisfaction
JOHN 4:14-18

Here's the picture Jesus paints: Every man and woman is in a desperate, life-and-death situation. Spiritually we're like travelers lost in the desert of sin and death. We need help. Our only hope for life is water. We try, over and over, again and again, to find water. We turn to this person, that activity, this good work, or that religious system, hoping to find the solution. Sometimes it seems like we've found it. For a while it seems we've stumbled on water to quench our thirst and meet our need, but before long we realize what we thought was the solution was not. So we start looking again. We search desperately for something, anything, that will dull the thirst, even if it's only for a moment. Yet all we can find apart from Christ is saltwater. It seems to help, but we end up more parched than we were before.

C. S. Lewis called this "an ever-increasing craving for an ever-diminishing pleasure" (*Screwtape*, 44). Have you ever felt that? Everyone who's looked at pornography has. Each look at the screen produces more cravings and less pleasure. Everyone who has been addicted to a substance has. It takes more to get high, and the high gets shorter. Everyone who's been in a codependent relationship has. As the relationship gets worse, the feeling of needing the other person gets stronger. Everyone who's proud has. We need more and more applause, even as it matters less and less. Everyone who's self-righteous has. We write more and more rules and find less and less joy.

The root of sin is pursuing happiness in something other than God, and sin produces an ever-increasing craving for an ever-diminishing pleasure. Now look closely at Jesus's promise to this woman. If she will turn to him and take one sip of the living water, her thirst will be quenched. But the promise continues: not only is her thirst quenched, but she will always have access to the living water. The living water will become a spring of water within her. We never need to be desperate again. Once we turn to Jesus and discover in him the fulfilling, satisfying source of spiritual nourishment, we can drink again and again. The spring always flows.

I love John Piper's well-known quote, "God is most glorified in us when we are most satisfied in him." We demonstrate the surpassing worth of Christ when we reject earthly, empty pleasures and embrace him as our all-consuming desire. A Christian who doesn't seek satisfaction in money, vacation, leisure, healthy children, or a good job but seeks Jesus instead makes a statement about the value of Jesus. When we find our greatest satisfaction in him, we bring him the most glory. But a Christian who constantly drinks from the pleasures of this world calls Jesus a liar because he comes to that woman standing by the well and contradicts the offer of Jesus. He says, "Don't listen to him. His water doesn't really satisfy."

Only Jesus can quench your thirst. Whatever you crave, whatever you long for, whatever you need, only Jesus can provide. Stop drinking from the wells of sin and come to Jesus. He offers living water. He offers what can truly satisfy.

Reflect and Discuss

1. Why does Jesus first focus on the woman's need for living water? What can we learn from his example in our own ministry opportunities?
2. What are some ways you try to quench your spiritual thirst? How does the good news of Jesus satisfy those desires?
3. Take a moment to reflect on Ecclesiastes 2:10-11, then thank God for Jesus's work and the changed heart he has given you.
4. How does one find living water? How does this change the way we fight against desires for lesser things?
5. Do you struggle to believe you will find fulfillment in Jesus? What good news is there for you in this passage?
6. What is living water? What does it mean to be satisfied by it?
7. Describe sin in the context of this passage. How does the definition inform our satisfaction?
8. Reflect on your own story of belief in Jesus. Where were you seeking fulfillment? How has belief in Jesus satisfied and changed your desires?
9. How is a Christian who constantly drinks from the pleasures of this world testifying against Jesus?
10. Why is the woman's ability to worship in Spirit and truth an issue of belief and not knowledge?

Jesus Saves

JOHN 4:16-26

Main Idea: Jesus focuses the woman's attention on the three main truths of Christianity: she is a sinner, he is the Savior, and salvation comes through faith in him.

I. **Every Person Is a Sinner (4:16-18).**
II. **Jesus Saves Us from Our Sin (4:25-26).**
III. **Salvation Comes through Faith in the Savior (4:20-24).**

There are all kinds of bumper stickers—funny ones, crude ones, political ones, and personal ones. All of them have a message. It got me thinking about the different messages people claim are Christian. Many of them would look great on a bumper sticker, but good luck finding them in the Bible. One popular bumper-sticker version of Christianity says, "God wants you to be happy just as you are." In other words, Christianity is nothing more than a spiritualized journey of self-affirmation. Another version says, "You do your part, and God will do his." That suggests God and I are equal partners in accomplishing my salvation.

Is this really the Christian message? The best way to answer the question—What is the message of Christianity?—is by turning to Jesus Christ. In his conversation with the woman at the well in Samaria, Jesus delivers and defines the greatest message in the world. You can't boil Christianity down to a bumper-sticker slogan. It's impossible to capture the depth of Christianity in a single phrase. But in this conversation Jesus focuses on three main truths. If this woman is to properly understand what following Jesus is all about, she must understand sin, the Savior, and salvation.

Every Person Is a Sinner
JOHN 4:16-18

Jesus focuses her attention on the sin that makes her guilty before God. She is an adulteress (v. 18). She has not only married five different men, but she is currently living immorally. She's moved in with a man who is not her husband. Her problem is not the particular sin (immorality) but that she is a sinner. She has broken covenant with the God of the universe and lives in rebellion against him. Sin is the starting point of the Christian message. From the beginning of humanity's story when sin burrowed into paradise, the pages of history are written in bright, vivid strokes of rebellion against God. Unless we understand our own sin and our identity as lawbreakers, the following truths won't matter to us.

Thomas Watson, a seventeenth-century Puritan pastor, wrote, "Till sin be bitter, Christ will not be sweet" (cited in Harvey, *When Sinners*, 16). Until this woman understands the depth of her sin, she will not long for the salvation Jesus offers. The gospel without sin is no gospel at all. Yet around the world a sinless, condemnation-free message is being held out as the Christian message. But without an awareness of our standing before God—that we are guilty rebels who fully deserve eternal punishment—grace is meaningless. Where there is no recognition of sin, there will be no joy. True joy comes when we understand that we were enemies of God who have now been reconciled to him.

The bumper-sticker Christianity that says "God wants you to be happy just as you are" is a lie. It's impossible for you to be happy just as you are. You're a sinner in need of rescue. The Bible describes you as dead, estranged, blind, sick, and enslaved. How happy does that sound? It's not fun to talk about sin. I'm sure it's not your favorite subject. But if you're to understand the basics of Christianity, you must first take an honest look at your heart—your deceitful, desperately wicked heart. Any message that ignores the reality of human sin is a lie. Just like the woman at the well, we are all sinners. We have all broken covenant with God. Charles Spurgeon, the Prince of Preachers, wrote,

> Too many think lightly of sin, and therefore think lightly of
> the Savior. He who has stood before his God, convicted and
> condemned, with the rope about his neck, is the man to weep
> for joy when he is pardoned, to hate the evil which has been
> forgiven him, and to live to the honor of the Redeemer by
> whose blood he has been cleansed. (Cited in Harvey, *When
> Sinners*, 38)

If we don't understand sin, we'll never understand the message of Jesus Christ, but when we start to understand that we are rotten to the core and sin has been eating away inside us like a cancer, then we're ready for the next truth of Christianity.

Jesus Saves Us from Our Sin
JOHN 4:25-26

This is in many ways the message of the Gospel of John. John wrote so that we "may believe that Jesus is the Messiah, the Son of God" (20:31). This was Jesus's message to the woman. Once she arrived at the understanding she was a sinner, she needed to understand he was there to save her. In the earlier part of his conversation, Jesus told her about living water. The first thing he did was point her to her need and then to the solution.

> *If you knew the gift of God, and who is saying to you, "Give me a drink," you would ask him, and he would give you living water.*
> *. . . But whoever drinks from the water that I will give him will never get thirsty again. In fact, the water I will give him will become a well of water springing up in him for eternal life.* (4:10-14; emphasis added)

Salvation from her sin was only possible as she came to a right understanding of Jesus Christ. She needed to understand he was the Messiah—the one sent by God to rescue people from sin (vv. 25-26). No man or woman can be saved apart from Jesus Christ. He is the only way of salvation. This has been the message from God since the beginning of time.

When mankind first sinned in the garden of Eden, God promised he would send a Savior to rescue them from their sin. Over and over, throughout Israel's history, this promise was portrayed.

When Jacob and his family were going to die because of a famine, they went to Egypt to get help. In Egypt they found one of Jacob's sons, Joseph, who had gone through humiliation and abuse before being exalted to a place of prominence. From this place of prominence, he was able to save his family, God's chosen people, from death. His example of suffering, exaltation, and salvation pictured the one who would be sent by God to suffer in order to provide salvation for all of God's people.

What did God do when his people were enslaved in Egypt? He sent a rescuer, and he had them celebrate that rescue each year, waiting in faith and anticipation for the ultimate Rescuer who would save them from a more powerful enemy—sin.

Later, Israel's armies were facing certain defeat as they stood on the opposite side of a valley from the Philistine army and their champion

Goliath. It was a hopeless situation. A period of slavery was certain until God brought an unexpected champion to defeat the giant and provide salvation for his people. A promise was made soon after: a greater champion would come from the line of David and provide a greater salvation for God's people. In each situation God delivered his people apart from any work on their part. Each time he was foreshadowing the salvation, deliverance, and redemption that would come through his Son Jesus.

This is why Jesus told this woman, "Salvation is from the Jews" (v. 22). He's not saying only Jews can be saved but that the message of salvation came through the Jews. The Old Testament Jewish Scriptures were God's way of revealing the promised salvation in Jesus Christ. He's also referring to God's promise to Abraham in Genesis 12. When God promised Abraham a son, he told him, "All the peoples on earth will be blessed through you" (Gen 12:3). From the seed of Abraham, the blessing of salvation would come to all people. Ethnicity, gender, and nationality don't matter. God's promise of a worldwide Savior was fulfilled in Jesus Christ.

Christianity is both inclusive and exclusive. It's *inclusive* because the invitation extends to everyone. Everyone, everywhere needs Jesus, and the death of Jesus Christ was enough to save all people from all ages. It's also *exclusive* because there's only one way to be saved. Acts 4:12 says only one name can bring salvation: Jesus Christ. Christianity says Jesus is the only way to God. If you come to Jesus, he will get you home. He is the only road that leads to the presence of God. He is the only door into God's house. Jesus is the all-sufficient and only Savior we need.

Salvation Comes through Faith in the Savior
JOHN 4:20-24

When Jesus points out this woman's sin, her first thought was that Jesus would want her to go to Jerusalem to worship at the temple (v. 20). She thought salvation was something she did, but Jesus instructs her about the true nature of salvation. Salvation is not something we do; it's something God does for us. He saves us.

Many times verses 23-24 are interpreted as referring to what Christians do on Sunday mornings—how we worship as a congregation. That misses the point. The context of these remarks is not a corporate worship service but an explanation of the gospel to a non-Christian.

Notice the words "in Spirit and in truth" in verse 24. In 3:31 John is describing Jesus and points out that Jesus is a reliable witness to what God desires because Jesus has been with God and bears witness to what he's seen and heard. However, despite the reliability of Jesus, no one receives his testimony.

> *The one who has accepted his testimony has affirmed that God is* true.
> *For the one whom God sent speaks God's words, since he gives the*
> Spirit *without measure.* (3:33-34; emphasis added)

To worship God in spirit and in truth means we have received the truth—the testimony about who Jesus Christ is—and we have received the Spirit. Jesus is describing salvation. We turn from the lies and error of this world and embrace the truth about Jesus and receive his Spirit, who then dwells inside each one who believes.

Jesus says in effect, "I have come to bring salvation. True salvation makes people worshipers of God. They have turned from self-worship—vowing allegiance to their own efforts and own desires and own glory—and have knelt in obedience and allegiance to the one true God. The only way people turn from self-worship to God worship, from rebellion to obedience, is by embracing the truth about me and receiving the Holy Spirit. This is the salvation I bring."

This whole discussion on salvation is set within the context of Jesus's death. Twice in these verses (4:21,23) Jesus refers to the "hour." That "hour" is his death and resurrection. Salvation is not found at the temple but at the cross. It's not found in religious ceremony but in the Messiah's death. Salvation from sin and reconciliation with God will only come as she turns from her sin and self-worship and trusts in the atoning sacrifice of Jesus on her behalf. She was hoping her religious experience would be enough. She was trusting in her obedience to her fathers (v. 20), but Jesus makes clear her only hope is coming through him to the Father.

Conclusion

Jesus clearly defines our message; he leaves no room for doubt, no possibility of error, no hesitation or waffling. If we are to understand and share the message of Christianity, we must focus on sin, the Savior, and salvation.

On a trip to Eastern Europe, I entered a cathedral filled with statues and covered in paintings. One painting of Jesus covered by glass stood waist high in the front of the room. A lady went up to it, and with tears in her eyes, she kissed it. Then she bowed, crossed herself, and walked to the back of the room to buy candles. Where she kissed it, the glass was worn down from years of worshipers kissing that glass. Perhaps she hoped going somewhere (the cathedral) and doing something (kissing a portrait) and giving something (money for candles) would save her from her sin.

The message of Christianity is not a bumper-sticker slogan about doing good things or being a better person. The message of Christianity is a call to worship the God of the universe. It's a call to the soul-expanding, heart-enlarging, world-shaking worship of the God who reigns over all. It's a call to turn from our sinful rebellion and to be saved from our self-worship by the power of Jesus Christ. John Newton, near the end of his life, summed up the message of Christianity perfectly: "My memory is nearly gone, but I remember two things: that I am a great sinner, and that Christ is a great Savior" (cited in Pollock, *Amazing Grace*, 182).

Reflect and Discuss

1. What are the three main truths of Christianity?
2. What are some false bumper-sticker interpretations of Christianity? How does the Bible address them?
3. What is the ultimate problem the woman at the well faces?
4. Why does it matter that the woman understands the depths of her sin? Why not just call her a sinner in general terms?
5. What is the danger of thinking too lightly of your own sin?
6. Why does Jesus tell the Samaritan woman that "salvation is from the Jews"?
7. How is Christianity both inclusive and exclusive? How does this change the nature of your relationship with unbelievers?
8. How has your worship changed as a result of salvation?
9. How is the message of Christianity a call to worship the God of the universe?
10. Why is the woman's ability to worship in spirit and truth an issue of belief and not of knowledge?

Excuses That Impede Evangelism

JOHN 4:27-42

Main Idea: Jesus refutes our excuses for not sharing the gospel with nonbelievers and challenges us to share the gospel right now.

I. **Three Excuses for Evangelistic Failure (4:27-35)**
   A. They won't be interested (4:27-30).
   B. I'm too busy (4:31-34).
   C. I'll do it later (4:35).

II. **An Encouragement to Evangelize (4:36-42)**

A n old gospel song called "Excuses" has a chorus that goes like this:

Excuses, excuses, we hear them every day,
And the devil will supply them, if from church we stay away.
When people come to know the Lord the devil always loses,
So to keep those folks away from church, he offers them
  excuses. (The Kingsmen Quartet, "Excuses").

It's a strange song, but it does capture our amazing ability to make excuses. From the moment we're old enough to speak, we learn to make excuses. No one has to teach us. I've always been amazed that after dinner when it's time to clean up the dishes, our kids have to use the bathroom. They magically emerge the moment the last dish is put away. We are all master excuse makers. Here are three excuses Christians often make for not sharing the gospel with non-Christians.

Three Excuses for Evangelistic Failure
JOHN 4:27-35

They Won't Be Interested (vv. 27-30)

The disciples have just returned from their shopping trip in town, and they're shocked to see Jesus talking with this woman. They wonder why Jesus would waste time talking with, of all people, this Samaritan woman. They could understand why Jesus would talk to Nicodemus (ch. 3). After all, he was a religious man. He was worth spending time with. But this woman? Look at the question they wanted to ask Jesus, but didn't: "Why are you talking with her?" (v. 27).

Don't judge who will respond to the gospel. Share it with everyone. The gospel doesn't discriminate. Neither should we. But it's easy for us to judge ahead of time how we think someone will respond to the good news about Jesus Christ.

I love the contrast between the disciples' reaction to this conversation and the woman's reaction. She didn't stop to think about who would listen to her or who she thought might respond to the gospel. She ran back into town so quickly that she left her water jar at the well. The urgency of the gospel—it's a message of life and death—demands we freely share it with all people. It doesn't allow us to make the excuse that people won't listen.

I'm Too Busy (vv. 31-34)

The disciples had bought some food in the town, and they attempt to give some to Jesus to eat. His response is cryptic (v. 32). The disciples are confused and try to understand what Jesus means. Jesus clarifies his comment: "My food is to do the will of him who sent me and to finish his work" (v. 34). Jesus is so absorbed with the matter at hand he doesn't want to stop and eat. He doesn't want to get distracted by anything else. It demonstrates the urgency of the gospel. It's not something we get to when we feel like it. It's not something that takes a backseat to breakfast.

The *Raleigh News & Observer* reported a story a few years ago about a man who died at a hospital in Goldsboro, North Carolina. Apparently he choked on his medication and fell and hit his head on the floor. A nurse helped him start breathing and sat him in a chair in the waiting room. He sat in that chair for the next twenty-two hours before having a heart attack and dying. During those twenty-two hours he was virtually ignored by the staff; in fact, after the choking incident, no one checked his vital signs for over an hour. They were too busy playing cards in the break room next door (Biesecker, "Tape Shows"). The men and women responsible for keeping him alive were distracted by something as worthless as a game of cards. What distracts us from our mission? What distracts us from sharing the message of eternal life with those all around us who are spiritually dying?

John Calvin, commenting on this passage, wrote, "By his example, [Jesus] shows us that the kingdom of God should have priority over all bodily comforts" (*John*, 107). Jesus's food was to accomplish the work God gave him to do. That work was "to advance God's kingdom, to restore lost souls to life, to spread the light of the gospel, and to bring salvation to the world" (ibid., 108).

Too many churches have gotten distracted from the mission God has given them. The older and bigger a church is, the easier it is to get distracted. There's an old story about a harbor town located in a treacherous area where boats frequently capsized on the rocks in bad weather. The town was known for its faithful rescue team. Whenever the bell sounded, a group of men rowed quickly to the scene of the disaster, risking their lives to remove sailors from sinking vessels or to pluck them from heaving waves. After a few years the town collected money to build a rescue station near the shore to store all of their equipment, thus making their rescue work easier. Also, special training was offered to others who wanted to become rescuers. The operation became efficient, saving hundreds of lives from the raging waters. But as time went by, comforts and conveniences were added to the building—cupboards full of food, a dining room, a lounge with stuffed chairs and recliners, and sleeping quarters. The lovely building became a club where townspeople loved to eat, meet, play games, and socialize. The bell still sounded when a wreck occurred, but only a handful of people responded. Later, no one even bothered to answer the rescue call, for they didn't want to leave the comfortable club (Davey, *When Heaven*, 28).

I'll Do It Later (v. 35)

Jesus asks the disciples a pointed question: "Don't you say, 'There are still four more months, and then comes the harvest'?" (v. 35). He's saying, "Do you guys think you need to wait before reaping the fruit of the gospel? Are you hoping it will come later? You're wrong; look at the Samaritans coming right now. What are you waiting for? The time is now!" Jesus is driving the urgency of the gospel home to the hearts of his disciples. We don't wait for a different time or a better time; the harvest is now. Go, do the work of sharing the gospel right now. Charles Spurgeon, preaching on this passage, challenged his congregation:

> Some of you good people, who do nothing except go to public
> meetings, the Bible readings, and prophetic conferences,
> and other forms of spiritual [indulgence], would be a good
> deal better Christians if you would look after the poor and

needy around you. If you would just tuck up your sleeves for work, and go and tell the gospel to dying men, you would find your spiritual health mightily restored, for very much of the sickness of Christians comes through their having nothing to do. All feeding and no working gives men spiritual indigestion. Be idle, careless, with nothing to live for, nothing to care for, no sinner to pray for, no backslider to lead back to the cross, no trembler to encourage, no little child to tell of a Savior, no grey-headed man to enlighten in the things of God, no object, in fact, to live for; and who wonders if you begin to groan, and to murmur, and to look within, until you are ready to die of despair? (Cited in Hughes, *John*, 132)

We've seen three excuses—*they won't be interested, I'm too busy,* and *I'll do it later.* Now notice three ways to engage right here, right now.

An Encouragement to Evangelize
JOHN 4:36-42

There's an old saying, "The road to hell is paved with good intentions." The road to hell for *others* is often paved with *our* good intentions. It's time to stop making excuses. No more intentions. We need action. Jesus told us the harvest time is now. Not tomorrow. Not in a week. Now! Get started now sharing the gospel with those God has uniquely placed in your circle of influence. Think about your coworkers, your neighbors, and your family. Start with them. It's time to turn your intentions into actions.

If you decide to do something out of guilt, it won't last. Guilt, like a sparkler on the Fourth of July, burns out quickly. This passage ends with encouragement to get busy (vv. 36-42). Do you see what has happened? Men and women have turned from their sin and turned to Jesus for salvation. Men and women have tossed aside their jars filled with their own good works and effort and have come to drink from the fountain of living water.

When the gospel is clearly explained and faithfully shared, men and women will come to Christ. That's the beauty of the gospel. It's God's good news, and God does a great work in the hearts of rebels, causing them to turn from their self-worship and turn to him in true worship. What did they discover when they came to Christ and believed in him? Look at their confession: they realized Jesus is indeed the "Savior of the world" (v. 42). They found hope instead of uncertainty, salvation instead of slavery, peace instead of misery, and grace instead of judgment.

Maybe it would be more accurate to say hope found them, salvation found them, peace found them, and grace found them. Our motivation for sharing the message of Christianity is that it's not dependent on our power, our wisdom, or our strength. It rests solely on the power of God. We don't win souls. God rescues sinners and graciously gives us front-row seats! God wants people (v. 23). He is seeking people, drawing them. There are people from every tribe, tongue, and nation—there are people in your city—that God is drawing to himself.

Our role is twofold. First, we share the *message* of Christ. God draws people through his gospel proclaimed. Second, we share in the *joy* of the sinner who comes to Christ (v. 36). People will come to Christ when we share the gospel, and we will get the privilege of rejoicing in their new birth with them. God will draw sinners to himself, and they will find joy in him. This reality should motivate us to labor with all our might to make Jesus Christ and his gospel known and loved throughout the world. Augustine wrote this beautiful reflection about Jesus Christ:

> You are ever active, yet always at rest. You gather all things to yourself, though you suffer no need. . . . You welcome those who come to you, though you never lost them. You release us from our debts, but you lose nothing thereby. You are my God, my Life, my holy Delight, but is this enough to say of you? Can any man say enough when he speaks of you? Yet woe betide those who are silent about you! (*Confessions* [IX 1], 181)

May we, by the grace of God, never be silent.

Reflect and Discuss

1. Do you feel an urgency to share the gospel with people in your life? How might a sense of urgency change your interaction with your neighbors, coworkers, or classmates?
2. What are some excuses you use for not sharing the gospel? How are these excuses an evidence of unbelief?
3. How does belief give you a sense of urgency in mission?
4. How might study or preparation become a replacement for mission?
5. What comforts in your life have caused you to step back from the dangers of the mission field?

6. Is there someone in your life you need to share the gospel with right now? What is stopping you? What will you say to that person?

7. Take time to pray specifically for the opportunity and courage to share the gospel with some specific people in your life.

8. Is there anyone in your life who has the gift of evangelism? How might you learn from that individual?

9. How does the sovereignty of God to rescue sinners give us freedom to share the gospel without fear of rejection?

10. What is our role in salvation, and what is God's role? Why is this good news?

Authentic Faith

JOHN 4:39-54

Main Idea: The contrast between the Jews' and the Samaritans' responses to Jesus reveal what authentic faith looks like.

I. Authentic Faith Is Not Spiritual Curiosity but Actual Commitment.
II. Authentic Faith Is Not an Emotional Feeling but an Informed Belief.
III. Authentic Faith Is Not a Single Decision but a Growing Dependence.

In verses 39-45 Jesus has concluded a wonderful few days with a group of Samaritans, who've turned from the darkness of sin and embraced the light of the world. They've repented of their sin and placed their faith in Jesus. Then Jesus leaves them and heads back to his own people—the Jews. Jesus is fully aware of what awaits him. Unlike the Samaritans who've believed in him, he's heading back to a people who will reject him. Though the overall response Jesus receives is unbelief, there are occasions of real faith, and the contrast between these two responses teaches us what authentic faith looks like.

Authentic Faith Is Not Spiritual Curiosity but Actual Commitment

John contrasts the Jews' reception of Jesus and the Samaritans'. The Jews demonstrate unbelief (vv. 46-48), and the Samaritans model genuine belief. The Jews came to see Jesus. They welcomed him because they were curious about what he could do. They'd been in Jerusalem and seen what Jesus did there. They saw him cleanse the temple. They heard about his miracle of turning the water into wine, so they came out to watch him. This still happens today. People come to church or buy books or listen to Christian radio because they're curious about Jesus. This curiosity uses words like "spirituality" and "faith" and "higher consciousness" but never anything more concrete than that.

Celebrities like Deepak Chopra, the Dalai Lama, and Oprah Winfrey epitomize this bland spiritual curiosity. Chopra wrote in *Time* magazine,

The most inspiring thing [the Dalai Lama] ever told me
was to ignore all organized faiths and keep to the road of
higher consciousness. "Without relying on religion, we look
to common sense, common experience and the findings of
science for understanding," he said. ("Dalai Lama," 43)

In a *USA Today* article titled "The Divine Miss Winfrey?," Oprah is quoted
as saying, "I live inside God's dream for me. I don't try to tell God what
I'm supposed to do. God can dream a bigger dream for you than you
can dream for yourself." A professor at the University of Florida dissects
Winfrey's message:

> Winfrey pushes the idea that you have a life out there, and
> it's better than the one you have now and go get it. It's most
> apparent in the setting of her show. The guest is sitting beside
> her, but what she's really doing is exuding this powerful
> message of "You are a sinner, yes, you are, but you can also
> find salvation." What I find intriguing about it is it's delivered
> with no religiosity at all . . . it has to do with this deep
> American faith and yearning to be reborn. To start again.
> (Oldenburg, "The Divine Miss Winfrey?")

Spiritual curiosity is not just an American thing. It's universal. But
spiritual curiosity is not authentic faith. In fact, Jesus harshly condemns
the Jews for their lack of faith—their curiosity clothed in religious garments. As Jesus returns to Galilee, he's met by an official whose son is
dying. He begs Jesus to come with him to his home and heal his son.
Look again at Jesus's rebuke: "Unless you people see signs and wonders, you will not believe" (v. 48). This rebuke is aimed at the watching
crowd; the "you" is plural. Jesus knows they only care about watching
him perform. He knows their faith is not in him but in the miracles. The
Samaritans demonstrate real, authentic faith. They come to Jesus for
salvation from their sin, not to witness a show. They stay with him, listen
to his words, and place their faith in him alone.

Authentic Faith Is Not an Emotional
Feeling but an Informed Belief

Turning to Jesus Christ in faith requires understanding certain truths
about him. There is *content* to our faith. A lot of people say they've

trusted Jesus Christ because they had an experience, some sort of emotional epiphany. We see this in Jesus's interaction with the men and women of his day. They came and rallied around him and watched him perform a miracle, so out of excitement or enthusiasm they jump on the Jesus bandwagon. If you asked them, "Are you a follower of Jesus?" "Sure," they would respond, "Didn't you see what he did for us?"

In John 6 Jesus does an amazing miracle. He turns five loaves of bread and two fish into enough food to feed five thousand men, plus women and children. What was the response of the people? John writes, "They were about to come and take him by force to make him king" (6:15). They were excited. They were on board, but they weren't trusting in Jesus. They just wanted free food (v. 26). By the end of the chapter, "many of his disciples turned back and no longer accompanied him" (6:66).

The Jewish royal official asks Jesus again to come and heal his son (4:49-50). By this point we can almost hear the desperation in his voice: "Please! I'm begging you! Help him!" Jesus doesn't rebuke him. He doesn't turn him away. He simply says, "Go, your son will live." What does the official do? He believes. He trusts Jesus, and his trust is more than an emotional response to Jesus. His trust is based on something concrete: "what Jesus said." How significant! This man wasn't riding an emotional high. He was responding to the truth Jesus proclaimed. The words of Jesus caused this man's faith. Compare that to what brought about authentic faith in the Samaritans: "Many more believed because of *what he said*" (v. 41; emphasis added).

Authentic faith is not a blind leap in the dark or a ride on the crest of an emotional wave. Authentic faith is an informed belief about Jesus Christ. John has stressed this throughout his Gospel. His purpose is to inform everyone who picks up his Gospel and reads that Jesus is the Christ, the Son of God. Armed with this information, the reader can then choose to trust Jesus and receive eternal life. But we can't trust Jesus unless we understand the truth about him. We need a basis for our belief.

So far we've studied four chapters of truth about Jesus. In those chapters Jesus has been revealed not only through his acts—like turning water into wine and cleansing the temple—but also through his titles. We've already seen eight different titles of Jesus; these titles help us know whom we're trusting.

- In 1:1 Jesus was announced as the *Word*, the one who could perfectly reveal God to man.
- In 1:29 and 36 Jesus is declared to be the *Lamb of God*, the one who would offer his life as a sacrifice for the sin of each man and woman.
- In 1:34 Jesus is called the *Son of God*, the one, unique Son who was sent by the Father as a love gift for his people.
- In 1:38 and 3:2 Jesus is identified as *Rabbi*, the one who could perfectly teach us what God is like and how to be reconciled to him.
- In 1:41 Jesus is described as the *Messiah*, the one who would completely fulfill the promises of God given in the Old Testament.
- In 1:49 Jesus is welcomed as the *King of Israel*, the one who would sit on the throne and rule over his kingdom.
- In 1:51 Jesus is called the *Son of Man*, the one whom Daniel prophesied would have an everlasting dominion that would never pass away, filled with people from every nation and language who would serve him.
- In 4:42 Jesus is proclaimed to be the *Savior of the world*, the one who would shed his blood to bring salvation to all mankind.

Authentic faith is not rooted in emotional experience but in the truth about Jesus Christ.

Authentic Faith Is Not a Single Decision but a Growing Dependence

Twice the text says this man believed (4:51-53). We find the same pattern with the Samaritans (vv. 39-41). In neither case are we told *when* the individual was saved. John is showing us how authentic faith always results in *continued* belief. Don't misunderstand what he's teaching. He's not saying a person needs to be saved over and over. He's not denying genuine conversion happens at the moment when a person turns from sin and trusts Christ. What he is saying is that those who are genuinely converted will continue to believe on Jesus Christ.

I've talked with a number of individuals who claim to be Christians, and when you ask them how they know Jesus Christ has saved them, they point to a past decision. As you continue to talk with them, there's no evidence in their lives they are indeed believers, but they're holding on to some experiences in their past. They base their hope on the words of a prayer or a religious experience from the past. Authentic faith always continues. It doesn't stop. It doesn't give up. It doesn't turn away. Genuine believers will continue to follow Jesus Christ.

Throughout John's Gospel we see those who seem to believe but then turn back from following Jesus Christ.

> *From that moment many of his disciples turned back and no longer accompanied him. So Jesus said to the Twelve, "You don't want to go away too, do you?"*
>
> *Simon Peter answered, "Lord, to whom will we go? You have the words of eternal life. We have come to believe and know that you are the Holy One of God." (6:66-69)*

How are we to understand what happened to these disciples who turned away? As readers we're forced to ask, "What is genuine belief?" Genuine belief is belief that continues. Look at the contrast between those who turned away and the Twelve. Jesus asks them if they want to leave as well. Peter, answering for the group, says in effect, "Where would we go?" Then he acknowledges who Jesus is and says, "We believe." Do you see the contrast? Those who left Jesus demonstrated by leaving that their faith was not authentic (cf. 1 John 2:19). On the other hand, the disciples, by persevering in the faith, demonstrate that their faith is indeed authentic.

This discussion of authentic faith continues throughout the New Testament. Authentic faith always continues; authentic faith is evident when we persevere in believing and trusting Jesus Christ.

> *Once you were alienated and hostile in your minds expressed in your evil actions. But now he has reconciled you by his physical body through his death, to present you holy, faultless, and blameless before him—*if indeed you remain grounded and steadfast in the faith and are not shifted away from the hope of the gospel that you heard. (Col 1:21-23; emphasis added)

> *Watch out, brothers and sisters, so that there won't be in any of you an evil, unbelieving heart that turns away from the living God. But encourage each other daily, while it is still called today, so that none of you is hardened by sin's deception. For we have become participants in Christ* if we hold firmly until the end the reality that we had at the start. (Heb 3:12-14; emphasis added)

Believing Jesus is not something we do one time. We must keep believing, keep depending, keep trusting. From the beginning—the opening verses of the Gospel of John—the need for continual trust is emphasized. Those who become children of God are those who received Christ (John 1:12), those who *are believing* (present tense) in his name.

Why is continued belief so important to John? Where did he learn this emphasis? "Then Jesus said to the Jews who had believed him, 'If you continue in my word, you really are my disciples'" (8:31). To *continue* is to "abide," to "remain," and to "persevere." True disciples continue in the faith, growing more and more in their dependence on Jesus Christ. Authentic faith is more than spiritual curiosity about Jesus. Authentic faith is more than emotional feelings about him. Authentic faith is not a single decision for him. Authentic faith is an actual commitment, an informed belief, and a growing dependence on Jesus Christ.

We can think of faith in Jesus Christ the way we think about marriage. If an acquaintance were to ask me if I was married, I would say yes. If he asked me how I knew I was married, I might mention my wedding ceremony years ago. He could respond, "I know a lot of people who had a wedding ceremony but who aren't married." So how do I know I'm married? Is it because of the piece of paper I received years ago from a county clerk? Is it because of some photos in an album? Is it because I'm wearing a ring? Those all testify to a past event and remind me I had a wedding. But the real way I know I'm married is because I go home each night to my wife. She gives me a kiss, we spend the evening wrangling kids together, collapse into bed, and wake up to start again the next day. I know I'm married because every day I live out my marriage.

Are you a believer in Jesus Christ? Don't point to a past event. Show me how you live out your faith every day. For Christians, faith starts again each morning when our feet hit the floor. Faith goes to work and comes back home at night. Faith falls asleep with us. For two thousand years a synonym for *Christian* has been *believer*. Not believed but believer. Are you a believer in Jesus Christ? Is your faith authentic?

Reflect and Discuss

1. What does authentic faith look like?
2. How is authentic faith different from the faith prescribed by people like Oprah or Deepak Chopra?
3. Why does Jesus rebuke the crowd when asked by a father to heal his son?

4. How do the Samaritans demonstrate authentic faith?
5. Why did the same crowd who wanted to make Jesus king soon turn back and no longer walk with him?
6. How is informed belief about Jesus necessary for authentic faith?
7. What titles have been used for Jesus through the first four chapters of John, and what do they tell us about Jesus?
8. Why should we not place our confidence in salvation on a single prayer or experience?
9. Why is continued belief so important to John?
10. What warning can we take from the disciples who turned away?

Lord of Sickness and Sabbath

JOHN 5:1-18

Main Idea: The persecution of Jesus provides him with an opportunity to reveal his authority over all mankind and to confront the religious leaders with their rebellion against God.

I. **Jesus Is Lord over Sickness (5:1-9).**
   A. It's Not a Fake Healing.
   B. It's Not a Faith Healing.
   C. It's a Free Healing.
   D. It's a Full Healing.
II. **Jesus Is Lord over the Sabbath (5:9-18).**

The IRS employs more than 80,000 people and has a budget of nearly a billion dollars.[2] Imagine how much time and money could be saved by Americans simply submitting to the IRS's authority. But we don't like to submit to someone else's authority.

Human history is the history of how man has rebelled against authority. Beginning in the garden, people demonstrated they wanted to answer to no one, including God. It continues throughout the Old Testament, whether you're reading the account of Israel complaining in the wilderness or rebelling against God in the book of Judges. The natural bent of our hearts is antiauthority. We're rebels by nature. Only the supernatural work of God in our hearts allows us to turn from our rebellious ways to submit to Jesus as our Lord and Master.

Our rebellious nature and our struggle with authority—particularly Jesus's authority as Lord—become clear the more we study the Gospel of John. In chapter 5 Jesus heals a lame man and is persecuted because of it. This persecution provides him with the perfect opportunity to reveal his authority over all mankind and to confront the religious leaders with their rebellion against God. By this point a transition has taken place in

---

[2] Church Marr and Cecile Murray, "IRS Funding Cuts Compromise Taxpayer Service and Weaken Enforcement," Center on Budget and Policy Priorities, April 4, 2016, accessed May 5, 2017, http://www.cbpp.org/research/federal-tax/irs-funding-cuts-compromise -taxpayer-service-and-weaken-enforcement.

the Gospel. Chapter 1 is an introduction to the entire book, and chapters 2–4 reveal how people were interested in Jesus and his miracles, but chapters 5–7 chronicle the shift from curiosity to opposition and from interest to persecution. The shift in attitude toward Jesus corresponds with Jesus's further establishing his authority. Jesus's authority is seen as he reveals himself to be Lord over sickness and Lord over the Sabbath.

Jesus Is Lord over Sickness
JOHN 5:1-9

Jesus is in charge. This miracle reveals the authority and deity of Jesus Christ. I want to point out four things about this miracle.

It's Not a Fake Healing

It begins with the healing of a lame man. This man, chosen by Jesus, had been lame for thirty-eight years. He's not faking it. Jesus is now in his early thirties—probably thirty-one or thirty-two. For this to have been fake, the man would have had to plan it six years before Jesus was born. Depending on your translation, you may or may not have a verse 4. In the CSB, NIV, and ESV it's missing. However, a footnote in the CSB reads,

> Some mss include vv. 3b-4:—*waiting for the moving of the water, because an angel would go down into the pool from time to time and stir up the water. Then the first one who got in after the water was stirred up recovered from whatever ailment he had.*

Most New Testament scholars believe this section is not original and was added in the margin of a manuscript by one of the scribes who was copying the text. However, it does show us what many thought in that time, and it explains the words of the invalid in verse 7.

It's Not a Faith Healing

Many books and television programs promise people if they just have enough faith, all their physical infirmities will be miraculously cured. One such faith healer was Peter Popoff. He was a widely popular televangelist in the 1970s and 1980s who claimed he could heal those who had enough faith. He would call out the names and ailments of those in the audience, claiming to have received divine revelation. He was exposed as a fraud on the *Johnny Carson Show* when one of the radio transmissions between Popoff and his wife was aired. It came to light that Popoff's wife and workers would mingle with the crowd before the service and pick up information. This information would then be relayed from Popoff's wife to a tiny receiver in Popoff's ear. Everything he had said was a lie.

This account in John's Gospel in no way supports the claims of faith healers. The man who was healed is no example of faith. Look at verse 7. His response to Jesus's question, "Do you want to get well?" was to complain that he had no one to help him. I love one writer's description of this man's response:

> [Verse] 7 reads less as an apt and subtle response to Jesus's question than as the crotchety grumblings of an old and not very perceptive man who thinks he is answering a stupid question. (Carson, *John*, 243)

We learn more unflattering details about this man later in the account. In verse 10, when the Jews ask him why he's breaking their law by carrying his mat on the Sabbath, he responds by blaming Jesus: "The man who made me well told me, 'Pick up your mat and walk'" (v. 11).

Later Jesus comes back to him and tells him, "Do not sin anymore, so that something worse doesn't happen to you" (v. 14). He's implying the man's condition was the result of sin he had committed. It's clear later in John's Gospel that sickness and disease are not always the result of sin (ch. 9). In fact, they may rarely be the result of it, but they can be sometimes: the person who contracts HIV from immoral behavior or who kills her liver through drunkenness demonstrates that sin can have physical consequences.

It's a Free Healing

This man didn't purchase the healing. He didn't win the sweepstakes or find the golden ticket. He certainly didn't deserve to be healed. It was only because Jesus graciously chose to heal him that he was healed. Here is an old, angry, embittered man who's broken and helpless. He's done nothing to deserve the kindness of Jesus. Even when Jesus seeks him out, he responds with an ugly comment, complaining about no help. What does Jesus do? He doesn't say, "Well, if only he had asked me," or, "He deserves to be alone and miserable," or, "I gave him a chance, and he failed." In his grace he looks past the man's failure, the man's sin, and he restores him. He makes him whole. Jesus can do the same for you. He has eyes to see past your hard exterior, past your brokenness, and he can make you whole.

It's a Full Healing

The man wasn't partially healed. He was completely and "instantly" healed (v. 9). When Jesus told this lame man to get up and walk, sickness and disease fled. How much physical therapy did this man require after the disease left his body? How many days of working out before his strength returned? None. The words of Jesus brought total and complete restoration.

Sometimes we forget about the power of Jesus. He is Lord over sickness. If he commands it to go, sickness must obey. This is why Christians pray for physical healing. It isn't always Jesus's will to heal his people, but if it is his will, he can do it. Often he's doing a thousand other things through the sickness—things we are unaware of, but we pray because sickness is no match for him.

Jesus Is Lord over the Sabbath
JOHN 5:9-18

The story doesn't end here. It isn't as simple as Jesus healing a man and the man going his own way. Look at the last phrase of verse 9: "Now that day was the Sabbath." Jesus chose to heal this man on this specific day to make a point to the religious leaders. He wants them to see their lack of submission to God and his authority.

Word has spread about this lame man being healed, and the Jewish religious leaders find him before he returns home. They say in essence, "It's the Sabbath, and you're working by carrying your bed. How dare you?" (v. 10). Doesn't this reveal their values? First, they're more concerned about their rules than they are about God's rules, and second, they're more concerned about their rules than they are about people. A man has just been healed! Shouldn't this be an occasion to celebrate? The love of rules, traditions, and possessions more than people can creep into our lives in subtle and dangerous ways.

The religious leaders would have claimed to love this man, but their actions told the real story. Eventually they find out Jesus is the one who healed the lame man, and they persecute Jesus "because he was doing these things on the Sabbath" (v. 16). In the coming chapters we will see the persecution grow until these same men are inciting a mob to scream, "Take him away! Crucify him!" (19:15) Here Jesus gets the opportunity to defend himself: "Jesus responded to them, 'My Father is still working, and I am working also'" (5:17).

Jesus could have rightfully set them straight on their misunderstanding and misinterpretation of the Sabbath. The Sabbath day was instituted in Exodus 20, when God delivered to Moses the Ten Commandments and the Sabbath was intended to be a blessing. As Jesus said, "The Sabbath was made for man and not man for the Sabbath" (Mark 2:27). The Sabbath was to give people a day of rest from their labor and a day consecrated to him. The work they were to refrain from doing was their regular employment (Carson, *John*, 224). Acts of mercy—works of kindness that benefited other people—fit the spirit of the command exactly. To forbid them was a complete and utter perversion of what God intended. However, here Jesus did not defend himself by clarifying the purpose of the Sabbath. His defense was that God was working on the Sabbath. They would all have to agree with that; none of them would say that God took a day off each week. Therefore, if God was working, then it was perfectly legitimate for Jesus to work as well.

We need to understand Jesus's logic. He's not saying that because God works on the Sabbath, *anyone* can work on the Sabbath. No, he's saying that because God works on the Sabbath, *he* can. For Jesus's defense to be valid, all the factors that apply to God must apply to Jesus. Jesus is insisting that whatever factors justify God's continuous work on the Sabbath justify his. The Jews understand that Jesus is claiming equality with God (John 5:18).

The showdown that had been brewing is now taking place. The religious leaders of Israel are faced with a decision. Will they submit to the authority of Jesus Christ, or will they rebel against his authority and choose to live autonomously? Will they honor his instructions, or will they ignore his commands and elevate their man-made rules above his will? This battle surfaces throughout the rest of John's Gospel, and it's a battle we're familiar with as well. Each day we have to decide if we'll submit to Jesus as Lord.

Our hearts are a battlefield. Two opposing forces clash violently each day. Our desire for autonomous self-rule engages in a fierce battle with an appropriate desire to submit to the lordship of Jesus Christ. Regardless of who we are or what situation we are in, we must diligently fight to obey Christ, putting to death our desire to be in charge. It's a battle we can win only by the powerful work of Christ within us.

Jesus is Lord over sickness and Lord over the Sabbath. What that means is that Jesus can heal and give rest. Jesus can heal your broken bone or your broken heart or your broken relationship. If you're tired and weary and don't have the strength to go on, Jesus can give you rest. The Lord of healing and the Lord of rest invites you to come and be refreshed and restored as you follow him.

Reflect and Discuss

1. What does this passage want us to believe about Jesus?
2. What other Scripture passages show Jesus's authority over all things?
3. Why is it important to note that the healing in this passage is not a faith healing?
4. How do God's people display to the world God's sovereignty through obedience of his command to rest?
5. Do you have patterns of rest in your life? How can rest be an active fight for submission?
6. How had the Pharisees misunderstood the purpose of the Sabbath?
7. What claim does Jesus make in response to the accusations of the Pharisees?
8. Do you ever think of how each day you're faced with a decision to submit to Christ's authority or rebel? How might that change the way you live?
9. What steps are you taking to fight to obey Christ?
10. How can the battle for obedience be won?

Answering to a Higher Authority

JOHN 5:19-29

Main Idea: Jesus's authority stems from his deity, and his authority demands obedience.

I. **Jesus Does What Only God Can Do.**
II. **Jesus Receives Honor Only God Deserves.**
III. **Jesus Has Power Only God Can Claim.**

In the first part of chapter 5, Jesus Christ reveals himself as Lord. His words and works show his power and authority. Because of his authority, there's a claim on our lives to obey him. In verses 19-29 we see that Jesus's authority stems from his deity, and his authority demands obedience.

The religious leaders wanted to kill Jesus because he was "making himself equal to God" (v. 18). Their response was wrong, but their understanding of Jesus's statement was not. Jesus was revealing himself as God. This is the basis for his authority. Jesus stresses his deity by describing his unity with the Father in these verses. Once we see his deity, his authority over us becomes obvious. Jesus reveals his deity and authority in three ways.

Jesus Does What Only God Can Do

Jesus does not do "anything on his own" (v. 19). Everything he does is perfectly in concert with the Father's work and will. "For whatever the Father does, the Son likewise does these things." Let me put that in our modern vernacular: Jesus isn't a trust-fund kid trying to distance himself from his Father. He's not the black sheep trying to make a name for himself. He's not the type-A firstborn trying to outdo his dad and make it on his own. He's perfectly in sync with his Father. He's not a second god come to steal the worship and adoration that belongs only to the true God. *He is the true God.* He and the Father are *one.* To worship God is to worship Jesus, and to worship Jesus is to worship God. Remember his defense for working on the Sabbath: "If the Father has the authority to work on the Sabbath, then I do as well" (v. 17; my paraphrase).

Jesus is making a clear statement of deity and authority by revealing his ability to do works only God can do. He has the authority to give a person life (v. 21), and he has the authority to judge men (v. 22). These two characteristics are unique to God; if Jesus has the authority to do them, then he must be God. Maybe someone else could heal a person, but Jesus will do far greater works: He will raise the dead to life. He personally will rise from the dead. When he does so, those who opposed him will marvel (v. 20). Jesus is saying, "You saw me heal a lame man but explained it away and said, 'He's got no authority over us.' What are you going to say when I raise someone from the dead? How will you explain that one? How will you avoid the clear conclusion that I am God and you must obey me?"

Jesus Receives Honor Only God Deserves

This is ironclad evidence of Jesus's deity. Listen to what God says in Isaiah: "I will act for my own sake, indeed, my own, for how can I be defiled? *I will not give my glory to another*" (Isa 48:11; emphasis added). God will not give his glory or honor to someone else, yet he gives it to Jesus because Jesus is God (John 5:23). Since the Father and Son are one, to reject the Son is to dishonor the Father. Jesus is tying his authority directly to the authority of God himself. It's as if he is looking square in the eyes of these religious leaders—these guardians of monotheistic teaching—and saying to them, "You cannot honor God if you do not honor me. You pious and sanctimonious men, your lives are supposed to be the paragon of obedience and submission to God, but if you do not submit to my authority, you are in absolute rebellion against God."

This is a compelling reminder of the centrality of Jesus Christ to God-pleasing worship. We live in a pluralistic society, a society that promotes the equality of all religions. God's Word is clear: any system of worship that does not honor Jesus Christ as the true God is from hell. It's a lie of Satan.

One of the current ways Satan is trying to attack the deity of Jesus Christ is through the religion of tolerance. There's a loud cry for tolerance in our society, but it's not really tolerance that's wanted. True tolerance says, "All people have the right to choose what to believe." As Christians, we gladly support this type of tolerance. We don't want to force or coerce someone to become a Christian. We know doing so is impossible anyway; it's a decision of the heart. This is why Christians have always been at the front lines in the fight for religious liberty. We believe people should have the right to believe whatever they choose, even if they choose to believe something stupid. They can set up a religion that worships a toaster as god. The religion of tolerance has a completely different agenda. It says we must affirm, "All religions are equally true." That's not tolerance; that's an entirely new religion. Satan pushes the religion of tolerance because it undermines the worship of Jesus as the one true God. Though we believe every person has the right to believe whatever he wants, we also believe that only one thing can be true.

Only the true God is worthy of worship, and the only way to worship him is through his Son, Jesus. John Calvin's words, written 450 years ago, are still true and timely:

> Muslims and Jews give the God they worship beautiful and magnificent titles. However, we should remember that whenever God's name is separated from Christ, it is nothing more than empty imagination. (*John*, 129)

What good is an imagination that's empty? The only useful imagination is a full one. An empty imagination is worthless, as is worshiping God apart from Jesus.

I remember hearing a knock on our front door. When I opened the door, I saw two ladies standing on my step holding Bibles and some religious literature. My suspicion was soon confirmed: these two ladies were Jehovah's Witnesses going from door to door sharing their false gospel. As rapidly as I could, I told them we believed differently about Jesus, and the Bible clearly says Jesus is truly God. "Oh, we believe he's God," they said. "No, you don't. You believe he's a god, but you do not believe he's of the same essence as the Father. You do not believe he's one with the Father." At that point they admitted they viewed Jesus differently, and the conversation ended a few moments later. Those two ladies, as sweet as they were, standing on my porch with Bibles in hand, were rebelling against God. Anyone who does not submit to Jesus Christ—anyone who dishonors the Son—does not honor the Father.

What does submission to God look like? Well, it begins by following Jesus's instructions to believe him (v. 24). Any talk of obeying God or following God or pleasing him is empty and meaningless until you've accepted the sacrifice of Jesus on your behalf. It's easy to think about Jesus and say things like, "I really respect him." "I think he's pretty cool." "He says some really good things." Think about those statements from

God's perspective. God made you, but you rebelled against him. Instead of punishing you, he put in motion a plan to rescue you. This plan required his Son to be born as a man, live a perfect life, and then die a horrible death so you could be forgiven and freed. You hear all this, and you think, *Wow. I respect Jesus.* God didn't send his Son to die so you'd respect him. He sent his Son to die so that you'd throw yourself at his feet and ask him to rescue you. God is not after your respect. God is after you. He says anything short of coming in faith to Jesus Christ to save you amounts to disrespect. The only way to honor God is to embrace the gift of mercy and forgiveness Jesus won for you on the cross.

Jesus Has Power Only God Can Claim

Jesus has authority over all men and their eternal destiny. He's the giver of salvation, and his salvation has two perspectives. In verse 25 it's a current perspective. Right now Jesus is giving life to those who are spiritually dead. Verses 28-29 have a future perspective. Jesus will raise the dead to eternal life. Jesus has the prerogative to give life because he has "life in himself" (v. 26).

If I were to walk into your house, take a painting down off your wall, and give it away, what would you think? You would probably think I had no right to give away your painting. But if I were to walk into my house, take a painting down off my wall, and give it away, would you think twice about it? No. It's mine to give. Jesus has the authority to give life because he owns life.

To whom does he give this life? The spiritually dead. The dead "will hear [his] voice" (v. 25). I've heard numerous funeral sermons and never seen the corpse say amen. How can the spiritually dead hear and obey Christ's message? I think the best way to answer that question is to ask another one: How can a lame man take up his bed and walk? Only if the commander provides the power (5:1-18). Apart from Jesus Christ no person can choose spiritual life. Just like the lame man, we're unable to heal ourselves. Yet, when Jesus calls us to life, he instantly makes us alive. Salvation is wholly the work of Christ; he transforms dead sinners into living sons.

However, the authority of Jesus extends beyond calling spiritually dead sinners to life. It also encompasses calling the physically dead back to life. The final two verses (vv. 28-29) focus on a future day when Jesus returns to take believers into heaven and cast unbelievers into hell. On that day those in the grave will hear his voice. Just as Jesus told the

lame man to "get up," he will shout to those in the grave, "Get up!" and
they will. What authority! Jesus will call all men to stand before him and
receive his judgment. Those who have believed in him and submitted
to his commands will receive eternal life, and those who have not will
experience eternal judgment.

In John 11 Jesus raises Lazarus from the dead. How amazing it
would have been to stand there that day and see this man rise from the
grave and come walking out! In 5:29 Jesus tells of a day when every dead
person will be called out of the grave by one simple command: "Get
up!" Jesus will speak, and every single corpse from all of human history
will obey. Now that's authority!

> A bugler could stand at the edge of a graveyard and play
> reveille, but nothing would happen. He could travel to the
> greatest of our national cemeteries, where military men, noted
> for their obedience throughout life, lie buried. No matter how
> well or loudly he played, nothing would happen. Those dead
> men need a far greater authority to bring them to life, and
> that authority is the voice of Jesus Christ. (Hughes, *John*, 166)

Verse 27 contains one final reminder of Jesus's authority. Jesus
describes himself with the title *Son of Man*. This title is taken from Daniel
7. In that chapter Daniel is experiencing a vision from God that reveals
God's sovereignty over all the nations and kingdoms in the world. In
verses 9-10 he describes a scene from God's throne room:

> *As I kept watching, thrones were set in place, and the Ancient of Days
> took his seat. His clothing was white like snow, and the hair of his
> head like whitest wool. His throne was flaming fire; its wheels were
> blazing fire. A river of fire was flowing, coming out from his presence.
> Thousands upon thousands served him; ten thousand times ten
> thousand stood before him. The court was convened, and the books
> were opened.* (Dan 7:9-10)

Here's what we find a few verses later:

> *I continued watching in the night visions, and suddenly one like a
> son of man was coming with the clouds of heaven. He approached the
> Ancient of Days and was escorted before him. He was given dominion,
> and glory, and a kingdom; so that those of every people, nation, and
> language should serve him. His dominion is an everlasting dominion*

that will not pass away, and his kingdom is one that will not be destroyed. (Dan 7:13-14)

Jesus is the Son of Man. He's been given dominion, glory, and a kingdom. He is to be served by all peoples, nations, and languages. His dominion is everlasting and shall never pass away or be destroyed. The story of the gospel is that the King has come. Will his subjects obey? The most pressing question this text poses to us is this: Will we submit to the authority of Jesus Christ? Will we seek to bring every area of our lives under his control?

Hebrew National makes 100 percent premium kosher beef hot dogs. On the hot dog package, right underneath the bright yellow letters, "Hebrew National," are the words, "We answer to a higher authority." The same slogan should be written on everything we do. Is the authority of Christ affecting how you talk to your spouse? discipline your children? discipline yourself? respond to criticism? spend your time? spend your money? As Christians, our confession is Jesus Christ is Lord, and our commitment is to submit to his lordship in every area of our lives. We do, indeed, answer to a higher authority.

Reflect and Discuss

1. What does it mean that Jesus "is not able to do anything on his own" (John 5:19)?
2. How is Jesus making a clear statement of both deity and authority?
3. How can Jesus have the authority to give a person life and judge people?
4. How has he displayed this authority?
5. Why is rejection of Jesus dishonoring to God? What is the difference between admiring Jesus and believing in Jesus?
6. What words would you use to lovingly tell someone that any system of worship not honoring Jesus as the true God is a lie?
7. What does submission to God look like?
8. How can the spiritually dead hear and obey Jesus?
9. What claim does Jesus make by calling himself the Son of Man?
10. How is the authority of Christ affecting the way you live?

Witnesses to Deity

JOHN 5:30-39

Main Idea: Jesus introduces four witnesses to his deity, leaving the religious leaders with no excuse for rejecting him.

I. Witness 1: John the Baptist (5:33-35)
II. Witness 2: The Works of Jesus (5:36)
III. Witness 3: The Words of Scripture (5:39)
IV. Witness 4: God the Father (5:37-38)

One of the foundational truths of Christianity is belief in the deity of Jesus Christ. This doctrine undergirds the Christian faith. Without it everything else will crumble and fail. This is why the devil has always attacked this truth. If he can chip away at the foundation and weaken the support, then he may be able to topple the faith of the saints and stem the advance of the gospel. We must guard against apathy and indifference about Christ's deity. We should regularly remind ourselves and one another of what upholds and buttresses the rest of our doctrine. What a tragedy to discover one day that through our negligence the foundation of faith has been subtly chipped away.

We cannot devote too much time or attention to the deity of Jesus Christ, for without it we have no genuine faith. C. S. Lewis, writing to a dear friend who had rejected Christ and embraced atheism, wrote,

> If [Christ] was not God, who or what was He? . . . The doctrine of Christ's divinity seems to me not something stuck on . . . but something that peeps out at every point [of the New Testament] so that you have to unravel the whole web to get rid of it . . . and if you take away the Godhead of Christ, what is Christianity all *about?* (Cited in Townsend, "C. S. Lewis' Theology"; emphasis original)

The answer to Lewis's question is a resounding, "Nothing!" Without the deity of Jesus Christ, there's no Christian faith, no gospel, no power to save.

In verse 30 Jesus continues the theme that he and the Father are one. The obvious implication is that to oppose Jesus is to oppose God, to reject Jesus is to reject God, and to rebel against Jesus is to rebel against God. Jesus's testimony about himself is clear.

At first glance Jesus appears to contradict himself in verse 31. He seems to be saying, "I know that I said I was God, but you have no reason to believe me." In Old Testament law multiple witnesses were needed for a truth to be established as certain. For instance, in Deuteronomy 19:15 we find this legal requirement for a person to be convicted of a crime:

> *One witness cannot establish any iniquity or sin against a person, whatever that person has done. A fact must be established by the testimony of two or three witnesses.*

Testimony without validation wasn't accepted as true. So, Jesus is going to call witnesses to validate his deity right in front of the leaders, leaving them with no excuse for rejecting him.

Witness 1: John the Baptist
JOHN 5:33-35

We were first introduced to John the Baptist in chapter 1.

> *And John testified, "I saw the Spirit descending from heaven like a dove, and he rested on him. I didn't know him, but he who sent me to baptize with water told me, 'The one you see the Spirit descending and resting on—he is the one who baptizes with the Holy Spirit.' I have seen and testified that this is the Son of God."* (1:32-34)

John is convinced Jesus is the Messiah, and he makes it known. At this point, the religious leaders Jesus is talking with have heard John's message. They know what John thinks about Jesus. They know John's witness, but they reject it. Jesus doesn't let them off the hook that easy. He doesn't say, "Well, John says this about me, but you've rejected it so let's move on." He reminds them they had at one time listened to John and valued what he said. They hadn't just heard John's testimony; they had requested it! They had "sent messengers to John" (5:33) to find out what he had to say. In fact, they had even liked what John said for a time. They "were willing to rejoice for a while in his light" (v. 35).

Before Jesus burst on the scene, John was preaching the Messiah was coming. They liked that message. They were excited about the dawning of the messianic age. But when Jesus appeared and John pointed to Jesus as the Messiah, they didn't like that as much. Jesus didn't fit their image of what the Messiah should be. He didn't come in riding a white horse and ready to overthrow the Roman oppression. Instead, he overthrew money tables in the temple and exposed their hypocrisy. That's when they stopped listening to John—not because his message changed but because their comfort level changed.

Jesus describes John as a lamp, a description that provides many helpful applications for us and our witness. A lamp must be lit. You could even translate that word "burning" as "ignited" (v. 35). Our witness will only be effective if God ignites it. That's one reason we pray. A lamp provides guidance and direction; it's not the destination. It's not the center of attention. The lamp simply illuminates the way to something else; it serves a greater purpose. A lamp eventually burns out. The verbs used to describe John's ministry are all in the past tense. John *has* borne witness. He *was* a lamp. John's life and ministry served a purpose for a time, but it eventually ended. We only have a short time on this earth to impact people for Jesus.

However, there's more to this image of a lamp. The same word translated "lamp" is found in the Greek translation of the Old Testament, the Septuagint (LXX). This is the Bible Jesus and the Jews would have regularly used. This word for "lamp" is found in Psalm 132:17: "There I will make a horn grow for David; I have prepared a lamp for my anointed one." The "horn" for David is a reference to the Messiah—also called God's anointed. The Messiah will have a lamp prepared for him. Jesus and John the Baptist are the fulfillment of this promise. John was the lamp prepared for Jesus, the Messiah. But there's still more. In the previous verse of Psalm 132, we read, "I will clothe its priests with salvation, and its faithful people will shout for joy." The same word translated "shout for joy" is found in our passage in John 5. In verse 35 Jesus says, "You were willing *to rejoice* [same word] for a while in his light." If you put all of this together, you see a strong indictment against the religious leaders. The psalmist prophesied that true saints would see the lamp prepared for the Messiah and rejoice. Jesus reminded them that they rejoiced "for a while," but they stopped rejoicing. What does that say about them? They are not genuine saints. Genuine saints would not stop rejoicing in the light.

Jesus doesn't need John's testimony to convince himself of what is happening (v. 34). He's got three more witnesses even greater than John. The reason he included John's witness was so some of them who had heard it might remember, turn from their rebellion, and be saved. Jesus mentioned John's testimony as an act of grace.

Witness 2: The Works of Jesus
JOHN 5:36

If they don't believe because of John's witness, they should believe when they see Jesus's works, which make his deity self-apparent. When Nicodemus came to Jesus, he was motivated, at least in part, by the works of Jesus. He said, "Rabbi, we know that you are a teacher who has come from God, for no one could perform these signs you do unless God were with him" (John 3:2). All that Jesus does testifies he is God. There's no natural explanation for Jesus's works; there has to be a supernatural cause. The most obvious explanation and the explanation the religious leaders should arrive at is that Jesus is the Messiah. The coming of the Messiah would be marked by miracles and signs that could only be attributed to God. In chapter 7, verse 31, the crowds understand that Jesus is doing supernatural works: "However, many from the crowd believed in him and said, 'When the Messiah comes, he won't perform more signs than this man has done, will he?'" There is a saying, "If it walks like a duck and quacks like a duck, it must be a duck." Jesus walks like the Messiah, talks like the Messiah, and does works that only the Messiah can do. The only logical conclusion is that Jesus is the Messiah. He is God.

This is why Jesus performs the miracles he does. His miracles aren't motivated solely by compassion for the sick or love for the dying. They're signs pointing people to a right understanding of who he is. Can't Jesus heal sick and dying people without anyone knowing it's him? In fact, can't he stop people from ever getting sick or dying? So, why does he perform miracles? Peter answers that question in a sermon he gave on the day of Pentecost:

> Fellow Israelites, listen to these words: This Jesus of Nazareth was a man attested to you by God with miracles, wonders, and signs that God did among you through him, just as you yourselves know. (Acts 2:22)

The works of Jesus make it clear he's divine. By themselves, his works should be enough to convince them of the deity of Jesus Christ.

Witness 3: The Words of Scripture
JOHN 5:39

Jesus acknowledges the seriousness of the religious leaders' study of the Scriptures. They diligently search through the Scriptures, and the Scriptures present a detailed witness to Jesus Christ. When Jesus mentions the Scriptures here, he's referring to the Old Testament. In many ways you can boil the teaching of the Old Testament down to two main themes. The first theme is that man is hopelessly rebellious and unable to save himself. From the moment Adam and Eve disobeyed God and ate the forbidden fruit, they became captive to sin. Their children were sinners (one was a murderer), and their grandchildren were sinners. Nothing they could ever do would be enough to save themselves from their sin. Apart from God they had no hope for rescue.

Have you noticed that even the heroes of the faith are recorded in unflattering terms? Think about Noah. After the ark landed, he got drunk and naked. Or Abraham—the friend of God, the father of Israel didn't trust God enough to wait for a legitimate son. Moses led God's people out of Egypt but was forbidden to enter the promised land because of his disobedience. Even David, a man after God's own heart, committed adultery and then murder to cover it up. Why does the Bible display all their dirty laundry? Because we need to understand that every person is a sinner in need of a Savior. Every single one of us, no matter how noble we may appear, is a rebel without hope, alienated from God.

The second theme that runs throughout the Old Testament is that God will send a Savior. From the moment mankind fell into sin, God promised a Rescuer. The Old Testament describes in great detail this one who would come. He's called the promised Seed, the Lion of Judah, the Son of Man, the Suffering Servant, the Passover Lamb, and the Messiah. These are just a few of the descriptions of Jesus that saturate the pages of the Old Testament. The entire weight of the Old Testament stands behind the claims of Jesus. Every word is a witness to who he is.

Witness 4: God the Father
JOHN 5:37-38

Standing behind the previous three witnesses is the greatest witness of all—God himself. Now these Jews have not seen God, and they have not heard God's voice. How could they possibly know what God wants?

The only way they can know him is through his revelation to them. God reveals himself to mankind through his messengers, through his works, and through his Word. What does Jesus present as support for his claim of deity? A prophet, supernatural works, and the Scriptures. In the same way and manner God reveals himself to mankind, Jesus reveals his deity to man. To doubt the claims of Jesus is to disregard God's revelation about himself.

Just like the religious leaders, we are completely cut off from God because of our sin. We have no way of knowing who God is and what God wants apart from his revelation to us, and his revelation to us makes clear the deity of Jesus Christ. Denying the deity of Jesus Christ is to set ourselves up as greater than God; it is to exalt our opinion over God's. That's a frightening place to be.

It all boils down to this: if Jesus is not God, he could not have paid the penalty for our sin. If Jesus is not God, we would be unable to cling to his righteousness. If Jesus is not God, we would be without hope. But Jesus is God. Phillis Wheatly, a young slave girl, wrote a poem at the age of thirteen to the students at the University of Cambridge. I can think of few words that more beautifully and accurately exalt the deity of Jesus Christ and the effects of his sacrifice.

> Students, to you 'tis giv'n to scan the heights
> Above, to traverse the ethereal space,
> And mark the systems of revolving worlds.
> Still more, ye sons of science ye receive
> The blissful news by messengers from heav'n,
> How Jesus' blood for your redemption flows.
> See him with hands out-strecht upon the cross;
> Immense compassion in his bosom glows;
> He hears revilers, nor resents their scorn:
> What matchless mercy in the Son of God!
> When the whole human race by sin had fall'n,
> He deign'd to die that they might rise again,
> And share with him in the sublimest skies,
> Life without death, and glory without end. ("To the University
>   of Cambridge, in New England")

Eternal life and eternal glory with Jesus are at stake. The deity of Jesus Christ is the foundation of our hope. May we never fail to know, defend, and share the truth that Jesus Christ is God.

Reflect and Discuss

1. What are we to believe about Jesus from this passage?
2. How are you guarding against apathy and indifference about Christ's deity? Who in your life is encouraging and standing watch with you?
3. Why does Jesus describe John the Baptist as a lamp?
4. How is Psalm 132 used as a reference in this passage?
5. Why does Jesus list John as a witness when the other three witnesses are so much greater?
6. Why does Jesus perform miracles? What should be the people's response?
7. What two major themes run throughout the Old Testament? How do they point to Jesus?
8. Why does God choose to work through sinful, flawed people like Moses and David and then tell everyone their faults through Scripture?
9. If someone were to write down your story of salvation, what would Jesus have delivered you from? How would the unmerited love and mercy of God to you be evidenced from your past?
10. If the Jews haven't seen God or heard his voice, how can Jesus list God as a witness to his deity?

Truth or Consequences?

JOHN 5:38-47

Main Idea: Jesus warns the religious leaders about the serious consequences of denying his deity.

I.   **You Cannot Properly Interpret Scripture (5:38-40).**
II. **You Cannot Love God (5:42-43).**
III. **You Cannot Honor God (5:44).**
IV. **You Cannot Avoid Judgment (5:45-47).**

For almost thirty years you could turn on NBC and watch the game show *Truth or Consequences*. The format of the show was simple. Contestants would be given about two seconds to answer an obscure trivia question. If they couldn't figure out the answer (i.e., the truth), they would have to suffer the consequences. If a contestant got an answer correct, he usually faced a quick second or third question to trip him up. The consequences were participating in some ridiculous, embarrassing stunt. I saw part of one episode in which two men couldn't figure out the "truth," so they were forced to try to ride a unicycle on national TV.

Tell the truth or face the consequences. Every parent has said some variation of those words, and every child has heard them. John 5:1-37 reveals the truth that Jesus is God. Verses 38-47 consider four consequences for denying this truth.

You Cannot Properly Interpret Scripture
JOHN 5:38-40

If we read the Bible and don't worship Jesus Christ as the one true God, we've completely missed the point. James Boice asks,

> What is the primary purpose of Scripture? Is it to record
> the history of God's dealings with men? It does record such
> history, but that is not its primary function. Is it to reveal
> certain truths to men? Although it does reveal truths, this

is not its primary function either. The primary purpose of
Scripture is to point men and women to Christ. (*John*, 2:407)

Many devote a significant amount of time and effort to studying the
Scriptures and yet fail to see, understand, and exalt Jesus Christ as Lord
and Savior. They fail to see Jesus in Scripture because they misunderstand the purpose of the Bible.

Some think the Bible is a book of *ancient tales*. It's not much different from Aesop's *Fables*. The Bible's full of stories and tales like "The
Tortoise and the Hare," illustrating ideas such as slow and steady wins
the race.

Others think the Bible is a book full of *moralistic lessons*. It's a book
of virtues. It includes many different genres, everything from fairy tales
to history lessons, Greek mythology to English poetry. Each is included
to help instill certain positive character traits.

Still others think the Bible is like a *driver's manual*. It tells you to turn
here, yield over there, and stop when you reach this line. It tells you how
to navigate through life. It's our road map. "Doesn't the word *Bible* stand
for *Basic Instructions before Leaving Earth?*"

Finally, some people think the Bible is full of *secret codes*. The extreme
end of this view has people searching the Bible for hidden messages and
trying to decipher numerology. A less extreme view is taken by those
who search the Bible for inspirational nuggets to impact each day—a
little chicken soup for their souls.

To miss the promise of God to send a Savior to rescue mankind
from sin, and not to see the fulfillment of that promise in the person
of Jesus Christ, is to miss everything! Everything in Scripture serves as
a sign pointing us to Jesus. When I was growing up, my parents took
the family on a trip from Michigan to Florida. We were so excited! All
we could talk about for weeks—maybe months—leading up to that trip
was Florida. Just mentioning "Florida" would bring squeals of delight
from us as we anticipated all the fun that lay in store. When we finally
took that trip, we couldn't wait to get there. We drove and drove and
finally we saw it. There on the side of the highway was a big blue sign
with a bright orange sun on it and the word "Florida." We were so
excited my parents pulled the van off the road, and we went over to
the sign, lined up around it, and took a picture. Then we took all of
our stuff out of the van, made camp around that sign, and spent the

next week and a half enjoying the big, blue Florida sign. Of course we didn't. We got back in the van and drove into Florida and spent a week and a half enjoying it.

Studying the Scriptures without seeing, worshiping, and obeying Jesus Christ is as foolish as making camp around the Florida sign. The whole point of the sign was to encourage us to keep going and to tell us what awaited us. The whole point of the Word of God is to point us to Jesus. God gave us his Word so that we might come to Jesus Christ. I love how Sally Lloyd-Jones captures it:

> Now, some people think the Bible is a book of rules, telling you what you should do and shouldn't do. The Bible certainly does have some rules in it. They show you how life works best. But the Bible isn't mainly about you and what you should be doing. It's about God and what he has done. Other people think the Bible is a book of heroes, showing you people you should copy. The Bible does have some heroes in it, but . . . most of the people in the Bible aren't heroes at all. They make some big mistakes (sometimes on purpose). They get afraid and run away. At times they are downright mean. No, the Bible isn't a book of rules, or a book of heroes. The Bible is most of all a Story. It's an adventure story about a young Hero who comes from a far country to win back his lost treasure. It's a love story about a brave Prince who leaves his palace, his throne—everything—to rescue the one he loves. It's like the most wonderful of fairy tales that has come true in real life! You see, the best thing about the Story is—it's true. There are lots of stories in the Bible, but all the stories are telling one Big Story. The Story of how God loves his children and comes to rescue them. It takes the whole Bible to tell this Story. And at the center of the Story, there is a baby. Every Story in the Bible whispers his name. He is like the missing piece in a puzzle—the piece that makes all the other pieces fit together, and suddenly you can see a beautiful picture. (*The Jesus Storybook Bible*, 14–17)

Jesus makes clear that the whole Bible tells his story. In Luke two disciples are walking down the road when Jesus, freshly resurrected, joins them. He asks them why they're so sad. They don't recognize him, so they tell him all about Jesus and his death. Jesus responds:

"How foolish and slow you are to believe all that the prophets have spoken! Wasn't it necessary for the Messiah to suffer these things and enter into his glory?" Then beginning with Moses and all the Prophets, he interpreted for them the things concerning himself in all the Scriptures. (Luke 24:25-27)

Jesus wanted them to see that all the Scriptures pointed to him (Luke 24:44; Acts 26:22-23). Everything that had happened to him—his suffering, death, and resurrection—was prophesied already. He had to suffer: Genesis 3—he was the Son whose heel would be bruised. He had to be rejected: Psalm 118—he was the Stone who would be cast out. He had to be killed: Isaiah 53—he was the Lamb led to the slaughter. He had to be victorious: the bruised heel would crush the serpent's head. The rejected stone would become the cornerstone. The sacrificed Lamb would see his offspring.

The Bible is about Jesus Christ. As the subtitle of *The Jesus Storybook Bible* indicates, every story whispers his name. Law, poetry, narrative, and prophecy all work together to point us to Jesus Christ. The reason we read this book is to see him. If we miss him, we miss it all.

These religious leaders thought the act of studying God's Word would bring them favor with God. They assumed their devotion to the Scriptures would cause God to accept them. But God's Word isn't a lucky charm. It's a sign that points us to Jesus Christ. Martin Luther preached on this passage just a few months before his death:

Here Christ would indicate the principal reason why the Scripture was given by God. Men are to study and search in it and to learn that He, He, Mary's Son, is the one who is able to give eternal life to all who come to Him and believe on Him. Therefore he who would correctly and profitably read Scripture should see to it that he finds Christ in it; then he finds eternal life without fail. On the other hand, if I do not so study and understand Moses and the prophets as to find that Christ came from Heaven for the sake of my salvation, became man, suffered, died, was buried, rose, and ascended to Heaven so that through Him I enjoy reconciliation with God, forgiveness of all my sins, grace, righteousness, and life eternal, then my reading in Scripture is of no help whatsoever to my salvation. I may, of course, become a learned man by reading and studying Scripture and may preach what I have acquired; yet all this would do me no good whatsoever. For if I do not know and do not find the Christ, neither do I find salvation and life eternal. In fact, I actually find bitter death; for our good God has decreed that no other name is given among men whereby they may be saved except the name of Jesus. (Cited in Boice, *John*, 2:421–22)

Do you realize it's possible to focus on the minutiae in the text and miss the larger point? Many people I've met argue vehemently over peripheral issues while neglecting foundational ones. They argue about the length of a skirt or the beat in the music while ignoring the centrality of the gospel to our lives as believers. If you're a Christian and you read the Bible while missing the point, you're going to struggle with confusion, discouragement, frustration, ineffectiveness, and stagnation:

- Confusion because the parts won't make sense by themselves.
- Discouragement because it will seem like a duty instead of a delight.
- Frustration because your love for the Scriptures won't grow.
- Ineffectiveness because you won't understand why it matters in your life.
- Stagnation because you won't see growth in understanding or maturity.

It's about Jesus. It's all about him. We need to guard against being distracted by secondary concerns. A church should be defined by its commitment to Christ, not personal preferences. As Christians, we must be vigilant to help one another keep the main thing the main thing. The main thing is "Jesus Christ and him crucified" (1 Cor 2:2).

You Cannot Love God
JOHN 5:42-43

If you deny the deity of Jesus Christ, it's impossible for you to love God. You can write songs to God. You can go on mission trips. You can feed the poor. You can give money to the church. But if you don't worship Jesus Christ as the true God, you cannot love God. If one of your children was completely rebellious, constantly disobeying your instructions, directly defying everything you said, would you believe her when she said, "I love you"? No. You'd probably say, "You don't love me. You only love yourself." Her actions reveal her heart's condition. Jesus says these men who claim to love God reveal a lack of love by their refusal to believe God. They're unwilling to accept the one God sent. Four times in this passage Jesus describes himself as having been sent by God (vv. 30,36,37,38). Yet he was being rejected by those who claimed to love God. Their declaration of love does not square with their lives. If they loved God, they wouldn't receive false prophets while rejecting God's Son. Right after my wife and I got engaged, we spent the summer apart. Because we were apart and busy, with infrequent opportunities to call each other, we wrote letters—a lot of letters. Partway through the summer, I went to visit her at camp. Imagine if I had walked in and seen all of my letters unopened and filling the wastebasket. "What's going on? I thought you loved me," I'd say. "Oh, I do," she'd reply. "Then why haven't you read any of my letters? If you loved me, you would listen to what I have to say," I could argue. We can claim to love God, but if we don't listen to what he says, we don't love him (cf. 14:23-24).

The reality of our love for God is seen in our submission to Jesus Christ. Love is more than the declaration of our lips. Love is seen in our actions. The proof of love is not what we say but what we do. In high school I took geometry. You generate a hypothesis, and then you prove your hypothesis. You couldn't just turn in your hypothesis to your teacher. You had to prove why your hypothesis was true through a series of logical steps. You may think you love God, but where is your proof? You need to think about what would prove your love is true. Maybe you look at your works and think, *I give money in the offering. I go to church. I pray before meals. I try to do the right things. Therefore, I love God.* Didn't the religious leaders do all of these things and more? Yet Jesus said they didn't love God. The only proof of your love for God that matters is your submission to Jesus Christ. If you refuse to submit to Jesus as Lord, if you deny his deity, then you can write poems to God and paint murals of Bible scenes on the walls of your house, but it doesn't matter. You cannot love God if you refuse to submit to Jesus Christ as God.

You Cannot Honor God
JOHN 5:44

These men were more concerned about how they would appear to others than they were about the glory of God. They were unwilling to humble themselves, believe on Jesus, and submit to his will. Like them, we care too much about what other people think about us. Why do you choose the clothes you wear? Is it not to craft a certain image? Some people wear a certain kind of thing to church each week for one reason—to impress people. They want people to think they're spiritual. Often the same motive causes one person to dress fancy and another person to dress immodestly. Both are trying to draw praise. Both are hoping to be noticed. Both are worried about what people might think or say. So the one dresses to catch the eye of the righteous, and the other dresses to catch the eye of the rebellious. Both are still making decisions based on what others might think and say about them. They both want honor from others.

The religious leaders in Jesus's day could spout great truths about the glory of God. They could wax eloquent about the Shekinah glory and regale you with all the details of God's glory revealed in Israel's history. But when it came down to it, they were more concerned about being honored by men than they were about honoring God.

To embrace the deity of Jesus Christ is inherently humbling. If you embrace the gospel message, you're admitting your life is so messed up that God's Son had to enter the human race in order to fix you. In order to believe the gospel, you must admit you're not righteous. You must admit you're a sinner who desperately needs a Savior. The sad testimony of these men is they liked flattery more than the truth. They swapped God's salvation for man's admiration. What a terrible trade! If you were to chart the trajectory of your life on a graph, would it look like you were aiming at man's applause, man's acceptance, and man's appreciation, or God's approval? The only way to honor God is to humble yourself and admit that he sent his own Son, Jesus, into the world to rescue you. You cannot deny the deity of Jesus and still honor God.

You Cannot Avoid Judgment
JOHN 5:45-47

Rejecting Jesus Christ is going to bring the religious leaders under God's judgment. In verse 45 Jesus tells them directly, "You will stand accused before God." Jesus won't accuse them though; Moses will. They will make their defense: "We held to the law. We obeyed what Moses wrote." The divine decree will judge them guilty.

Moses wrote that mankind was sinful and rebellious and needed a Savior. That's what the Ten Commandments are all about. They show us what it means to obey God, and they also show us that we each fail.

No one has worshiped God alone. No one has loved his neighbor like himself. No one but Jesus, that is.

Moses wrote that a promised Deliverer would come. The Son of God would come to redeem his people from their sin. These men who put their hope and confidence in Moses's writings missed the point of what he wrote. He wrote about Christ. He wrote about the coming of Jesus.

In spite of all their religious training, these men had misplaced their hope. Their hope was in their own righteousness. They were trusting in their commitment to reading and obeying the Scriptures. Hope in anything other than the finished work of Jesus Christ on the cross for your sin is a fool's hope. The sad verdict of their lives is offered by Jesus in verse 40: "You are not willing to come to me so that you may have life." The only way to have life is to come to Jesus, and the only possibility for the man or woman who rejects Jesus Christ is judgment.

When Bob Barker hosted *Truth or Consequences*, he ended every show by saying, "Hoping all your consequences are happy ones." If you deny the truth about Jesus, your consequences are not going to be happy.

- You won't understand the Bible.
- You won't love God.
- You won't honor God.
- You won't avoid judgment.

But if you embrace the truth about Jesus, these four consequences flip around and become happy ones.

- Because of Jesus, you will avoid judgment.
- Because of Jesus, you will honor God.
- Because of Jesus, you will love God.
- Because of Jesus, you will understand the Bible. In fact, the Bible will come to life as you start to see Jesus on every page.

Reflect and Discuss

1. What consequences will you face if you deny or miss the truth that Jesus is God?
2. What is the primary purpose of Scripture?
3. What are some ways people misunderstand the purpose of Scripture?
4. In your own study of Scripture, how is your focus moving to Jesus?

5. What steps can you take to ensure Jesus remains at the center of your Bible study?
6. What Old Testament passages can you think of that point to Jesus?
7. What is the danger in focusing on the minutiae in a text and missing the larger point?
8. What results will occur in our theology and doctrine if we read Scripture and miss the point of Jesus?
9. How is it humbling to embrace the gospel of Jesus?
10. How can Moses accuse those who claim to have kept the law?

A Greater Moses

JOHN 6:1-21

Main Idea: In Jesus, God sent a greater Moses to rescue his people.

I. **Jesus Miraculously Feeds the People.**
II. **Jesus Miraculously Crosses the Sea.**
III. **Jesus Is Greater Than Moses.**

George Washington's impact on the birth of the United States is reflected across the country. A state is named after him, as well as the nation's capital. Two hundred forty-one townships and twenty-six cities are named Washington. Four forts, five mountains, and three ports bear his name. Bridges and parks and at least a dozen colleges are named after him. Imagine if you combined George Washington with the Pope or with Billy Graham, so that Washington was not only the founder of the nation, but he was also the leader of your religion. Even if you did that, you still wouldn't come close to matching how the Jews felt about Moses. Moses was their great hero. Not only was he responsible for bringing them out of Egypt and governing them as a nation for the first time, but he was also the greatest religious leader in their history. He's the one who went up the mountain to meet with God and receive the Ten Commandments.

The Jews' reverence for Moses is the background for John 6. Moses was mentioned at the end of chapter 5 when Jesus told the religious leaders they failed to believe Moses because Moses wrote about him (v. 46). One day Moses himself would condemn these men for their failure to believe on Jesus. In chapter 6 we discover God sent a greater Moses to rescue his people. The first few verses of chapter 6 set the context that Jesus is to be understood as a Moses-type figure. Four details in the opening verses connect Jesus to Moses and show us Jesus is like Moses. None of these details are especially significant in themselves, but when you put them together, you see Jesus doing what Moses did.

First, Jesus is leading a crowd just like Moses did. Moses was the leader of Israel when Israel escaped from slavery in Egypt. When we think of Moses, we think of a man leading a large crowd from Egypt to the promised land.

Second, the crowd is following Jesus because they saw the signs he did. Why did the crowd follow Moses? They saw the signs he did in Egypt. Moses was the one God used to bring the ten plagues on Egypt. Those signs authenticated his role as one sent by God.

Third, Jesus and his disciples went up on the mountain. After performing signs and leading Israel out of Egypt, Moses and his servant Joshua went up on the mountain to receive the law from God.

Fourth, these events took place during the Passover, a yearly Jewish festival celebrating when God rescued his people from Egypt. The final plague was the death of the firstborn. God commanded Moses to have each family kill a lamb and spread its blood on the doorposts of their house. If they did, death would pass over them, and their firstborn would be spared.

The context of the next two events shows us that Jesus is walking in the footsteps of Moses. What follows these two events is a discussion about how Moses fed them with manna in the wilderness on the way to the promised land. Jesus is revealing himself to be like Moses, but the convincing proof comes in the next two events. Anyone could have led a crowd up a mountain at Passover. That by itself wouldn't make a person like Moses. So, how is Jesus like Moses?

Jesus Miraculously Feeds the People

Moses was tasked with leading the nation of Israel from slavery in Egypt across the wilderness to a new home in the land God had promised to give them. It was no easy task. The size of the nation alone—between one and two million people—made it almost impossible. Can you imagine trying to lead that many people to do anything, much less traverse the wilderness in search of a new home? One of the main problems was how to feed a group this large. Where would the food come from for them to survive this trek? You couldn't plant crops out in the wilderness and wait for them to grow. You couldn't leave Egypt with forty years' worth of food in your saddlebags.

How would they eat? God would provide their food. He told Moses to tell the people he would send bread from heaven for them to eat. Every morning this bread (called *manna*) would be on the ground, and they could take baskets and collect enough to feed their families that day. Any extra would spoil overnight. The next day the manna would be back on the ground for that day's meals.

Jesus faced a similar circumstance. He had a great crowd and no way to feed them (vv. 5-6). He asks one of his disciples what to do. Why did Jesus ask? So that he could see how Philip would respond, and so that when he did something miraculous the disciples would understand how amazing it was. Jesus wants his disciples to fully understand who he is. He could have solved the problem without involving them, but he wanted them to see. He wanted them to understand his power, so they would believe. The miracle isn't just for the hungry people. It's for the disciples, so they would not underestimate the power of Jesus.

Philip says it would cost more than "two hundred denarii" (v. 7). A denarius is equal to one day's labor. Philip's answer shows the immensity of the problem. Even if they were to spend eight months' salary on bread, it wouldn't be enough for each person there to get a bite. They didn't have the money to feed the people, and even if they did, where would the bread come from? Human ingenuity couldn't solve the problem. Because we live in an age of great technological advance, we sometimes act as if we're invincible. This passage is a great reminder that we will always be confronted with problems too big for us to solve. Death, disease, war—those are the big ones. Even when we shrink them down to a personal size, we realize how powerless we are. Who can stop himself from getting sick? Who can make sure he's never misunderstood or mistreated? Who can make sure everyone likes him all the time? We are powerless, just like Philip. Like Philip we're quick to look for human solutions. A problem comes and our minds start going. We're going to fix it. And like Philip, we forget who's standing with us. Jesus asked Philip the question so Philip would learn that no problem is a match for Jesus's power.

Another disciple, Andrew, brings Jesus a boy who has a lunch with him (vv. 8-9). It seems like a great act of faith until it's undermined by his final comment, "But what are they for so many?" It's as if he were saying, "Here you go, Jesus, but I don't know what good it will do." If you grew up in a home with a bunch of men, you understand Andrew's comment. Five loaves wouldn't have been enough. What chance would they have of feeding five thousand men? That's one thousand men per loaf. These loaves weren't large. We would probably call them biscuits. Imagine five thousand men show up for breakfast, and there are five biscuits and a small bowl of gravy for the whole group. That's the situation here.

We can be really hard on the disciples. They had already seen Jesus turn water into wine. Of course he can feed five thousand with five loaves! But I don't think that's fair. How many times do we have to see God work before we stop doubting? I don't know. I certainly haven't reached that point. When I face a situation that seems impossible, I look for human solutions (as Philip did), and if I don't see any, then I despair (as Andrew did), thinking, *What good will it do? What difference will it make?* There's a small boy with a small lunch of small fish. It's hopeless. It looks like everyone's going hungry.

Then just like Moses, Jesus fed the multitude miraculously (vv. 10-11). There was no sleight of hand. He prayed, thanked his Father for what he was about to do, and turned five loaves and two fishes into an all-you-can-eat buffet: "as much as they wanted" (v. 11). When Jesus supplies, it's never too little. He never runs out. Jesus loves to go above and beyond not only what we can ask but even what we can think (Eph 3:20). Jesus has never yet run into a problem he can't solve.

- No wine at the wedding. No problem.
- No food in the wilderness. No problem.
- No life in the tomb. No problem.

When you follow Jesus, you never reach a dead end.

After he finished, he had the disciples collect the leftovers into baskets (vv. 12-13), so that none would be "wasted" or lost (v. 12). The concept comes up again later in the chapter. Jesus says, "This is the will of him who sent me: that I should *lose* none of those he has given me but should raise them up on the last day" (6:39; emphasis added). Jesus never wastes anything. Nothing of his will ever be lost. He's showing the disciples his care and illustrating what it means that he will not lose any of those who belong to him. If Jesus cares enough to make sure none of the leftovers are lost, how much more will he make sure none of his people are lost? Just like Moses thousands of years earlier, Jesus cares for each one of his people. He provides the food they need in a way that shatters all human expectations.

Jesus Miraculously Crosses the Sea

After leading the nation of Israel out of the land of Egypt, Moses found himself in a terrible predicament. The Egyptian army led by a vengeful Pharaoh was approaching from the rear, and the Red Sea was cutting them off in the front. What should Moses do? If they didn't keep moving, Pharaoh's army would cut them down, but there was nowhere to go. God told Moses to stretch his staff out toward the sea. When Moses did, God divided the sea, and the people marched through on dry ground.

Pharaoh's army tried to follow, and the walls of water collapsed on them, drowning them and their horses.

Jesus sends the disciples across the sea without him (vv. 16-17). I'm not sure they knew how he would cross. It's too far to swim—six miles across—but he sends them and they go. The sea starts to get choppy (v. 18). In fact, it's so bad these experienced fishermen spend most of the night rowing and only make it halfway across (v. 19). Why is the water so choppy? Because a "high wind," a powerful wind, was blowing. Do you know what God sent to part the Red Sea when the Israelite nation needed to cross?

Then Moses stretched out his hand over the sea. The LORD drove the sea back with a powerful east wind all that night and turned the sea into dry land. So the waters were divided, and the Israelites went through the sea on dry ground, with the waters like a wall to them on their right and their left. (Exod 14:21-22; emphasis added)

God caused a powerful wind to blow so that Moses could miraculously lead his people across the sea.

Jesus walks across the sea as effortlessly as if he were walking on dry ground (John 6:19). Can you imagine? That's mind-boggling. Why'd he do it? Why not just meet them on the other side? Jesus walked to them on the water for the same reason he fed the five thousand: so they would witness his power and understand who he is.

When they see Jesus, they're scared. They're witnesses to deity. They've seen something that is far beyond what's natural. They're confronted with a being far more powerful than they can fathom. Here, in the midst of the storm, they don't fear the storm. They fear the Maker of the storm. At this moment on the Sea of Galilee, the disciples were confronted with a power beyond their reckoning. They saw the power of God, and they were afraid. But what does Jesus say? "Don't be afraid" (v. 20). There is a God with power our minds cannot fathom. He is just and will someday use his power to right all wrongs and judge all sin. Yet, through his Son, Jesus, he reaches out to each of us and says, "You don't need to be afraid. If you believe in Jesus, if you receive him, there's no need to fear."

With these two acts, Jesus identifies himself as one like Moses: he feeds the people and crosses the sea, both in ways that require divine help. Some who see him make the connection (v. 14). They don't call Jesus *a prophet*. They call him *the Prophet*. He's a particular prophet the nation of Israel has been anticipating. All the way back in

Deuteronomy 18:15, Moses wrote, "The LORD your God will raise up for you a prophet like me from among your own brothers. You must listen to him." Jesus was making clear he was the prophet like Moses. The book of Deuteronomy ends with these words:

> No prophet has arisen again in Israel like Moses, whom the LORD knew face to face. He was unparalleled for all the signs and wonders the LORD sent him to do against the land of Egypt—to Pharaoh, to all his officials, and to all his land, and for all the mighty acts of power and terrifying deeds that Moses performed in the sight of all Israel. (Deut 34:10-12)

A special prophet would come who would do mighty signs and wonders just as Moses did. Century after century, Israel waited for the prophet like Moses, and here he is. They see the works of Jesus, and they recognize the fulfillment of Moses's prophecy.

Jesus Is Greater Than Moses

What was Moses's greatest accomplishment? His defining legacy was leading the nation of Israel out of slavery in Egypt and bringing them to a new land, the land God promised them. Moses was the great liberator of Israel. When Jesus was born, Israel was in slavery again, not in Egypt but in their own land. The Romans had conquered Israel and made it part of the empire. When someone like Moses shows up, what do you think the Israelites want him to do? They want him to lead them out of slavery. They want to start a revolution and overthrow their foreign captors.

Here's a crowd of five thousand Jewish men, chafing under Roman oppression. They recognize the second Moses, and they think, *Finally! Finally we'll be free from Rome. No longer will we be slaves in our own cities. Let's make Jesus king and take back the kingdom* (see John 6:15). Jesus thwarted their plans. He saw the revolution in their eyes, and he left. Was it fear? Was it doubt? Why leave? Because Jesus wasn't worried about victory over Rome. He was after a greater victory. Jesus came to wage war against sin and suffering. He came to duel with death.

They wanted to make Jesus king, but before he would wear the crown of gold, he chose to wear a crown of thorns. Before he would sit on the throne, he would hang on a cross. The crucifixion would come before the coronation. Moses won a great victory, but it pales in comparison to the victory Jesus won when he rose from the grave, triumphant over death and hell.

Application

Think about how you approach Jesus. The Israelites wanted to make Jesus their king by force (v. 15). So they did want Jesus, but they wanted him to be their puppet. They would follow Jesus as their king as long as he did what they wanted, as long as he overthrew Rome. That is not Christianity. The Jesus of the Bible is no man's puppet, but how often we come to him telling him what we want him to do. We bargain with him. We claim to follow him as long as he doesn't say or do something we dislike. We want the kingdom without the King. We want the liberty without the liberator. We want all of the blessings Jesus can secure for us without actually having to obey and follow him.

If we want Jesus to fix all of our problems but we don't want to have to follow Jesus, all we want is a puppet king. We want another Moses— someone to get us out of trouble and make our lives a little more comfortable. Jesus is so much more, so much greater.

The only way to come to Jesus is to lay down your expectations, put aside your requirements, let go of the strings, and follow him. When you do, you will find that not only is Jesus greater than Moses, but Jesus is far greater than anything you can ever imagine.

Reflect and Discuss

1. What four details in John 6:1-4 connect Jesus to Moses?
2. Why is Moses used as a comparison for Jesus?
3. What is different about the way Jesus feeds the crowd and the way Moses fed the Israelites?
4. How do you think you would respond if you were one of the five thousand?
5. Why does Jesus have the disciples gather the leftovers?
6. Why does Jesus walk across the water to his disciples? Why not just go with them on the boat?
7. Why does Jesus withdraw when he sees the crowd coming to make him king?
8. Compare Moses's leading the Israelites out of slavery to Jesus's death and resurrection. What are the similarities? How is Jesus's victory greater?
9. Describe what it looks like to approach Jesus to get something from him.
10. Describe what it looks like to approach Jesus to get him.

Bread of Life

JOHN 6:22-60

Main Idea: Eternal life comes only to those who eat the bread of life.

I. **God Gives Bread to Those Who Are Hungry.**
II. **Only God's Bread Can Give Life.**
III. **We Must Eat the Bread to Live.**

We all know what it's like to be hungry. From the moment we emerged from our mothers' wombs, we've wanted to eat.

There's not a day that goes by in my house when someone doesn't say, "I'm so hungry." God created our bodies to run on food, and hunger is the warning system telling us we're getting low. We feel the hunger. We hear the growling, and it causes us to think, *I need to eat.* That's what keeps us alive. We're also spiritually hungry. There's a growling of the soul that indicates emptiness inside. We were made to live on some sort of fuel, but we're not sure where to find it. We feel hungry, so we look for something to fill the emptiness inside us—something to quiet the hunger pangs in our hearts.

In this passage Jesus tells us about the bread of life, the only thing satisfying enough to quiet our cravings and fill our souls. He stands in front of a crowd and says in essence, "The only way to live is to eat the bread of life." Jesus makes this offer in the midst of a lengthy sermon. He repeats three truths multiple times to make clear that life comes only to those who eat the bread of life.

God Gives Bread to Those Who Are Hungry

The previous day Jesus had five thousand men plus their families take a seat on the hillside. He then prayed over five small loaves of bread and two pieces of dried fish. He turned that meager meal into an abundant stream of fish and bread, feeding everyone who was hungry. The miraculous work of Jesus reminded the people of something similar in the history of Israel (vv. 31-32). When the nation of Israel had journeyed from Egypt to the promised land, God sustained them with manna. Every morning they would wake up to see the ground covered with sweet, flaky white bread. I love the people's reaction the first time God sent them manna.

> *When the layer of dew evaporated, there were fine flakes on the desert surface, as fine as frost on the ground. When the Israelites saw it, they asked one another, "What is it?" because they didn't know what it was. Moses told them, "It is the bread the LORD has given you to eat."*
> (Exod 16:14-15)

Why did God send them bread? First, they were hungry. They were traveling across the wilderness with no way to gather enough food to sustain a nation. Second, he loved them and wanted them to know he would provide for them. He wanted them to unmistakably experience his kind provision. The manna was a picture of what was to come. Just as God sent his people bread when they were physically hungry, he would send them bread to quench their spiritual hunger. God would send the true bread from heaven, a greater provision for a deeper hunger (John 6:33-35). God sent the true bread, but it didn't appear on the ground first thing in the morning. It appeared in a manger late at night. The bread was a person: Jesus Christ, sent by God to meet man's spiritual hunger.

We often hunger for the wrong bread. Why do you think the people got in boats and traveled across the sea to find Jesus (vv. 22-25)? Was it because they understood he was the one who could quench their spiritual hunger, he was the one who could fill the emptiness inside their souls? Jesus said they were seeking him because they wanted more bread to eat (v. 26). One author said, "They were moved not by full hearts, but by full bellies" (Morris, *John*, 358).

We are often captives to our physical longings. Consider how much time, effort, and energy you put into making sure your physical hunger is met. You get up in the morning, and the first thing you think about is what you're going to eat or drink. Throughout the day we're running here or there for lunch or dinner, spending time making food, or heading to the store for more groceries. We make sure we don't go hungry. Compare that to how much time and energy and effort we put into making sure our spiritual hunger is met. Do we even think about it? Do we give any thought to what sustains our spiritual lives, what nourishes our souls? Even when we attend church, are we thinking about anything other than what we want and what we like?

If your life consists of working day after day to put food on the table, it's going to feel empty. If all your energy is targeted at meeting your physical needs—needs that never take a day off—your life will feel wasted. I wonder if the reason so many Christians feel bored and restless is that their lives are spent pursuing that which cannot satisfy: another promotion at work, another vacation away, another sports victory, or another fancy meal. Jesus is the bread of life; he's the only one who can fill the emptiness inside us. A full life is a life spent in pursuit of Jesus. A life spent any other way will feel barren and unfulfilled.

Only God's Bread Can Give Life

No matter how good the meal tastes, no matter how much money you spend on it, no matter how amazing it is, at some point in the future, you'll be hungry. Jesus makes this point to the crowd. He says in essence, "You are after more bread, but it won't last. The bread you want may fill you up for the moment, but it will be temporary. Bread may sustain your life, but only for a time." Even those who ate the manna God sent from heaven still died (v. 49). The bread couldn't keep them alive indefinitely. This is a subtle reminder to the crowd that even though they ate the miraculous meal the day before, they were still going to die.

The bread we crave never lasts long enough. All of the physical things we look to for meaning eventually fade. I love how C. S. Lewis put it: "I cannot find a cup of tea which is big enough or a book that is long enough" (cited in Hughes, *John*, 206). Do you know what he means? That which we think gives our lives so much meaning is never quite enough. We always need more, but even more won't do it. We think when this event happens or this goal is achieved or we reach this milestone, then finally life will be worth living. But even those who reach their goals still die. That's where each of our stories is heading. Eventually, food won't keep us alive. Neither will medicine or money or friendship or family. Is there any hope?

Jesus is the bread of life, and he promises life to all who receive him.

> *Don't work for the food that perishes but for the food that lasts for* eternal life, *which the Son of Man will give you, because God the Father has set his seal of approval on him.* (6:27; emphasis added)

> *For the bread of God is the one who comes down from heaven and gives* life *to the world.* (6:33; emphasis added)

For this is the will of my Father: that everyone who sees the Son and believes in him will have eternal life, *and I will raise him up on the last day.* (6:40; emphasis added)

Truly I tell you, anyone who believes has eternal life. (6:47; emphasis added)

This is the bread that comes down from heaven so that anyone may eat of it and not die. (6:50; emphasis added)

I am the living bread that came down from heaven. If anyone eats of this bread he will live forever. *The bread that I will give for the* life *of the world is my flesh.* (6:51; emphasis added)

The one who eats my flesh and drinks my blood has eternal life, *and I will raise him up on the last day.* (6:54; emphasis added)

Just as the living Father sent me and I live because of the Father, so the one who feeds on me will live *because of me.* (6:57; emphasis added)

This is the bread that came down from heaven; it is not like the manna your ancestors ate—and they died. The one who eats this bread will live forever. (6:58; emphasis added)

Jesus is the bread that gives life that never ends, and the life Jesus promises has two dimensions. First, it makes a person alive spiritually right now. Jesus brings you into a life-giving relationship with the God of the universe. His life flows through you, and you are able to relate to him. Where before your sin had cut you off from him, Jesus has now brought you into a relationship with the living God. Second, it means that after you die physically, you will be resurrected to live with Jesus forever. Four different times in our text Jesus promises to raise his people up on the last day (vv. 39,40,44,54). He is the bread of life, and the life he gives will never falter, never fade, and never fail.

We Must Eat the Bread to Live

Imagine being famished. You've had an extremely busy day and just haven't had time to eat. Your stomach's growling, and all you can think about is food. You sit down at the table, and a plate of fresh dinner rolls is set in front of you. What would you do? You'd take one (or two or three) and start eating. Why? Because the only way to satisfy your hunger is to eat. Bread only does you good if you eat it. How do you eat the bread of life? Jesus tells the crowd to eat his flesh and drink his blood. Is he endorsing cannibalism? No, to *eat* means to *believe.*

> *"I am the bread of life," Jesus told them. "No one who comes to me will ever be hungry, and no one who believes in me will ever be thirsty again."* (6:35; emphasis added)

> *Truly I tell you, anyone who believes has eternal life.* (6:47; emphasis added)

When you take a bite of bread, you believe it's safe for you to eat (it's not going to kill you); plus you believe it will give you strength. You can't eat halfway. Chewing and spitting out is not eating. You either eat or you don't. The same is true of believing on Jesus. You either believe him or you don't. You either trust he will give you life so you receive him fully and completely, or you don't. There's no middle ground when it comes to believing on Jesus. When you eat, you internalize the food.

- Thinking about eating is not the same as eating.
- Knowing nutritional facts is not the same as eating.
- Understanding how food is processed by the body is not the same as eating.

To believe is to internalize the truth about Jesus. It's to receive him into your soul.

- Thinking about Jesus is not the same as believing.
- Knowing facts about Jesus is not the same as believing.
- Understanding how Jesus saves a person is not the same as believing.

Believing is staking your life on the fact that the only way to live is to receive him. It's placing all your hope on him to sustain you. It's a deep sense that you will die without him. It's placing all your confidence in him as the only one who can give you life and strength and a future. And the best part of eating the bread of life is there's no bill. All you have to do is receive it.

Sadly the crowd predominantly chose to reject the bread of life (v. 36). They made excuses (v. 42) and said it was too hard to believe (v. 60). They grumbled about what Jesus said (v. 41), just as the Israelites of old grumbled about the manna in the wilderness. Believing on Jesus is hard. Believing demands relinquishing all other means of salvation. It means saying, "I cannot do it on my own. I cannot make it on my own. I will die apart from Jesus. I'm helpless and hopeless. Jesus, save me! Jesus, forgive me! Jesus, give me life!" That's not easy, but it's true, and it's your only hope.

Saint Augustine famously said, "You made us for yourself, and our hearts find no peace until they rest in you." I want to keep the spirit of his statement but tweak the words just a bit. If he was reading this passage, he might say, "You made us to hunger for you, and our starving souls find no nourishment until they feast on you." Only Jesus can fill the emptiness inside. Only Jesus can quiet the growling of your soul. Only Jesus can give you life.

Reflect and Discuss

1. Have you ever noticed your own spiritual hunger?
2. Summarize Jesus's sermon with three major truths.
3. What two reasons did God have for sending bread to the Israelites in the wilderness?
4. Why does Jesus call himself the bread of life?
5. Why do the people follow Jesus across the Sea of Galilee?
6. How much time and effort do you put into making sure your spiritual hunger is met?
7. Do you feel bored and restless in life? Are you seeking fulfillment in Jesus?
8. Why does Jesus point out that the Israelites ate manna in the wilderness and died?
9. How often does Jesus mention "life" in this section?
10. How do you "eat" the bread of life?

Understanding Election

JOHN 6:35-40,61-65

Main Idea: Jesus teaches that God has chosen a people for himself.

I. **The Elect Have Been Given to Jesus by God.**
II. **The Elect Will Come to Jesus Because the Father Draws Them.**
 A. We are unable to come to God on our own.
 B. God uses the gospel to draw the elect to saving faith in Jesus.
III. **The Elect Will Be Raised by Jesus on the Last Day.**
IV. **Application**
 A. Let the doctrine of election encourage you to examine yourself.
 B. Let the doctrine of election encourage you to exalt God.

Every couple of years in the United States, we have an election. We go to a polling place and choose which officials we want to represent us. That's what an election is—it's a choice. In fact, the word *election* is defined as "the exercise of deliberate choice" (Dictionary.com). During seminary I discovered that *election* and *choice* were not just talked about every four years in American politics, but they were scattered throughout the pages of Scripture. I had been in church all my life. I added it up, and by the time I was twenty, I had heard more than three thousand sermons and one thousand other Bible lessons. Yet I was shockingly unfamiliar with how frequently the term *election* or *elect* was found in Scripture. Here's a quick sampling:

> *He will send out his angels with a loud trumpet, and they will gather his* elect *from the four winds, from one end of the sky to the other.* (Matt 24:31; emphasis added)

> *But he cut those days short for the sake of the* elect, *whom he chose.* (Mark 13:20; emphasis added)

> *Who can bring an accusation against God's* elect? *God is the one who justifies.* (Rom 8:33; emphasis added)

This is why I endure all things for the elect: *so that they also may obtain salvation, which is in Christ Jesus, with eternal glory.* (2 Tim 2:10; emphasis added)

Paul, a servant of God and an apostle of Jesus Christ, for the faith of God's elect *and their knowledge of the truth that leads to godliness.* (Titus 1:1; emphasis added)

Therefore, brothers and sisters, make every effort to confirm your calling and election, *because if you do these things you will never stumble.* (2 Pet 1:10; emphasis added)

I was talking with a lady who had been a Christian for many years, and she told me she didn't believe *election* was in the Bible. I didn't know what to say. You may disagree with a certain view of election, but there's no denying it's in the Bible. You find the word used over and over, and the truth of God's sovereign election is present in numerous passages that don't even use the word. What she was objecting to was not the word but the theology behind the word. What does the Bible teach about election? Wayne Grudem defines *election* this way:

Election is an act of God before creation in which he chooses some people to be saved, not on account of any foreseen merit in them, but only because of his sovereign good pleasure. (*Systematic Theology*, 670)

Election—God's absolute sovereignty in salvation—can be difficult to embrace. When I was first confronted with this teaching, I wasn't sure I could believe it, but the more I studied God's Word and the more I committed myself to digging into Scripture, the more my eyes were opened to the truth God had chosen a people for himself. That was the only way I could explain passages like these:

When the Gentiles heard this, they rejoiced and honored the word of the Lord, and all who had been appointed to eternal life *believed.* (Acts 13:48; emphasis added)

Therefore, as God's chosen ones, holy and dearly loved, put on compassion, kindness, humility, gentleness, and patience. (Col 3:12; emphasis added)

For we know, brothers and sisters loved by God, that he has chosen you. (1 Thess 1:4; emphasis added)

> *Listen, my dear brothers and sisters:* Didn't God choose *the poor
> in this world to be rich in faith and heirs of the kingdom that he has
> promised to those who love him?* (Jas 2:5; emphasis added)

As the Spirit of God opened my eyes to this truth, I began to understand how vital it is for us as Christians to embrace God's sovereignty. In John 6 Jesus clearly states that God has chosen a people for himself. In just a few short verses he delivers three God-exalting truths of sovereign election.

The Elect Have Been Given to Jesus by God

There is a people—a group of men and women—that have been given to Jesus by God (vv. 37,39). We see this spelled out again in chapter 10. In that passage Jesus refers to his sheep, and he says, "My Father, *who has given them to me,* is greater than all. No one is able to snatch them out of the Father's hand" (10:29; emphasis added). The verb *has given* is in the perfect tense, which means a past action has present results. In the past God gave Jesus a specific group of sheep that are his and remain his in the present. In chapter 17 we see Jesus again emphasize the Father has given him a group of people.

> *I have revealed your name to the people* you gave me *from the world.
> They were yours,* you gave them to me, *and they have kept your
> word.* (17:6; emphasis added)

> *I am not praying for the world but for those* you have given me,
> *because they are yours.* (17:9; emphasis added)

> Father, I want those you have given me *to be with me where I am.*
> (17:24; emphasis added)

In eternity past God chose people, not based on any merit of their own, and gave them as a gift to his Son. Paul told the Christians in Ephesus they were chosen in Christ before the foundation of the world (Eph 1:4). I love John MacArthur's explanation of this mind-boggling, Christ-magnifying truth:

> The plan of God from eternity past was to redeem a segment
> of fallen humanity through the work of the Son and for
> the glory of the Son. There was a moment in eternity

past when the Father desired to express His perfect and incomprehensible love for the Son. To do this, He chose to give to the Son a redeemed humanity as a love gift—a company of men and women whose purpose would be, throughout all the eons of eternity, to praise and glorify the Son, and to serve Him perfectly. ("Foreword," 15)

The Elect Will Come to Jesus Because the Father Draws Them

The context of Jesus's teaching on election is the response of the Jews. Jesus just fed five thousand men, as well as women and children. After he feeds them and crosses the sea, they find him and begin to ask him questions. Jesus tells them he is the bread of life. They don't understand, and more than that, they don't believe. Their lack of faith doesn't discourage Jesus. He's not wringing his hands and shaking his head, concerned his coming to earth is a failure. He's confident and expresses his confidence that all whom the Father has given him will come to him because the Father will draw them (John 6:37). Jesus's confidence is supported by two reasons.

We Are Unable to Come to God on Our Own

Apart from the effective working of God, we are completely and utterly unwilling and unable to come to Jesus (vv. 44,64-65). Down to our core we are rebels against God. Nothing in us wants to turn from our sin and come to Jesus for salvation. The Bible describes every one of us as unrighteous and says none of us seek God (Rom 3:10-11). We don't seek God because we can't. We're not free to seek him. As much as we like to trumpet our freedom, we're not free. Many people talk about free will. Your will isn't free. You are a slave to sin (Rom 6:6). Sin enslaves everyone. That's why we can't come to God. The chains of sin hold us so tightly that we cannot, will not, and have no desire to break free. We think we're free, but what we think is freedom is actually slavery. It's impossible for us to come to Christ on our own.

You may struggle with the biblical teaching of God's sovereignty because you feel it invalidates the invitation extended by Jesus. You think, *Don't the Scriptures say, "Whosoever will may come"?* That's a good question. The Bible does teach that, but that leads to another question:

Who wills to come? Jesus makes clear in John 6:44 and again in 65 that no one comes to the Father because of their own will. The doctrine of election is easier to embrace when you understand your own slavery to sin.

The great nineteenth-century preacher, Charles Spurgeon, was preaching about God's sovereignty from Romans 9, explaining verse 13, "I have loved Jacob, but I have hated Esau." Afterwards a woman came up to him and said, "I don't understand how God could say he hated Esau." Spurgeon responded, "Ma'am, I find it more difficult to understand how he could love Jacob" (cited by Davey, "Sovereignty"). The real mystery of election is not that some are not chosen but that God would choose anyone at all. It's the doctrine of God's sovereignty that allows us to come to the place where we can say, like the apostle Paul before us, "But *by the grace of God* I am what I am" (1 Cor 15:10; emphasis added). Salvation does not glorify me. It glorifies him.

God Uses the Gospel to Draw the Elect to Saving Faith in Jesus

The word translated "draws" is interesting (John 6:44). John later uses it to describe the disciples' action when they were pulling their nets, filled with fish, onto the deck of the boat (21:11). Like fish swimming in the murky waters of sin, we are graciously drawn to salvation by God. But the means he uses is not a net; it's the preaching of the gospel and the life-giving work of the Spirit (v. 63). God uses means to accomplish his purposes. We could think, wrongly, that since God will draw the elect to salvation we don't need to preach the gospel. To say that would be to deny the clear command of Scripture and to misunderstand the work of God. Just as God has ordained the result, so also he ordained the means. The only way the elect will come to him is through the proclamation of the gospel (Jas 1:18).

Election is wholly a result of God's mercy, but we're responsible to respond. Divine sovereignty doesn't negate human responsibility. As fiercely as Jesus proclaims the sovereignty of God, he also welcomes sinners to come to him for salvation. If you immerse yourself in this Gospel, you will discover it written by an apostle who is a staunch defender of the biblical doctrine of election, and you will hear him repeatedly call sinners to turn from their sin and come to Jesus Christ for salvation. You see, it's not our duty to try to guess who the elect are but to share the gospel faithfully and to believe it ourselves.

The Elect Will Be Raised by Jesus on the Last Day

Jesus came to the earth to secure salvation for the elect (John 6:37-39). This is God's will, and Jesus will certainly accomplish it (v. 44). Jesus doesn't hesitate or equivocate. He says simply and with complete certainty that every single one whom God has given him will come to him and will not be cast out but will be raised with him on the last day. Martin Luther, commenting on this passage, wrote,

> Here Christ says: "This is the will of Him who sent Me, that I should lose nothing." He will not only refrain from expelling and rejecting anyone, but He is also resolved to keep them with Him and prevent anyone else from taking them from Him. (Cited in Boice, *John*, 2:500)

The security of your eternal future rests in the hands of Jesus. The basis of your eternal security is election. Jesus connected the security of believers with the sovereignty of God when he said,

> *My sheep hear my voice, I know them, and they follow me. I give them eternal life, and they will never perish. No one will snatch them out of my hand. My Father, who has given them to me, is greater than all. No one is able to snatch them out of the Father's hand. I and the Father are one.* (John 10:27-30)

A. W. Pink wrote,

> Our coming to Christ is not attributed to man's fickle will, but as the effect of the Father's drawing to the Saviour each one given to Him in the counsels of that Father's love before the foundation of the world! So, too, the reception of them is not merely because of Christ's compassion for the lost, but as the obedient Servant of the Father's will, He welcomes each one brought to Him—brought by the unseen drawings of the Father's love. Thus our security rests not upon anything in us or from us, but upon the Father's choice and the Son's obedient love! (*John*, 331)

Application

Let the Doctrine of Election Encourage You to Examine Yourself

"Therefore, brothers and sisters, make every effort to confirm your calling and election" (2 Pet 1:10). How do I know if I'm elect? That question may be rattling around in your mind right now. The answer is fairly simple. Have you turned from your sin and believed in Jesus as your Lord and Savior? "For this is the will of my Father: that everyone who sees the Son and believes in him will have eternal life, and I will raise him up on the last day" (John 6:40). Who will be raised up on the last day? In this passage we get two descriptions: the first description is the elect (v. 37), and the second is those who believe in the Son (v. 40). How do you know if you're elect? Those whom the Father has given to Jesus have turned from their sin and believed in him.

Let the Doctrine of Election Encourage You to Exalt God

John Piper tells the story of Peter Cameron Scott:

> [He] was born in Glasgow, Scotland, in 1867 and founded the African Inland Mission. His efforts to take the gospel to Africa met with tragedy and discouragement. His brother John had joined him in the mission, but within months John fell victim to fever. Alone in the jungle, Scott buried him, and at the grave rededicated himself to preach the gospel. But, to compound his heartache, his health broke, and utterly discouraged, he had to return to England.
>
> In London, something wonderful happened. Scott needed a fresh source of inspiration and he found it at a tomb in Westminster Abbey that held the remains of a man who had inspired so many others in their mission to Africa. The spirit of David Livingston seemed to be prodding Scott onward as he knelt reverently and read the inscription [on Livingston's tomb]:
> OTHER SHEEP I HAVE WHICH ARE NOT OF THIS FOLD; THEM ALSO I MUST BRING. (John 10:16)
> He would return to Africa and lay down his life, if need be, for the cause for which this great man had lived and died. It is the truth of election ("I have other sheep")— the sovereign freedom of God in saving a people for

Himself—that guarantees the triumph of the gospel and the universal fame of God's grace. (Piper, *Pleasures of God*, 151)

The fame of God's grace will grow in our eyes as we embrace his sovereign grace. We need to cling to this truth, so that we can with awe and amazement and assurance declare, "God is sovereign. He's in charge. He has a plan, and it *will* come to pass!"

Reflect and Discuss

1. What three truths about the elect do we see in this passage?
2. What difficulties do you have in embracing the doctrine of election?
3. Who are the elect?
4. Why are you unable to come to God on your own?
5. Why do the elect come to Jesus? Why is this good news?
6. How does election glorify God?
7. What means does God use to draw the elect to saving faith? Can we neglect mission because of election?
8. What promise does Jesus make about the ultimate fate of the elect?
9. How does election provide security for a believer?
10. How does the doctrine of election encourage believers?

True or False?

JOHN 6:66-71

Main Idea: Not all who call themselves disciples really are, for there are key differences between true and false disciples of Jesus Christ.

I. **True Disciples Make a Commitment to Follow Jesus.**
II. **True Disciples Make a Confession of Faith in Jesus.**
   A. You have to know who Jesus is.
   B. You have to trust Jesus completely.

I read the story of a man named Charles who went from relative anonymity to great notoriety in a short time. His name was unfamiliar to those living in Boston in 1920, but like a shooting star this millionaire burst on the local scene. Charles made his millions by encouraging others to invest their money with him. He began a company called the "Securities Exchange Company" that promised 50 percent interest on investments in forty-five days or a full 100 percent in ninety days. In just a few months forty thousand people handed him nearly fifteen million dollars. Some even mortgaged their homes and emptied their life savings to invest their money with Charles. In August of that year, Charles Ponzi was arrested and charged with multiple counts of fraud and larceny. Since that time the name *Ponzi* has become synonymous with fraudulent investment.

Sometimes the difference between true and false is almost imperceptible. As humans we're masters at pawning the false off as true, but we're not always that great at spotting the difference. Sometimes it doesn't matter. It makes no difference whether you can tell leather from pleather or if you can distinguish ham from Spam. But there are certain areas where being able to discern the difference between real and fake matters.

In John 6 we discover the difference between real and fake. The issue in question has consequences that extend beyond investment accounts and life savings. The issue at stake is eternal life and salvation from the wrath of God. This passage focuses on a large group of men who've taken the title of disciple, and it reveals some key differences between true and false disciples of Jesus Christ. What is a disciple of Jesus? We discover in the book of John that a disciple is someone who believes on Jesus and continues to follow him. We find some who are called disciples for a time eventually stop following Christ, and the lesson we're supposed to learn is that some who call themselves Christians are not. Some who appear to follow Jesus for a while eventually reveal themselves to be false disciples when they turn from following him.

True Disciples Make a Commitment to Follow Jesus

The saddest verse in the Gospel of John may be 6:66: "From that moment many of his disciples turned back and no longer accompanied him." A true disciple of Jesus Christ does not turn from following him. These professing disciples revealed their discipleship was fraudulent when they stopped following Jesus. It is impossible to be a genuine disciple merely for a time. You either turn from your sin, place your faith in Jesus Christ, and follow him until you get to heaven, or you don't. There is no middle ground!

Many professing believers see a distinction between being a Christian and being a disciple, as if one can be saved but not follow Jesus. The notion of salvation apart from following Jesus is foreign to the New Testament. Francis Chan writes,

> Some people claim that we can be Christians without necessarily becoming disciples. I wonder, then, why the last thing Jesus told us was to go into the world, making *disciples* of all nations, teaching them to *obey all* that He commanded? You'll notice that He *didn't* add, "But hey, if that's too much to ask, tell them to just become Christians—you know, the people who get to go to heaven without having to commit to anything." (*Crazy Love*, 87; emphasis original)

In verse 66 we find a group of men and women who've been boasting that they're disciples of the Messiah. When some of their friends called him a phony, they defended him. They've wandered around following Jesus from place to place. They've cheered with the rest of the crowd when he healed the lame man and made the blind man see. Their minds had raced wildly when they tasted the bread he had created from a small boy's lunch—all of their problems appeared to be solved. They had pushed forward with the surging crowd, desiring to make him their king. But now they turn from him, and with shoulders slumped and heads bowed low, they slink away, their sandals kicking up small clouds of dust. They looked like real disciples, they acted like genuine believers, but they stopped following him, and in that moment it became clear that they were fakes.

False disciples come to Jesus for reasons other than Jesus. In this passage men came to Jesus for miracles (v. 2), to have their bellies filled (vv. 13-14,34), for political freedom and power (v. 15). This fraudulent gospel is preached from the pulpits of churches around the world: "Come to Jesus to get wealthy and well. Come to Jesus to succeed and prosper. Come to Jesus for everything but him."

Time magazine ran a cover story with this headline: "Does God Want You to Be Rich?" In this story they discovered that

> of the four biggest megachurches in the country, three
> are Prosperity or Prosperity Lite pulpits. While they don't
> exclusively teach that God's riches want to be in believers'
> wallets, it is a key part of their doctrine. (Biema and Chu,
> "Does God Want You to Be Rich?")

They quoted television preacher and author Joyce Meyer:

> Who would want to get in on something where you're
> miserable, poor, broke and ugly and you just have to muddle
> through until you get to heaven? I believe God wants to give us
> nice things. (Ibid.)

Nice things? Like miracles, food, political freedom, and power? False disciples come to Jesus to get something they want from him. Genuine disciples are drawn to Jesus by God. Their eyes are opened, and they see the light of the good news of the glory of Jesus Christ (2 Cor 4:4-6).

Genuine disciples come to Jesus because he is the bread. This is why God must do a work in us. Without that work, we would only come to Jesus to get stuff. We'd come to get money, a house, or a better job, but God has shown us the glories of Jesus and drawn us to his Son. Our coming to Jesus is no testimony to our discernment but to his grace.

Here's a great question to determine whether you've come to Jesus for Jesus. If the Father has drawn you to the Son, you will love Jesus, not just his gifts. You will desire him, not just his works. John Piper writes,

The critical question for our generation—and for every generation—is this: If you could have heaven, with no sickness, and with all the friends you ever had on earth, and all the food you ever liked, and all the leisure activities you ever enjoyed, and all the natural beauties you ever saw, all the physical pleasures you ever tasted, and no human conflict or any natural disasters, could you be satisfied with heaven, if Christ was not there? (*God Is the Gospel*, 15)

False disciples look at Jesus and see a genie in a bottle. He's there simply to grant their requests. True disciples come to Jesus because he is the prize, not because he dispenses prizes.

On the afternoon described in our text, thousands of false disciples walked away from Jesus. Why did they stop following? They left because it got too difficult (John 6:66). This wasn't what they signed on for. They signed on for miracles, popularity, and freedom, but not for this. What they heard was too difficult to accept. What part was too difficult, we're not sure. Maybe they realized Jesus was really claiming to be God, and they said, "Whoa, that's too much. That's crazy. I can't go for that!" Maybe it was because he talked about dying. "Wait, we want you to be king. If you die, how are we going to be fed and taken care of?"

Jesus knew they were grumbling and complaining about what he said: "Does [what I've just been saying] offend you?" he asked (v. 61). The word translated "offend" means to "give up believing" or to "fall away." Eventually, all false disciples will find some reason to fall away, to stop believing. It's almost as if Jesus were offering them the excuse they were looking for: "I know you guys are looking for a reason to leave; is this it?" Being a disciple is more than saying the right words or being part of a group. Being a disciple of Jesus Christ is making a commitment to follow him with all your life for the rest of your life. Later the apostle John will offer this insight to the local church:

> *They went out from us, but they did not belong to us; for if they had belonged to us, they would have remained with us. However, they went out so that it might be made clear that none of them belongs to us.*
> (1 John 2:19)

They left. They stopped. They quit. They went out. They fell away. They turned back and no longer walked with Jesus. "Many" of his disciples stopped following him.

True Disciples Make a Confession of Faith in Jesus

After watching these false disciples turn away, Jesus turns to the Twelve and asks them if they want to leave as well. Jesus didn't ask this question for his sake. He wasn't alarmed that so many had left. Jesus knew which disciples were his, and he was actively preserving them. This question wasn't intended to assure Jesus of their commitment to him. It was an opportunity for the disciples to make a confession of faith, which they did (John 6:67-69). Every genuine confession of faith has two parts.

You Have to Know Who Jesus Is

Unless you've come to know that Jesus is God, you cannot be his disciple. Simon Peter makes a clear affirmation of Christ's deity: "We have come to believe and know that you are the Holy One of God" (v. 69). The title *the Holy One of God* comes from Isaiah, who wrote extensively about the holiness of God. In Isaiah 6 the prophet was transported through a vision into the throne room of God. He's struck with the awesomeness of God and cries out, "Woe is me for I am ruined!" (v. 5). Circling the throne of God are angels, covering their feet and faces with wings and crying out with voices so loud they shake the foundations of the room. What do they cry? "Holy, holy, holy is the LORD of Armies" (v. 3). The impact on Isaiah was so profound that the truth of God's holiness flowed from his pen. Sixty-two times Isaiah writes about God's holiness. He can't get over it. To him the characteristic that defines God is his holiness. He is unlike anyone or anything else. He has an unmatched weightiness and worthiness.

Throughout the book that bears his name, Isaiah refers to God as the "Holy One of Israel." He does it twenty-five times! So when Peter opens his mouth to confess his faith, he unmistakably declares that Jesus is God: "The Holy One"—a title that could only be used for God. True discipleship can only begin when you know who Jesus is; he is God!

You Have to Trust Jesus Completely

Genuine disciples believe Jesus. They come to him for salvation from their sin and for eternal life. They reject any other way and any other path. Peter's question in John 6:68, "Lord, to whom will we go?" is stated in such a way that the implied answer is "No one." We reject anyone else as Savior, Lord, and Master, including ourselves, and we turn to Jesus alone.

Before getting married, many couples draw up a prenuptial agreement. It's a legal document that details what will happen to the couple's assets in the case of divorce. Some "experts" in this field suggest videotaping the signing and including in the agreement what will happen to any children in the case of a divorce. After completing this agreement, this couple will at some point in the future stand before a minister or government official and promise, "With this ring I thee wed, and all my worldly goods I thee endow. In sickness and in health, in poverty or in wealth, 'til death do us part." Shouldn't they rephrase it this way: "All my worldly goods I thee endow, except for the ones listed in the prenup. 'Til death do us part, or sooner on amicable terms as spelled out in the opening lines of our agreement"? Wouldn't that be more accurate? Probably not as romantic but definitely more authentic.

We excel at adding the little phrase "but just in case" onto the end of many of our major decisions. The prenuptial agreement is the ultimate "but just in case." A person stands in front of another person, pledging everything, but with certain things already withheld, just in case. A genuine disciple of Jesus Christ rejects the phrase "but just in case." A genuine disciple of Jesus Christ depends completely, totally, solely on Jesus for his or her salvation. Like Peter, with clear eyes and resolute will, we proclaim to Jesus, "To whom would we go? You have the words of eternal life."

Reflect and Discuss

1. Who is a disciple of Jesus? Is it possible to be a Christian without being a disciple?
2. Why did the people in this text walk away?
3. What lesson should we learn from those "disciples" who follow Jesus for a time and then leave?
4. What marks of genuine discipleship are shown in this passage?
5. Why might false disciples follow Jesus for a time? How is this different from true disciples?
6. What marks true disciples' commitment to follow Jesus?
7. Could you be satisfied with heaven if Christ was not there?
8. Why does Jesus ask the disciples if they, too, want to leave?
9. What are the two parts of every genuine confession of faith?
10. Describe the connection between Isaiah's and Peter's confessions.

Tough Questions

JOHN 7

Main Idea: John records twenty questions—asked of Jesus or by Jesus—and the answers provide insight into who Jesus is and why he came.

I. Where Is Jesus (7:1-13)?
II. How Does Jesus Know So Much (7:14-18)?
III. Who Wants to Kill Jesus (7:19-24)?
IV. Who Is Jesus (7:25-31)?
V. Will You Come to Jesus (7:32-39)?
VI. Do You Believe Jesus (7:40-52)?

One day one of my children told me he had a Bible question for me. That's great. I can handle it. "What's a mustard seed taste like?" he asked. "Can you eat it?" I have spent hours in Greek, Hebrew, theology, church history, even practical theology, yet nothing prepared me for this question. Not one professor had discussed the flavor of mustard seeds. We sometimes get the toughest questions from the most unlikely sources. Questions help us better understand the truth. Often the tougher the question, the more helpful the answer. In John 7 we find twenty questions—more than one question every three verses. John has made the case for Jesus's identity in the previous chapters by recording different miracles and some long talks in which Jesus explains to the people who he is. But in this chapter he takes a different approach. He records all these questions, and the answers provide insight into who Jesus is and why he came. We can boil the twenty questions down to these six major ones.

Where Is Jesus?

JOHN 7:1-13

The half brothers and half sisters of Jesus think he should go up to Jerusalem for the Festival of Shelters (or Booths or Tabernacles) since most Jewish men make that trip each year. They don't believe Jesus is the Messiah, and they think his appearance in Jerusalem will expose him as a fraud (7:3-5). They challenge him, essentially saying, "If you're really the Messiah, go make it public! What are you trying to hide?" But Jesus's timetable is not their timetable because his purpose is not their purpose. Sometimes we get frustrated when God doesn't do something on our timetable. We have everything planned, everything ready, but he fails to do our bidding. Could it be that God is doing something greater than we realize? Could it be that the God who has always existed may have a plan that you, with your twenty years or forty years or eighty years of wisdom, don't understand? To follow Jesus means we give up control of our timetable and our purpose. We turn over the keys, the map, and the schedule to him.

Jesus wasn't in Jerusalem because he was busy doing the work of God (7:6-8). Jesus didn't come to earth to gather a crowd. In chapter 6 his hard sayings pushed the crowd away, revealing those who were following him for entertainment. Jesus came to expose and then die for sin. "You don't understand," Jesus tells his brothers. "People don't hate you, but they hate me because my presence exposes their sin" (my paraphrase). Jesus isn't complaining about being unpopular. He was pretty popular. Crowds flocked to him wherever he went. He's stating a fact. He, the light of the world, exposes the darkness of man's sin (3:19-20). I know how tempting sin is. I know how easy it would be to do wrong things if no one were around to see me. I understand all too well Jesus's statement that men love darkness rather than light because they love their sin. But an encounter with Jesus exposes that sin. He turns the lights on, and our sin can't be hidden. When our sin is held up against his perfect righteousness, we can't help but see how filthy we are. At that point we have two options: come to him for cleansing or hate him for exposing our dirtiness.

If Jesus were just some run-of-the-mill, glory-seeking, fame-craving false prophet, he could have gone up to Jerusalem, done mighty works, gathered large crowds, and basked in their adoration. But Jesus is the light of the world, and when the light enters darkness, everything is exposed for what it really is. This is what Jesus's family doesn't understand. The religious leaders were plotting to kill him because he broke their religious monopoly (7:1). Everyone else looked at the Jewish religious leaders and saw their good deeds, but Jesus saw their pride and self-righteousness. He exposed their sin. But he didn't just come to expose sin; he came to die for sin.

The Gospel of John is an ever-progressing journey. From the first words, it points us to a specific place—the cross. Seven of its twenty-one chapters focus on the time between the Last Supper and the resurrection. Here it was not Jesus's time to die (7:6,8). This chapter begins by telling us that Jesus did not go up to Judea because that's where people were waiting to kill him. But lest we think Jesus was a coward, he says, "My time has *not yet* arrived" (v. 6; emphasis added). Jesus was moving toward the cross, but he was doing so on God's timing. The crucifixion of Jesus was part of God's eternal plan to provide our salvation. It was God's will to crush his Son to save us. The giving of his life for our guilt was the only perfect remedy for our sin. His righteous life offered in place of ours was the only acceptable means whereby our iniquities could be paid for.

Jesus exposed sin, but then he died for it. There's a pattern here that his disciples can follow. Jesus was like a doctor explaining the symptoms and then offering the cure. He exposed in order to heal. The Pharisees were good at exposing sin. They loved to point out everyone else's mistakes. They loved to sit in court and hand out punishments for people's crimes. One time they brought a woman to Jesus who was caught committing adultery. No one would doubt her guilt. They wanted Jesus to lead her stoning, but he didn't. Instead he exposed their sin: "The one without sin among you should be the first to throw a stone at her" (8:7). They all left. Only Jesus was without sin. Only *he* could throw the first stone, but he didn't. He offered forgiveness.

As his followers, we have a similar mandate (Eph 5:11). We aren't the light of the world, but we are to reflect the light into the world and in so doing expose the works of darkness. But we don't expose sin to make ourselves look better or gloat in our goodness. We expose sin to offer a cure—the blood of Jesus.

Sometimes Christians think exposing sin turns a person into a self-righteous ogre. Maybe they think of the command, "Judge not!" Maybe into their heads pops a picture of Hester Prynne slinking around New England with a scarlet letter sewn to her bodice. These images of exposing sin are probably the reason most churches refuse to confront sin on any level. Even though Jesus commands church discipline, and the commands are reiterated throughout the New Testament, most churches practice selective amnesia, conveniently forgetting God's command to deal with sin in the church. How we deal with sin as a church either distorts or clarifies the gospel of Jesus. We distort the gospel when we ignore sin, pretending it doesn't exist. We distort the gospel when we expose sin without offering the hope of forgiveness. But when we expose sin as sin and then extend the promise of healing in Jesus, we clarify the gospel.

Churches need to take sin seriously. Christians need to love one another enough to be willing to say, "Hold on! You're going down a bad path. That's the way of foolishness that leads to death." But we must say it in love and always for the purpose of healing and happiness. Jesus exposed sin and then died to defeat it. We expose sin and then tell people they can have victory over it through the blood of Jesus.

In John 7:11 the crowds asked, "Where is he?" The answer is that Jesus was waiting for the right moment to head to Jerusalem. At the appointed hour he would head to Jerusalem to crush sin once and for all. But not yet. His time had not come.

How Does Jesus Know So Much?
JOHN 7:14-18

George Whitefield lived during the eighteenth century and was one of the human catalysts of the Great Awakening. God used Whitefield powerfully in both England and America as he preached the gospel in open fields to thousands. Whitefield was a man of incredible spiritual power, and he possessed remarkable physical gifts. One biographer wrote,

> [Whitefield] recounts that in Philadelphia that same year on Wednesday, April 6, he preached on Society Hill twice in the morning to about 6,000, and in the evening to near 8,000. On Thursday, he spoke to "upwards of ten thousand," and it was reported at one of these events the words, "'He opened his mouth and taught them saying,' were distinctly heard at Gloucester point, a distance of two miles by water down the Delaware River. . . . And there were times when the crowds reached 20,000 or more." (Cited in Piper, "Velvet-Mouthed Preacher")

Two miles! Twenty thousand people! Outdoors! No microphones! I would have loved to hear George Whitefield preach. But Whitefield's preaching was nothing compared to Jesus Christ's. When he spoke, people marveled; they were awestruck by his command of the Scriptures. "How is this man so learned, since he hasn't been trained?" (v. 15). Jesus could have answered simply, "I know so much because I'm God." That's true, but he gave a different reason. He said he knew so much because he was sent by God. Remember who Jesus is speaking with: devout Jews—men and women who hold the writings of the Old Testament in high esteem. They would have been hesitant to believe someone was God, but they had for centuries believed God sent people to deliver his message.

However, Jesus goes even further. He claims to have a message from God, and then he says in effect, "If you don't recognize it, it's because your hearts are unwilling to submit to God" (v. 17). He connects the head and the heart. He says submission comes before understanding. The gateway to the mind is the heart. When we rebel against God's will, our ability to understand and comprehend spiritual truth is compromised. Or to put it simply: *Unbelief causes misunderstanding.* Understanding spiritual truth isn't simply an intellectual exercise. It's spiritual. You can study Greek, Hebrew, and Aramaic; you can memorize all of the notes in your favorite study Bible; but until you submit to the will of God, it won't make sense. Jesus says faith, which includes trusting him and submitting to his will, precedes understanding.

John wrote this Gospel so we can understand who Jesus is, and by understanding we can exercise faith. God wants us to use our minds; that's why he gave them to us. However, Jesus cautions us about putting too much confidence in our own understanding. At some point we have to come to the place where we say, "God, I don't understand it all. I can't understand it all. But this I know: I'm a sinner, and I need a Savior. Jesus died to be my Savior. I'm asking you to show me mercy because of what Jesus did." When you reach that point, then you'll understand the truth about Jesus.

Imagine walking across a frozen pond and seeing something under the surface. You bend down for a closer look, and you can make out some details but not enough to know for sure what it is. Day after day you come back and look, but you're never sure whether it is what you think it is. The ice on top of the pond distorts the object just enough so that you're not absolutely sure. How will you figure out what it is? How will you come to know for sure? You've got to break the ice. Your will is the ice. Until your will is broken, until your will gets out of the way, you'll never reach the depth of understanding you desire. We can never separate our will and our understanding.

Some Christians think spiritual growth is simply about more Bible knowledge. We think attending a certain Bible study and gaining more information means we're growing spiritually. We think reading some books means our faith is growing. We think a certain person who can quote a bunch of verses is a spiritual giant. We confuse Bible knowledge with actual spiritual maturity. Spiritual maturity means we're submitting our will to the Father's. Spiritual maturity means I value assembling with God's people, I place the needs of others before my own, and I stop grumbling and complaining about what I don't like. Don't stop reading books and attending Bible studies—those can be great tools for spiritual growth—but don't confuse the accumulation of Bible knowledge with a growing love for Christ and submission to his will. Remember, no one studied the Bible more than the Pharisees, and according to Jesus, no one misunderstood spiritual maturity like the Pharisees.

Who Wants to Kill Jesus?

JOHN 7:19-24

Israel's religious leaders wanted to kill Jesus. They first planned to kill him after he healed a lame man on the Sabbath (5:18). Jesus pinpoints the real reason they wanted to kill him, when he says in effect, "You want to kill me because you say I broke the law, but your desire to kill me violates the law. Doesn't Moses say, 'Do not murder'?" (see 7:19). The reason they hated Jesus was because he exposed their self-righteousness.

Few things are as dangerous as self-righteousness. What motivates a group of self-professing law keepers to break the law flagrantly? Self-righteousness. We should understand the appeal of self-righteousness. No one wants to think of himself or herself as a bad person. Self-righteousness—viewing myself as pretty good, pretty righteous—is natural, but it's dangerous because it's deceptive. It deceives me about how good I am. The Jewish religious leaders loved to compare themselves to the worst in society: the tax collectors (basically a group of thieves) and the prostitutes. When Jesus came, he forced them to compare themselves to him: God in the flesh.

Self-righteousness also deceives us about how self-righteous we are. I've never met a person who admits to being self-righteous. One of the famous villains in *Batman* is called Two-Face. One side of his face looks normal, and the other side was disfigured in a horrible accident. So when he looks in the mirror, if he turns a certain direction, he looks normal—handsome even. There's some of Two-Face in all of us. We struggle with sin. We battle pride, anger, despair, lust, and greed. But when we look in the mirror, self-righteousness turns our faces to one side. Our ugliness is hidden, and all we see are the good things we've done. We don't see the ugly side; even the ugliness of self-righteousness is out of view. Don't think you're free from the seductive power of self-righteousness. The moment you stop suspecting yourself is the moment self-righteousness seizes control. Do you think the religious leaders thought they were being self-righteous? No, they thought they were just doing what was right. Self-righteousness often feels right. That's why it's so deceptive.

The ultimate danger of self-righteousness is that it squeezes out any space for grace. The religious leaders lacked grace. They didn't extend grace to others. They didn't speak with grace. Why? Because they didn't see their own need for grace. They saw their righteousness and thought they were fine. Grace was irrelevant, unnecessary. Those who see grace as unnecessary for them will never show grace to others. If self-righteousness is given a room, before we know it or realize it, it will spread to every corner, and grace will be evicted. And due to the deceptive nature of self-righteousness, we'll even feel good about it.

The religious leaders wanted to kill Jesus because he healed a man on the Sabbath, but Jesus said healing and circumcision are no different (vv. 21-23). Both are ways to bless, care for, and show grace to others. Due to their self-righteousness, they couldn't bring themselves to see Jesus's kindness to a man as a good thing. They were anti-grace. Here are two questions to diagnose self-righteousness.

How do you treat people who are different from you? For the Jewish leaders circumcision on the Sabbath was fine but not healing. For us the distinction may be age, music, dress, and priorities. But self-righteousness is evident in how we handle differences. The whole point of self-righteousness is that self is the standard for what's righteous. So self-righteousness can appear anywhere someone does something different from what I do. Are you the standard for what's right or wrong?

Do you excuse in yourself what you accuse in others? The Jewish leaders could do something on the Sabbath—circumcise—and it was OK. But Jesus couldn't do something on the Sabbath—heal—because it was wrong. If they did it, it must be OK. If someone else did it, it was worthy of scorn and ridicule and judgment. When you find yourself accusing someone else, ask if you would excuse or rationalize the same behavior in yourself. If so, you've found where self-righteousness is hiding.

Who Is Jesus?

JOHN 7:25-31

Many of the Jewish people were trying to piece together the puzzle of Jesus. "Maybe it's possible he's the Messiah. Maybe he's the one God promised long ago through Moses and the Prophets. Could he really be the one?" The question of Jesus's identity permeates this chapter. Everyone seems to have an opinion. Some say he's a good man; others say he's a deceiver (v. 12). Some think he's demon possessed (v. 20), while others believe he's the Messiah (v. 40). Is Jesus the Messiah? That's the question the crowd is asking, and it's the question of the Gospel of John. We find a clear answer when we consider chapters 6 and 7 together.

Chapter 6 started with Jesus miraculously feeding the Jews with bread while they are out in the wilderness. Next, Jesus miraculously crosses the sea. On the other side of the sea, he talked about Moses, manna, and the new covenant. The people didn't like what he said, so they began to grumble and complain; many turned and walked away in unbelief. It sounds familiar if you've read the Pentateuch. In Exodus God brought the children of Israel out of Egypt and into the wilderness. While they were there, he fed them with bread from heaven, called *manna*. To get them to the wilderness, he miraculously parted the sea so they could get across. While in the wilderness, he delivered to Moses the old covenant. The people began to grumble and complain, and by the time they made it to the promised land, the nation turned and walked away in unbelief, unwilling to follow God and his chosen leader into the land of promise.

John 7 continues this theme. The setting is the Festival of Shelters, a commemoration instituted in Leviticus 23. The purpose of the festival was to remind the Israelites and their descendants that God brought them out of Egypt (Lev 23:42-43). God provided for his people when they were on their way to the promised land. Here's the ironic part. That time of Israel's wandering—when God was meeting their needs in the wilderness—was characterized by grumbling, complaining, and unbelief. Centuries later we find the Jews celebrating God's salvation from Egypt and the way he provided for them. Jesus comes into town during the celebration, and he reveals himself as the greater Moses, as the ultimate provision of God sent to bring salvation to God's people. This time will they believe in him? Some did (7:30-31). They believed because Jesus perfectly fit the criteria for the Messiah. They looked at the promises of God, and they looked at the life of Jesus, and the two were a perfect match.

Will You Come to Jesus?
JOHN 7:32-39

The Pharisees don't like Jesus. In fact, they want to kill Jesus because he's honest with them. He's not afraid to point out their hypocrisy and self-righteousness. His unwillingness to coddle them has enraged them to the point where they're actively seeking to murder him. Everyone in Jerusalem is talking about Jesus. People are murmuring about Jesus. You could translate the word *murmuring* as "whispering." They're afraid to speak publicly about Jesus because they don't want to suffer the wrath of the Pharisees. Verse 32 said the crowd was whispering "these things." What things? They were wondering if Jesus could possibly be the Messiah. Everything he said and did pointed to him being the one sent by God to defeat sin and rescue people from death. Imagine crowds of people walking through Jerusalem, saying, "Could Jesus really be the Messiah?" And every time a Pharisee walks by, they look down and become quiet.

Before Jesus invites the crowds to come to him, he warns them they must make a decision (vv. 33-34). He will be leaving soon to return to his Father. Things are going to change. They can't wait indefinitely to decide whether to come to him. The crowds respond with confusion. They don't understand what Jesus means about leaving. They wonder if he is leaving to live with the Greeks due to the dispersion (vv. 35-36). At first the inclusion of their speculation seems pointless, but their question about the dispersion and the Greeks is included because it's foreshadowing. After Jesus dies, is buried, and rises again, he teaches his disciples for forty days and then ascends to heaven. Once he leaves, his disciples begin to tell others about him. They come under severe persecution and are dispersed from Jerusalem. Many of them travel and begin to tell non-Jewish people (the Greeks) about Jesus. Eventually the message of Jesus will make its way to all people. It will spread because the invitation Jesus gives is for everyone. No country, no ethnicity, no gender, no class, no language, no people are excluded from the invitation Jesus gives.

On the last day of the Festival of Shelters, Jesus extends an amazing invitation to the people (vv. 37-39). To understand the invitation, we need to understand the Scripture Jesus quotes. His statement, "Streams of living water [will] flow from deep within him," points us back to Isaiah. The first thirty-nine chapters of Isaiah talk primarily about judgment: on Judah, on Jerusalem, and on the nations surrounding Israel. There are even chapters prophesying judgment on the whole world. The judgment is due to the wickedness of each of these nations. Though there are many glimpses of hope in the first thirty-nine chapters, the book really takes a turn in chapter 40. Instead of judgment, we find promises of salvation that dominate the remaining twenty-six chapters, which center on someone called "the Servant."

- In chapter 52 we find out the Servant is God. He's described as "raised and lifted up" (52:13)—the same phrase in Hebrew that Isaiah uses to describe God (6:1).
- In chapter 53 we find out that the Servant will bring salvation by hanging on a tree, suffering, and dying in the place of sinners.
- In chapter 54 we find out that the death and resurrection of the Servant allows God to offer us an eternal covenant of peace, and we can live free from fear of judgment.

If you read Isaiah's book, by the time you reach chapter 55 (the chapter Jesus references in John 7), you know God will send his Servant—who is God—to save his people from judgment. Now compare these two invitations:

If anyone is thirsty, let him come to me and drink. (John 7:37)
Come, everyone who is thirsty, come to the water. (Isa 55:1)

Jesus, the Messiah, the Servant, the Son of God, invites thirsty people to come to him and drink. When we hear the invitation to come and drink, we don't get how important it is. We're spoiled by our unlimited selection of beverages. When Jesus says he'll give the thirsty water, we must understand the gravity of the situation. Remember he's saying this on the final day of the Festival of Shelters. The Festival of Shelters commemorates a time in Israel's history when they were stuck in the desert. Those who are thirsty in a desert are dying. This is why so many of the miracles during the time of Israel's wandering in the desert had to do with water: Moses striking a rock and water pouring out, Moses commanded to speak to a rock so water would come out, and God providing water in the midst of the desert. In a desert water means life. In a desert, if you're thirsty, you're dying.

Jesus is inviting the dying to come to him for life. Are you dying? Yes, we're all dying. What can we do about it? Jesus invites the dying to come to him. The one in the desert with his strength fading, struggling to go on, hears the promise of water, and he knows that's his only hope. Your only hope is Jesus. Only Jesus can give you water. Only Jesus can give you life. Look at what Jesus promises: not only will he give you a drink, but he will put a river of water in your heart (John 7:38). To those in the desert, a cup of water is great, but a river of water changes their lives: it guarantees life; it is a source of unending life. This is what Jesus promises. If you come to him, he will give you unending life by putting his Spirit inside you. He will actually put some of him inside you.

He says in effect, "If you're dying (and you all are), come to me. Not only will I give you life, but I will put my Spirit inside of you so that you will always have life. My Spirit inside of you will become a river of unending life." The Spirit will be a river of water inside you, and no desert or drought can ever cause it to run dry. Water to the thirsty, life to the dying—Jesus is all of this and more.

Now, I know how some people think: *But this sounds too good to be true. I'd love some water. I need life, but I don't have anything to offer Jesus. I don't deserve it, and I've got no way to get it.* God says,

> "Come, everyone who is thirsty, come to the water; and you without
> silver, come, buy, and eat! Come, buy wine and milk without silver
> and without cost!" (Isa 55:1)

Jesus doesn't want your money. He wants you. He invites you to come empty-handed to him, and when you do, you'll never be empty-handed again. We have nothing, but for some reason God still wants us, so he invites us to come. Come empty-handed. Come with no money. Come with nothing. Come dying. But you must come. Remember the warning Jesus gave, that some would seek him and not find him (John 7:34). That sounds a lot like Isaiah 55:6: "Seek the LORD while he may be found; call to him while he is near." If you don't find life before death, you can't find life after death. If you don't drink the water before you die, you won't have the chance afterward. How do you come to Jesus?

> Let the wicked one abandon his way and the sinful one his thoughts;
> let him return to the LORD, so he may have compassion on him, and to
> our God, for he will freely forgive. (Isa 55:7)

Do You Believe Jesus?

JOHN 7:40-52

You won't come to Jesus if you don't believe him. If you believe he's God, if you believe he's the only source of life, if you believe he will give you his Spirit, if you believe he loves you, if you believe he's gracious and merciful, if you believe he's the fulfillment of all God's promises, then you'll come to him. If not, then you won't. If you're wrestling with whether to believe, you're not alone (vv. 40-44). But if you have already decided you don't want to believe him, then you'll find an excuse not to. We see it here. They thought his hometown ruled him out as the Messiah, but they were wrong about where he was born. But if you want to find the truth, if you want to know if this is real, then you need to examine what the Bible says about Jesus. Is he the Son of God?

Those who were unbiased saw something unique about Jesus, and they couldn't help but be affected (vv. 45-46). I love their response: "You ask why didn't we arrest him? Have you heard him speak? There's no one like him" (my paraphrase). But the Pharisees had decided, and no amount of evidence would change it. They had chosen not to believe, so they came up with lame excuses to make their unbelief seem reasonable (vv. 47-52). They didn't believe Jesus because they didn't want to believe Jesus. Their unbelief was rooted in an unwillingness to discern the truth.

Conclusion

For decades one of the first places immigrants to America landed was Ellis Island. They came hoping for a better life, longing for a chance to find happiness. Near Ellis Island was a statue, and the statue was an invitation. A poem by Emma Lazarus captured the invitation:

"Keep, ancient lands, your storied pomp!" cries she
With silent lips. "Give me your tired, your poor,
Your huddled masses yearning to breathe free,
The wretched refuse of your teeming shore.
Send these, the homeless, tempest-tossed to me,
I lift my lamp beside the golden door!"

What a beautiful invitation. "Give me your tired, your poor, your huddled masses." Jesus extends a better invitation. "Come, weary and broken. Come, thirsty and dying. Come to me and find life."

Reflect and Discuss

1. Why do Jesus's half siblings want him to go to Jerusalem?
2. Do you ever bargain with God in the same way Jesus's siblings do, asking him to show himself as God in order to get something you want?
3. Why do the people begin to hate Jesus?
4. Why does Jesus expose sin?
5. How can the way we deal with sin either distort or clarify the gospel?
6. How is it possible for someone to know a lot of information about Scripture and still not understand it?
7. Why do the religious leaders hate Jesus and want to kill him?
8. What ways does self-righteousness deceive us? Why is this deception so dangerous?
9. Use the two self-righteousness self-diagnosis questions. Is there anything in your life you need to confess and repent of?
10. How does Jesus use Isaiah 55:1 to invite the people to come drink? What is he inviting them to believe and do?

An Issue with Authority

JOHN 8:1-12

Main Idea: Jesus Christ has the authority to do and to say everything he's done and said.

I. **Jesus Acts with Authority (8:1-11).**
II. **Jesus Claims Authority (8:12).**

Consider this scenario: You're standing in a bank. You're in line waiting for the next teller to become available when you see a man walk into the bank. He's got a visible firearm, and he begins to give people instructions. You see a second man. He walks right past you and all the other people waiting in line to talk to the tellers. He opens that little, swinging half door (I've never understood the point of that door anyway—who's it going to stop?), and he walks over to the safe and begins to open it. A third man has a handful of empty bags. He begins to fill up each bag. Once the bags are full, he leaves out the back door of the bank. What's going through your mind?

Now picture that scenario with a few more details. The man who's filling up his bags is a custodian, and the bags he's carrying are garbage bags. The reason he's exiting out the back of the bank is because that's where the Dumpsters are. The man who marched by you and all the other customers, he's the bank manager. He opens the safe every morning. It's part of his job. The man with the visible firearm is the bank security guard. The details make a difference, don't they? Imagine if you attempted to walk past the tellers and open the safe. They'd call 911, slap handcuffs on you, and throw you in the slammer! You don't have the authority to do what the bank manager does. In John 8 Jesus Christ makes clear he has the authority to do and to say everything he's done and said.

Chapter 8 begins with Jesus doing something that, if he were not God, would be absolutely insane. He will forgive a woman caught in adultery. Who has the authority to forgive sin? After that, he stands up and again claims to be the Messiah. He calls himself the light of the world, and he tells each person listening to him that they live in darkness and they need to follow him. Either Jesus is the Son of God, or he's utterly insane. Either he has the authority to do the things he does, or he's nothing more than a madman who should be ridiculed, then forgotten.

Jesus Acts with Authority
JOHN 8:1-11

The scribes and Pharisees are trying to trap Jesus. They think they have all of the pieces in place to bait him into their trap. They have a woman who was caught in the act of adultery. She is guilty with no reasonable doubt. Why did they think bringing this woman to Jesus would trap him? In their minds Jesus had set himself above the law in the past, and they thought he might do it again. Back in chapter 5 there was a controversy over the Sabbath (5:16). Jesus healed a man on the Sabbath, and they thought he was breaking the law. He wasn't. He was doing what they should have done on the Sabbath: he was helping people. But in their opinion he was violating the law.

Why do they think this particular situation will cause him to violate the law? The Mosaic law is clear that adultery is wrong, and the punishment for it is death. They know how compassionate Jesus is, particularly for those everyone considered sinners. Knowing his compassion, they thought Jesus might, in violation of the law, excuse her sin. They thought they could trip Jesus up due to his compassion. Jesus ignores their plan. He doesn't address the law or this woman's condition. He just tells them to go ahead and stone her, with one condition: as long as *they* were not guilty of breaking the law. With one statement Jesus shines the light on their sin. Only Jesus could have thrown the first stone, but he didn't. They all slink away, none of them willing to stand before Jesus and claim to be sinless.

Up to this point nothing Jesus has done has required any special authority. All he did was properly interpret the law, but what comes next demands unique authority. *Jesus forgives her sin.* He tells her he will not condemn her. Who has the right to forgive sin? We can forgive someone who sinned against us, but our forgiveness doesn't absolve guilt. Suppose you're in Jesus's position and you forgive this woman. All of a sudden the wife of the adulterous man comes up to you and says, "What right do you have to forgive this woman? How dare you? Did she sin against you?" What would you say? It's not up to you to forgive someone else's sin. You don't have the authority. Now, if the angry wife walked up to Jesus and asked the same question, "What right do you have to forgive her? Did she sin against you?" he could say, "Yes, she did. Not only did she sin against me, but I will take that sin upon myself—I even will become her sin for her. That's why I have forgiven her." Jesus does not ignore or excuse her sin. He acknowledges her sin, but he came to save sinners. When he spoke to this woman, she heard Jesus say, "I'm not like those hypocritical men who only care about condemning you. I care about you, and I forgive your sin. Now, go, and by my power live a transformed life." She was guilty. She was ashamed. She was humiliated. It looked like her life was over, both metaphorically and literally. Caught in the act of adultery, she was going to be executed. A group of religious men drag her to the holiest man around. They drop her at his feet and say, "She's guilty. We have multiple witnesses. Do we have your permission to stone her?" At that moment stoning, as horrible as it seems, may be welcome. She's been disgraced. Then Jesus covers her disgrace with his grace. He levels the playing field by quietly making each man admit his own sin, and then instead of condemning her, he forgives her. Not only does he forgive her, but he also transforms her future. He doesn't give her a license to keep sinning. He gives her a reason to stop.

Your sin never surprises Jesus. When he took your sin on himself as he hung on the cross, he bore judgment for every single sinful action, attitude, and thought you'd ever have. Your sin can't surprise him because he's already received the punishment for it. As a Christian, you are free from condemnation. Jesus paid it all. Rest in his grace. Rest in his goodness. Rest in his forgiveness. Jesus won't stone you, so don't stone yourself.

Jesus Claims Authority
JOHN 8:12

One of John's favorite descriptions of Jesus in his Gospel is that he is the light. John describes Jesus this way twenty-two times in the book. The "light of the world" is a clear messianic title. When the people heard Jesus make this statement, they should have remembered that Isaiah describes the Messiah as "a light for the nations" who would bring God's salvation to the ends of the earth (Isa 49:6). So, when Jesus stands up and calls out to the crowd, "I am the light of the world," he's identifying himself as the Christ, the Messiah, the one who fulfills God's promise to make the world right again.

However, the title "light of the world" does more than identify Jesus as the Messiah. It also identifies him as God. Throughout the Old Testament, God is called the light. For instance, in Psalm 27:1, "The LORD [Yahweh] is my light and my salvation." So add that to Jesus's claim. He's not just a messenger from God. He *is* God. He's divine.

With the claim to be God comes unique authority, which we see by understanding more specifically what Jesus means when he says he's the light of the world.

In chapter 6 Jesus replayed the history of the nation of Israel. He fed them miraculously with bread in the wilderness. He crossed a sea miraculously. The crowds grumbled and complained, then acted in unbelief.

In chapter 7 he celebrated the Festival of Shelters, which commemorated a specific time in Israel's history—the time of wandering in the wilderness, being fed miraculously by God after miraculously crossing a sea. It was a time characterized by grumbling, complaining, and unbelief.

Also in chapter 7, while celebrating the way God provided for them in the wilderness, Jesus invites thirsty people to come to him and drink—in the same way God provided water for the nation when they were thirsty.

Now here in chapter 8 we see this little word *again* (v. 12) that connects these words back to Jesus's statement about the water in chapter 7. We should understand this metaphor in the context of Israel's wilderness wanderings. After God brought the nation of Israel out of slavery in Egypt, they found themselves trapped on the banks of the Red Sea with Pharaoh closing in on them from behind. They began to doubt, to grumble, and to disbelieve the word of God. Moses told them to trust in God and watch his salvation:

> *Then the angel of God, who was going in front of the Israelite forces, moved and went behind them. The pillar of cloud moved from in front of them and stood behind them. It came between the Egyptian and Israelite forces. There was cloud and darkness, it lit up the night, and neither group came near the other all night long.* (Exod 14:19-20)

From this point forward God leads his people through the wilderness and to the promised land with a cloud and a pillar of fire. They just have to follow him.

When Jesus calls himself the "light of the world," he is not just identifying himself as God; he's commanding them to follow him. Jesus is telling them, in no uncertain terms, the only way for them to leave slavery is to submit to him. The only way for them to make it through the desert and reach the promised land is to submit to him. His claim of authority is no different today. The only way to escape slavery to sin is to follow Jesus. The only way to know where to walk and also make it to heaven is to follow Jesus.

C. S. Lewis wrote, "I believe in Christianity as I believe that the Sun has risen: not only because I see it, but because by it I see everything else" ("Is Theology Poetry?," 141). By claiming to be the light of the world, Jesus is saying, "Only by me can you see and understand everything else. Only by me can you see and understand this world." Apart from Jesus, this world is simply unknowable. The parts only make sense because of Jesus. Your life will only make sense as you submit to Jesus. Until the light of the world illuminates your world, you'll never make sense of the world.

The imagery here is pretty simple—if our world didn't have the sun, not only would we not know the sun, but we wouldn't see to understand our world. Jesus is like the sun. We can't make sense of a world that has so much evil and so much good without Jesus. Jesus helps us see it. He helps us understand it. In Jesus's light we can embrace the reality that this world is broken because of sin, but we can do so with hope, for Jesus has promised to fix it. Our hope isn't a fool's dream. It's rooted in the reality of the resurrection. Jesus already defeated death, so we have confidence he will one day banish death forever. Jesus is the light of the world, and only by following him can we see.

Reflect and Discuss

1. Does Jesus ignore the woman's sin in dealing with the scribes and Pharisees?
2. How is the act of forgiving the woman's sins different from the previous times Jesus has acted?
3. In forgiving the woman's sin, what is Jesus saying about himself?
4. Have you ever felt shame and disgrace over your sin? How is this passage a message of hope concerning those feelings?

5. How can you rest in the forgiveness of Jesus?
6. What Old Testament texts are being referenced by calling Jesus "the light of the world"?
7. How do Isaiah 49 and Psalm 27:1 point to Jesus as God rather than just as a messenger from God?
8. How do Jesus's claims of himself as bread, water, and light point back to the exodus?
9. How does the light of the world help us make sense of the world around us?
10. How can you leave a life of slavery by submission to Jesus?

Giving Up Heaven

JOHN 8:13-30

Main Idea: Jesus gave up heaven to give us heaven.

I. **Jesus Came from Heaven.**
II. **Jesus Promises Entrance to Heaven.**

Arland Williams and five others knew their situation was hopeless. Floating in the icy Potomac River, the six survivors of Air Florida Flight 90 knew there was no way to reach the shore just forty yards away. They could hear the rescuers trying to reach them, but each attempt to cross the icy waters failed. Just as they were giving up hope, they heard the sound of an approaching helicopter. A life ring fell into the hands of one of the survivors, and he was pulled to safety. Next it fell in Arland's hands. He could be saved. But before the helicopter could pull him up, he handed the life ring to someone else. The chopper could only hold two, so it turned toward the shore and sped away. Just a few minutes later it returned. Again the life ring fell into Arland's hands, and again he handed it to someone else. The third time he did the same. There would be no fourth opportunity. By the time the helicopter had returned, Arland had disappeared below the surface.

In 2007 an article was written about Arland Williams's sacrifice and appeared in *Men's Health* magazine. After recounting Williams's story, the author of the article asks,

> Why would anyone put the lives of strangers ahead of his own?
> He couldn't even see the faces of the people he was saving,
> because they were on the opposite side of the wreckage, yet
> he made a sacrifice for them that their best friends might have
> refused. (McDougall, "The Hidden Cost of Heroism")

The concepts of heroism and self-sacrifice puzzle the writer. Why would someone die for someone he didn't know? He tries to analyze it scientifically and concludes,

> Extreme heroism springs from something that no scientific
> theory can fully explain; it's an illogical impulse that flies in

the face of biology, psychology, actuarial statistics, and basic common sense. (Ibid.)

He even quotes Charles Darwin, who "couldn't figure out how to crowbar heroism into his survival-of-the-fittest theory" (ibid.). Darwin said,

> He who was ready to sacrifice his life, as many a savage has been, rather than betray his comrades, would often leave no offspring to inherit his noble nature. (Ibid.)

After examining the story and different theories, the writer concludes that though the act was heroic, there would be no one to pass down the family name.

How can a purely humanistic understanding of life explain self-sacrifice? If man is simply a highly evolved animal and we got this way through natural selection, then self-sacrifice can only make sense in specific situations. It might make sense to protect one's family, ensuring your genes are passed on to the next generation. It might make sense to defend the leadership of a colony or country. But sacrificing one's life for strangers is not survival of the fittest; it's survival of the weakest, survival of the least fit. Humanism doesn't have an answer for why Arland Williams's decision to give up the life ring is noble. His heroism doesn't make sense within a humanistic framework. But his act makes perfect sense within a Christian understanding of the world. In a Christian understanding of the world, we see his act through the lens of the words of Jesus Christ, who said, "No one has greater love than this: to lay down his life for his friends" (15:13).

A Christian worldview doesn't see self-sacrifice as a foolish choice that goes against biological instinct and may possibly corrupt the gene pool. A Christian worldview sees self-sacrifice as the highest act of love. We arrive at this view of the world not only by listening to Jesus's words but also by seeing Jesus's example. In spite of many conversations with Jesus, the religious leaders don't understand him. Jesus makes it simple. He summarizes what he's doing and why he came. *Jesus gave up heaven to give us heaven.* That's why he's there. It's what he came to do.

Jesus Came from Heaven

Before this conversation Jesus stood up during one of the Jewish festivals and invited those who were dying to come to him for life. Then the religious leaders brought a woman to him to be put to death for adultery, and Jesus responded by forgiving her and giving her life, after which he called himself the light of the world and called all of them to follow him. Following him was the only way to find life, but the religious leaders, the Pharisees, would not listen or believe (8:13). How does Jesus answer this charge of dishonesty and deal with their unbelief? Seven times in this conversation he tells them that he came from heaven (vv. 14,16,18,23,26,29).

The lifeblood of Christianity is self-sacrifice. In a society where power, wealth, and authority are the great goals, Jesus shows us a different way. He shows us a path stained with blood and says, "Follow me." He tells us to give up our rights for the good of someone else. He tells us the way to be great is to serve. Jesus shows us a radical way of living, the way of self-sacrifice. He made a sacrifice that is far greater than any sacrifice you or I could make: he gave up heaven.

Jesus Promises Entrance to Heaven

Jesus gave up heaven to give us heaven. He tells these leaders, in no uncertain terms, they cannot get to heaven. The way to heaven has been barred by their sin (v. 21). Here's the human dilemma. We were made to know God, enjoy God, live with and for God, but we rebelled. Our rebellion has made it impossible to know, enjoy, and live with God. Human religion is an attempt to get back to God. It's our effort to regain what was lost by our rebellion. But here is Jesus essentially saying to the most religious men around, "You can't do it. You can't get to God. You can't get to heaven. Your sin will always bar the way."

Attempting to get to God apart from Jesus Christ is like being in a futile religious maze. You turn this corner labeled "good works" and find a barricade. This corner is marked "sincerity," but there's no way through. Each turn is a dead end. There's no relief. But Jesus came to make a way. He came to knock over sin's barricade. He gave up heaven to give us heaven. How?

First, he lived a perfect life. In verse 29 he says he always does the things that are pleasing in God's sight. No one other than Jesus can say that. Only Jesus is without sin. Second, he died for sinners. In verse 28 he talks about how he will be lifted up. He's referring to his death on the cross. He will take the penalty we deserve in order to give us what he deserves. He will take our death and give us his life.

Jesus lived perfectly and died in our place in order to give us heaven, but something is required from us. Not work, effort, or religious ritual, but faith. The word *unless* is a beautiful word. "You will die in your sins *unless . . .*" (v. 24 RSV; emphasis added). Unless you believe that Jesus is the Son of God, that he gave up heaven, that he took your sin, and that he can give you life and hope and joy and heaven. It really is that simple. All it takes is faith. All that's required is to believe. The difference between heaven and hell is faith in Jesus Christ.

However, faith isn't simple. Jesus points this out to the Pharisees. He says in verse 15, "You judge by human standards." He's pointing out their limitations. We need to do what the Pharisees were unwilling to do. We need to wrestle with the limitations of our own understanding. We are in the flesh. We are in one place at one time. Our understanding will always be affected by our limitations. We have to decide what we will identify as the ultimate authority in life. The Pharisees would have said, "Our ultimate authority is God." But Jesus tells them, "No. You are your ultimate authority. You judge according to what you think. You judge according to how you feel. You judge according to the flesh" (v. 15; my paraphrase).

All the time we each decide whom to trust. When we pick up medicine from the pharmacy, we trust our doctor who prescribed it and our pharmacist who prepared it. We also trust the company that developed it and the government that approved it, plus the people who trained the doctor and pharmacist and the many hands at the drug company who prepared and packaged it. When it comes to physical life, we trust our care to a lot of people. When it comes to your spiritual life, whom do you trust? Your authority is either yourself—what you think, how you feel, what you have experienced—or it's God and what he says. Do you really want to trust yourself with your eternal future? You are flesh. You didn't exist until thirty or fifty or eighty years ago. You can't keep yourself from getting sick or hurt. You cannot guarantee you will be alive tomorrow. Do you really think you're the best choice to be the ultimate authority in your life?

There are many reasons Jesus is trustworthy—he's God, he never lies, he never sins, he's loving, and the list goes on—but here's one key reason to trust him: he gave up heaven to give us heaven. If you can find someone who sacrificed more for you than Jesus did, trust him, but if you can't, then Jesus has earned your trust.

Reflect and Discuss

1. Can a purely humanistic understanding of life explain self-sacrifice? Why or why not?
2. Would others say your life is marked by self-sacrifice?
3. How does the Christian worldview differ from the world's in its understanding of self-sacrifice?
4. What does Jesus benefit from his sacrifice on the cross?
5. Why does Jesus sacrifice on our behalf?
6. What does Jesus do after forgiving the woman's sins?
7. What is the human dilemma?
8. According to Jesus, all men will die in their sins *unless* what happens?
9. Who is the ultimate authority in your life? If it's not Jesus, what is keeping you from submission to him?
10. List all the reasons you can believe Jesus is trustworthy.

Bleed the Bible

JOHN 8:31-47

Main Idea: A genuine disciple holds to the Word.

I.   **Disciples Hold On to the Word of God.**
II. **Disciples Discover Truth in the Word about Jesus.**
III. **Disciples Find Freedom in the Truth.**

When Jesus came to the Festival of Shelters (ch. 7), he taught he was the Messiah and all men needed to come to him so they would not die in their sin. Some responded to this message in belief (7:31; 8:30), but in the Gospel of John, whenever we see that someone believed, we should ask, "Was their faith genuine?" Not all claims to faith are genuine (2:23-25). Not everyone who says he is a believer in Jesus really is. Jesus understood there would be many who claimed to be his disciples that would turn and walk away, revealing their faith was false (6:66).

The words of Jesus, beginning in verse 31, clarify whether the faith of these men was genuine. Verse 31 begins with the word *then* (Gk *oun*), which shows us we're to interpret these words in light of the declaration of faith made by these men. Was their faith genuine? Jesus reveals that genuine disciples "continue" or abide in the Bible.

Disciples Hold On to the Word of God

The litmus test of true discipleship is continuing, abiding, remaining, and persevering in the Bible. These Jews were not genuine disciples. Jesus said his word found no place in them (v. 37), and they could not bear to listen to his word (v. 43). We know their faith is false because the teachings that would become part of the Bible didn't find a warm and receptive home in their hearts. They may have reacted gladly to it at first, but ultimately they tossed his word aside.

What does it mean to "continue" in his word (v. 31)? We can understand it better if we look at the negative example found in verse 37. The opposite of abiding in his word is that his word finds "no place" in us. This expression is found only two other times in John's Gospel. The first is in chapter 2, verse 6, when Jesus turns the water into wine. The jars "each *contained* twenty or thirty gallons" (emphasis added). The second use is in chapter 21: "And there are also many other things that Jesus did, which, if every one of them were written down, I suppose not even the world itself could *contain* the books that would be written" (v. 25). The problem was their hearts would not hold on to the words of Jesus. They were unwilling to *contain* the Bible.

To *abide* in the Bible means to hold on to the teachings of Christ and never let go. It means the Bible so fills us up that we can barely contain it. It means we're willing to let the Bible dominate us. It means every area of our lives is being brought under the control of the Word of God. Every thought, deed, and action seeks conformity to the Scriptures. It means even when we don't like something in the Bible, we still obey, asking God to change our hearts so the truth of the Bible will find a warm and friendly reception in us.

Abiding in Scripture also means we take a much longer-term perspective on things. We aren't seeking immediate, instantaneous results. We understand genuine faith is proved over time, but false faith flickers and dies. It's easy for us to focus on instant results—instant coffee, instant pudding, instant news—but the Christian life is not lived in the instant but in the eternal. Anyone can follow Jesus for a day, but a genuine believer will follow him for a lifetime. He or she will hold tightly to his words and never let go.

Our problem is we want the Bible to validate what we already think or feel. We love sermons that agree with how we think. We don't like sermons that disagree with us. We don't like the suggestion that something we believe could be wrong. We want our opinions and beliefs to be validated. Do we really think we have the Bible mastered to the point that our thinking is never going to be changed? If you've got it all down, then you don't need the Bible. But you don't have it all down. None of us do. We should find ourselves constantly rethinking things. We should regularly have our thinking challenged. That's how God changes us. That's how we grow.

The Bible is clear from cover to cover that we need constant contact with it in order to grow. Wisdom comes from prolonged exposure to the Bible. God told Joshua the Scripture should be meditated on day and night (Josh 1:8). The psalmist echoes God's words and calls meditation a delight (Ps 1:2). Jesus isn't changing the Bible's teachings; he's affirming what has always been its clear message: genuine disciples are marked by a commitment to God's Word. The Bible is the means God has chosen to reveal himself to us, and through the Bible we grow in our understanding and worship of him.

When we hold to the Word of God, Jesus says, "You will know the truth" (John 8:32). The only pathway to truth is the Bible. The truth isn't cloaked in obscure, vague ambiguity. We don't have to learn special codes or study numerology. We just have to hold to the Bible. The longer we persevere in it, the clearer the truth becomes.

Truth is under attack. Some go so far as to suggest that the search for truth is pointless. On June 13, 2014, new age guru Deepak Chopra tweeted, "All belief is a cover up for insecurity."[3] In other words, there's no such thing as truth. Even the notion of truth itself is ridiculous. There's no such thing as right and wrong, no moral absolutes, just experience. So, Chopra advises, experience it. This false thinking has made its way into the church. We find ourselves pulled into a search for new spiritual experiences. We forfeit objective biblical revelation for private, mystical experience. We have our quiet time hoping to find some hidden jewel in the text that speaks right to our emotions and experiences and gives us a nice, warm buzz for the day. That's not what Jesus promises! When we hold to the Bible and discover truth, here's what we discover: truth is found in the person of Jesus Christ. We find him in his Word. That's why we reject emotionalism, sentimentality, and other such drivel as being "God's word to us" and instead rely solely on the Word of God, which focuses on the person of Jesus Christ.

Disciples Discover Truth in the Word of God

True disciples hold tightly to the Word of God, and as they do, they learn more and more about genuine reality, which is sourced in and centered on Jesus Christ (v. 32). To seek truth apart from Jesus Christ is inherently self-defeating because he alone is "the way, the truth, and the life" (14:6). If we reject the Word of God, we'll not be able to discern, understand, or even desire the truth. These false disciples rejected the Word of God, so they could not know or appreciate the truth (8:40,45).

When the Word of God is rejected, truth is lost. The apostle Paul warned Timothy a day would come when men would no longer endure the teaching of the Word, and instead they would desire that which made

---

[3] Deepak Chopra, blog, @DeepakChopra, June 13, 2014, accessed July 12, 2017, Https://twitter.com/deepakchopra/status/477434125163298816?lang=en.

them feel good about themselves (2 Tim 4:3). Look at the popular books in bookstores right now, and let me know whether that day has come.

Disciples Find Freedom in the Truth

When we hold tightly to the Bible, we discover the truth about Jesus, and that truth sets us free. "You will know the truth, and the truth will set you free" (v. 32). Every person who is thrown in jail and claims they are innocent quotes this verse. Every politician lamenting corrupt government and promising drastic changes uses it in a speech. Every anti-establishment hippie paints it in neon colors on the side of his VW van. But this is not a general proverb to be applied however we want, whenever we want, in whatever situation we want.

First of all, it's given in the context of abiding in the Word of God. Second, it's not referring to one's private situation but to something much bigger and universally applicable: the truth of the gospel revealed in Jesus Christ. Third, the freedom that is being promised is a specific freedom. It's freedom from sin. Jesus said we're all enslaved to sin (v. 34). Whether we want to admit it or not, each of us is a slave to sin. In this passage these men couldn't see their own slavery. Jesus promises them freedom, and they answer spitefully: "We have never been enslaved to anyone" (v. 33). Jesus makes clear they're slaves to sin, and at some point the slave is kicked out of the house, and only the family remains. "So, you need the Son," Jesus says in essence, "to set you free."

Do you see the progression? We believe on Jesus Christ, hold fiercely to his Word, learn more about him, and find greater freedom and victory over sin in our lives. This is true freedom.

> True freedom is not the liberty to do anything we please, but the liberty to do what we ought; and it is genuine liberty because doing what we ought now pleases us. (Carson, *John*, 350)

We can be free from sin through Jesus Christ. Charles Wesley describes this freedom beautifully in his great hymn "And Can It Be?"

> Long my imprisoned spirit lay
> > fast bound in sin and nature's night;
> Thine eye diffused a quickening ray—
> > I woke, the dungeon flamed with light;
> My chains fell off, my heart was free,
> > I rose, went forth, and followed Thee.

Genuine freedom comes from submission to the Word of God. We think freedom is throwing off all social restraints and doing whatever we want, but that's not freedom. That's slavery—slavery to our passions and lusts, slavery to sin. Real freedom is the ability to say no to the fleeting pleasures of sin and hold out for the fulfilling joy that comes in Christ. Those who are mature understand that genuine freedom is the ability to say no to anything that's going to hinder their enjoyment of Christ. The Word of God, the Bible, the truth of Jesus, sets us free from sin to enjoy God. It removes the chains of sin and gives us the freedom of a Son! As we persevere in the Word of God, we will—Jesus promises—understand more about him, and we will be increasingly liberated from the sin that shackles us to joylessness.

Part of this text is sad and scary. These religious men think they're doing just fine spiritually, but they've been deceived. They see themselves as free men (v. 33), sons of Abraham (v. 39), and children of God (v. 41). But here's what Jesus says about them: they're enslaved to sin (vv. 34-35), they're intolerant of truth (vv. 40,45), and they're the offspring of Satan (vv. 44-45).

If we're not careful, an emphasis on reading and studying the Bible could push us to legalism. We could think, *I'm a failure if I miss a single devotional time,* or *If I don't do my Bible study today, God is not going to be happy with me,* or *A real Christian wouldn't struggle with having to read her Bible.* That's not at all what Jesus is teaching in this passage. Verse 47 helps us see the gospel—what Jesus did for us—in relation to these truths.

Our hope is not found in ourselves and in our ability to perfectly fulfill a list of Bible-reading requirements. Our position in Christ is not rooted in our capacity to mark off boxes on a spiritual-discipline checklist. If we've turned from our sin and turned to Christ, then God will do that work in us. He will create in us a growing desire for his Word. He will give us the strength to say no to our lazy flesh and be diligent in our study of the Scripture. That doesn't mean we will never have dry spells and difficulty, but it does mean that over the long haul God will work in us, giving us the desire to hold to his Word, the ability to see Christ in it, and the freedom that comes from it.

John Bunyan—the wonderful, Puritan pastor and author of *Pilgrim's Progress,* the man whom Charles Spurgeon said bled the Bible—described the Bible this way:

> I tell thee, friend, there are some promises that the Lord hath helped me to lay hold of Jesus Christ through, . . . that I would

not have [these promises taken] out of the Bible for as much gold and silver as can lie between York and London piled up to the stars. (Bunyan, *Sighs from Hell*, 3:721)

Like Bunyan, read the Book, treasure it, immerse yourself in it, and do so for the long haul. Spend as much time as possible in the Bible so that it becomes a part of you, and then maybe one day you will cut your finger and bleed the Bible.

Reflect and Discuss

1. What are three marks of a genuine disciple?
2. What does it mean to abide in Jesus's word?
3. How should we respond when we see something in the Bible we don't like or understand?
4. Do you feel your time in Scripture frequently challenges your thinking and beliefs? Why or why not?
5. How can we grow in wisdom and delight in Scripture?
6. What are some ways you might seek truth apart from Jesus?
7. How can truth, and knowing it, set you free? What can the truth of Jesus set you free from?
8. How would you define true freedom in light of this passage?
9. How is the Christian understanding of freedom different from the world's understanding?
10. How might you find yourself slipping into legalism in your pursuit of Jesus?

Never See Death

JOHN 8:48-59

Main Idea: Jesus promises his disciples that if they hold to his word they will never experience death.

I. **What Does This Promise Mean?**
II. **Who Is This Promise For?**
III. **Why Should I Believe This Promise?**

A fascinating story appeared in *Time* magazine a few years ago. By day, Randolfe Wicker, 63, runs a lighting shop in New York City. But in his spare time, as spokesman for the Human Cloning Foundation, he is the face of cloning fervor in the U.S. "I took one step in this adventure, and it took over me like quicksand," says Wicker. He is planning to have some of his skin cells stored for future cloning. "If I'm not cloned before I die, my estate will be set up so that I can be cloned after," he says, admitting, however, that he hasn't found a lawyer willing to help. "It's hard to write a will with all these uncertainties," he concedes. "A lot of lawyers will look at me crazy."

As a gay man, Wicker has long been frustrated that he cannot readily have children of his own; as he gets older, his desire to reproduce grows stronger. He knows that a clone would not be a photocopy of him but talks about the traits the boy might possess: "He will like the color blue, Middle Eastern food and romantic Spanish music that's out of fashion." And then he hints at the heart of his motive. "I can thumb my nose at Mr. Death and say, 'You might get me, but you're not going to get all of me,'" he says. "The special formula that is me will live on into another lifetime. It's a partial triumph over death. I would leave my imprint not in sand but in cement." (Gibbs, "Baby, It's You!")

Because of death's certainty, it's natural to fear death. English philosopher Francis Bacon wrote, "Men fear death as children fear to go in the dark" (*The Essays*, 343). Because of the fear of death, we hope for victory over death. We hope something will happen to keep the cold, dark clutches of death from overtaking us. Is there hope for immortality? Is there any way to triumph over death? Jesus makes a promise in verse 51 that anyone who keeps his word will never see death. To understand this promise made by Jesus, we need to answer a few questions.

What Does This Promise Mean?

Death is fundamentally *separation*. As I noted before, at death the spiritual part of man—his soul—is separated from the physical part of man—his body. We feel this separation when we attend a funeral. We walk into the room, greet the family who are mourning over the separation that has taken place between them and the one they love, and then we walk to the front of the room and look into the coffin. In that coffin we see a shell. Though the body is still with us, the person—the part of that person that really makes her who she is—is no longer there. It's gone. Her soul has been separated from her body, and all that remains is an empty shell.

Where does that immaterial part of a person—the soul—go at death? If we're being honest, we hope that it goes somewhere in some form, and something inside us says this life isn't all there is. We know deep down that we'll live on somewhere, somehow after this life. God has placed eternity in our hearts (Eccl 3:11). He has implanted the knowledge that there's more than this life.

If physical death is the separation of the soul from the body, then spiritual death is the separation of the soul from God. Jesus talks a lot about spiritual life and death. Earlier in the Gospel of John, Jesus told Nicodemus that every single man and woman needs to be born again (John 3:3). Nicodemus was understandably confused. "How can I be born when I'm old?" he asked. "Am I supposed to crawl back into my mother's womb?" Of course not. Jesus was referring to *spiritual* birth. Nicodemus, like every other individual, needed to be given spiritual life. In other words, each one of us is spiritually dead. Because of our sin, we've been separated from God. We need something to happen so that we can be reunited or reconciled to God, so that we can have spiritual life.

Immediately after that conversation with Nicodemus, we find one of the most famous verses in the entire Bible: "For God loved the world in this way: He gave his one and only Son, so that everyone who believes in him will not perish but have eternal life" (3:16). The promise Jesus makes—"he will never see death" (8:51)—goes beyond physical death to spiritual death. Physical death pictures the far more terrifying reality of spiritual death. Our sin separates us from the sinless God of the universe. That separation is made permanent after physical death, when God, the just Judge, punishes that sin with eternal separation from him in the horrors of hell.

Understanding that reality makes the promise of Jesus even sweeter. We don't have to remain spiritually dead, awaiting that day of judgment. Instead, we can be made alive and can look forward to eternal life with God in heaven forever. Jesus came to bring spiritual life to the spiritually dead. He came to remove the alienation that exists between God and us because of our sin and to reconcile us to God, promising us the joy of his presence forever.

In chapter 11 John records that Jesus attended a funeral. There Jesus expanded on the promise he makes here: "I am the resurrection and the life. The one who believes in me, even if he dies, will live. Everyone who lives and believes in me will never die" (11:25-26). Jesus promises, "Even if he dies, [he] will live." Though we still experience physical death, we will not experience eternal, spiritual death.

When we think about the fear of death, we really fear two things: death's uncertainty and its significance. When we receive the life that Jesus promises, the *uncertainty* is gone. We may not know when or how our physical death will take place, but we are certain about what will happen the moment it takes place. As one author wrote, "Death is only the introduction to the nearer presence of God" (Barclay, *John*, 2:38). For the Christian physical death is not a separation but a homecoming. Death means being ushered into the presence of Jesus. The *significance* of physical death has also been irrevocably altered. Before, it signified the eternal separation we would experience from God in conscious torment because of our sin, but not anymore. Those who've believed on Jesus have been given life that physical death cannot extinguish. Death has lost its finality. Nothing can sever the life-giving relationship we now enjoy with God.

Donald Barnhouse was the pastor of Philadelphia's Tenth Presbyterian Church when his wife died and left him with young daughters to raise alone. While driving to her funeral he realized that he had to say something to explain all of this to his girls, to somehow put in perspective for them something with which he himself was already struggling. They stopped at a traffic light while driving to the funeral. It was a bright day, and the sun was streaming into the car and warming it. A truck pulled up next to them, and the shadow that came with the truck darkened the inside of the car. He turned to his daughters and asked, "Would you rather be hit by the shadow or by the truck?" One of them responded, "Oh, Daddy, that's a silly question! The shadow can't hurt you. I would rather be hit by the shadow than by a truck." He tried to explain to them that their mother had died, and it was as if she had been hit by a shadow. It was as if Jesus had stepped in the way in her place, and it was he who had been hit by the truck. He quoted the familiar words of Psalm 23: "Even though I walk through the valley of the shadow of death, I will fear no evil, for you are with me" (Anderson, "Valley").

That's the promise Jesus makes. We who believe will never experience death, just its shadow. We will never be cut off from God. We will only be cut off from our physical bodies.

Who Is This Promise For?

This promise is conditional. It begins with the word *if.* Something must be done in order for this promise to apply to us. Jesus says in John 8:51, "If anyone keeps my word . . ." So this promise is only true for those who keep his word. To keep Jesus's word means that we embrace and hold to what he says. We hold to the teaching of Jesus that apart from him we are lost, sinful, spiritually dead, and without hope. We must recognize the only remedy for our sin is to turn *from* that sin and *to* Jesus Christ as our Savior. To believe in him is to reject any and all attempts to reach God on our own and to trust singularly in his saving work on our behalf.

The beauty of this promise is it's free and available to all men (v. 51). He said "anyone." Jesus excludes no one from this offer of salvation. No one is excluded because of being too *bad* to be given eternal life through Jesus, and no one is included because of being *good enough* to earn eternal life apart from Jesus.

We each relate to God in one of two ways. While Jesus was on earth, he interacted with people from all different backgrounds, but the Gospel writers and Jesus himself lump them into these two broad categories. We could call them the *sinners* and the *self-righteous.*

The sinners were those who knew they were lost and cut off from God. They would be the nonreligious, the men and women who either didn't care that they were sinners or thought they weren't salvageable.

The self-righteous were those who thought their good behavior and good works earned favor with God. They kept from the "really bad sins" like immorality, stealing, and murder. On the outside they looked good. However, each good deed they did was their attempt to put God in their debt. With each righteous act, they grew more confident in their own efforts to please God.

Jesus told both groups the same thing: "You're spiritually dead, and apart from me you can never experience spiritual life. However, if you turn from your sin and from your self-righteousness and place your faith in me alone, I will give you eternal life. You will never be cut off from God" (my paraphrase). In John 3 Jesus spoke one-on-one with a religious leader, and in chapter 4 he had a private conversation with an immoral outcast. As different as they were on the outside, they shared a common state: spiritual death, a common future: separation from God, and a common need: a Savior. Jesus gave them both the same message—the message he gives these Jews in chapter 8, and the message that applies to us today: believe on me and you will not see death.

Why Should I Believe This Promise?

You don't believe everything you hear or read. What criteria do you use to determine what's believable, to decide who's trustworthy? A couple of criteria guide all of us. First are a person's **qualifications**. What about them makes them trustworthy? Jesus lists his qualifications in verses 54-58. He's the one and only Son of God who came down to this earth as a man to save mankind from the penalty that our sin demands. But he's not just the Son of God; he's God himself.

Abraham had been dead for nearly two thousand years, and Jesus claimed to exist prior to him. Jesus is not to be regarded as a good man or a moral teacher but as God in the flesh. Jesus demonstrates he is God by taking the divine name and claiming it as his own. In the Old Testament God revealed himself using the name "I AM" (Exod 3:14). Here Jesus takes that name to himself (John 8:58). Jesus is not a man God adopted. He himself is divine. Jesus is also the promised Savior (v. 56).

When God created the world, he created it perfect. Mankind was made to live in perfect harmony and communion with God. We were designed to worship and enjoy him in his presence forever. However, man sinned, and with that sin came the awful penalty of death—separation from God. In that moment when God revealed to the first humans the penalty for their sin, he also made a promise that one day he would send a Savior who would reconcile man to God, who would restore that broken relationship (Gen 3:15). A number of generations later, God promised Abraham that this Savior would come through his offspring and that through this child all of the families of the earth would be blessed (Gen 12:3). The rest of the Old Testament is tracing this lineage with anticipation for the fulfillment of this promise.

The New Testament begins with a record of births. From Abraham's line of descendants, Jesus of Nazareth was born. But he was no ordinary baby. God had sent his own Son to take on human flesh and be born as a man. This was the fulfillment of God's promise. The coming of Jesus as the Savior of mankind was what Abraham was rejoicing about. He believed God would fulfill his promise of a Savior who would reconcile sinners to a perfect God. We can believe Jesus's promise because he is the Son of God who came to this world to bring life. His qualifications are impeccable.

A second reason we believe someone is because of their **experience**. If you're scheduled to have surgery and are nervous about it, the best people to talk to are a doctor (because of his qualifications) or a patient who's successfully gone through the procedure (because of his experience). Best of all would be a doctor who had the surgery successfully performed on himself. We not only believe Jesus's promise of victory over death because of who he is but also because of what he's done.

Sadly the religious leaders rejected Jesus Christ and attempted to kill him (John 8:59). Though this attempt failed they would later succeed. The religious leaders would turn Jesus over to the Romans to die the cruel death of a criminal. He was beaten, mocked, tortured, and then stretched out to hang on a cross until dead in chapter 19. If the story ended there, we'd have no reason to believe his promise. But in chapter 20 a woman visits his tomb and finds it empty. She weeps, thinking his body has been stolen. All of a sudden, Jesus, resurrected from the dead, appears to her. He's no longer dead; he's alive!

We believe his promise of victory over death because he has experienced it. He has triumphed over death—both physical and spiritual—and now he stands ready to allow us to experience the same victory. If we turn from our sin and trust in him as our Savior, then we too can be assured that death will not conquer *us* because Jesus has conquered *death*. The separation from God that our sin demanded was taken by Jesus upon himself so that we don't have to bear it, and the resurrection of Jesus Christ has left death powerless. "Death has been swallowed up in victory" (1 Cor 15:54). Because of the resurrection of Jesus from the dead, we have nothing to fear—we will never see death. His death in our place has freed us from the paralyzing fear of physical death. The beautiful lyrics penned by Henri Malan, a nineteenth-century Swiss pastor and hymn writer, capture the confident hope available to every Christian.

> It is not death to die—to leave this weary road,
> and join the saints who dwell on high who've found their
> home with God.
> It is not death to close the eyes long dimmed by tears,
> and wake in joy before Your throne delivered from our fears.
> It is not death to fling aside this earthly dust
> and rise with strong and noble wing to live among the just.
> It is not death to hear the key unlock the door
> that sets us free from mortal years to praise You evermore.
> O Jesus, conquering the grave
> Your precious blood has power to save.
> Those who trust in You will in Your mercy find
> that it is not death to die.

Reflect and Discuss

1. What does Jesus's promise mean?
2. How will those who keep Jesus's word never experience death?
3. What is death?
4. Where does the soul go at death?
5. What does Ecclesiastes 3:11 teach us about man's understanding of life?
6. How does the gospel change the significance of physical death?
7. Who will receive the promise Jesus makes in this passage?
8. How is keeping Jesus's word different from the Pharisees' attempts to keep the law of Moses?
9. How is Jesus's promise available to all men? Does this conflict with Jesus's teaching on election in chapter 6?
10. Why should you believe Jesus's promise?

The Blind Will See

JOHN 9

Main Idea: Only Jesus, the light of the world, has the power to give sight to the blind.

I. **The Miracle (9:1-7)**
II. **The Reaction (9:8-12)**
   A. Interrogation 1 (9:13-17)
   B. Interrogation 2 (9:18-23)
   C. Interrogation 3 (9:24-34)
III. **Application**
   A. If you recognize your blindness, Jesus will give you sight (9:39).
   B. If you think you can see on your own, you can't (9:39-41).

I can't imagine losing the ability to see. One moment everything is bright and clear, and the next moment you're in complete darkness. In John 9 we're introduced to a man who has only known darkness. He has never seen light, never seen beauty, never experienced sight. He serves as an illustration of fallen mankind. We are spiritually blind and cannot see the beauty of God.

The Miracle

JOHN 9:1-7

We're intended to understand this miracle in connection with what Jesus taught during the Festival of Shelters. Jesus stood before the crowd and said he was "the light of the world" (8:12). He makes the same claim here in verse 5, and this miracle authenticates his claim. He is indeed the light of the world. He has the power to remove the darkness and give light. Healing a blind man is the perfect illustration of his unique power and prerogative.

Prior to the healing, his disciples ask whose sin caused the man's blindness (v. 2). Was it the man's sin or his parents'? This question reveals a legalistic outlook on life—an outlook fostered by the example

207

of the religious establishment. Legalism is the attempt to earn God's favor through our own righteous works. A legalist operates under the (usually unspoken) assumption that people earn or keep God's favor through righteous deeds, so legalists begin to view themselves as deserving of certain blessings. In other words, if I can *earn* God's favor by my good works, then the more good works I do, the more God becomes indebted to me. He *must* reward my good deeds with blessings. If something "bad" happens to me, it must be because I did something bad.

The disciples look at this man born blind and conclude that he or his parents had sinned, because if they had not done something wicked, then God would be forced to respond with blessing. That's textbook legalism. Jesus has no sympathy for legalism. This man's blindness had nothing to do with his sin (though birth defects and disease are indicators of the world's fallen state due to sin in general). His blindness had a far greater purpose. This man was born blind so Jesus could teach the profound truth of spiritual blindness and reveal himself as the light of the world. That puts a different perspective on trials we face.

Whenever I face a trial, I struggle with viewing it legalistically: "God, how could you allow this to happen to me? Haven't you noticed everything I'm doing for you?" My next response is to see how quickly I can make the trial stop, all the time missing the fact that God has a bigger purpose in mind for my suffering. To short-circuit the trial would be to miss out on the display of God's glory *in* the trial.

Jesus is going to display his glory by healing this man. He bends over, makes little mud balls, places them in the man's eyes, and sends him off to wash his eyes in the pool of Siloam. He chooses that particular pool for two reasons. First, the word *Siloam* (as we're told in v. 7) means "sent." Jesus has repeatedly referred to himself as the one sent by God. This action is another reminder of who he is. Second, the waters of Siloam are mentioned in Isaiah 8:6, a chapter that contains a prophecy about the Messiah. God warns the Israelites of impending judgment because they refused the waters of Shiloah (the Hebrew name for Siloam) that God provided. Will history repeat itself? Will the Jews again reject what God has sent? Regardless of what others will decide, this blind man obeys the words of Jesus and is miraculously healed (John 9:7).

John records the healing in an understated way. A man born blind can now see. For the first time he sees colors and shapes. He's heard people describe a flower. Now he sees one. He's heard men talk of physical beauty, and now he understands. Jesus's amazing power makes this man see. It's not the combination of clay and saliva, the chemicals in the pool of Siloam, or the man's obedience. It's the power of Jesus. This man could do nothing to make himself see. The only thing he could do was do what Jesus said.

The Reaction
JOHN 9:8-12

His neighbors don't know what to make of the miracle, so they bring him to the Pharisees for their perspective. The Pharisees are the religious establishment. They don't like Jesus, primarily because he condemns their self-righteous hypocrisy. They decide to investigate the miracle, and the purpose of their investigation is to squelch the story and condemn Jesus. Their investigation consists of three interrogations.

Interrogation 1 (9:13-17)

Right from the start, the Pharisees have determined Jesus is guilty (v. 16). Their regulations about the Sabbath were more significant than a never-before-seen display of healing power, even though the regulations were man-made, not divinely given. Since they're unsure how to reconcile this apparent violation with the miraculous power, they ask the (formerly) blind man, "What do you say about him?" He responds, "He's a prophet" (v. 17). In other words, "He must be from God if he can do something like this." Unsatisfied with his answer, they begin a second interrogation.

Interrogation 2 (9:18-23)

Their new goal is to disprove the miracle, so they question the parents about his blindness: "Was he really blind from birth?" "Yes. We don't know how he can see, but he can. He's an adult, why don't you ask him?" (vv. 19-21; my paraphrase). Well, they had; they just didn't like his answer. Verse 22 is an important editorial comment by John. Believing on Jesus and publicly confessing belief was not a popular thing to do. Public faith in Jesus had serious consequences. Unsuccessful, the Pharisees embark on a third interrogation.

Interrogation 3 (9:24-34)

The religious leaders are stuck. They can't dispute the miracle, nor can they acknowledge that Jesus is from God. If they do, that would mean his diagnosis of their spiritual hypocrisy is true. It would require them to humble themselves before him. Their last-ditch effort is to have this healed man denigrate the character of Christ. At least this might save some face. They tell him to "give glory to God" (v. 24). In other words, "With God as your witness, tell the truth. This man (Jesus) is a sinner."

We see clearly the deceptive power of sin. Sin has twisted their minds so much they find it impossible to see things clearly. Sin causes confusion and breeds spiritual ignorance. Their foolishness is exposed by the simple, logical answers of the man who has been healed. All he knows is he was blind but now he can see (v. 25). What a great truth we've sung many times: "Amazing grace, how sweet the sound that saved a wretch like me. I once was lost, but now am found; was blind, but now I see."

He answers their questions honestly, but you can hear the sarcasm dripping from his lips. "Are you kidding me? You don't know where he's from. Look at what he's done!" (vv. 30-33; my paraphrase). Then he uses their own words against them. He says, "We know that God doesn't listen to sinners" (v. 31). This is in response to their earlier question, "This man is not from God, because he doesn't keep the Sabbath. . . . How can a sinful man perform such signs?" (v. 16). Their question implies that a sinner could never do these signs because God would not listen to him. The blind man is saying, "You're right. Only someone who is from God can do these things. That means Jesus must be from God." What a clear, logical deduction! In spite of the overwhelming evidence, the religious leaders continue to find reasons to ignore what's so clear. So a blind beggar shames the spiritually elite by seeing what they could not.

The Pharisees respond by excommunicating him from the synagogue. He's cut off religiously and socially for stating the obvious: Jesus must have come from God. God never promises following his Son will make life easier. You may have heard some wrong teaching that claims turning to Jesus will make your problems go away. That's not what Jesus says. Jesus says, "Don't be surprised if they hate you. They hated me, and you follow me" (15:18-21; my paraphrase; cf. 1 Pet 4:12-17; 1 John 3:13). Following Jesus is worth it; the difficulties of following Christ on this earth cannot even be compared with the future joy still to be revealed (Rom 8:18). He is the greatest treasure! We come to him because we understand that in his "presence is fullness of joy " (Ps 16:11 NKJV). But that doesn't always correspond with earthly happiness. Sometimes your faith will bring rejection and mistreatment.

John 9:35 says Jesus "found him." Do you see the divine initiative? Without any prompting, Jesus reached down when this man was blind and gave him physical sight, and now he seeks him out and gives him spiritual sight. Before people can receive spiritual sight, they must first acknowledge they need it. Jesus pointed out this man's need in verse 35. He essentially asked, "Have you placed your faith in the Son of God who became a man? Do you recognize your need of a Savior, and are you willing to turn from your own attempts and trust in him alone to save you?" The man asks, "Who is he?" Jesus responds, "You have seen him." This man was blind, and Jesus doesn't just say to him, "I am the Son of Man." He says, "You have seen him" (vv. 35-36). Earlier in the day this man could not see anything, but now he's seen the Messiah. His eyes have beheld the Savior. Instantly he begins to worship Jesus.

Application

If You Recognize Your Blindness, Jesus Will Give You Sight (9:39)

Imagine if the story began this way. Jesus and his disciples meet a man born blind. Jesus promises to heal the man's eyes. He makes little mud packs, places them in the man's eyes, and tells him to go wash his eyes in the pool of Siloam. A couple of hours later, a friend of the blind man walks by and sees him begging in his normal spot, but his eyes are caked with mud.

"What's going on?" his friend asks.

"Not much! What's up with you?"

"Nothing. What's all over your eyes?"

"It's mud. Some guy came by and put this mud on my eyes and said it would help me see. I let him do it, but it didn't make sense. I'm fine. There's nothing wrong with me."

Could it be possible for a man who was born blind to assume he was fine? Only someone who realized he was blind would long for sight. Only the one who understands his condition will allow Jesus to fill his eyes with mud and then go through town looking ridiculous in the hopes of healing. Only when a person understands his spiritual blindness will he turn to Jesus for healing. We are blind, and once we realize that, then we can come to Jesus to receive sight.

If You Think You Can See on Your Own, You Can't (9:39-41)

Those who think they see are blind to their own blindness and will remain that way. They reject the light because they live in and love the darkness.

> Those who [are] blind are the ones who do not realize their need. Those who receive sight are the ones who sense their darkness. The Pharisees thought they had it all together, that they had arrived. Through their acquaintance with the Law they knew they were not perfect, but they did not understand how deeply infected they were with sin. So they adopted the external appearance of having dealt with sin though actually they had never faced the darkness of their hearts. They were self-satisfied. They said, "We see" when in reality they were blind. (Hughes, *John*, 259)

One of the great promises God made to his people was that he would send a Savior to help those who were desperate—a promise that would be fulfilled by Jesus (Isa 42:6-7). God's people were in the darkness of sin and unbelief, and the Messiah came to bring them light. But the religious leaders missed him because they could not perceive their own blindness. Charles Spurgeon wrote,

> It is not our littleness that hinders Christ; but our bigness. It is not our weakness that hinders Christ; it is our strength. It is not our darkness that hinders Christ; it is our supposed light that holds back His hand. ("Sermon #1795," 30:489)

If we want more of Christ, we must recognize a growing need for him. Those who drink the most are the ones who feel the thirstiest. Those who eat the most are the ones who feel the hungriest. Those who see and enjoy and experience the most are the ones who flee the darkness and run to the light!

Reflect and Discuss

1. Define legalism. Why is it contrary to the message of the gospel?
2. How might you fall into legalism during suffering? What can you do to fight against it?
3. Why does Jesus send the blind man to the pool of Siloam?
4. What do you think the man thought when his sight was restored?

5. Why do the Pharisees instruct the man to give glory to God? What are they actually telling him to do?

6. What does the man mean when he says, "We know that God doesn't listen to sinners"?

7. What happens to the man when he refuses to do anything other than testify for Jesus?

8. What condition were you in when Jesus found you? In what ways has he healed you?

9. Have you taken time today to worship Jesus?

10. Are you daily aware of your need for Jesus? What are some things in your life that might hinder this awareness?

The Good Shepherd

JOHN 10:1-21

Main Idea: Jesus is the good shepherd who cares for God's people.

I.   **Jesus Gathers His Sheep (10:1-6).**
II   **Jesus Guards His Sheep (10:7-10).**
III. **Jesus Gives His Life for His Sheep (10:11-18).**

God pictures his care of his people through the image of a shepherd and his sheep (Ps 23:1-4). In Psalm 80:1 God is called the "Shepherd of Israel." In Isaiah 40:11 God promises to bring his people back from exile in Babylon like a shepherd gathering his lambs in his arms. God wanted his people to understand his grace, his mercy, and his love.

One of the ways God cared for Israel was by appointing human shepherds, leaders who were supposed to serve as God's representatives, demonstrating God's care for his flock. But those who were supposed to lead the Israelites—who were in positions of religious influence and who were to be God's representatives to his people—were not caring for the sheep. They were hurting the sheep. Instead of leading them to encounter and obey God, they were leading the people away from God and into empty religious ritual. Instead of bringing the people of God to graze in the pastures of God's grace, the religious leaders were loading them up with the weight of religion and man-made requirements and making them plow the barren fields of legalism. Instead of guarding the flock of God, they were goading them to turn from God to their own efforts. Instead of leading them to the overflowing fountains of grace, they were leaving them distressed, diseased, and spiritually dead.

In Ezekiel 34 God condemned the religious leaders of Israel for their mistreatment of his sheep (34:1-10). He says the shepherds have left the sheep exposed. They've forced them to fend for themselves. They've even killed the sheep for their wool and meat. In response, God will set up "one shepherd" over the flock—his servant David (34:22-24). At the time of this prophecy, King David was dead and had been for a long time. We understand this promise refers to a King who would come from the line of David. It's a promise about the Messiah.

All of this is background to help us interpret Jesus's words in John 10. In the previous chapter Jesus healed a blind man. When the man who had been healed would not denounce Jesus, he was kicked out of the synagogue. The religious leaders left him to wander alone, fending for himself, but he didn't remain alone for long. Jesus found him.

Jesus fulfills Ezekiel 34. The shepherds of Israel neglected the sheep. They were reckless and destructive. But God hadn't forgotten his flock. He sent a shepherd to rescue and care for his sheep. Jesus is the good shepherd who cares for God's people. How does Jesus care for his sheep?

Jesus Gathers His Sheep
JOHN 10:1-6

If you have believed on Jesus, you are his sheep and will never be forgotten. Religious leaders may cast you aside, but your shepherd will come and gather you to himself. Jesus highlights the relationship between the shepherd and his sheep. The sheep are in a sheepfold. The only legitimate way to collect the sheep is through the gate. The shepherd calls each sheep gently by name. Jesus knows each of his sheep personally. He's a personal shepherd. He knows your strengths and weaknesses. He knows if you're an older sheep who walks a little slower now. He knows if you're a younger sheep full of energy and enthusiasm who likes to wander away and explore. He knows when you need to rest and when you need to eat. He knows everything about you.

He calls his sheep by name because his sheep aren't alone. In this sheepfold are other sheep (10:3). He doesn't bring out all the sheep. Many would rather stay in the fold of religion. He only brings out those who are his own. Before Jesus even calls them, they belong to him. God gave sheep to his Son. Jesus said, "Everyone the Father gives me will come to me" (6:37). Jesus approaches the pen of religion and speaks the truth. Those given to him by the Father before the foundation of the world hear him calling, and they come to him. They don't *become* his sheep because they follow him. They follow him because they *are* his sheep. The Shepherd, not the sheep, takes the initiative. Just as the prophets foretold, God sent a shepherd to draw God's sheep back to God. Jesus came and his sheep responded. Their response is simple: they hear, and they follow.

All the credit and glory go to the shepherd, not the sheep. We tend to make the sinner the focus of salvation. The glory does not belong to the sinner but to the Savior. Being called a sheep is not a compliment; sheep aren't known for their intelligence. The reason they need a shepherd is because they're dull and defenseless. They'll wander off a cliff or into a gully. They've no natural means to defend themselves from predators. This image should curb our rampant self-exaltation. On our best days we're still helpless sheep desperately in need of a shepherd. The religious leaders didn't understand the illustration (10:6). They did not know his voice because they were not his sheep.

Jesus Guards His Sheep
JOHN 10:7-10

Jesus changes the metaphor slightly. He's not just the Shepherd; he's also the gate for the sheep. The gate keeps out those who intend to harm the sheep. Jesus promises to guard and protect his sheep from those who desire to hurt them. Remember what just happened: the religious leaders just excommunicated a man because he publicly confessed his faith in Jesus. In response Jesus reminds them that God called the religious leaders wicked shepherds who harm the sheep.

Imagine how this struck those listening. They'd been taught by the religious leaders that it was only through them and keeping their list of good deeds that a man could be in God's favor. They've dutifully obeyed these men. Their families have listened and responded to their teaching. Their hope was in following the words of these shepherds who turn out to be wicked! Imagine not being able to trust those you thought were looking out for you. Imagine hearing that not only what they taught you was wrong; it was also destructive. At this point, wouldn't you be thinking, *Jesus, if that's true, what do I do? Whom can I trust? If I was so wrong about these men, how will I know whom to listen to?* The answer is to come to Jesus (vv. 7-10). Come through him, and you'll find protection from the thieves and robbers. Enter the flock of Jesus, and the religious leaders can no longer damage you. Jesus will guard you.

This isn't merely a first-century warning. There are still robbers and thieves attempting to crawl over the fence and into the church with the goal of doing as much damage as possible (Jude 3-4). Until Jesus returns, there will always be wolves that walk around disguised as sheep, and their selfishness will ravage the flock. You need to be careful to whom you listen and whom you follow. It's one of the reasons God has given the church pastors (Latin for *shepherds*). Pastors protect you from wolves (Acts 20:28-31). The greatest danger to your spiritual health will most likely come from someone claiming to be a Christian, someone who quotes a lot of verses and distracts you from the gospel of Jesus. That's why everything must center on Jesus Christ. He's our Shepherd. He bids us come through him into the fold. He's the gate, and the gate offers us protection, peace, and security from those who would through false teaching attempt to turn us from following the Shepherd.

Entering the flock of God through Jesus Christ not only protects us from danger, but it also protects us from hunger (v. 9). Some Christians only think of Jesus saving us from sin. They picture the Christian life as being pulled away from the danger of sin and corruption of any kind and locked, nice and secure, in the fold. They would be content to live in the safe confines of the sheepfold, never venturing out, never making contact with anything outside the fold. What good would it do to be protected from the dangers outside the fold if you're going to starve to death inside the fold? Jesus doesn't call us to a life of hunkering down safely inside the fold, protected from danger but starving to death. Jesus wants us to have life and have it abundantly. He protects us wherever we go, so through him we find the best pasture and feast to our hearts' content. The Christian life is not simply being saved *from* something. We're also saved *to* something.

We're not just protected from the destruction of sin. We're given the joy of walking with Jesus. That doesn't mean we constantly frolic in the meadow, where life is easy. Jesus doesn't promise us a trouble-free life. He promises us joy that is bigger and lasts longer than our troubles. Even when we walk through the valley of the shadow of death, we will not fear. Even when we feel like armies are encamped around us, Jesus will spread out a banquet table for us in the sight of those enemies. If you think Christianity is primarily about obeying rules, you're wrong. Christianity is about joy. God made us to enjoy him and his world. The first humans were only given one rule, and that rule was intended to protect their joy. God is not a cosmic bully, arbitrarily enforcing rules to make us miserable. God is infinitely happy, and he gives us rules to protect happiness, not prevent it.

If your life is about anything other than Jesus Christ, that thing will steal your joy (v. 10). It will rob you of the delight God wants you to have in Jesus. If you pursue anything as ultimate in your life other than Jesus, it will fail. But in Jesus Christ, regardless of your circumstances, you can discover unshakeable joy and abundant life—not an abundance of possessions or even an abundance of laughs but a life overflowing with joy in Jesus. He promises the closer we walk with him and the more intimately we follow him, the greater our joy will be and the fuller our lives will be. Jesus didn't call us out of the emptiness of sin to live in mediocrity. He called us to feast at his table, to rejoice in his presence. Stop wandering away from the Shepherd to seek out your own pasture and to find your own water. Every time you do, you will find the grass withered and the water bitter.

Jesus is the gate. Through him we rest in the safety of the fold and rejoice in the sweetness of the field. The false shepherds of Israel cast the sheep aside, endangering their lives, but Jesus, the good shepherd, lovingly gathers his sheep to himself and then guards them from all danger.

Jesus Gives His Life for His Sheep
JOHN 10:11-18

In one act we see most clearly the shepherd's care for the sheep. When the sheep are in imminent danger, the shepherd gives his life to save them. Jesus is different from the religious leaders in many ways. Jesus points to their relationship with the sheep and says in effect, "You're simply hired hands" (v. 12). To them tending the sheep was a job, a way to make extra cash. If tending the sheep is your job, what happens when the predator attacks the flock in the middle of the night? You run, and you don't look back! As long as you're faster than the slowest sheep, you're fine. Those sheep are not yours, and no job (and definitely no sheep) is worth losing your life. A hired hand loves his life more than he loves the sheep. But Jesus is not a hired hand. These sheep are his, and he loves them more than he loves his life. That's why he lays down his life to protect his sheep. Five times in four verses Jesus promises to lay down his life for the sheep (vv. 11,15,17,18).

Jesus is the hero of the story. When he sees the wolf coming, he doesn't run away. He steps in front of the sheep. He will not allow anything to hurt or harm his sheep. No price is too great to pay for his sheep. What are the dangers to the sheep that Jesus must fight?

The next day John saw Jesus coming toward him and said, "Here is the Lamb of God, who takes away the sin *of the world!"* (1:29; emphasis added)

Truly I tell you, anyone who hears my word and believes him who sent me has eternal life and will not come under judgment *but has passed from* death *to life.* (5:24; emphasis added)

Jesus, the Good Shepherd, gave his life to protect his sheep from predators—from sin, from judgment, and from death. He didn't die simply to be an example or to demonstrate the depth of his love. He died because his sheep were in real danger. He died in our place, and by his death we are saved (Isa 53:6). Where does that leave us? Are we shepherdless? I like the way John Piper says it: "The story doesn't end with a mangled shepherd lying dead among three dead wolves, and sheep scattered thirsting and starving in the desert" ("I Have Authority"). Jesus's death defeated sin and death and judgment because he did not stay dead (John 10:17-18). He arose and continues to shepherd his sheep. Jesus is a victorious, risen, and living shepherd.

If Jesus is the Good Shepherd, then what you need to do is simple: follow Jesus. Don't look elsewhere. Don't wander away. Recognize that in him we have everything we would ever need. When we're tired, he brings us to rest in green pastures. When we're thirsty, he guides us to the refreshing spring. When we're uncertain, he leads us on the paths of righteousness. When we're afraid, he comforts us with his presence. Follow the good shepherd. As you follow him, goodness and mercy will follow you all the days of your life, and on his timetable he will lead you to his house where you will dwell with him forever.

Reflect and Discuss

1. What image does God give to convey how he cares for his people?
2. Why does God appoint human shepherds for his people? How had the Israelite leaders failed this purpose?
3. How does God respond to the failure of the Israelite leaders in Ezekiel 34?
4. In what ways does Jesus care for his sheep?
5. Take time to reflect on the fact that Jesus knows and calls you by name. In what ways does this stir your emotions?
6. What significance is there in Jesus's knowing his sheep by name?
7. Why do Jesus's sheep follow him?
8. How is Jesus the gate for the sheep?
9. What have you been saved *from* and saved *to* as a Christian?
10. What hope does the formerly blind man, who was cast out of the synagogue, have in Jesus the good shepherd?

Unbelief Exposed

Main Idea: Jesus confronts unbelief, exposes it for what it is, and challenges unbelievers to believe on him.

I. **Jesus Exposes the Reasons for Unbelief (10:22-26).**
II. **Jesus Exposes the Consequence of Unbelief (10:25-31).**
III. **Jesus Exposes the Folly of Unbelief (10:32-42).**

Six percent of Americans believe the moon landing was faked. Another 5 percent are uncertain ("Conspiracy Theories"). If you were to walk down the street asking people if man walked on the moon, one out of every nine would say either "no" or "I don't know," which proves people are crazy. The conspiracy theorists remind me a bit of the religious leaders in Jesus's day. In spite of the overwhelming evidence that Jesus is the Messiah, they refuse to believe. They persist in unbelief despite all they see and experience.

In John 10 Jesus graciously exposes their unbelief. He speaks to a group of men and women who've heard him teach and seen his miracles, yet they persist in their opposition and antagonism toward him. This account takes place at the end of Jesus's public ministry. In the following chapters Jesus focuses primarily on teaching his disciples. What's so remarkable about this passage is that he doesn't leave the public eye before coming face-to-face with those who don't believe. One more time, he confronts their unbelief, exposes it for what it is, and challenges them to believe on him.

Jesus Exposes the Reasons for Unbelief
JOHN 10:22-26

The Jews begin this conversation with Jesus by asking a question that sounds innocent. They ask him who he is, and they beg him to answer clearly whether he's the Messiah—the Christ. It seems like a great request. Hopefully he'll set them straight. What a great opportunity for Jesus! They want to know who he is so they can believe on him (vv. 22-24).

But the spirit behind their question is not genuine. The word translated "surrounded" (v. 24) is only used four times in Scripture, and two of those times it refers to encircling armies. The reason they want him to state his identity plainly is not so they can believe but to have grounds to condemn him. They surround Jesus and want him to publicly declare he's the Messiah so they can string him up for blasphemy.

To this point in the Gospel of John, Jesus has only claimed the title of "Messiah" once in chapter 4 when he was speaking to the Samaritan woman. Why didn't he claim this title more often? He didn't claim the title because the Jews had a misunderstanding of the purpose of the Messiah's coming. They were looking for a political leader who would overthrow Rome (6:14-15). Even the religious leaders—the Pharisees and chief priests—were under this impression (11:48). Though Jesus hadn't used the term *Messiah*, his works and words make his identity clear (10:25). He's the promised Messiah, sent by God to redeem his people. There's no denying the miracles of Jesus, and they serve as an unmistakable sign that he's sent by God. Yet the Jews persist in their unbelief.

As the conversation continues, Jesus continues to expose their unbelief. He begins by eliminating their excuse. They place the blame for their unbelief on him, claiming he has kept them in suspense (v. 24). They essentially say, "It's your fault. You haven't made it clear. We don't know what to think." But they don't lack information. They've seen and heard enough to understand who he was and why he had come. Consider what we've studied in the Gospel of John, which records just a small sliver of Jesus's works.

Chapter 2—Jesus turned water into wine. After that, he went into Jerusalem and kicked the extortionists out of the temple, embodying the OT prophecies regarding the Messiah's zeal for the temple.

Chapter 3—John the Baptist testified that Jesus is the Messiah, and John's ministry is simply to point others to him. "He must increase," John said, "but I must decrease" (v. 30).

Chapter 4—Jesus healed the son of a royal official without ever taking a step in the direction of the child, who was sick and dying in another town.

Chapter 5—Jesus healed a man who had been lame for thirty-eight years. He then called God his Father and called himself both the Son of God and the Son of Man, the latter being a title for the Messiah found in the book of Daniel.

Chapter 6—Jesus miraculously fed five thousand men plus women and children. He then miraculously crossed a sea. The chapter ends with him calling himself the bread of life and the Son of Man.

Chapter 7—Jesus stood up at the Festival of Shelters and applied a messianic passage from Isaiah 55 to himself. He begged the watching crowds to come to him and receive the gift of the Spirit—a gift only the Messiah could give.

Chapter 8—Jesus continued to preach to those at the Festival of Shelters. This time he applied a messianic passage from Isaiah 4 to himself, promising the light of life to all those who walk in darkness. He also called God his Father and referred to himself as the Son of Man and I AM—the name of deity.

Chapter 9—Jesus healed a man born blind.

Chapter 10—Jesus applied the messianic promises about the coming of a good shepherd to himself, making clear that he fulfills them.

In case that's not clear enough, Jesus claimed repeatedly to have been sent by God and said he was doing the work of his Father. Their problem is not intellectual ignorance but spiritual ignorance. Jesus said in chapter 9 they're spiritually blind (9:39). They know what Jesus said and who he claims to be, but they are lost and in darkness. From a human perspective the reason they don't believe is because they're **unwilling** to embrace the truth about Jesus.

Jesus shows them a second reason for their unbelief. He just placed the responsibility on them for their unbelief, but then he shows them the divine perspective. The reason they don't believe is because faith has **not been granted** to them (10:26). Jesus interweaves human responsibility and divine sovereignty. We have a tendency to look at this verse and interpret it, "You are not part of my flock because you do not believe," but that's not what Jesus says. He says, "You don't believe *because* [for this reason:] you are not of my sheep." We don't believe to *become* God's sheep. We believe because we *are* God's sheep.

Maybe you're wondering why Jesus tells them this. It's easy for us to think this truth is inappropriate to share with someone who does not believe. We may think it gives them a built-in excuse for rejecting Jesus. But anyone looking for an excuse to ignore Jesus will find one. We can always rationalize what we've already made up our minds to do. This truth compels each of us to listen for the Master's voice. Jesus shows us our inability to save ourselves. Unless God gives us the ability to hear the voice of Jesus, we will not be able to hear it. We must recognize our

utter helplessness apart from Jesus to receive salvation and turn to him
alone. We don't do anyone a favor by suggesting they can in some way
assist God in saving themselves. This truth is pictured in the miracles
on either side of this passage. Could the blind man make himself see
(ch. 9)? Could Lazarus raise himself from the dead (ch. 11)? Can a
blind and dead sinner give himself sight and life? Only God can save.

Jesus Exposes the Consequence of Unbelief
JOHN 10:25-31

We see the consequence of unbelief by paying close attention to the
beautiful promises Jesus gives to those who are his sheep. Those who
believe are given a gift that can never be earned: eternal life (v. 28). The
opposite is true for those who do not believe. Death is their destiny. A
believer will never be separated from God and will be free to enjoy his
presence forever, but an unbeliever will be cut off from God forever; he
will never know and experience the abundant life Jesus promises. The
result of belief is safety and security in the presence of God. Jesus knows
you and protects you forever. You do not need to fear what may happen because the basis of your security is not in your 401k, your physical
strength, or your good works.

This passage powerfully argues for what theologians call "eternal
security" or "perseverance of the saints." It's the truth that if Jesus saves
you, you are saved for good. If Jesus makes you alive, you'll never die.
If Jesus gives you sight, you'll never go blind. If Jesus adopts you, you'll
never be alone. If Jesus takes you in his hands, you will be in those
hands beyond the bounds of time. When this age is a faint whisper in
the annals of time, Jesus will still be holding you safe and secure in his
hands. Nothing and no one can touch you there. In Mark 8:36 Jesus
asked, "For what does it benefit someone to gain the whole world and
yet lose his life?" The man who turns in faith to Jesus Christ gains his life
and in the process gains everything, but the one who persists in unbelief
loses everything, including his life for eternity. There's no safety apart
from Jesus Christ. There's only death and uncertainty.

These verses may cause fear in those who've not believed, but they
should bring believers tremendous hope, encouragement, and comfort.
If God has called us to his Son, nothing can ever pull us away from
him. The apostle Paul said nothing can separate us from the love of
Christ (Rom 8:35-39). Satan may attempt to convince us that our guilt

is too great for God to forgive, but our hope is Jesus's promise, not our performance.

How can Jesus make this promise of eternal security? He can because he and the Father are one (John 10:30). They're distinct in person but perfectly united in essence. We can rest in the person of Jesus Christ because he is divine. After Jesus made this claim of deity, the Jews attempted to kill him (v. 31). This is the third time (cf. 5:18; 8:59), each because he claimed equality with God. The Jews perfectly understand Jesus's claim to be God. Jesus would have been entirely justified to leave them, unhappy and unbelieving, to die in their sin, but before his public ministry ends, he makes one more call for them to believe on him by exposing the folly of their unbelief.

Jesus Exposes the Folly of Unbelief
JOHN 10:32-42

Jesus exposes their folly by reminding them of two things they've had to ignore in order to reach their conclusion: his works and God's Word. Jesus describes his works in a couple of different ways (v. 32). He calls them "good"—this term carries the idea of not just being morally excellent but also beautiful or praiseworthy. Imagine if Rembrandt went back to elementary school. He gets his report card and notices that among all of the As he has an F in art class. He goes to the kindergarten art teacher and spreads out all of his finest paintings on the table in front of her. All over the walls are plastered the scribbling and finger-painting efforts of kindergarten students. He points down at his priceless masterpieces. "Which one of these beautiful pictures," he asks, "is the reason I failed your class?" Here Jesus, the perfect Son of God, is living in the midst of a wicked, godless world. Every action, every word, and every conversation is spotless. Not only is he free from sin, but he travels around healing the helpless—restoring sight to the blind, making the lame walk, and curing the leper. He spreads his works out on the table in the sight of these men and says in effect, "Which one of these beautiful works is the reason you want to kill me?"

He adds a second phrase, which makes their indictment even sillier. He points out that these works are all "from the Father" (v. 32). So he's essentially asking, "Which beautiful work *of God* do you want to kill me over?" These men are so wrapped up in religion they miss the beauty and glory of the Son of God on display right in front of them. They're like a person who visits the Grand Canyon and is so fascinated by the pot-holes in the parking lot he fails to see one of the wonders of the world. Their religion—full of man-made requirements designed to impress God—is weak and worthless in the presence of Jesus. How weak a religion that opposes healing a blind man! How worthless a religion that wants to kill a man for helping the downcast and oppressed! They can't see how amazing Jesus is. They think Jesus is a man who is making himself God (v. 33). They've tragically reversed the truth. He's God who made himself a man. His display of power and grace can only be explained by God's becoming a man. Three times they've tried to kill Jesus, but Jesus still calls them to come to him to receive salvation from sin and death through him. He pleads with them to believe on him if for no other reason than the works he's been doing (vv. 37-39). He says, "There's only one explanation for what I have done: I've come from the Father, and I'm one with the Father. Believe on me! Don't persist in your unbelief" (my paraphrase). Would you offer salvation to people trying to kill you? Jesus does, and it's a good thing because each one of us is described as an enemy of God. Jesus in his grace pleads with them to turn from their sin and follow him.

They've ignored his works, and they've also ignored God's Word. They wanted to stone him because he called himself God—the Son of God (vv. 33,36). Jesus shows them how foolish they are by appealing to Psalm 82, particularly verses 6-7. This is a much-debated passage. Who is God referring to here? Some think he's talking to corrupt judges in Israel. Others view it as referring to angelic powers. Most scholars think he is talking to the nation of Israel, focusing on when God gave them the law on Mount Sinai. Regardless of to whom God is speaking in Psalm 82, he calls them "gods" and "sons of the Most High" because they're functioning as someone sent by him—someone acting on his behalf. If those who acted unjustly on God's behalf were called sons of God, how is it not appropriate for Jesus who came from God and did beautiful works for God to refer to himself as the Son of God?

Jesus subtly and sarcastically reminds them, "The Scripture cannot be broken" (v. 35). In other words, you can't set aside the law just because you don't like it. But that's exactly what they do. They ignore the testimony and character of Jesus. They disregard the works of Jesus and the Word of God, and they seek to harm him (v. 39). With their rejection the bulk of Jesus's public ministry comes to a close. It ends with rejection and unbelief. Jesus graciously called men to himself, revealing himself as the Messiah, but the religious men and women persisted in unbelief.

After their rejection, Jesus went away from the city, out into the pasture, away from the religious center, and called his sheep to follow him (vv. 40-42). Men and women there heard the truth about Jesus and believed. It really is that simple: belief or unbelief?

Reflect and Discuss

1. Why do the Jews ask Jesus one final time to tell them plainly whether he is the Messiah?
2. Why doesn't Jesus claim the title Messiah in this passage?
3. Why do the Jews have no excuse for their failure to believe Jesus is the Messiah?
4. What two reasons does John give concerning why the Jewish leaders don't believe?
5. What reason does Jesus give them for why they don't believe?
6. What promises does Jesus make for those who are his sheep?
7. Describe eternal security. What does this mean for you right now? How does it affect your life?
8. How can you respond to the lies of Satan that your guilt is too great for God to forgive?
9. How can Jesus make the promise of eternal security?
10. Would you offer salvation to those who were trying to kill you?

The Final Word

JOHN 11:1-44

Main Idea: When we learn to trust Jesus, we will experience the triumph of life over death.

I. **Mary's and Martha's Plan (11:1-16)**
II. **Mary's and Martha's Pain (11:17-37)**
III. **Jesus's Power over Death (11:38-44)**

When our plans fail, it hurts. In John 11 two sisters—Mary and Martha—have a great plan. They're confident it will work, but it doesn't. And they come face-to-face with the person who could have made it work, but he didn't. Through their failed plans and in the midst of broken hearts, they learn Jesus has something much bigger and much better than their plans. Jesus doesn't conform to their preconceived ideas, and it's a good thing because he knows what he's doing and he can do whatever he wants. When they learn to trust him, they see and experience things they could never have seen and experienced on their own.

Mary's and Martha's Plan

JOHN 11:1-16

Mary and Martha know Jesus well (vv. 1-2). That they send the note to Jesus shows a close relationship. They know their note will get to Jesus, and they know Jesus will want to know. The sisters have a plan (v. 3). They're telling Jesus about their situation so he will do something about it. They think, *If we tell Jesus Lazarus is sick, Jesus will heal Lazarus.*

When Jesus gets the message, he responds in a couple of headscratching ways: he says the sickness won't lead to death (v. 4), but we find out ten verses later (from Jesus's own mouth) that Lazarus is dead. Then Jesus, because he loves Lazarus and the sisters so much, decides to stay where he is and not go visit them (vv. 5-6). At first blush that's puzzling behavior. He does give a reason: the purpose of the illness is to glorify both him and the Father.

Nothing happens by chance. Nothing is without purpose. Whether sorrow, sickness, or death, nothing happens to you that God does not permit for a reason. You will encounter no situation in life in which God cannot be glorified. It doesn't matter if it's an impossible boss, a loveless marriage, a crushing tuition bill, or a dysfunctional family; God can be glorified in every situation. You need to learn to ask, no matter the situation, "How can I glorify God in this?" Our normal response is to ask, "What's the fastest way out of this situation?" Christian maturity is learning to look at a situation and knowing that, whatever you face, you face it so God can be glorified through you. Does that make it feel like your life is insignificant and you're a pawn in God's global chess game? On the contrary, this passage shows that the glory of God and the love of God are not at odds. Jesus stayed for two reasons: the glory of God (v. 4), and his love for the family (v. 5). God's glory and his love for you are not enemies. Reject the temptation to pit the two against each other. God's glory is displayed chiefly in his bottomless love for his people.

Was it unloving for Jesus to stay two extra days? If you were Mary and found out Jesus delayed, would it have *felt* unloving? It would have felt like betrayal. But your feelings are fallible. They are pathological liars. Your feelings say, "Jesus doesn't love you. See? He won't come. He won't act." Don't trust your feelings. Let the truth shape your emotions, not your emotions the truth.

Jesus decides to go visit Lazarus, but his disciples aren't keen on the idea, for good reason (vv. 7-8). I can imagine the disciples looking at Peter, and Peter stepping forward, clearing his throat, and saying, "Uh, Lord, have you forgotten what happened last time we were there? The religious leaders tried to kill you. I think getting that close to Jerusalem is a bad idea." Jesus responds with a metaphor (vv. 9-10). Just as it's safer to travel during the day when the world's light (the sun) is out, it's safe to travel with Jesus, the true light of the world. This is a subtle and sweet rebuke: "Thank you for your concern, but I have nothing to worry about. I am the light of the world, and the light won't be darkened until time runs out. I've still got time" (my paraphrase). He then lets them know why he wants to head to Judea. "Lazarus has fallen asleep," and Jesus wants to wake him up (vv. 11-16).

Why does Jesus call death "sleep"? He's showing them a distinctly different perspective on death. They fear death. They see death as the ultimate winner. It's why they don't want to go to Judea. Jesus sees death much differently. Death is no worse than sleep, and there's no reason to fear sleep. This is the reason he can say he's glad he waited for Lazarus to die. It's not because he dislikes Lazarus; it's because he knows death is powerless before him. He can wake Lazarus up from death. It is no harder for Jesus to rouse Lazarus from death than for you to rouse your child from bed. On second thought, Jesus may have the easier task.

I love Thomas's response. He's like Eeyore in *Winnie the Pooh*. I can almost hear him: "We might as well go and die with him" (v. 16; my paraphrase). Now, Thomas has earned the nickname of Doubting Thomas not only for this account but also because he doubts Jesus's resurrection. The nickname is unfair, however. I think we should call him "Logical Thomas." It's not illogical to think they might die with Jesus if they go up to Judea. Later on Jesus will die there, and eleven of the twelve disciples will die because of their faith in him. Thomas isn't crazy; he's logical. The problem is that our logic can't account for the power and plan of God. Human reasoning falls well short of the divine. Like Thomas we're tempted to believe only when we can figure it all out. I wonder how often our logic keeps us from seeing God do something miraculous. I wonder how often our critical thinking blinds us to God's glory.

Mary's and Martha's Pain
JOHN 11:17-37

By the time Jesus arrives in Bethany of Judea, Lazarus has been dead four days (vv. 17-18). The timing is not an accident. After four days there's no doubt Lazarus is dead. It's too long for it to be a mistake. It also allows a crowd of mourners to gather and witness the power of Jesus. However, before Jesus reaches their house, Martha comes out and meets him and expresses her disappointment (vv. 20-22). She had a plan. She called Jesus, and he could have fixed Lazarus, but he didn't come in time. Her intense disappointment reveals her deep confidence in Jesus. She knew, beyond any shadow of a doubt, that Jesus could have healed Lazarus. Now here he is four days late! Nevertheless, she still expresses great faith (v. 22). She essentially tells Jesus, "I don't know what you can do now, but I know you can do whatever you want."

Jesus responds with a simple statement with profound implications: "Your brother will rise again" (v. 23). Martha knows the Old Testament. She understands God's promise that this life is not all there is. She knows the grave is not the end (v. 24). But Jesus is talking about something even bigger, even more remarkable. Jesus says, "I am the resurrection and the life" (v. 25). He doesn't say, "I can resurrect people, and I have life." He says, "*I am* resurrection, and *I am* life" (emphasis added). Our hope is not in an event (resurrection) but in a person (Jesus). Nothing can hinder him from giving life because he doesn't *have* life; he *is* life. This is just one of the ways Jesus is different from you and me. You *have* life. He *is* life. You can lose your life. He cannot and will not lose his life. He laid it down, but his resurrection was proof that death could not take life from him.

Jesus then makes a promise that goes beyond what he's going to do for Lazarus (v. 26). What he does for Lazarus proves that he has the power to keep his promise. He promises that those who believe, though they die physically, will live on forever. Those who live spiritually will never have to worry about their spiritual life ending. Christians live with great hope for the future. We hope in Jesus Christ. We believe, like Martha, that he is the Son of God, come into the world, just as God promised, to rescue us from death and hell. We know that he is the only one we can trust with our lives, so we give our lives to him.

After Martha responds in faith, she goes to get her sister Mary (vv. 28-30). Mary says the same thing, word for word, to Jesus that Martha said (v. 32; cf. v. 21). How many times before Jesus got there had they discussed it? How many times in their grief had they said, "If only Jesus had been here, our brother would not have died"? This was their plan. They were sure Jesus would heal Lazarus. But he didn't, and it hurt.

The next few verses show Jesus's response to Mary's and Martha's sorrow (vv. 33-38). Jesus knows what he's going to do, but before he does it, he responds with deep compassion. Followers of Jesus are commanded in Romans 12:15 to "weep with those who weep." We do what Jesus did. We love others enough to enter their suffering. Oh, to be more like Jesus. Oh, to willingly enter others' suffering. The most remarkable part is that Jesus is going to do something that takes their suffering away, but before he fixes their problem, he joins their pain. He enters their grief before he exiles it. We can't be afraid to enter other people's pain. We need to be more like Jesus in this way. So often we shy away from the uncomfortable. We try to smooth over the brokenness. We need to, out of love, sit and weep with those who weep. Pray for a heart that breaks with heaviness when others suffer.

Jesus's Power over Death
JOHN 11:38-44

After entering their grief, Jesus moves to end it (vv. 39-42). Why did Jesus let this happen if he knew he was going to raise Lazarus from the dead? Why did he let those he loved experience four days of grief? Jesus is doing things we can never grasp. He's God. He's got purposes far beyond what we can even imagine. We don't know all that Jesus is doing, but we should never doubt his love for us, his desire for us to experience his glory, and his call for us to trust him. His love, his glory, and our need for faith are often most clear in the darkest times. This miracle was about something bigger than removing their grief. This miracle was about the power of Jesus over death. They were intimate witnesses to death's demise. It was high noon, and they were lining the streets to watch the duel between Jesus and death. That never would have happened if Jesus had submitted to the sisters' plan.

The end of the story is almost anticlimactic (vv. 43-44). It seems more should be said. Why so few words about the resurrection of Lazarus? Because if Jesus really is life, then this wasn't a fair fight. The outcome had been decided long ago. It was a mismatch from the moment Jesus was born. When Lazarus walks out of the tomb, he is still wrapped in the funeral garments. Ten chapters later we read about another resurrection. As big as this one is, that one's even bigger. If this is the first blow, the next resurrection is the knockout punch. Jesus is life, and death never stood a chance.

Jesus and death fought, and Jesus got the last word. Up to this point, death always won. Death would sweep in, and whoever was in the way lost. Death always got the final word. Even if a person seemed to rally, death would eventually silence him. Back in verse 4 Jesus told the disciples, "This sickness will not end in death." But it did, didn't it? Yes and no. For Lazarus the train stopped at death, but the journey didn't end there. The train started up again. Death didn't get the last word. The sickness didn't end in death but in resurrection.

Few passages are filled with more hope than this one, because no occasions feel more hopeless than when a person dies. It's all over. No more chances. No more hope. Death has spoken, and it is final. Not anymore! Jesus has spoken. He has the final word, and the final word is this: "I am the resurrection and the life" (v. 25).

Reflect and Discuss

1. How does Jesus's waiting to go to Lazarus display his love for Lazarus and the sisters?
2. What assurance can we find in this passage during our own times of suffering?
3. Why do the disciples not want to go to Lazarus? What is Jesus's response?
4. Why does Jesus call death "sleep"?
5. Does your response to Jesus's teachings ever mirror Thomas's? What hope do you have from this passage?
6. What does it mean that Jesus is the resurrection and the life? Why is this good news for his followers?
7. Why does Jesus weep at Lazarus's death?
8. Why does Jesus let Lazarus die? Why did he let those he loved experience four days of grief?
9. What is one explanation for how abruptly this story ends?
10. What did Jesus mean by "this sickness will not end in death"?

One Man's Death

JOHN 11:45-57

Main Idea: John answers the question of why Jesus died both from the perspective of the religious leaders and from God's perspective.

I. The Death of Jesus Was Politically Expedient (11:45-50).
II. The Death of Jesus Was Spiritually Effective (11:51-52).
   A. His death satisfied the just wrath of God.
   B. His death secured redemption for his children.

The cross is violent, bloody, and the pivotal moment in the Bible's overarching story; everything that came before the cross pointed ahead to it, and everything that has come after looks back. Our focus on the cruel and bloody death of Jesus Christ does not stem from an unhealthy fascination with violence. It flows from a proper understanding of God's Word. From this point forward the Gospel of John is focused on the cross. Beginning with the death and resurrection of Lazarus, the focus of this Gospel is the impending sacrifice of Jesus on the cross. The raising of Lazarus from the dead assures us of Jesus's power over death *before* he goes to the cross to die.

This passage contains a clear, powerful, and somewhat ironic instruction about the purpose of his death. Historically, the death of Jesus Christ cannot be denied. Too many valid sources record the death of Jesus of Nazareth on a cross. The real question revolves around its purpose. What was accomplished on the cross? This passage offers two perspectives on the death of Jesus: that of the religious leaders and that of God.

The Death of Jesus Was Politically Expedient
JOHN 11:45-50

After the resurrection of Lazarus, several people believed on Jesus (v. 45), but some present informed the religious leaders—the Pharisees—of what happened (v. 46). The Pharisees called the other religious leaders—the Sadducees—together for a meeting of the Sanhedrin (v. 47).

The Sanhedrin was the highest judicial body in Israel. They had both political and spiritual power but served under Roman authority. For them the power and popularity of Jesus was a significant problem. They accepted the eyewitness testimony as true and then went about trying to figure out how to stop Jesus (vv. 47-48). They couldn't bear the thought of a man running loose who could heal people and raise them from the dead. They didn't protest the authenticity of the healing. (They tried that when Jesus healed the man born blind—ch. 9—and it made them look foolish.) They say matter-of-factly, "This man is doing many signs" (v. 47). They acknowledge Jesus has supernatural power to raise the dead. Even their word choice is remarkable. They used the word *sign* (*semeion*), which means "an event which is regarded as having some special meaning; something which points to a reality with even greater significance" (Louw and Nida, *Lexicon*, 33.477). They acknowledge that the works of Jesus are so phenomenal that they must point to something more significant, yet they refuse to ask what the works point to. These religious leaders see all of these signs and fail to consider what's being advertised: Jesus is the Messiah. How do we explain their failure to see the truth? The answer is not a lack of information. Jesus gave the answer back in chapter 9 when he told them they were blinded by their sin.

Their unbelief is even more startling when you consider the occupation of these men. They each had years, if not decades, of religious service. These were supposed to be the most spiritual men in the nation. If we could have been present at the meeting, we would have listened as they opened the meeting in prayer. We would have been impressed by the priestly robes of the Sadducees and the phylacteries—little boxes containing Scripture—on the hands and foreheads of the Pharisees. All of this religion and all of this biblical knowledge were theirs, yet they were unable to see the glory of God's Son. You can be religious but lost. You can memorize Scripture and still be ignorant of its truth. You can say all of the right things but have a heart that has not been transformed by the power of Jesus Christ.

Their primary concern was maintaining control. Jesus threatened their position and influence. If people continued to believe Jesus was the Messiah, then Rome would sweep in and take away the leaders' authority. They would lose their position and their freedom. You could better translate the end of verse 48, "The Romans will come and take away *from us* both our place and our nation." Their concern wasn't for the people but for themselves. They were focused on maintaining their own positions of power. We see in them a clear and striking picture of the self-centeredness of empty religion. Empty religion—practiced by people who come to church, give money, say and do the right thing, and are moral but have no relationship with Jesus Christ—is always revealed by a person's focus. If someone has been truly converted and is following Jesus, his focus will be first on Jesus, second on other people, and finally on himself. But empty religion is focused first on me. It's based on my effort. It's about maintaining my good works. It's primarily concerned with my blessing and my safety. Ultimately, I am the one who receives the praise for it: "Look at all the good choices he's made."

A similar error is apparent when we begin to evaluate spiritual realities by how we will be affected. Their concern wasn't whether Jesus was right or good but how his actions would affect them. This is a dangerous path but one we so easily travel. When our decisions are not based on clear, biblical standards of holiness but on how they will affect our own comfort and convenience, then we're committing the error of the Pharisees and Sadducees. Their fear of loss of influence and loss of income pushed them to disobey God's will.

In response to their problem, Caiaphas, the high priest, offers a plan (vv. 49-50). Jesus was a problem, and problems need to be eliminated. With cunning and coldness, the high priest calls for Jesus's death. His statement reveals another reality of religion. Religion is self-centered and fear motivated, and it always leads to spiritual rationalization. Since it's not rooted in the unchanging grace of God, it will waver based on circumstances. We will make decisions based on our own perception of what benefits us—what we think keeps us in God's favor. Ultimately, religion is *our* attempt to maintain *our* position. It's rooted in what we believe others think about us and what we believe God thinks about us. So we begin to play this game: we look at an action that is wrong, and we begin to justify why it's really not that bad. What we're doing is coming up with a defense for our actions; we're justifying ourselves. Christian, our justification doesn't rest on us! It can't. Our justification comes through Jesus and him alone.

What Caiaphas is doing here is self-justification. The religious leaders wanted to kill an innocent man because it benefitted them—it was politically expedient—but they needed to come up with some type of justification. If they could justify it (their thinking goes), then God could not hold it against them. On the scales of good and bad, their good motive would outweigh the evil of the actual deed. Caiaphas's speech must have been convincing because they made plans to kill Jesus (v. 53). It's gone beyond impulsive attempts to stone him and become premeditated murder. However, Jesus avoided them until the appropriate time (v. 54). He would not die because of the whims and wishes of the religious establishment. His death was not the tragic death of a religious zealot. He would die at the time chosen by his Father. His life would not be taken from him, but he would willingly sacrifice it.

The Death of Jesus Was Spiritually Effective
JOHN 11:51-52

Caiaphas's words reveal a second perspective on Jesus's death. God planned Caiaphas's words to serve his own purpose. They held greater meaning than Caiaphas had planned. Caiaphas's intention was evil, but God had ordained the death of Jesus. Peter makes this point clearly during his sermon on the Day of Pentecost: "Though he was delivered up according to God's determined plan and foreknowledge, you used lawless people to nail him to a cross and kill him" (Acts 2:23).

God decided for Jesus to die. His death was not an accidental tragedy. It fulfilled God's eternal plan. But that doesn't get Caiaphas off the hook. He was not an unwilling puppet. We shouldn't look at him as a spiritual dummy with God's hand up his back moving his mouth. Once again we see the interplay between divine sovereignty and human responsibility. As John MacArthur wrote, "God sovereignly turned his wicked, blasphemous words into truth" (*John*, 484). The death of Jesus Christ may have been politically expedient for the leadership of Israel, but it accomplished more important purposes.

His Death Satisfied the Just Wrath of God

There's a key word that's easy to overlook both in Caiaphas's prophecy (John 11:50) and John's interpretation of it (vv. 51-52): *for*. You understand the significance a little more if you substitute the words "in place of" or "on behalf of." Jesus was dying in place of someone else. This is the language of temple sacrifice. The Gospel of John constantly points us to the Passover Festival, when lambs would be brought into Jerusalem and sacrificed in the temple. In chapter 1 John the Baptist twice introduced Jesus by saying, "Here is the Lamb of God" (vv. 29,36). Beginning in chapter 12, the rest of the Gospel takes place during the Passover Festival. To understand this prophecy, we need to understand what took place at Passover.

The first Passover is recorded in Exodus 12. God had just brought nine plagues on the Egyptians, warning Pharaoh to let the people of God go. Pharaoh wouldn't, so one final plague was coming: the killing of the firstborn. However, God made a provision so that his people would not have to suffer the death of their firstborn sons. They needed to take an unblemished lamb, kill it, and put some of its blood on the doorposts of their house. When God saw the blood, he would pass over them, and their sons would be safe. To save the life of their son, each family had to take the life of a lamb.

Another significant time on the Jewish calendar focused on a sacrifice. It was called the Day of Atonement. On that day two goats were brought to the priest. One of them was sacrificed to the Lord, and the other was released into the wilderness as the scapegoat. It's a beautiful picture of what was necessary to atone for the sins of man. The goat that was released pictured *expiation*: the removing or covering of sin. The goat that was slaughtered pictured *propitiation*: pacifying the just wrath of God. One goat would not have been enough. God could not just place the sin of the people on the back of the scapegoat and send it away. His holiness and justice demands blood be shed for the forgiveness of sin. Whenever sin is forgiven, someone must pay. If I get angry and smash your windshield and you forgive me, someone still pays. We sometimes view God's forgiveness as him sending our sin away into oblivion, but the reality is that our sin is still counted, just not against us. Sacrifice is necessary because of our guilt (Isa 53:6).

When Caiaphas prophesied that Jesus would die *for* or *on behalf of* the children of God, he reminds us that someone must satisfy the debt of sin. Only a perfect Lamb could do that and only by shedding his blood. Jesus was not a helpless child; he was a willing Savior. This sacrifice was not contrary to love; it was the ultimate expression of it. Through the perfect sacrifice of Jesus, the just wrath of God has been removed, and forgiveness can be offered and fellowship restored between Creator and creature. John Piper says it clearly:

> There was only one hope for me—that the infinite wisdom of God might make a way for the love of God to satisfy the wrath of God so that I might become a son of God. ("Foreword," 14)

His Death Secured Redemption for His Children

As John interprets Caiaphas's words, he adds a note of great certainty. The death of Jesus Christ "was going to" accomplish what God intended. It *was going to* save those it was intended to save, and it *was going to* gather them into one people. The certainty is unmistakable. The death of Jesus Christ did not secure the possibility of salvation. It actually secured salvation for those whom God had chosen—those referred to as the "children of God."

Sometimes Christians talk like the death of Christ simply made atonement for sins possible. That's not what the Bible teaches. The death of Christ actually atoned for the sins of those, both Jew and Gentile, who were the children of God. Who are the children of God? Those who were chosen by God and who responded by believing on the name of Jesus (1:12-13). In the classic book *Redemption Accomplished and Applied*, John Murray helps us better understand what was accomplished on the cross:

> Did Christ come to make the salvation of all men possible, to remove obstacles that stood in the way of salvation, and merely to make provision for salvation? Or did he come to save his people? Did he come to put all men in a salvable state? Or did he come to secure the salvation of all those who are ordained to eternal life? Did he come to make men redeemable? Or did he come effectually and infallibly to redeem? . . .
>
> What is offered to men in the gospel? It is not the possibility of salvation, not simply the opportunity of salvation. What is offered is salvation. To be more specific, it is Christ himself in all the glory of his person and in all the perfection of his finished work who is offered. And he is offered as the one who made expiation for sin and wrought redemption. He could not be offered as Savior and as the one who embodies in himself salvation full and free if he had simply made the salvation of all men possible or merely had made provision for the salvation of all. It is the very doctrine that Christ procured and secured redemption that invests the free offer of the gospel with richness and power. It is that doctrine alone that allows for a presentation of Christ that will be worthy of the glory of his accomplishment and of his person. It is because Christ procured and secured redemption that he is an

all-sufficient and suitable Savior. (*Redemption Accomplished and Applied*, 63, 65).

The death of Christ would gather all of his sheep into one fold with one shepherd. None would be lost. None would be forgotten. All would, by the power of the shepherd and through the offering of his life, be brought safely into the flock of God. We sing and preach and meditate on the death of Jesus, not to bask in the gory details but to celebrate the glorious victory. "Bearing shame and scoffing rude, in my place condemned he stood; sealed my pardon with his blood. Hallelujah! What a Savior!" (Philip Bliss, "Hallelujah! What a Savior!").

Reflect and Discuss

1. According to the Jewish leaders, why did Jesus die?
2. What caution should we take from the leaders' acknowledging the "signs" Jesus performs while still plotting to kill him?
3. Compare the empty religion of the religious leaders with the true faith of those who believe in Jesus.
4. How will the focus of a true follower of Jesus change?
5. Why can those who believe in Jesus have unchanging confidence despite circumstances?
6. Describe how this passage reveals both the responsibility of man and the sovereignty of God in salvation.
7. What did Jesus accomplish on your behalf on the cross?
8. Why is the preposition *for* in verses 50-51 so significant?
9. Why were two goats needed for the Day of Atonement sacrifices? How does Jesus meet those needs on the cross?
10. Why is it incorrect to speak of the cross as making atonement for sins *possible*?

The Gift

JOHN 12:1-11

Main Idea: Jesus receives a gift of great significance and promises it will never be forgotten.

I. **Mary's Gift Is a Reminder of His Impending Death.**
II. **Mary's Gift Is a Picture of Extravagant Love.**
III. **Mary's Gift Is an Illustration of Humble Service.**
IV. **Mary's Gift Is a Rebuke to Self-Centered Religion.**

If you were to take a minute and think about what gifts meant a lot to you, I bet you'd discover the most meaningful gifts were personal and sacrificial. When a person gladly sacrifices for your benefit, it shows the depth of his or her love for you. The gift is greater than the materials it's made from. It's a tangible demonstration of love.

In John 12 we find a gift of great significance. Jesus promises this gift will never be forgotten; wherever the gospel is preached, the story of this gift will be shared. In the previous chapter Jesus received a message that a good friend was sick, and because of his love for his friend, he waited to visit him until he was dead. Jesus arrives and interrupts the funeral by bringing his dead friend back to life, but the chapter doesn't end with the big celebration you might expect. If you were at a friend's funeral, what would you do if he rose from the dead? Once you picked your jaw up off the floor, you'd throw a party. You'd feast on all the casseroles intended for the postfuneral meal. The scene that follows the resurrection of Lazarus is not a party but a secret meeting where the self-righteous religious leaders decide Jesus needs to die. It's not until this meeting ends with a signed death warrant that we visit the small celebration for Lazarus.

Look who's sitting at the table with Jesus: Lazarus himself. What was Lazarus doing in the previous days? He was lying dead in the grave. What do you think the conversation was like at dinner? What would you say to Lazarus?

Lazarus is a picture of everyone who is a Christian. We find him, after his death, feasting in the presence of Jesus. That's our destiny. As with Lazarus, death holds no finality for us. Death is the appetizer for a feast with Jesus. The main focus of this account is not Lazarus but the gift Mary gives to Jesus. What is the significance of her gift?

Mary's Gift Is a Reminder of His Impending Death

John includes many markers in his retelling of these events that force us to see this act against the background of the sacrificial death of Jesus, including the accounts on either side of this story. Before we read about this gift, we're told of the secret meeting where the religious leaders decide to kill Jesus (11:53). Immediately following this gift, we discover that the chief priests have issued a death warrant for Lazarus as well (12:10).

The next clue is the mention of Passover (12:1). Passover was when each Jewish man brought a lamb into Jerusalem to be offered in his place. Jesus is the Lamb of God: he's our Passover Lamb, whose death will take away our sins.

Next, the description of Lazarus is "the one Jesus had raised from the dead." One of the main purposes of the account of Lazarus's resurrection was to give us confidence in Jesus's victory over the grave. Jesus has the power to defeat his own death.

What about the gift itself? The gift is ointment that normally serves as a burial spice. After a person died, perfumes and spices would be placed on his body to prepare it for burial. As Mary prepares Jesus's body for the coming grave, her gift prepares us for his death.

In verse 4 we're introduced to Judas Iscariot. He's called the one "who was about to betray" Jesus. That description points us to a night less than a week away when Judas will lead a group of soldiers and religious leaders to the garden of Gethsemane. There he will give Jesus a kiss of betrayal, starting a chain of events that ends fewer than twenty-four hours later with Jesus's corpse being taken off the cross.

Finally, the last recorded words from dinner are Jesus's own reminder (v. 8): "But you do not always have me." He reminds them he came into the world to lay down his life as the perfect sacrifice for the sins of mankind.

This gift offered by Mary serves a similar function to the gifts we give at Christmas. Christmas isn't a celebration of our generosity. The gifts we give point to the greatest gift ever given: a Savior.

Mary's Gift Is a Picture of Extravagant Love

The gift amounted to a Roman pound, which converts to between eleven and twelve ounces—about the size of a can of soda. John describes it as "expensive" (v. 3). It was equivalent to three hundred denarii (v. 5)—one denarius was equal to a day's wage for the average worker. The cost was approximately one year's salary. The gift is "pure"—it's not an imitation, not a cheap knockoff. Her gift reminds us of the surpassing value of Jesus Christ. Mary realizes it's worth it to give all to Jesus. She doesn't pick the cheap perfume. She doesn't dab a little bit on the inside of his wrists. She brings out the best, most extravagant, most expensive ointment of the day, and she pours every ounce on him. Her gift is her way of yelling from the top of a mountain, "Jesus is worth it!"

The example of Mary forces us to consider what a right response to Jesus looks like. If we really see Jesus for who he is—the almighty, infinite God of the universe who condescended to take on human form so that he could die a brutal death in the place of his rebellious creatures—if we understand his beauty—that he is the all-satisfying, wondrous, joyful God who promises to give peace, blessing, and satisfaction in himself to those who come to him—if we get this, how can we possibly withhold anything from him?

When was the last time you demonstrated extravagant love for him? What does extravagant love for Christ look like now? He's not physically present. We can't copy Mary's act by giving him tens of thousands of dollars' worth of perfume. There's not a simple, one-size-fits-all answer. Her extravagant love was revealed in the fact she didn't robotically respond to someone's command. She knew him and loved him so much she did the hard work of thinking about what he would love and how she could demonstrate her love to him.

Mary's Gift Is an Illustration of Humble Service

In verse 3 Mary pours this perfume on Jesus's feet. Twice John mentions it, and then he states that she wiped his feet with her hair—an act of great humility. In spite of her extravagant love, Mary never lost sight of the glory of Jesus. Her act of love was carried out with deep reverence. What a contrast to the arrogance of the religious leaders in chapter 11, who think they have the right to kill an innocent man.

The emphasis on the washing of Jesus's feet points us ahead to the next chapter where Jesus humbles himself and washes the feet of his disciples; then he commands them to go and do likewise. Mary exhibits the rare combination of generosity and humility. She gives a tremendous gift with no desire for the spotlight. How easily our most sacrificial acts of love can turn into a platform for self-promotion. Like Mary, may we give extravagantly, all the while directing the glory and praise to Jesus.

Mary's Gift Is a Rebuke to Self-Centered Religion

John intends for us to see a contrast between Mary and Judas. John often portrays the truth by using contrasts. His favorite is the contrast between light and darkness.

For everyone who does evil hates the light and avoids it, so that his deeds may not be exposed. But anyone who lives by the truth comes to the light, so that his works may be shown to be accomplished by God. (3:20-21)

We see this perfectly illustrated by two who attended the banquet. Judas does wicked things and hates (even condemns and then betrays) the light. Mary has come to the light, and it's clear her works have been carried out by the grace and power of God. Mary's love rings authentic. Judas is a hypocrite. His cold, faithless heart is masked by a cloak of self-righteous piety.

Judas serves as a warning. He looked and spoke the part of a disciple. He could have supported his suggestion to give the money to the poor with hundreds of Old Testament verses. However, his motive was self-centered. He was only concerned about what he could get from Jesus. Judas looks good on the outside. At a glance he seems moral, but money and possessions are more important to him than Jesus. What did he do when faced with the decision to give up his stuff or give up Jesus? Stuff wins. Sorry, Jesus. Mary, on the other hand, viewed possessions as an opportunity to bless Jesus. How do you view possessions?

In verse 3 John says, "the house was filled with the fragrance of the perfume." Love has an undeniable fragrance, and when you smell it, you want to linger there. You can't get enough. Mary's gift helps us catch the faint whiff of love and leaves us longing for more. We wait for the day when the fragrance of love fills the whole world.

Reflect and Discuss

1. Picture Lazarus at the festival. How might all of Jesus's followers one day resemble Lazarus?
2. How should the reader understand the significance of John's mention of the Passover as this story starts?
3. How might Mary's gift remind us of Christmas?
4. Why was Mary's gift itself so significant? How was it foreshadowing the cross?
5. Why is Mary's gift a picture of extravagant love?
6. How does Mary's example help us consider what a right response to Jesus looks like?
7. What might extravagant love for Christ look like now?
8. When was the last time you demonstrated extravagant love for Jesus?
9. How does John contrast Mary and Judas?
10. Take inventory of your life. How do you view your possessions? If Jesus asked you to give up everything, would it be easy or hard? Why?

A Different Kind of King

JOHN 12:12-36

Main Idea: Jesus is the victorious King, but his victory is not what the crowds anticipated.

I. His Victory Is Not Political.
II. His Victory Comes through Death.
III. His Victory Honors Another.

What image do you have in your mind of a good leader? What does Prince Charming look like? He's tall, dark, handsome, and comes riding in on a majestic white stallion. I've never heard a version of the story where a short, pudgy, balding, middle-aged prince comes panting and wheezing to the rescue. We've fashioned a picture of what the quintessential hero looks like. Anything else just doesn't work.

The Jews living in the time of Jesus had fashioned a picture of the Messiah that would rival any Disney hero: a tall, dark, and handsome king riding into Jerusalem on a white stallion, ready to lead the forces of Israel in overthrowing the tyranny of Rome. That's what they wanted; that's what they were hoping and longing for. When Jesus appears on the scene and people begin to wonder if he's the Messiah, they expect him to raise an army to lead them to a great military victory. They are waiting for him to fulfill the promise of a victorious king. Earlier in the Gospel of John, after Jesus fed the five thousand, they wanted to take him by force and make him king. They had been waiting and watching and hoping for this powerful and victorious king to swoop in and rescue them; now he's here. What's he waiting for?

Jesus is the Messiah and has come as the victorious King, but not in the way they expect. They selectively read the promises of the Old Testament. All they saw was a political savior for Israel, but the promise of a victorious king was far greater and far more comprehensive than they understood. The Messiah came to bring spiritual salvation from sin's tyranny, not political salvation from the tyranny of Rome. The problem was the Jews' vision: they were shortsighted. They thought the big enemy was Rome (11:48). Jesus wasn't concerned with the Romans.

He was focused on enemies far greater and far more powerful: he came to defeat sin and death. Jesus is the victorious King prophesied in the Old Testament, but his victory takes a form the Jews never anticipated. As Jesus enters the city, the people see him as their king (vv. 12-13). They call him "the King of Israel," but their desire for a king and the King's actual purpose are worlds apart. Jesus is the victorious King, but his victory is not what the crowds expected.

His Victory Is Not Political

Everything the crowd says is correct. It's biblical and accurate. They quote from Psalm 118:25-26. They cry, "Hosanna," which means "Save us, Lord." Then they take the next verse and apply it to Jesus: "Blessed is he who comes in the name of the Lord!" Everything they say has messianic overtones. They recognize Jesus for who he is. He's the anointed King. However, their understanding of his kingship is too narrow. John has shown us on two different occasions they wanted a political savior (chs. 6 and 11), but Jesus's coming supersedes any political concerns.

When political figures came to Jerusalem, every aspect of their entrance was choreographed to demonstrate power and authority. Their entrance was announced by trumpets. They were preceded by soldiers in full military regalia. Finally, they made their entrance riding on a brilliant white stallion or in a gleaming gold chariot pulled by magnificent horses.

Jesus comes with no soldiers. He doesn't choose a warhorse but a young donkey. He shows what kind of King he really is. In verse 15 John quotes Zechariah 9:9-10 about the promise of a coming King. This prophecy says a lot about the kind of King who was coming. He is different from the average political ruler. The choice of the donkey reveals this King will achieve his victory through humility. The salvation he secures will come through meekness. He doesn't come to destroy other nations but to "proclaim peace to the nations." The Jews expect the Messiah to liberate them, crushing the nations in the process, but the King comes to bring peace to all nations.

God's plan has always been for all the nations, not just Israel, to bow in worship before him. In the book of Acts, the gospel spreads to both Jew and Gentile and brings them into this new, unique community of faith called the church. But the seeds had been sown throughout the Old Testament. In Genesis 12:3, God promised Abraham that "all the peoples on earth will be blessed through you." Isaiah prepares the people for the coming king and calls him "a light to the nations" (42:6). Through him

God's salvation will reach the end of the earth (49:6). The Messiah was never only a king for Israel. He was coming to call worshipers from every nation and every tribe and every people to the true God. Though Israel was hoping for a nationalistic, political savior, God sent Jesus to be a light to all men—to call both Jew and Gentile to saving faith through his work. This vision fuels the Christian commitment to global missions. We have a passion to see people from every nation turn in faith to Jesus Christ and worship him with their lives. Too often we view missions as an event—I go on a *missions* trip—or an occupation—we support *missionaries*—when the Bible calls us to view missions as an adjective to describe each believer's life. Every day we are called to *missional* living, spending every moment on a mission to share the gospel. Cross-cultural, worldwide missions should be an overflow of our daily mission in the neighborhoods, offices, and relationships God has given us. Our mantra should be, "I will go where I can, send others to go where I can't, and pray diligently for the gospel to be fruitful in both places."

We shouldn't expect our vocational missionaries to be faithful in missions overseas if we aren't faithful in missions in our communities. As we faithfully share the gospel, we have confidence that men and women will respond in faith because Jesus sets before us the vision of a kingdom filled with worshipers from every tribe, tongue, and nation. The fulfillment of Zechariah's prophecy is also seen in the account that immediately follows Jesus's entry into Jerusalem. The King who comes to proclaim peace to men and women from every nation is sought out by Greek-speaking Gentiles (John 12:20-21). Jesus fulfills the promise that the Messiah will be a light to the Gentiles. His kingdom isn't one nation but is worldwide and includes both Jew and Gentile.

The religious leaders couldn't see past their own situation. They missed the massive promise of God to bring together a people from all nations to worship and serve him. Jesus didn't come to overthrow political leaders. God has been and continues to be sovereign over kings and nations. Jesus is building a global nation: Jew and Gentile, slave and free—all released from the shackles of sin and brought into the people of God by the work of the promised King.

In verse 32 Jesus again affirms that his kingdom will include "all people," not just Jews. As we read his promise in the larger context of this passage, we understand he's not suggesting all men will be saved or all men will be drawn to him in some way. He's clearly saying that, just as God promised in the Old Testament, his death will effectively draw *all* men—that is, not just Jews but men and women from *all* nations—to him for salvation.

His victory is not political, and neither is our hope. Be a good steward of your vote. Be wise in selecting leaders. But do so without fear. Jesus isn't on the ballot. We don't vote on the King of kings. Our hope has never been and will never be in Washington, DC. Our hope is sitting on a throne in heaven.

His Victory Comes through Death

Charles Ross Weed wrote a thought-provoking poem contrasting Jesus and Alexander the Great:

> Jesus and Alexander died at thirty-three,
> One died in Babylon and one on Calvary.
> One gained all for self, and one Himself He gave.
> One conquered every throne, the other every grave.
> When died the Greek, forever fell his throne of swords,
> But Jesus died to live forever Lord of lords.
>
> Jesus and Alexander died at thirty-three.
> The Greek made all men slaves, the Jew made all men free.
> One built a throne on blood, the other built on love.
> The one was born of earth, the other from above.
> One won all this earth to lose all earth and Heaven.
> The other gave up all that all to Him be given.
> The Greek forever died, the Jew forever lives.
> He loses all who gets and wins all things who gives. (Quoted in
>   Hughes, *John*, 303)

What a unique King is this King of Israel. His kingdom and reign are unlike any earthly kingdom. Not only is it not political, but it was secured when the King died. Most kings enter the city to the cheers of their subjects on their way to take a seat on the throne and to reign. Jesus entered the city to the cheers of the crowd so that he could take his place on a cross and die. The coming of the Greeks to see him signals that the time for Jesus to die is coming soon. The hour appointed for Jesus's death on the cross is here. Jesus lived to die. His midnight birth in Bethlehem was the first step on the road to Calvary.

The Jews missed this when they read the Old Testament. In Isaiah 52, Isaiah is prophesying about the one who would come to bring salvation to God's people. He refers to him as the Servant. The Jews read about this Servant and focused on verses like 13. They thought, *Great! A king to rule over Israel. A king who is high and exalted.* They could picture him, greater than David and Solomon, sitting and ruling from the throne in Jerusalem, all other kings bowing before him and bringing him gifts. What they missed was how this King would achieve victory (Isa 52:14; 53:2-3). They were looking for the highly exalted King to bring salvation from pagan nations, but God promised them a King who would suffer to bring salvation from sin's penalty. Victory would cost the King his life.

Jesus taught his death in a parable after the Greeks came to him (John 12:24). Jesus's death will reap a great harvest. Jesus is going to die so that others can live. His death makes it possible for others to experience life. He will achieve victory over the grave by going to the grave himself and then vanquishing its hold through his resurrection. We are the great recipients of Jesus's death. He died so each one of us could have life. He died in your place. Don't ever get over that. Don't let his death become routine to you. We must not minimize the horror of Jesus's death (v. 27). Though he came into the world to die in our place on the cross, his death was not simple or easy. He took upon himself the curse that our sin demanded. He refers to his death in verse 32 as being "lifted up from the earth," that is, death by crucifixion. "Christ redeemed us from the curse of the law by becoming a curse for us, because it is written, Cursed is everyone who is hung on a tree" (Gal 3:13). When Jesus hung on that cross, he was *cursed* in our place. The full fury of God's wrath toward sin was poured out on him. For the first and only time, the perfect fellowship that existed between Father and Son was torn apart, so that Jesus in deep anguish would cry, "My God, my God, why have you abandoned me?" (Matt 27:46). R. C. Sproul describes the cry of Jesus:

> This cry represents the most agonizing protest ever uttered on this planet. It burst forth in a moment of unparalleled pain. It is the scream of the damned—for us. (Quoted in Mahaney, *Living*, 89)

This is the kind of King God promised—a King who would lay down his life so we could be rescued. He is a King who would take the punishment we deserve so we could enjoy a life we do *not* deserve. Like a grain of wheat falling into the dirt and producing a harvest, Jesus refuses to stay in the ground. He crushes death by rising from the grave. He wins. Death is defeated and Jesus reigns over everything.

Jesus then turns and applies the principle of the seed to his disciples. He calls every disciple to follow his example (John 12:25-26). Listen to John Piper's helpful explanation:

Here the destination is eternal life. And you can miss it by loving your life—that is, by making your goal in life to be safe and secure and comfortable and surrounded only by pleasant things. That is the pathway to perishing. Or, Jesus says, you can take another path and arrive at eternal life. That path is called hating your life in this world. Notice that he adds "in this world." Hating your life in this world means that you will choose to do things that look foolish to the world. You will deny yourself things, and take risks, and embrace the path of suffering for the sake of love. This, Jesus says, will lead to eternal life, not death. ("Where I Am")

How is it possible to hate our life in this world? The answer is in verse 26: we follow Jesus. We don't focus on ourselves and our situations. We pursue Jesus with every fiber of our beings. The way to love your life is to focus exclusively on yourself, and the way to hate your life is to focus exclusively on Christ. Seek him and you will deny yourself. Jesus holds out a great motivation to seek him and hate yourself: we will be where he is, and we will be honored by the Father. Great joy and reward come from moving our attention from our own comfort and well-being and instead living lives of radical commitment to the only one who is worthy of it.

My goal in life is to help people find joy in Jesus; it's the only kind of joy that lasts. Here's how you find joy: die to yourself. Die to little dreams. Die to empty routines. Die to playing life safe. Die to protecting your reputation. Die to selfish, small living. Die to stingy self-centeredness. Die. Only then can you live, and only living brings joy.

His Victory Honors Another

Jesus is a King who glorifies someone else (v. 28). As Jesus walked the earth, he focused on doing what glorified his Father. In chapter 8 Jesus said he always does the things pleasing to his Father (v. 29) and that he did not come to seek his own glory (v. 50). The ultimate reason Jesus came to earth was for the Father's glory. Everything that was, is, and will be is working to glorify God. He is worthy of all the praise, honor, and glory that can ever be offered. The universe and every creature in it is designed for the glory of God. That doesn't change at the cross. The cross is not first about us. We are glad recipients of what was accomplished, but we are not the focus.

Here is an essential difference between genuine Christianity and the empty religion Jesus condemns: genuine Christianity has as its overarching goal the glory of God. Christianity is God centered. Religion is man centered. Religion revolves around man's position, man's influence, man's perspective, and man's work. Religion is all about me, what I feel I need, and what I do. Christianity is all about God, who he is, and what he says. We learn about true Christianity from Jesus Christ. He shows us what it means to live for the glory of God. What would your life look like if you demonstrated complete commitment to the glory of God like Jesus did? Complete commitment—every single motive, thought, and action of every single minute, hour, and day. The life of Jesus shows the world that God is worthy of our praise and affection. What does your life show?

Jesus glorifies God, especially in the cross (12:31-32). In the cross God demonstrates his justice. God would be a wicked Judge if he excused our wickedness. How could his love for sinners be reconciled with his justice? The answer is the cross. At the cross justice and mercy met in the body of Jesus Christ. In that act God judged our sins by executing justice on Jesus. This is good news for those who will be saved, but it's bad news for those who reject Jesus. If you reject Jesus, the cross has sealed your fate; your rejection of God's perfect sacrifice means you'll have to bear sin's penalty yourself. Since you have sinned against an infinitely holy God, your penalty will be infinitely terrible.

Jesus's death glorifies God by demonstrating his holiness and by defeating Satan. Though it appeared to be the opposite, Satan's ultimate defeat was accomplished on the cross. The cross was his moment of bruising Jesus's heel, but just as God promised Adam and Eve, the King crushed the serpent's head. When Jesus rose from the grave, he liberated us from the grip of sin. Sin and condemnation no longer have power over us who have been rescued. The cross assured the victory of Jesus and sealed the defeat of Satan (Col 2:15).

Jesus's death also brings glory to God by reconciling sinners to God. When Jesus is lifted up, he will draw people to himself. God's mercy and compassion are seen in saving those who do not deserve it. Sinclair Ferguson writes,

> The cross is at the heart of the gospel; it makes the gospel good news. Christ died for us; He has stood in our place before God's judgment seat; He has borne our sins. God has done something on the cross which we could never do

for ourselves. But God does something *to us* as well as *for us* through the cross. He persuades us that He loves us. (*Grow in Grace*, 58; emphasis original)

Are you persuaded God loves you? What more could he do to demonstrate his love for you than offer his Son in your place?

Jesus, our victorious King, offered his life to bring his Father glory, yet in giving his life on the cross, the Father glorified him as well. In verses 16 and 23 we read that in the cross Jesus would be glorified. In the cross God would reveal to the world the matchless worth of his Son.

This section ends with an invitation from King Jesus (vv. 35-36). Our King is not barricaded in the castle, cold and distant from his lowly subjects. He's not your typical king. As Jesus heads to the cross, on his way to die he turns to invite us to come to him and receive the blessings his death will bring. He begs us to believe in the light, to become sons of the light. Listen to the words of Jesus. He invites you to come out of the darkness of sin and death and come to the light. Jesus offers you a home and an inheritance, a seat at God's royal table, and entrance into a kingdom of love and grace.

Reflect and Discuss

1. When you think of a hero, what image comes to mind?
2. Who do the crowds believe Jesus is? What were they expecting Jesus to do?
3. Why were the Jews so wrong in their understanding of what the Messiah would be and do?
4. How is Jesus better than any king the Israelites could have hoped for or imagined?
5. Why does Jesus ride in on a donkey rather than a warhorse?
6. What Old Testament texts show the Messiah would come for all nations?
7. How does Galatians 3:13 give us further understanding of the words of Jesus in verses 31-32?
8. What does it mean to hate your life in this world? Why would anyone do this?
9. What is the overarching goal of Christianity?
10. What would your life look like if you demonstrated complete commitment to the glory of God as Jesus did? Would anything be different?

The Theology of Unbelief

JOHN 12:37-50

Main Idea: Jesus explains why the crowds persist in their unbelief in spite of witnessing his many miracles.

I. **What Is Unbelief?**
II. **Why Don't People Believe in Jesus?**

God used George Whitefield in a way seldom seen in this world. He was the main instrument in the spiritual revival known as the Great Awakening, which swept across the United States in the mid-1700s. Whitefield was also good friends with Benjamin Franklin. Their friendship began when Whitefield came to Philadelphia in 1739 and lasted until his death in 1770. During the course of this thirty-one-year friendship, Franklin was the primary publisher of all of Whitefield's sermons and journals. Forty-five times Whitefield's sermons were reprinted in Franklin's newspaper, *The Pennsylvania Gazette*, and eight times the sermon filled the entire front page. Franklin published ten editions of Whitefield's journals and sold thousands of reprints of Whitefield's sermons.

Their relationship extended beyond a business relationship. On more than one occasion when Whitefield came to Philadelphia, he stayed with Franklin in his home. When some of the religious elite criticized Whitefield in another local paper, Franklin wrote a rebuttal. His support for Whitefield, along with a regular correspondence between the two, continued for the next thirty years. Despite their friendship and Whitefield's continued presentation of the gospel, Franklin never responded in faith. In his autobiography Franklin wrote about Whitefield: "He used sometimes to pray for my conversion, but never had the satisfaction of believing that his prayers were heard" (quoted in Isaacson, *Benjamin Franklin*, 113). How do we explain Franklin's rejection of the gospel? He heard and read hundreds of the sermons of America's greatest evangelist. He spent hours with him discussing the gospel. He received dozens of letters over the span of thirty years, yet he was unmoved. Why didn't Benjamin Franklin believe? Why does anyone reject the gospel of Jesus Christ?

As Christians, we have a strong desire to call men and women in faith to Jesus. Because of God's grace, we understand the joy that comes from a restored relationship with our Creator. Our methods in calling men and women to faith will flow from our understanding of unbelief. If we don't know the answer to why people choose not to believe, then we'll constantly be asking the question, Will they believe if we do this? Can we convince them to believe if we try that? Our theology determines our methods.

Though the crowds had seen and witnessed so many of Jesus's miracles, they persisted in their unbelief. This is exactly what John prepared us for in the opening of his Gospel: Jesus "came to his own, and his own people did not receive him" (John 1:11). This passage answers the two most important questions about unbelief.

What Is Unbelief?

It's easy to equate unbelief with indecision. Have you ever spoken with one of your children and afterwards turned to your spouse and asked, "Do you believe her?" If you're not certain, you'll do some investigating. You may call another child in and get his account of the situation, or you'll call the same child back in and ask some deeper, more probing questions. In this situation your unbelief is really indecision. You'll know whether you believe your child when you get more information. That's not what unbelief means in this context. Their unbelief is not the result of a lack of information. They've seen and heard enough to make a well-informed decision. *Unbelief is the conscious rejection of God and his Word.* That's how Jesus defines unbelief. John 12:44-50 contains a summary of Jesus's message in which he emphasizes the close relationship between himself and his Father and between himself and his words. He's making the point that choosing not to believe in him means rejecting God himself (v. 44).

Belief in Jesus is equivalent to embracing God; to choose unbelief is to willfully reject God. Notice how closely Jesus ties himself to God in these verses:

- To *believe* in Jesus is to *believe* in God (v. 44).
- To *see* Jesus is to *see* God (v. 45).
- To *listen* to Jesus is to *listen* to God (v. 49).

If you fail to turn to Jesus in faith, don't think you'll be accepted by God. In fact, if you choose not to believe in Jesus, then God will judge you for your unbelief on the last day (v. 48). These words from Jesus force us to recognize the seriousness of unbelief. There's no way to stand accepted before God apart from faith in Jesus Christ.

Unbelief is the conscious rejection of God and his Word. Jesus draws a close relationship between himself and his words:

> *If anyone hears my words* . . . *The one who rejects me and doesn't receive my sayings has this as his judge: The word I have* spoken.
> . . . *For I have not spoken on my own, but the Father himself who sent me has given me a command to say everything I have said. I know that his command is eternal life. So the things that I speak, I speak just as the Father has told me.* (12:47-50; emphasis added)

God always moves and works by his word. Beginning in Genesis 1, God brought forth life by his word. Throughout the Old Testament God's word has been the pathway to life and blessing. In the New Testament we're told, "Faith comes from what is heard, and what is heard comes through the *message* about Christ" (Rom 10:17; emphasis added). God has always worked through his word. He has always used his word to call men to life and salvation. Therefore, to believe in Jesus means we accept and embrace the word of God. Unbelief, then, is the rejection of the word of God. It comes in many forms—from outright criticism and denial to neglect and questions about relevance—but the simple truth is that to reject Jesus's word is to reject his person. You cannot have Jesus without embracing his teaching on everything from false religion to judgment to hell. You can't pursue a relationship with God apart from Jesus, and you can't pursue a relationship with Jesus apart from his word.

Why Don't People Believe in Jesus?

This is the harder question to answer. In spite of overwhelming evidence that substantiated the claims of Christ, why did most Israelites not believe? The answer is multidimensional. Unbelief is not due to intellectual deficiency or a lack of knowledge. Unbelief is the response of a heart in rebellion against God. At the 2007 Shepherd's Conference Mark Dever said, "Unbelief never involves the mind alone; it is a spiritual state." Unbelief is the rebellious response of a man's heart. No amount of external pressure or coercion can ever make a person believe. That's why Christianity is not a religion that spreads by the sword. We could make people utter some form of a confession, but forced profession would be worthless, powerless, and empty. Unbelief stems from the heart of man. Any study of unbelief must begin by acknowledging the sinfulness of man. Bishop J. C. Ryle wrote,

> The prevalence of unbelief and indifference in the present ought not to surprise us. It is just one of the evidences of that mighty foundation-doctrine, the total corruption and fall of man. How feebly we grasp and realize that doctrine. We only half believe the heart's deceitfulness. (Quoted in Pink, *John*, 688)

John assigns the guilt of unbelief to man. Even the way he phrases verse 37—"*Even though* he had performed so many signs in their presence, they did not believe in him" (emphasis added)—makes clear they are culpable for their persistent refusal to believe in Jesus. The responsibility for rejecting Jesus as Savior falls squarely on the shoulders of unbelievers. They consciously reject salvation found only in Jesus Christ (cf. 3:19-20).

The depravity of man is not the only reason John provides for their unbelief. He says their unbelief is necessary in order to "fulfill the word of Isaiah the prophet" (v. 38). Their unbelief and rejection of Jesus were part of his substitutionary suffering for those who would believe. The first passage from Isaiah that John quotes is 53:1, where we find a detailed prophecy about how Jesus would suffer and die in the place of sinners. It was necessary for some to reject him so he could take his place on the cross and die the death we deserve. Jesus needed to die. He came to die. He did not come to earth to be cheered, accepted, and embraced by everyone. If that had happened, he never would have fulfilled the ultimate purpose of his coming: to die the brutal death of a criminal. John is showing how the unbelief of the Jews fulfills Isaiah's prophecy.

This raises a difficult, even troubling, question. If their unbelief is necessary to fulfill the prophecy of Jesus's rejection, is John saying that God planned their unbelief? The short answer is yes. No matter your view of God's sovereignty, there's no way you can get around the next few verses. Not only did they not believe, but John also says, "They were unable to believe" (v. 39). Why? John answers this difficult question by going back to Scripture, as we should. The reason they could not believe was God had blinded their eyes so they couldn't see and hardened their hearts so they couldn't understand and receive his healing. This isn't the first time we hear about God's hardening hearts and man's inability to believe. Moses, in one of his final charges to Israel, told them,

> You have seen with your own eyes everything the LORD did in Egypt to Pharaoh, to all his officials, and to his entire land. You saw with your own eyes the great trials and those great signs and wonders. Yet to this day the LORD has not given you a mind to understand, eyes to see, or ears to hear. (Deut 29:2-4)

This same language is picked up in Isaiah 6. God gives Isaiah the task of sharing his word with the children of Israel and says that Isaiah's message to them will be like this:

> Keep listening, but do not understand; keep looking, but do not perceive. Make the minds of these people dull; deafen their ears and blind their eyes; otherwise they might see with their eyes and hear with their ears, understand with their minds, turn back, and be healed. (Isa 6:9-10)

John says the unbelief of the Jews is the continued fulfillment of the words of Isaiah. They do not believe because God has not called them to believe. In fact, he has hardened their hearts even more than they already were. You could translate John 12:39 as: "They were powerless to believe" or "It was not possible for them to believe." What we see here are two interwoven truths in John's explanation of unbelief.

First, belief is not possible without God's direct work in man's heart. John Calvin explains: "Faith is not born in the ordinary human faculties but is a unique and rare gift of God" (*John*, 310). We see this clearly in John's quotation of the end of Isaiah's first prophecy: "To whom has the arm of the Lord been revealed?" (v. 38). God must reveal himself. God must take the initiative in salvation. God calls men to Jesus and saves them.

The second truth we see is that God can for his own purposes choose to harden those whom he chooses to harden (Rom 9:14-18). For his own reasons God chose to harden the already sinful, hard hearts of the Jews. We cannot completely understand God's purpose in calling some to faith and not others, but we submit to his authority and recognize the

Potter has the right to mold the clay however he sees fit. We are given a little glimpse as to God's purpose in hardening the Jews. The book of Acts ends with several Jews coming to speak with the apostle Paul while he was imprisoned in Rome. He preached a sermon to them that went from morning until evening. The reaction was mixed: some believed, some didn't, and a number were uncertain. Paul quoted Isaiah 6:10 about God's hardening the hearts of the Jews, and he gives us a glimpse as to why: "Therefore, let it be known to you that this salvation of God has been sent to the Gentiles; they will listen" (Acts 28:28). In the case of the Jews, one reason God confirmed them in their rejection and unbelief was that he was going to spread the gospel to the Gentiles. God has a plan. He's in control, and whatever he chooses to do in a person's heart is wise and just.

Whatever we do, we must not assign blame to God. D. A. Carson helps us put God's hardening in its proper perspective:

> God's judicial hardening is not presented as the capricious manipulation of an arbitrary potentate cursing morally neutral or even morally pure beings, but as a holy condemnation of a guilty people who are condemned to do and be what they themselves have chosen. (*John*, 448–49)

At some point we reach the end of our human understanding, and we are left to trust the goodness of God and recognize our finite comprehension of his way and plan. We need to affirm both truths John reveals in this passage, acknowledging that the Bible never pits divine sovereignty against human responsibility.

In Isaiah 6 God tells Isaiah his message would be about deaf ears and darkened hearts—which is discouraging—but if you keep reading, you find something hopeful. In verse 11 Isaiah asks God, "Until when, Lord?" He's asking, "How long will I preach a message that simply serves to harden the hearts of those who hear it?" The Lord's answer begins with the word *until*. *Until!* That means the hardening is temporary. God will call people to faith in him. That hope motivates evangelism. The sovereignty of God over belief and unbelief gives us confidence to share the gospel. If you don't think God is sovereign, why pray for those who don't believe? We need to see that God is God, and we are not. As God, he has the authority and power to give faith to whomever he chooses.

If God is sovereign over belief *and* unbelief, then it's his prerogative to determine who will and will not respond to the gospel. We see

Peter preach, and three thousand get saved. Paul saw hundreds, even thousands, turn in faith to Jesus, and we think God has also called us to preach the gospel. Yet God also used Moses and Isaiah and Ezekiel to share his message. If we judged them numerically, we'd consider them failures. The real question is, Can we continue to be faithful even if it appears that what we are doing is failing? Can we persist in sharing the gospel even if it takes us—like it took Adoniram Judson, the Baptist missionary to Burma—six years to see someone converted?

What we can't do is use this passage as an excuse not to share the gospel. That would be sin. A lack of evangelism is laziness. A lack of fruit in evangelism is not. Our goal needs to be biblically informed methods and a Christ-centered, theologically accurate understanding of the gospel. We leave the results up to God.

Not everyone in our passage rejects the gospel. In the summary of Jesus's message, he promises that those who believe in him will not remain in darkness (v. 46) but will have eternal life (v. 50). Belief in Jesus is not a sentimental salve for our guilt-ridden consciences.

- It's deliverance from the kingdom of darkness.
- It's redemption from the penalty of death.
- It's enjoyment of the new life—the life God intended for us.
- It's confidence in our renewed and restored relationship with the Creator.
- It's the bedrock of our souls and the source of lives of good works.

Genuine belief brings radical, complete, and lasting transformation of the whole person from the inside out.

There is one final group of people who seem to fall somewhere between belief and unbelief. They believe in Jesus—in some way—but are unwilling to confess that belief (v. 46). We might think they're merely shy or immature, but verse 43 tells us what motivates their decision. They love the glory that comes from man more than the glory that comes from God. What a stark contrast from the genuine belief of Isaiah, who saw the glory of God and placed his faith in Jesus Christ (v. 41). These silent, pseudo-believers are drawn to Jesus in some sense, but they value earthly applause more than Jesus, revealing a shallow, empty faith.

Jesus has no secret followers. The New Testament never mentions this category. God calls those who believe to be baptized, join a church, and participate in the Lord's Supper—all public expressions of a new internal reality. If you think you can be a secret follower, then you're deceived (v. 47). Jesus goes on to say that the Father will judge them on the last day. Some listen to the Word but do not follow it. They are Sunday Christians. They may come by after the service and thank the preacher for the message, but they do not obey God's Word. They do not follow Jesus Christ.

John wrote his Gospel to help us believe. He didn't provide us with an excuse for unbelief. This teaching on unbelief follows Jesus's pleading words to "believe in the light" (v. 36). This passage is about God's power to save, so trust him to save. Ask him to save. Tell people he can save. The most rigid unbelief shatters like glass when God swings his mighty hammer of grace. God is sovereign over unbelief, which means unbelief must bow before him. Unbelief cannot say no when God says yes. Someone's unbelief may seem like a roadblock too big to navigate, but God is bigger than unbelief. Trust him, pray to him, share the gospel, and then see the roadblock crumble as his grace sweeps in.

Reflect and Discuss

1. What is unbelief?
2. Can you have belief in Jesus apart from accepting and believing the Word of God?
3. How is unbelief a spiritual state rather than a mental one?
4. How does John make clear that the unbelief of the people is not for lack of evidence or signs from Jesus?
5. Why was the people's unbelief necessary?
6. How does Acts 28:28 shed light on why God would not open the hearts of many Jews to believe in Jesus?
7. When you come to a challenging problem in Scripture, what do you do?
8. What two truths do we see in John's explanation of unbelief?
9. How is election itself an example of belief in God's goodness and purposes?
10. Could this passage be used to excuse Christians from evangelism? Why or why not?

A Life of Humble Service

JOHN 13:1-17

Main Idea: The way to follow Jesus is to serve others humbly.

I. **Jesus Gives Us an Example of Humble Service (13:1-5).**
II. **Jesus Gives Us the Ability to Serve Humbly (13:6-17).**

Religion is focused on what I've done, what I do, and what I have the capacity to do in the future. When that's the case, every action I make is judged on the basis of what it does for me. Even my works of mercy and compassion will be attempts to balance my ledger sheet. The motivation stems from my desire to be a better person or my hope to remain in God's favor.

Jesus shows us a different approach. We are not the focus; in order to love and serve others selflessly, we need to look *beyond* our own lives. What he does, that Confucius or Ghandi cannot, goes beyond teaching what we should do and how we should live and actually gives us the power to live differently. Religion says, "Look inside yourself, and you will find the strength to live a life of service to others." Jesus says, "Look to me. I will show you the path to serving others, and I will give you the strength to live selflessly."

The Gospel of John calls us to follow Jesus. Following him is not a path to human greatness or man's acclaim. Following Jesus means we will put down the respect and riches of this world and pick up a wet, dirt-stained towel and use it to clean someone's muddy feet. The way to follow Jesus is to serve others humbly.

Jesus Gives Us an Example of Humble Service
JOHN 13:1-5

These verses are reported in shockingly simple language. It's almost like reading a newspaper report about last week's weather. But this isn't an average peasant from the streets of Jerusalem who's washing the dirty, smelly feet of these uneducated and illiterate fishermen. This is the Lord of all Creation; he simply speaks and universes are created from

261

nothing. One word from his mouth and Saturn with all of its rings bursts forth. What is he doing scrubbing these guys' toes?

The previous few verses make this act even more shocking. Verse 1 introduces the second half of the book. It locates the following events in the middle of the Passover celebration, but it's more than a chronological reference. It points us to the upcoming sacrifice of the Lamb of God. When Jesus burst on the public scene, John the Baptist cried out, "Here is the Lamb of God, who takes away the sin of the world!" (1:29). The Gospel of John has been building to this point, when the Lamb would take his place on the altar and his blood would spill out, bringing forgiveness of sin. We are marching deeper and deeper into the shadow of the cross; everything from this point on is leading us directly to that moment when Jesus would be suspended on that cursed tree for our sakes. For him to stop in the middle of that journey to wash the feet of his disciples is noteworthy. We need to feel the gravity of what he's teaching us.

Jesus's love for his disciples becomes one of the driving themes for the rest of the Gospel (13:1). This act of service demonstrates his love for these men, but it goes beyond that. In this example Jesus teaches us **no one is above serving**. Jesus doesn't deny his character by serving these men. His character makes this act of service even more profound. What follower of Jesus has the right ever to refuse serving? If our Master will humbly serve others, we are not exempt (v. 16). We have no standing to say, "I'm too good to do that." We need to beware the excuses we make for not serving others. We need to trace them back to their source. Is this excuse I'm making a legitimate reason, or is it a conscience-soothing way of saying, "I'm too good to serve them" or "I'm too important to serve in that way"? The service Jesus desires springs from humility. Nothing kills selfless service like pride.

In this example of humble service, we learn another vital lesson: **No one is below being served**. In this chapter we're reminded repeatedly about the upcoming betrayal by Judas. How many pairs of feet did Jesus wash? Twelve. Jesus even washed the feet of Judas, knowing full well what he was going to do (v. 2). Judas is in league with Satan at this point, but Jesus still stoops before him as a humble servant and slowly washes the caked dirt and grime off his feet. Would you have washed Judas's feet? I've decided I would have cleaned his feet with some paint thinner and a match. Not Jesus. He carefully washes the feet of a traitor, just as he washed the feet of Peter and James and John. Is anyone going to do worse things to you than Judas did to Jesus? No.

Though no one is below being served, in verse 14 Jesus narrows the focus of our humbleness to the family of God. Our brothers and sisters are to be the primary recipients of our selfless acts of kindness. We don't turn a blind eye and deaf ear to the needy outside the church, but our first order of business is to meet the needs of one another in the church. We have a unique bond with one another, namely that we are servants of the same Master. We all call Jesus "Lord." Our shared allegiance to Jesus is the root of our service to one another.

A trait of humble service, which simply cannot be counterfeited, is the willingness to be inconvenienced for someone else's benefit. Imagine a Christian woman who is the evangelical version of Martha Stewart. She loves to throw big events and have people into her home as long as she can plan and prepare for weeks in advance. Being inconvenienced for her might mean noticing a sister is struggling one Sunday morning, walking over to her, and inviting her and her family over for dinner even though she has nothing prepared. Or picture a man—spontaneous, outgoing, the life of the party—who sees a brother dealing with a problem that will take months of work, months of tedious and difficult effort. Being inconvenienced for him may mean spending weeks and weeks doing the tiresome labor necessary to help him through the situation.

Jesus Gives Us the Ability to Serve Humbly
JOHN 13:6-17

History gives us many great examples of selflessness. What sets apart this example of Jesus is not only that he is God (and therefore is the only one who legitimately deserves worship) but that through his selfless service we are given the ability to serve others as well. In this act of humble service, we're pointed to a greater, more powerful act of service. Jesus was showing them he had come not to be served but to serve. In just a few hours he would humble himself and serve them through his death on the cross. This becomes clearer in his conversation with Peter, in which he tells Peter they will understand "afterward" (vv. 6-7). Not after the act, but after the resurrection. Looking back on the foot washing, they would realize Jesus was portraying the necessity of humbling

himself in order to serve them. He had to become a servant for them
to have life.

Peter, of course, thinks he understands now. I love what Kent
Hughes writes: "Good old Peter. Sometimes the only time he opened his
mouth was to change feet!" (*John*, 314). Unless Jesus humbles himself
as a servant, unless Jesus selflessly offers his life in Peter's place, Peter
would have no ability to follow him (v. 8). Jesus's service on the cross
(pictured here by foot washing) is what makes discipleship possible.
That's why when Peter then asks Jesus to wash all of him, Jesus replies
that it's unnecessary. The point *right here* is not the depth of Peter's sin.
The point is the necessity of Jesus's sacrifice. His ultimate act of humble
service upholds all acts of Christian service and discipleship that follow.
If he had not taken on the form of a servant and humbled himself to
death, even the death on a cross, then we would have no ability to follow
him. If he had not done that, then his words and his example of washing
the disciples' feet would have been nothing more than a historical footnote. However, because of his humiliation, we have been made capable
of walking in his steps. He doesn't just provide the pattern for service;
he provides the power to serve.

He makes this point again in verse 15. When we read those words
"just as," we think it refers simply to being an example, but there's more
to it than that.

> [Just as] indicates not only similarity and adherence to a
> standard but also the ground on which this discipleship rests
> and the source from which it gains its strength . . . it directs
> them to Jesus' self-sacrificial love for them as the source
> and driving force for their love for each other. (Ridderbos,
> *John*, 463)

We will not humbly serve others in our own strength. We need Jesus's
help. Humble service flows from the gospel. The power to serve one
another is not found inside of us. We don't tap into inner strength or
discover secret power reserves. We fall on our faces before Jesus and beg
him to help us serve others. We rely on the Holy Spirit to enable us to
love others and put their needs before our own.

This kind of humble service has to be rooted in the gospel. What
Jesus commands is not an action but an attitude. Foot washing is not
the point. Some have taken this as a command to literally wash the

feet of others, but foot washing can be done arrogantly. It can be performed with a cold, dead, and uncaring heart. That's why the focus is on desire, not duty. To follow Jesus by humbly serving our brothers and sisters requires a fundamental transformation of our nature. We are selfish, independent, arrogant sinners with cold, hard hearts—what Jesus demands from us is to live as selfless, trusting, humble servants. The only way that's possible is if who I am fundamentally changes. Unless someone performs heart surgery on me, I cannot live a life of humble service.

Thankfully, when Jesus humbly sacrificed his life on the cross in my place, absorbing the wrath of God and giving me the gift of faith so that I would turn in repentance, faith, and obedience to him, he changed my nature. He gave me a new heart. Now what was impossible—a life of humble service—is not only possible; it's wonderful. It is the path of true joy (v. 17). Joy, happiness, and blessing come not from a life of selfish accumulation but from a life of self-denying compassion and service. But humble service is not natural. Sin, self-gratification, pride, and the desire for power and control are natural. Jesus is telling his disciples in essence, "My humble service to you on the cross, pictured by this act of foot washing, will enable you and empower you to live as you were intended to. It will change your desires and goals, your dreams and wishes. It will change your fundamental makeup. You'll learn that as you follow me, joy and happiness will find you: not standing on the throne, issuing edicts, and receiving tribute—blessing will find you kneeling on the floor, towel in hand."

Jesus does not call us to a life of leisure but of labor. He doesn't call us to follow him down paths sprinkled with gumdrops and lined with lollipops but down dirt-covered, sweat-stained paths—paths that stink, paths that are not simple or clean or neat. The cost of discipleship is high, but it's worth it. God's blessing comes to the genuine disciple—the one who follows Jesus into a life of humble service. Of all the marks of discipleship Jesus could have highlighted, he highlighted a willingness to pick up a towel and get our hands dirty. Few things we do make the gospel more beautiful and compelling than when someone sees Christians with dirty towels and clean feet. Dirty towels and clean feet make the gospel clear—everyday people doing everyday things to serve others. That's what humble service looks like. That's what following Jesus looks like.

Reflect and Discuss

1. How does Jesus show us a different path than religion?
2. How would you respond if Jesus were to wash your feet?
3. Why is Jesus's washing the feet of his disciples not a denial of his character as Master?
4. Do you find it hard to serve people you view as undeserving? What are some excuses you make?
5. Would you have washed Judas's feet? Why does Jesus?
6. What are some ways you can show loving service to fellow believers through inconvenience?
7. Describe the significance of the words "just as" to the Christian life (v. 15).
8. How is the focus of this passage desire rather than duty?
9. What is Jesus teaching his disciples by washing their feet?
10. How is humble service a picture of the gospel to an unbelieving world?

Belief and Betrayal

JOHN 13:18-30

Main Idea: The account of Judas's betrayal instills confidence in Jesus Christ.

1. Jesus Fulfills Messianic Prophecy (13:18-19).
2. Jesus Orchestrates the Coming Events (13:20-30).

In John 13 we read about Judas's betrayal, and we also find the prediction of Peter's denial. In this encounter between Jesus and the traitor Judas, the apostle John has a perfect seat to observe and record all that happens. He is the one, prompted by Peter, to ask Jesus who the betrayer is. Apparently he is also the only one close enough to Jesus to hear him reply (v. 26). None of the other disciples understood why Jesus sent Judas away with a command to do something quickly. John's report is firsthand, and he makes a reliable witness to the actual events of that Passover Festival. As we look at the events recorded in John 13, we see this passage was included to deepen our faith in the person and work of Jesus Christ.

Many passages we've studied in the Gospel of John have struck a note of hope, but this one echoes with chords of sadness. Here is a man who walked, talked, and lived with Jesus for a lengthy period, yet he walks away from the one who brings hope. The final chapter for Judas is a hopeless, tragic end. But there aren't simply negative lessons we can learn from this account ("Don't Be a Judas"). As we closely examine these verses, we discover a positive purpose in this act of treachery. The account of Judas's betrayal instills confidence in Jesus Christ.

John wrote this Gospel so that we would understand who the Messiah is (20:31). He wants us to come to the wonderful, life-changing, life-giving realization that Jesus Christ, a lowly carpenter from Nazareth, is the promised Messiah, the Son of the one, true God. Since this is his purpose, the events from the life of Jesus that John has recorded help us connect those dots. We have, on the one hand, a host of Old Testament teaching devoted to the coming Messiah. He was first promised to Adam and Eve in the garden of Eden, and that promise, like a scarlet thread, is woven throughout all the pages of the Old Testament. On the other side we have the life of Jesus Christ, a man who by all accounts lived a quiet, unremarkable life for about thirty years in a small village in Galilee but then roared onto the public stage, healing sickness, restoring sight, exorcising demons, controlling nature, and claiming to be the Son of God.

John wrote this Gospel so we could see that these events in the life of Jesus were not done to create a following or cause a spectacle. They were done to perfectly fulfill the promises made about the Messiah in the Old Testament. He wants us to connect the promise of the Messiah's power with the demonstration of Jesus's power. He wants us to see the works of Jesus as the fulfillment of those promises made so long before. His purpose is advanced in this account of Judas's betrayal. It is placed in this book, right here in this spot, to give us confidence that Jesus's claim to be the Messiah is accurate. We find two reasons to have greater confidence in Jesus.

Jesus Fulfills Messianic Prophecy
JOHN 13:18-19

Why did Jesus choose Judas as one of his disciples? Scripture is clear that Jesus wasn't surprised to discover treachery in the heart of Judas:

> *Jesus replied to them, "Didn't I choose you, the Twelve? Yet one of you is a devil." He was referring to Judas, Simon Iscariot's son, one of the Twelve, because he was going to betray him.* (6:70-71)

Jesus chose Judas because Judas's betrayal was necessary to demonstrate Jesus was the Messiah (v. 18). The quotation is from Psalm 41:9, where King David chronicles his suffering and mistreatment by those who'd been his friends. The reason this psalm is considered messianic is because much of David's life is a model for the coming Messiah (Carson, *John*, 470). Not everything, but the broad, general sweeping themes are seen as pointing toward the coming King, a son of David who would rule forever on the throne of David. The theme of David's life most frequently interpreted as pointing to the Messiah is his suffering. For instance, Jesus himself quoted David's prayer from Psalm 22:1: "My God, my God, why have you abandoned me?"

The disciples were going to have enough trouble understanding Jesus's death. On this night before he went to the cross, Jesus assures them that he was not a false Messiah. Even this sinister betrayal could give them confidence he is indeed the promised Son of David, the long-awaited Messiah. Jesus experienced an act of treachery at the hand of a trusted friend just as David did.

It's easy to look back on a past event and forget the bad and latch on to the good, thereby revising the truth of what really happened. Jesus wasn't betrayed by Judas, and then John and the disciples looked back on his life and revised history to make it fit their new version. Jesus actually discusses the betrayal before it ever happened. He told them about the betrayal beforehand so they wouldn't have to look back and wonder why it happened (v. 19). They wouldn't be forced to explain it away. He prophesied the betrayal and told them why it was necessary before it happened so they might believe. Judas's betrayal would serve as a steroid for the disciples' faith.

Jesus didn't want them to believe he was merely an insightful prophet, a good man, or an excellent teacher. Jesus said they were to believe that "I am he" (v. 19). The word *he* is not in the original manuscript; the translators supplied it. Jesus said they were to believe (in the Greek) "*ego eimi*" or "I AM." Throughout the Gospel of John, Jesus has called on them to believe that he is "I AM." *Ego eimi* is the Greek equivalent of the name given by God to Moses at the burning bush (Exod 3:14). Earlier in the Gospel of John, Jesus claimed this title, and the people understood exactly what he was saying. In fact, many of them attempted to stone him for what they considered blasphemy (8:58). Jesus is saying their faith would be strengthened by believing that Jesus is "I AM"—that Jesus was, is, and forever will be God.

Faith must have an object. By definition faith is not faith if there is no one in whom we place it. These days the word *faith* has become just another way to say that a person has a positive outlook or a hopeful attitude; that's not how the Bible discusses faith. Biblical faith must have Jesus Christ as its object. Biblical faith must embrace certain truths about the person and work of Jesus Christ. When we hear about someone's "faith," we need to listen with discernment. We do no one a favor by quietly and tacitly endorsing self-centered, humanistic thinking clothed in religious language. When we talk to a friend or neighbor, we must not call him merely to faith but to faith *in Jesus Christ*, the Son of God.

There's no way to come to God apart from a right belief in Jesus. Generic faith in God does nothing but damn a person's soul to hell. Right belief in Jesus (v. 20—through the testimony of those whom he has sent) will reconcile us wicked, vile sinners with the Holy God. Faith apart from Jesus is futile and hopeless, but faith in Jesus Christ as the promised Messiah will bring reconciliation with God. When we receive Jesus, we receive the one who sent him.

Jesus Orchestrates the Coming Events
JOHN 13:20-30

The backdrop of the events in John 13 is a battle. Not an isolated skirmish in some backwater village, but a cosmic battle that has been raging for thousands of years. Verse 1 relates Jesus's march to the cross. He is the Lamb of God making his way into the city to be sacrificed for the sins of man. He knew "his hour"—a phrase used throughout the book to speak of his death—had come. Verse 1 overviews one side of the conflict. Verse 2 spells out the enemy's plan. This is where we discover Judas is only a bit player. He's the puppet, and someone more powerful is pulling his strings: the devil is behind this betrayal.

This battle has a long history. It goes back to the beginning of civilization. God made a garden and placed man and woman in the middle. They were created to live in peace and harmony. Their responsibility was to serve God, enjoy his fellowship, and obey his word. He had given them one command: "Enjoy everything I've created for your benefit, but don't eat from the tree in the middle of the garden." The devil showed up disguised as a serpent and tricked the woman into eating from the tree. Adam followed her example. Soon God arrived and delivered a punishment for their disobedience. All the good things he had created would be cursed by sin. Instead of the ground serving man, man would serve the ground. Instead of marriage and children being a simple pleasure and perfect joy for the woman, these relationships would be plagued by sin.

They weren't the only ones who were cursed that day. The serpent was cursed as well. Earthly serpents were cursed above all animals, but the curse was extended to Satan (Gen 3:15). With that pronouncement the great serpent's fate was sealed. God promised a deliverer would come and liberate mankind from the oppressive rule of sin. When that deliverance came, the devil would be defeated, and his head would be crushed.

This promise is nearing its fulfillment in the upper room. Jesus and Satan are squaring off for the final battle, but the battle had been decided long before. Jesus is not surprised by the devil's move. He's not startled by Judas's treachery. Jesus is sovereign over everything that has happened and will happen, including his own betrayal. If you ever doubt the sovereign power of Jesus Christ, memorize verse 3. What had God given Jesus? "Everything." That's a word in Greek (*panta*) that means "all, every, the whole." Everything is in Jesus's hands. As the old spiritual says, "He's got the whole world in his hands."

- When someone mistreats you and justice seems far away, Jesus has everything in his hands.
- When the doctor calls with bad news, Jesus has everything in his hands.
- When your boss unexpectedly hands you a pink slip, Jesus has everything in his hands.
- When you've been faithful to teach your children, and they still walk away from the truth, Jesus has everything in his hands.
- When the person you pledge your love to discards you and you question your worth, Jesus has everything in his hands.
- When every waking thought is consumed by worry and anxiety, Jesus has everything in his hands.
- When your 401k plunges and there's no sign of recovery, Jesus has everything in his hands.
- When a friend seeks popularity by airing your dirty laundry, Jesus has everything in his hands.
- When you're pressured to do things you know you'll regret, Jesus has everything in his hands.

Few truths can engage our affections, calm our hearts, and influence our decisions like the reality of the sovereign power of Jesus.

I've heard people say, "You don't want to show up for a gunfight carrying a knife." I like to think Satan showed up for a nuclear war carrying a spoon. He is powerless. Jesus's life is not being taken from him. Satan can't defeat him. Jesus lays down his life willingly. After Satan enters into Judas, Jesus demonstrates his authority by telling Satan to leave and do what he's going to do quickly (v. 27). Even at this moment, he's in control. Jesus is not a powerless pawn in the struggle between Israel and Rome. He's not a tragic figure, shockingly betrayed by his old friend. He was and is the Son of God who marches to the cross in complete control of every event and circumstance. His journey to the cross is why we can say, "Where, death, is your victory? Where, death, is your sting?" (1 Cor 15:55). On that cross Jesus crushes the serpent's head. The cosmic battle culminates. Satan's prophesied defeat becomes a reality. Jesus triumphs over the serpent.

We understand the human drama of a friend betraying another friend, but the significance of this story extends far beyond a single traitorous act. The story of Judas should not bring despair and sadness, but it should remind us of the great power of Jesus Christ. In this circumstance, which seems like a great failure, Jesus wins a great victory. Against the backdrop of human wickedness, his character and his control are revealed in vivid and stunning detail.

Acts records Judas's tragic end, but John makes a powerful point about Judas. He concludes the account of betrayal with the phrase, "And it was night" (v. 30). Throughout this Gospel, John has recorded the words of Jesus about light and darkness. He calls Jesus the true light, who entered this world of darkness to bring light. We hear Jesus cry out, "I am the light of the world. Anyone who follows me will never walk in the darkness but will have the light of life" (8:12). When Judas walks out of the candlelit room into the dark street, he's walking away from the light of the world. As the door shuts behind him, his fate is sealed. He's turned his back on the only source of life. This is the end of Judas. He chose darkness over light. He chose death over life. And with his example comes a question: Will I embrace the light, or will I walk into the night?

Reflect and Discuss

1. How does Judas's betrayal give us confidence in Jesus?
2. Why did Jesus choose Judas to be one of his disciples?
3. What theme of David's life most frequently points to the Messiah?
4. Why does Jesus prophesy Judas's betrayal and tell his disciples of its necessity before it happened?
5. Why does Jesus say the disciples are to believe that "I am he" in verse 19?
6. How is the way the Bible speaks of *faith* different from our culture's use of the word?
7. Describe how Genesis 1–3 is the backdrop to the events in this passage.
8. Why is it good news that Jesus has been given all things?
9. If Jesus is sovereign over all things, what does it free you to do as his follower that you wouldn't do otherwise?
10. How does this passage demonstrate Jesus's power over Satan?

Fundamental Changes

JOHN 13:31-38

Main Idea: Jesus explains how his coming crucifixion fundamentally changes the disciples' future.

I. **The Cross and the Glory of God (13:31-32)**
II. **The Cross and the Disciples' Future (13:33-38)**
   A. The disciples cannot go with Jesus (13:33).
   B. The disciples are part of a new community (13:34-35).
   C. The disciples will be empowered to follow Jesus (13:36-38).

Have you ever been in a situation when a major life-change happened unexpectedly? The shock magnifies the pain, anxiety, and fear. It's hard enough to lose a loved one, but if it's unexpected, the world seems to stop, and it takes a long time for it to begin spinning again. The world is about to stop for the disciples of Jesus. Everything they've known and believed for the last three years is about to be tested. They've left their careers and families to follow Jesus. They've been ridiculed and mocked. They've seen friends turn away. They've committed every moment and every muscle to following him. Now Jesus is about to leave them.

Put yourself in their shoes. They've been following Jesus around every minute of every day for months and months. He called them to leave their homes and belongings, saying, "Follow me." Now he's essentially saying, "I'm leaving you. You can't follow me anymore." This is earthshaking. Dreams and visions of what they were going to build with Jesus are crumbling around them. The floor is swaying from side to side, and their next steps are clouded by doubt and confusion. But Jesus prepares them for his departure. Beginning in John 13:31 and extending through the end of chapter 17, we're allowed to eavesdrop on Jesus's final instructions to his disciples. We get to listen as Jesus teaches them why he's leaving and what they'll do after he's gone. These chapters make up the longest continuous section of Jesus's teaching in all of Scripture. The eight short verses at the end of chapter 13 introduce this extended section of teaching.

The Cross and the Glory of God

JOHN 13:31-32

Jesus begins by saying "Now" (v. 31). The *now* points us back to the preceding event. Judas just left to alert the authorities. The events have been set in motion that will lead to Jesus's trial, his beating, and ultimately his crucifixion. Notice Jesus doesn't simply say, "Now I am going to die." He talks about being glorified.

Jesus chooses language that not only describes what he's doing but also places what he's doing in its context. He's not simply informing the disciples of his next move; he's helping them see the significance of the next move. We do this all the time. If you're in the kitchen stirring flour into a bowl and your child asks you, "Hey, Mom, what are you doing?" You could say, "I'm moving this piece of wood in a circular motion." That's true, but it gives no context to your actions. You would probably say, "I'm making cookies." That's the big picture; that's what gives meaning to the action of stirring. If people can get the big picture, then they'll have a frame of reference to interpret the individual pieces.

Jesus helps his disciples see the upcoming events in the big picture of God's self-revelation. Twenty-three times in the Gospel of John we find a form of the word *glory*. Five of those twenty-three occurrences are found right here in verses 31-32. There are two aspects to God's glory. Romans 3:23 says, "For all have sinned and fall short of the glory of God." You could substitute *honor* or *excellent reputation* for *glory*, and the meaning wouldn't change (Grudem, *Systematic Theology*, 220–21). But there's a second aspect to God's glory, and that's the visible manifestation of his excellent character. One theologian says God's glory is "the revelation of His splendid activity" (Carson, *John*, 482). In the Old Testament God's glory was not simply the honor due him, but it was also the cloud or bright light that marked God's presence among his people. This revelation was referred to with the title "the glory of the Lord." In Exodus 16 God promised the people that in the morning they would see his glory. So God's *glory* is the visible expression of his excellence, and when that excellence is seen, then people are prompted to give him the *glory*—the honor and worship—he is due.

When Jesus speaks of the glory of God, he incorporates both aspects, but he applies them in a way that couldn't be done in the Old Testament. When the Israelites needed to be reminded of God's glory, he appeared to them—and revealed his character and attributes—in a bright light or a cloud. But how does God appear to man in the New Testament? How is God's excellence displayed in visible form? Through Jesus. Jesus is the glory of God. He is the manifestation of God's excellence. Because he himself is God, he perfectly reveals the excellent character of God. He is the exact imprint of God's perfect and holy nature.

- When we see Jesus, we see God.
- When we see Jesus, we understand who God is.
- When we see Jesus, we should recognize the honor and excellence God deserves, and we should respond with worship and praise—we should glorify him.

Now, to get to the bottom of why Jesus places his death and resurrection in the larger context of the glory of God, we need to consider another question: How does the mockery, beating, rejection, and murder of God's Son reveal God's character and cause anyone to recognize the excellence of God? Jesus doesn't say, "Now there is *a possibility* that the Son will be glorified. Now will God *hopefully* be glorified in me." He says, "Now the Son of Man *is* glorified, and God *is* glorified in him" (v. 31; emphasis added).

New Testament scholar D. A. Carson answers that question helpfully: "The supreme moment of divine disclosure, the greatest moment of displayed glory, was in the shame of the cross" (Carson, *John*, 482). There is no place we can look to better understand who God is than the cross. There is no place we can look and more clearly recognize that he is worthy of all honor and glory than the cross. The cross is the highest moment of God's revelation to mankind. In the cross we learn more about God's excellence than in any other moment in history. In the death of Jesus, we see God's holiness and love, righteousness and mercy, justice and grace, sovereignty and humility, wisdom and patience. If we want to understand God, we must study the cross. If we want to be transformed into the image of Jesus Christ, we must study the cross. A crossless Christianity is a Godless Christianity. Only through Jesus Christ—his suffering sacrifice—can God be known.

The cross is the place that fuels our worship of God. Every human being is a worshiper. You are worshiping someone or something every day. Only God merits undying allegiance and unqualified praise. What are we to do when our worship of God grows cold and stale? We go to the cross. God will never seem distant when we're standing on the hill where his Son was sacrificed in our place. True, passionate worship springs from a heart that has been gripped by the grace of God displayed in the cross. In those seasons of life when you're struggling to care—you want to care, but it's a chore—make frequent, daily pilgrimages to the cross. Watch as Jesus willingly took our bruises. Be reminded that through his stripes you have been healed. The old song says, "I'll cherish the old, rugged cross." Never get over the cross. The cross is not the starting line we quickly leave behind. The cross is Grand Central Station, and every part of our life runs out from it. Everything in the Christian life needs to revolve around Jesus Christ and him crucified (1 Cor 2:2). The cross is our message, the cross guides our methods, and the cross empowers our mission. When the cross is central, God causes true worship to flow from our hearts, through our lives, and out our lips.

The Cross and the Disciples' Future
JOHN 13:33-38

The Disciples Cannot Go with Jesus

Jesus prefaces this truth with a term he uses nowhere else in Scripture. It's translated "children," and it's filled with tremendous care and concern for the disciples (v. 33). Jesus's departure is not going to be easy for them. This is not a message he could simply drop into the middle of a conversation: "Hey, Peter, did you pick up the fish from the market? Oh, by the way, I'm leaving, and you can't come with me." The dynamics of the relationship are changing. They'll no longer be able to walk physically with him. So Jesus uses a term filled with care and overflowing with tenderness: my little *children*.

How could Jesus say to them here in chapter 13, "Where I am going, you cannot come" (v. 33), and just a few verses later tell them he was leaving to prepare a place for them so they could be where he was (14:2-3)? The key to solving this mystery lies in the phrase "just as I told the Jews." Back in chapter 8 Jesus told the Jews that he was going away and they would seek him and not find him: "Where I am going, you cannot come." The Jews wondered if Jesus was going to kill himself (8:22). They were wrong about the means of Jesus's death—he was not committing suicide—but they were right to understand that he was referring to his death when he said that. Now in chapter 13, as he speaks to his disciples, he is not saying, "I'm going to heaven. Sorry, you can't go there." He's saying, "I'm going to the cross, and I go alone. You cannot go to the cross with me." Only Jesus could go to the cross and pay the penalty that satisfies the demands of justice.

The Disciples Are Part of a New Community

Their relationship with Jesus is changing. They will still follow his teaching and commands, but they will no longer physically follow him. That's not the only relationship that's changing. Their relationship with one another is undergoing a radical overhaul. With Jesus's departure they are now being brought into a new community that will be defined by love.

When Jesus was on earth, how would someone know that a person was a disciple of Jesus? The answer is easy. They would watch them. If they followed Jesus around from place to place and listened to his teaching, then they were one of his disciples. That's fine when he's on the earth, but now what are they going to do? How will anyone recognize them as his disciples if he isn't around? "They will know you are my disciples because I am forming you into a new community that will operate on principles of love" (vv. 34-35; my paraphrase). Three times in these two verses Jesus says, "one another." The "one anothers" are his disciples. There is to be a community of disciples identifiable to the world by their love for one another. He is not leaving the disciples *alone*. He is leaving them *together*. Because of their relationship with him, they have a relationship with one another. He addresses them all as children, an intimate, family term. This is what he is leaving behind: a group of God's children, a band of brothers who serve one another in humility and love. That's what a church is.

He calls this command to love one another a "new" command, but there's nothing new about God giving a command to love others. All the way back in Leviticus we find the command to "love your neighbor as yourself" (19:18). In what sense is this command new?

First, it's new because it has its source in Christ's love for them. The command is to love one another *as* Christ has loved them. Here is a new standard for love. This is the ultimate example of our love for one another. We are to see Jesus's sacrificial, selfless love as the measure, goal, and enabling force of our love for one another. Also, our love for one another is only possible because of what Jesus did on the cross. Had he not paid for our sins and given us a new, righteous nature, we would be unable to love one another. I can love now *because* he first loved me. So it's a new command because of his love, which enables and exemplifies sacrificial love.

Second, it's new because it will define a community that is just coming into existence. Shortly after Jesus departs this earth, the church is established. This command is new because it's specifically given to this new institution made up of followers of Jesus.

Every organization is identified by certain characteristics. If you see a big, brown truck with yellow letters and a man dressed in brown steps out to deliver a package, you can identify the organization. Churches should not be identified by a white steeple, a sign with clever sayings, or a large wooden cross; they should be identified by the quality of one member's love for another. Genuine disciples of Jesus cannot be identified on the basis of a cross tattoo, fish decal, or "I ♥ Jesus" mug. Jesus says in effect, "My disciples will be distinct because of their love." People will see their love for one another and the only response they'll be able to make is, "Wow, they must be followers of Jesus."

Followers of Jesus will love others more than we love ourselves. That's a pretty tough standard. What does that look like on a practical level? If you love others like you love yourself, you'll give others the benefit of the doubt. We're so suspicious of other people. We distrust their motives. We often act like other people are criminal masterminds, intentionally weaving a web of lies, trying to entrap us. Instead, we should give others the benefit of the doubt.

I don't know if you've ever been around a hypochondriac—someone who always thinks she's sick. She gets a cough, looks online, and now is pretty sure she has the bubonic plague. Or he sees a red spot on his arm and thinks he's dying from leprosy when it's dried ketchup from lunch. Such people live suspiciously. Everything is a clue with a deeper meaning. Hypochondriacs are anxious, they're nervous, they're overwhelmed by fear. Too often we view others with greater suspicion than a hypochondriac views a sore throat. We don't give others the same benefit of the doubt we give ourselves. Love detests evil (Rom 12:9). It's patient, not suspicious of other people (1 Cor 13:4-7). Love doesn't say, "Why'd they do that? What did they mean when they said that? What they probably really meant was . . ." Those are unloving ways to treat other people. Are you continually plotting ways to hurt other people? Of course not! Then why do you think other people are doing that to you?

Two of the great ways to love people (and they go hand in hand) are to assume the best and have a sense of humor. When someone says something to you that could be interpreted two ways, assume the best possible interpretation and laugh about it. Even if you're wrong, you'll be happier. Sometimes we parse other people's words like we're back in high school English class. We've diagrammed their sentences to see if there's any possible way for what they said to be understood as offensive. If there's even a remote chance, we consider it hostile and get offended. Why? Because we don't love them as we love ourselves. Christian love intentionally assumes the best about people. It refuses to jump to conclusions. It doesn't judge motives. It is kind.

The Disciples Will Be Empowered to Follow Jesus

Peter brushes aside Jesus's command to love one another in a new community of faith. He's still struggling with Jesus's announcement that he is leaving and they can't come with him. He asks Jesus where he's going (v. 36). Look at the bold statement Peter makes: "I will lay down my life for you" (v. 37). Jesus challenges Peter: "Really? No. In fact, you're not even going to spend the rest of the evening following me. You will deny me three times before the rooster announces the dawn" (my paraphrase).

So Jesus tells Peter that he *will not* follow Jesus. He'll turn away. But if we back up, we see before that he tells Peter, "You *cannot* follow me" (v. 36). So Peter's not entirely to blame. It's true he won't follow Jesus, but that's because he can't follow him. Peter has no power within himself to continue as Jesus's disciple. Are we to conclude that in the face of difficult circumstances, there's no ability in us to follow Jesus? That might be true if it weren't for a small phrase tacked onto the end of verse 36: "But you *will* follow later" (emphasis added). After Jesus goes to the cross, Peter will be able to follow him. One of the themes Jesus instructs them on in the next few chapters is the gift of the Holy Spirit to indwell and empower them to follow him. Through suffering and persecution, into acts of love and mercy, they will be given the power through what Jesus accomplished to really live as his disciples.

Reflect and Discuss

1. How will the world identify Jesus's followers?
2. What do you think the disciples felt when they heard Jesus was leaving?
3. Define God's glory.
4. How does Jesus speak of God's glory in a way that couldn't be done in the Old Testament?
5. How does the suffering and shame Jesus is going to endure cause people to recognize the excellence of God?
6. What steps can we take when our worship of God grows cold and stale?
7. What can we learn about Jesus based on his calling disciples "children"?
8. Why does Jesus tell them, "Where I am going, you cannot come"?
9. In leaving the disciples, how is Jesus not leaving them alone?
10. How can Jesus call the command to love one another a "new" command?

The Promise of Heaven

JOHN 14:1-3

Main Idea: Jesus comforts his disciples with the promise of life forever with him in heaven.

I. Jesus Gives His Disciples a Command: Trust Me (14:1)!

II. Jesus Gives His Disciples Confidence: Here's Why You Can Trust Me (14:2-3)!

The book begins this way:

> I died on January 18, 1989.
>
> Paramedics reached the scene of the accident within minutes. They found no pulse and declared me dead. They covered me with a tarp so that onlookers wouldn't stare at me while they attended to the injuries of the others. I was completely unaware of the paramedics or anyone else around me.
>
> Immediately after I died, I went straight to heaven.
>
> While I was in heaven, a Baptist preacher came on the accident scene. Even though he knew I was dead, he rushed to my lifeless body and prayed for me. Despite the scoffing of the EMTs, he refused to stop praying.
>
> At least 90 minutes after the EMTs pronounced me dead, God answered that man's prayers.
>
> I returned to earth.
>
> This is my story. (Piper, *90 Minutes*, 13)

The following 192 pages chronicle Don Piper's tragic car accident and long, painful recovery, but the focus of the book is his story of visiting heaven for the ninety minutes between when he was pronounced dead and when he, in his words, "returned to earth." In the book he describes what God has done in his life since the accident and how his account of heaven has provided hope for so many. He writes, "I've changed the way I do funerals. Now I can speak authoritatively about heaven from first-hand knowledge" (ibid., 129).

Our hope is not supposed to be in the words of Don Piper. Our confidence about eternity doesn't come from someone else's experience. What he says is dangerous. He's replacing faith in the words of Jesus with faith in his own words. Piper's book ends with him recounting a number of times he has given hope to someone who has lost a loved one or was on the brink of death by telling of his experience in heaven. When we think about death, where are we supposed to look for hope and comfort?

The disciples are being forced to deal with the coming death of Jesus. The night before Jesus's crucifixion has been set aside for him to prepare them for life after the cross. He tells them he's leaving, and they cannot follow where he's going. They are confused. Simon Peter in chapter 13 and Thomas and Philip in chapter 14 pepper him with questions, trying to cut through the haze that has descended on them. His departure is also met with resistance. Peter proclaims his undying allegiance to Jesus, in effect saying Jesus is wrong and they *will* follow him wherever he goes.

The overwhelming response is not confusion or resistance. It's anxiety. Jesus begins chapter 14 by acknowledging the disciples' feelings. He understands his announcement is causing their hearts to be "troubled" (v. 1). Earlier in the Gospel of John, this same word *troubled* is used to describe what happened to a pool of water; it's translated "stirred up" (5:7). The disciples' hearts are stirred up. Like ingredients in a mixing bowl, doubt, confusion, uncertainty, and fear are being stirred around inside their hearts. This potent mixture of emotions is motivated by Jesus's departure. How can he leave them? Why can't they follow him? You take those questions and add them to the fact that one disciple will betray him and another will deny him, and you have a recipe for anxiety strong enough to paralyze the most mature disciple.

In this emotionally trying moment, Jesus comforts the disciples. It's remarkable he can even think of them at this time. Here he is about to take upon himself the sin of the world. He's on the verge of experiencing the wrath of God for our sin. Yet he compassionately reaches out to comfort his disciples.

Jesus Gives His Disciples a Command: Trust Me!
JOHN 14:1

Where do you look in difficult times? We try to find someone who has gone through a similar experience and look to his or her success as grounds for our hope. We seek some type of calming or soothing emotion: "Things are too up and down, I just need to get away from it all for a little while." In this time when the disciples' hearts were stirred up, Jesus reminds them to look to him. He gives his disciples two commands: "Believe in God; believe also in me" (v. 1). The focus of these commands is that they need to continue to do that which they've already done. Jesus is not telling them, "For the first time, you need to believe in me." He's saying, "You have believed in me; now keep believing, keep trusting, and keep relying on me." The antidote for the virus of anxiety is trust in Jesus. Not emotions, experiences, or others, but Jesus.

In the same breath he commands them to trust in him, he tells them to trust in God. He links these two commands together. It would have been natural for them as devout Jews to receive encouragement to trust in God. From a young age they would have been challenged with their need to believe in God. When called on to do so, they would say, "Of course I'll trust in God." Jesus links their belief in God with their belief in him to remind them that to trust in him is to trust in God, and the reverse is also true: trusting in God means placing their faith in Jesus.

In times of anxiety and stress, we tend to doubt whether God can be trusted. We begin to wonder if he really cares or if he knows what's best. Our hearts, like ships at sea, are battered by winds of uncertainty and taking on the waters of doubt. In those moments we need to be reminded that God controls the seas. The disciples are being buffeted by the winds of anxiety, and Jesus gives them this command: believe in me. Belief in Jesus will be their anchor in the coming turbulent days. Belief in Jesus will calm the troubled waters that rock their hearts.

Jesus Gives His Disciples Confidence: Here's Why You Can Trust Me!
JOHN 14:2-3

Throughout Scripture we're commanded to trust God, and we're given many reasons we can trust him. The Christian faith is not a mindless jump into a dark chasm of confusion. Jesus shines light into the darkness and explains it clearly, providing us with confidence that we can trust him. At the outset of this earth-shattering evening, Jesus assures them of the final outcome. Immediately after he announces he's leaving he promises, they will be with him where he is. By revealing the outcome to his disciples, Jesus is removing their fear and soothing their anxiety.

His explanation will provide them with the confidence they need in the coming tumultuous days.

Jesus tells his disciples they can have confidence because he is leaving to prepare a place for them. Jesus is heading to his Father's house. When a son heads to his father's house, he's returning home. Jesus is returning home, and his home has become their home. Jesus is preparing for them a new, different, and better home. Heaven is a real place. It's not a location from a science fiction novel, no more real than Santa's workshop. Look at how Jesus describes it. It's a "house" with "rooms," and twice he refers to it as a "place." Heaven is not a figment of the imagination or a state of mind. Heaven is a real place created by God for his people to dwell with him forever.

I love what C. S. Lewis writes about heaven in his timeless work *Mere Christianity*:

> Creatures are not born with desires unless satisfaction for
> those desires exists. A baby feels hunger: well, there is such
> a thing as food. A duckling wants to swim: well, there is such
> a thing as water. Men feel sexual desire: well, there is such a
> thing as sex. If I find in myself a desire which no experience
> in this world can satisfy, the most probable explanation is
> that I was made for another world. If none of my earthly
> pleasures satisfy it, that does not prove that the universe is a
> fraud. Probably earthly pleasures were never meant to satisfy
> it, but only to arouse it, to suggest the real thing. (Lewis, *Mere
> Christianity*, 136–37)

There's a desire that earth can't fulfill. This unfulfilled desire is a reminder heaven is real. God has planted within our hearts this desire for something more, something greater. The writer of Hebrews described men and women of faith as those who were looking for a different kind of city, one whose architect and builder is God (Heb 11:10). Jesus tells his disciples of such a city, a place designed specifically for those who follow him. It's a place with many rooms, which not only pictures how great and grand it is but how welcoming it is for the weary traveler. Their travels are about to take a turn down a long, lonely, deserted highway, but Jesus promises them they will find at their destination a room prepared for them by the Master's own Son.

We are not citizens of earth; we are citizens of heaven. If you follow Jesus, there will be unrest in your soul while you sojourn on this earth.

In the classic Christian allegory *Pilgrim's Progress*, John Bunyan tells the story of Christian's journey from the City of Destruction to the Celestial City. He meets a cast of characters, some good, some evil. His travels take him through many difficult places, and he is never at home until that day when he reaches the Celestial City. Don't waste your life trying to make your home here. Jesus promises that each person who follows him will have a room in the Father's house perfectly designed for him or her. No one who enters the Father's house will be turned away. There's room for everyone.

This promise must have lifted the disciples' hearts out of the murky waters of despair. Jesus promises them eternal rest in his home. This promise alone would remind them to trust him because if he is preparing a place for them, then he is not going to leave them on their own. Between the crucifixion and the resurrection the disciples were scared and helpless. They felt abandoned by their Lord. The promise of heaven was given to protect them from the temptation to feel forgotten. The devil likes to use that against us, saying, "God has forgotten you. If Jesus really cares about you, why is he leaving you all alone in this broken world?" This promise of heaven, like a battering ram, assaults that temptation. Jesus essentially says, "If I have a special place designed just for you, do you really think I wouldn't come back for you? Do you really think I'd leave you by yourself?" Next time the devil assaults you with feelings of loneliness and despair, trust Jesus who gave us the promise of heaven so we would never doubt his perfect plan for us.

I wonder if we hear the words of Jesus, "I am going away to prepare a place for you," and picture Jesus dressed in overalls and a tool belt, doing construction on a heavenly mansion. The preparation of the place is not with a hammer and nails. The instruments are a cross and a grave. The way Jesus prepares this special home for his disciples is by laying down his life so their sins can be forgiven. This promise should arouse in us a greater appetite for heaven. However, a few earthly snacks can spoil our appetite for heaven. The more we avoid them, the stronger our appetite for heaven grows.

The first threat to our appetite is *an unhealthy attachment to earthly things*. We can grow so attached to the things of this life that heaven seems like a punishment. The constant consumption of earthly candy has diminished our appetite for the transcendent feast promised in eternity. We need a better perspective on earthly things. Earthly joys are just a foretaste of the full and complete joy we will have in heaven.

Why do we love family vacations? Is it the rest and fellowship? That's a small, imperfect taste of our heavenly rest and fellowship. Why do we love sports? Is it the feelings of exultation and triumph and sharing that with others? That's a small sliver of the triumph and exultation we'll enjoy together in heaven. The pleasures we experience on this earth are gifts from God, but they are designed simply to whet our appetite for the eternally satisfying joys of heaven.

Randy Alcorn, author of a book on heaven, writes,

> Many assume heaven will be unlike earth. But why do we think this? God designed earth for human beings. And nearly every description of heaven includes references to earthly things—eating, music, animals, water, trees, fruits, and a city with gates and streets. The Bible speaks of the new heavens and a new earth—not a *non*heavens and *non*earth. "New" doesn't mean fundamentally different, but vastly superior. If someone says, "I'm going to give you a new car," you'd get excited. Why? Not because you have no idea what a car is, but because you *do* know. (*In Light of Eternity*, 31; emphasis original)

Don't allow earthly things—joys and pleasures—to diminish your appetite for heaven. Ask God to use them to prime your taste buds for heaven's glory.

A second appetite spoiler is *a wrong perspective on Jesus.* Have you ever spoken to someone who said he had no desire to go to heaven, sit on clouds, and strum a harp for all eternity? Some think heaven is endless boredom, like being a monk or nun forever. No, heaven is about Jesus. Our view of heaven reflects our view of Jesus. The less we think of Jesus here on earth, the less excited we'll be for heaven. If we think of Jesus as a boring, dull, cosmic killjoy, or if we view him as someone who is only to be tolerated, then we will have no appetite for heaven. It's no wonder some of us don't want to spend eternity in heaven with Jesus since we don't take the time here on earth to discover what an inexhaustibly delightful, satisfying, and magnificent Savior Jesus is. We should view our years here on earth as preparation for an eternity with Jesus. Use the seventy or eighty or one hundred years God gives you to prepare for an eternal retirement. Invest right now in your relationship with Jesus.

Jesus gives living water. He is the all-satisfying source of eternal refreshment. He is not only profoundly happy himself, but he created happiness. Not only is he beautiful, but ugliness flees from his presence. When we come to this realization, our appetite for heaven will grow, and we will no longer be content with the cotton candy of this world. The more our love for Jesus Christ grows, the more our appetite for heaven grows.

In the book of Revelation, we get a glimpse of heaven, and every scene centers on one person: Jesus. The worship of Jesus Christ to the glory of the Father is *the defining characteristic* of heaven. Heaven is not great because there is no sickness, death, or pain. It's not great because the streets will be made of gold and every tear will be wiped away. All those things are true, but heaven is great because Jesus is there. As Jesus makes this promise to his disciples, he doesn't promise the coolest bachelor pad in the sky where we can do whatever our hearts desire. Though heaven will comprise wonders we can barely imagine here on earth, the promise of heaven is that Jesus will be there. He tells them, "If I go away and prepare a place for you, I will come again and take you to myself, so that where I am you may be also" (14:3). The promise is that they will be with him. Nothing would ever separate them from Jesus Christ. Think of every word that describes what is good: *beautiful, peaceful, joyous, wonderful, great, amazing, happy, spectacular.* Heaven will be all of these things but only because Jesus is there. Sin will no longer separate us from his presence. We will forever enjoy the one we were created to enjoy.

Jonathan Edwards wrote,

> The redeemed have all their objective good in God. God himself is the great good which they are brought to the possession and enjoyment of by redemption. He is the highest good, and the sum of all that good which Christ purchased. God is the inheritance of the saints; he is the portion of their souls. God is their wealth and treasure, their food, their life, their dwelling place, their ornament and diadem, and their everlasting honor and glory. They have none in heaven but God; he is the great good which the redeemed are received to at death, and which they are to rise to at the end of the world. The Lord God, he is the light of the heavenly Jerusalem; and is the "river of the water of life" that runs, and the tree of life that grows, "in the midst of the paradise of God." The glorious excellencies and beauty of God will be what will forever entertain the minds of the saints, and the love of God will be their everlasting feast. The redeemed will indeed enjoy other things; they will enjoy the angels, and will enjoy one another:

but that which they shall enjoy in the angels, or each other, or in anything else whatsoever, that will yield them delight and happiness, will be what will be seen of God in them. ("God Glorified," 74–75)

Heaven is heaven because Jesus is there. At the apex of their distress, the disciples could remember this promise from Jesus: "You will be with me where I am." That promise sustained Abraham as he left his own country and looked for a new city. It was on the lips of David as he wrote: "You reveal the path of life to me; in your presence is abundant joy; at your right hand are eternal pleasures" (Ps 16:11). When an aged Peter took pen in hand to encourage suffering disciples, he reminded them of this promise:

> *The God of all grace, who called you to his eternal glory in Christ,*
> *will himself restore, establish, strengthen, and support you after*
> *you have suffered a little while. To him be dominion forever. Amen.*
> (1 Pet 5:10-11)

The presence of Jesus is the promise that sustains us in the midst of difficulties. Like the disciples, we need to cling to the words of Jesus as our hope and our confidence while we walk through this fallen, sin-plagued world.

A. W. Tozer called heaven "the long tomorrow" and reminded the church to "look to the long tomorrow" (quoted in Alcorn, *In Light of Eternity*, 160). Many days feel like they will never end. You wake up with a headache, the car doesn't start, your boss is grumpy, your lunch is cold, traffic is bad, the kids are out of control, and bedtime can't come soon enough. On those days, those never-ending days, we need to remember there is only one day that will never end, and it's a good day. Only the long tomorrow in heaven with Jesus will go on forever.

Reflect and Discuss

1. What remedy does Jesus give his disciples for their troubled hearts?
2. If the remedy for troubled hearts is faith in Jesus, what must be the root cause of troubled hearts?
3. What would it look like to trust in God in a recent anxiety in your life? What would look different?
4. Why can the disciples have confidence even though Jesus is leaving?

5. Why is it good news today that Jesus is preparing a place in his Father's house for his followers to go to in the future?

6. How has the promise that Jesus is preparing a place for you affected your life today?

7. Are there any things in your life that have become distractions to eternity?

8. What is the defining characteristic of heaven?

9. Are you growing in affection for Jesus so that you have a desire for heaven?

10. What are some earthly appetizers that extinguish your hunger for heaven?

More Promises

JOHN 14:4-14

Main Idea: Jesus assures his disciples that following him will lead to heaven, and he promises them help from heaven while they follow him on earth.

I.   **The Promise of a Path to Heaven**
II. **The Promise of Power from Heaven**
    A. Greater works
    B. Answered prayer

A t the turn of the century, a *USA Today* article was written about billionaire Ted Turner, the founder of CNN and owner of the Atlanta Braves. Toward the end of the article, Turner explains his view of life:

> You know, I'm not looking for any big rewards. I'm not a
> religious person. I believe this life is all we have. I'm not doing
> what I'm doing to be rewarded in heaven or punished in hell.
> I'm doing it because I feel it's the right thing to do. Almost
> every religion talks about a savior coming. When you look in
> the mirror in the morning, when you're putting on your lipstick
> or shaving, you're looking at the savior. Nobody else is going to
> save you but yourself. (Quoted in Lieber, "He Wants," 1–2C)

Though only a small minority of people would be bold enough to make that statement, it's the way the majority of people live. What Ted Turner so brazenly stated is the underlying philosophy of religion.

In Scripture we're forced to compare *religion* and the *gospel.* Religion is any system that teaches we have the ability to save ourselves. The gospel teaches we are completely unable to save ourselves. Religion says, "Look inside yourself for salvation." The gospel says, "The only hope for salvation is outside yourself." We clearly see the failure of religion in the Old Testament. The Israelites often fell into the trap of religion, assuming they could earn salvation by keeping the Old Testament law. The prophet Isaiah condemned the Israelites for living as if their works would justify them before God. They attempted to draw near to God with their mouths and honor him with their lips, but their hearts were far from him (29:13). In other words, they were trying to be good enough to earn God's favor. In the New Testament Jesus contrasted religion and the gospel in his interactions with the religious elite. They did a lot of religious things—they tithed on everything they owned (even down to herbs and spices from their gardens), they fasted multiple times a week, and they memorized copious amounts of Scripture—all with the goal of earning God's favor.

Jesus told them it was impossible, and in the place of religion he offered them the gospel. He promised his followers reconciliation with God, not through their effort and work but only through faith in him. Jesus did for us what we couldn't do for ourselves. This is what Jesus reminds his disciples of in chapter 14. In this section of the Gospel of John, the disciples are on a roller-coaster ride, and it's just beginning. So far this evening,

- They've had their feet washed by their Master.
- They've been warned of a traitor in their midst.
- They've seen Peter shot down as he proclaims his loyalty to Jesus.
- They've just found out that Jesus is leaving them.

After all the bad news, they finally receive some good news beginning in chapter 14. Jesus promises them he will return to collect them so they can be with him forever. He ends this promise with words of assurance: "You know the way to where I am going" (v. 4).

Thomas speaks for all of them when he expresses uncertainty: "Lord, we don't even understand where you're going, how could we possibly know the way?" (v. 5; my paraphrase). This question from the lips of Thomas brings a second promise from Jesus. These promises are given after Jesus gives them a command. He says, "Believe also in me" (14:1). The promises hinge on faith. These promises are given to those who have committed themselves to follow Jesus as his disciples.

The Promise of a Path to Heaven

This promise is not a future promise but a current one. Jesus doesn't say, "You *will know* [future tense] the way to heaven." Jesus tells them, "You *know* [present tense] the way to heaven" (v. 4). The significance of the perfect tense is it's a past action that has future results. So in effect Jesus is saying, "In the past you came to know the way; this knowledge will continue into the future." But the disciples aren't certain they know the way. In fact, Thomas says he's not even sure of the destination (v. 5). Jesus is the way to gain access to the Father. They may be confused, but they already know this path because they know Jesus.

This entire discussion is based on an understood, yet often overlooked, presupposition. Everyone who's religious realizes something needs to happen for him or her to get to God, to make it to heaven. Whether their answer is good works, giving to charity, penance, last rites, karma, reincarnation, or martyrdom, all religious people acknowledge what the Bible teaches throughout: the way to God is blocked. Something hinders us from being with God, and it must be overcome. In the Old Testament God taught Israel this truth through an object lesson. Hanging in the tabernacle and then in the temple was a thick, heavy curtain called "the veil." The purpose of the veil was to separate mankind from the earthly dwelling of God. The veil itself didn't separate man from God. It was just a symbol. What really separates man from God is sin. The abundance of organized religions reveals that most people feel they need to do something to get to God, something to get through the veil of sin.

Because of our sin, we need a mediator. We need someone who can bring us into God's presence. For the Jews, this person was the priest. Once a year he would pass through the veil and enter the presence of God to confess the sins of the nation. When Jesus died, the veil in the temple was torn from the top to the bottom. Just as the veil symbolized the separation of God and man, the tearing of the veil symbolized there is now a way to enter the presence of God. Jesus is the mediator. Being both man and God, he alone can bridge the chasm that separates a sinful person from a holy God. Jesus uses the imagery of a way, a path, a road to teach them he is able to take them from one point—their sinful, wicked state—to a different point—reconciliation with God.

The disciples don't need to concern themselves with a location or a destination. They don't need to obsess over a place. They need to focus all of their attention on a *person*. Just as heaven is about living with Jesus, salvation is about walking with Jesus. Jesus does not say he will point them in the right direction. He says he is the driver and the destination. One commentator wrote,

> [Jesus] does not only give advice and directions. He takes us by the hand and leads us; he strengthens us and guides us personally every day. He does not tell us about the way; he is the Way. (Barclay, *John*, 157)

Salvation is more than praying a prayer. It's putting your trust in a person. We create doubt when we view salvation improperly. We might worry about the words we said, or whether we were sincere, instead of trusting in Jesus. Through Jesus alone we are brought into a right relationship with the Father. The exclusivity of Jesus's statement often angers people. Why is it so offensive? It's offensive because it strikes a blow to our pride. What Jesus says to you and to me is, "You cannot make it to heaven on your own." It feeds our proud nature to attempt to save ourselves. To accept the true Jesus revealed in Scripture requires humility.

Jesus doesn't make this exclusive statement because he's trying to win a popularity contest. He says it because it's true. What Jesus says can be trusted because he himself is the truth. Jesus does not simply tell the truth; he embodies it. He is the source of truth, and the reason truth is absolute. Social commentators say we've been living in the age of postmodernism. Listen to these words on postmodern thinking from John MacArthur:

> [T]he one essential, non-negotiable demand postmodernism makes of everyone: We are not to think we know any objective truth. Postmodernists often suggest that every opinion should be shown equal respect. And therefore on the surface, postmodernism seems driven by a broad-minded concern for harmony and tolerance. It all sounds very charitable and altruistic. But what really underlies the postmodernist belief system is an utter *intolerance* for every worldview that makes any universal truth-claims—particularly biblical Christianity. (*Why One Way?*, 9)

I visited the website religioustolerance.org and read this in their statement of beliefs: "We do believe: that systems of truth in the field of morals, ethics, and religious belief are not absolute. They vary by culture, religion, and over time." Jesus condemns that thinking when he states, "I am the truth" (v. 6). If he is the true way to the Father, then only through him can we have life. He has driven this point home throughout the Gospel. Only through Jesus can anyone find life. Jesus repeatedly tells his disciples he is the source of life (cf. 1:3-4; 4:13-14; 5:21; 11:25). Why is it so important on this night for him to reassure them he is life? Because they will see him die. They will witness the life leave his physical body. They will watch as his lifeless flesh is taken down from the cross and carried to the tomb. Even as they watch this tragedy unfold, they will hear these words of reassurance echo: "I am the life."

These three descriptions—the way, the truth, and the life—lay the foundation for the exclusive statement Jesus makes at the end of verse 6: "No one comes to the Father except through me." Christianity is exclusive. But Christianity is not exclusive because of who it lets in. Jesus teaches, "Anyone may come" (see John 7:37; Rev 22:17). Christianity is exclusive because there's only *one way* to get in. Jesus alone brings men to God. He is *the* way, not *a* way.

The reason the disciples eventually came to believe Jesus's promise of a path to heaven is because Jesus is God. Their assurance is rooted in the deity of Christ. He has the right and authority to make these promises because he himself is God (John 14:7). Everything Jesus says and does demonstrates he is one with the Father (vv. 9-11). Jesus's words reveal he is in the Father, and Jesus's works reveal the Father is in him. The disciples should have realized Jesus is one with the Father by this point. He asks in effect, "How can you not yet believe?" There should be no way to miss it. He made the claim over and over, and his claim is backed up by such definitive acts that those acts alone should be enough to make them believe. Jesus can make the promise of heaven—both the reality of the place and the exclusivity of the path—for one simple reason: he is God.

The Promise of Power from Heaven

Here's a promise to comfort the disciples' hearts and calm their fears: Jesus is not withdrawing from them. He's not leaving the difficulty and challenges of this life so he can kick back in a heavenly La-Z-Boy. He's going ahead of them, but he will continue to actively work in them. He is going to heaven, and from there he will supply them with infinite resources. The power he will supply them will be seen through greater works and through answered prayer.

Greater Works

What does Jesus mean that his disciples will do greater works? He's not saying just the Twelve will do greater works. He says, "The one who believes in me" (v. 12). *Greater* can't simply mean "more spectacular." If he meant "more spectacular," then his disciples might have had this discussion:

"Hey, Peter, you're creative. Jesus said we'd do more spectacular works than he did. What's more spectacular than turning water into wine?"

Peter thinks for a second; "What about if someone walked on water? Oh wait, Jesus already did that."

So James jumps in: "Let's not worry about the water miracles, what's more spectacular than healing a man who's blind or lame or sick? . . . What's greater than healing a man that's half-dead?"

"Well," Peter responds, "you could resurrect a man who's all the way dead."

Nothing could be done that's more spectacular than what Jesus did, but if we look at this promise in the larger context of God's plan of redemption (which is its setting), we can understand what Jesus means. The works the disciples would do were not more spectacular, but they were greater in extent.

Greater geographically. One historian writes,

> Think of what Jesus in the days of his flesh had *actually done.*
> He had never preached outside of Palestine. Within his
> lifetime Europe had never heard the gospel. He had never
> personally met [the] moral degradation of a city like Rome.
> (Barclay, *John*, 165; emphasis original)

But his disciples have spread the gospel around the globe.

Greater ethnically. Jesus dealt almost exclusively with the Jews. However, his disciples would deal with both Jews and Gentiles.

Greater numerically. Acts begins with a few dozen disciples meeting in a room, but by Acts 2 three thousand are added to the church.

Greater spiritually. William Barclay writes, "The triumphs of the message of the Cross were even greater than the triumphs of Jesus in the days of his flesh" (*John*, 165). Jesus may have raised the physically dead, but the disciples were able to witness the spiritually dead come to life (Eph 2:4-7).

However, we set up a false dichotomy if we try to contrast the works of Jesus with the works of the disciples. The distinction is between what Jesus did on earth and what Jesus is accomplishing from heaven through his people here on earth.

Answered Prayer

The Spirit's power will not only be seen in greater works, but it will also be evident through answered prayer (vv. 13-14). Jesus promises to answer the prayers of his disciples. But lest we run home and fall on our knees begging for a new boat, notice Jesus defines genuine prayer as prayer in his name and prayer that when answered will bring glory to God. To pray in Jesus's name is not to recite a magical incantation but to pray in line with his will. It's to pray with the understanding the request you bring is one Jesus would sign his name to. It's a request that, if answered, would show the world who God is and what he cares about. Hudson Taylor, the faithful missionary to China, once said,

> I used to ask God to help me. Then, I asked Him if I might help Him. Finally, I ended up asking Him to do his work in me and through me, if He would be so pleased." (Quoted in Davey, *When Heaven*, 135)

That's praying in Jesus's name.

When we pray expecting him to answer, he will. Confident prayer in the name of Jesus—according to his will—will be answered, and when that answer comes, God will be glorified. John Piper writes,

> Prayer is the open admission that without Christ we can do nothing. And prayer is the turning away from ourselves to God in the confidence that he will provide the help we need. Prayer humbles us as needy and exalts God as wealthy. (*Desiring God*, 160–61)

This passage is packed with wonderful promises Jesus made to his disciples: the promise of a place called heaven, the promise of a path to heaven, and the promise of power from heaven. Like an engagement ring, these promises bring us hope and excitement for that day when we see Jesus face-to-face. But all of these promises come after a single command: "Believe in me." These promises are only for people who have placed their faith in Jesus Christ alone. Remember what Jesus promises:

- You do not need to rely on yourself, for he is the way.
- You do not need to live in uncertainty, for he is the truth.
- You do not need to fear death, for he is the life.

Reflect and Discuss

1. What is the underlying philosophy of religion? How is this different from the gospel?
2. How does the Old Testament display the failure of religion?
3. What does the Bible teach that all religions also acknowledge? What symbol does God give of this in the temple?
4. Why is Christianity exclusive?
5. What is so offensive about Jesus's statement of exclusivity?
6. How will Jesus's followers do greater works?
7. In what ways has Jesus's promise of greater works been seen?
8. What does it mean to pray in Jesus's name?
9. Why are Jesus's words on prayer good news we can believe?
10. What can we believe about Jesus based on his words on prayer?

Jesus Loves Me, This I Know

JOHN 14:15-31

Main Idea: Even though Jesus is leaving, the relationship between Jesus and his disciples will continue to be defined by love.

I. **The Disciples' Love for Jesus**
II. **Jesus's Love for His Disciples**
    A. The assurance of his resurrection
    B. The assurance of his Spirit
    C. The assurance of his peace

I wonder if the disciples' anxiety in John 14 is due in part to the change taking place in their relationship with Jesus. For months they've walked step for step with Jesus. They've experienced everything from the mundane to the miraculous *with* him. They've attended weddings and funerals. Some days they've eaten little, and some days they've had their fill of wonder bread created by Jesus's own hand. Now they fear it's all changing. Jesus is leaving them, and there's no way their relationship will survive.

But Jesus assures them their relationship with him is not finished. Their relationship will continue to grow and develop. Plus, it will be marked by a single, defining characteristic: love. They will grow in their love for Jesus and will demonstrate it through their actions. Jesus will continue to love them, and his love will be experienced through the gift of his Spirit.

Jesus begins this farewell conversation with his disciples by promising they will be with him in the future (14:1-3). Jesus doesn't only offer them promises about the *distant* future. He also assures them of what will happen in the *near* future. His promise of a future in heaven doesn't mean they're cut off from him until then. Though he is going before them, preparing their way to the Father, their relationship will continue. He describes how this relationship will continue in the future by focusing first on the disciples' love for him and then on his love for the disciples.

The Disciples' Love for Jesus

The disciples love Jesus. Their anguish over his departure is more than concern for their future. The reason this news hits them so hard is because they care deeply about their Teacher. Their hearts have been knit together with his through all their experiences over the previous few years. Jesus tells his disciples how they can show him they love him after he's gone to heaven. True disciples reveal their love through obedience (vv. 15,21,23-24). In verse 15 Jesus describes the proof of their love with the phrase, "You will keep my commands." He's not singling out a particular command or a select saying. He describes a life committed to following him no matter where he leads. He describes a person who has cast aside all concern except obedience to Jesus. Loving Jesus is not like bargain hunting at a garage sale: you can't comb through all that he says, then pick whatever commands you like, disregarding any you find unappealing. Love for Jesus means obeying even the most difficult commands. We might say, "Look, I love Jesus. See how I obey him," and then point to the commands easiest for us to obey: "I don't kill, and I don't have any graven images. See, I really love him." Our genuine love for him is truly revealed when we obey the challenging commands during difficult times.

The world knew Jesus loved the Father because he obeyed the Father's commands (v. 31), *especially* the difficult ones—like going to the cross and taking on himself the sins of the world. The world will see our love for Jesus as genuine when we gladly choose the tough things and obey him in those. Love when life is soft, safe, and easy proves little. Who do we know loves his wife? The elderly man who parades around with his healthy, beautiful, twenty-something trophy wife on his arm? Or the elderly husband bathing and feeding his disoriented wife as she slowly loses her memory? They may both love their wives, but we're certain one does. Jesus shows us what it means to love through difficult obedience.

Love for Jesus must also be our *motivation* to obey his commands. Obedience must flow out of a heart of love. Obedience without love is nothing more than the pursuit of self-righteousness. We will never obey his Word if all we feel is a sense of moral obligation. We will never obey his Word if all we want is to shore up our standing before God. If we look at the words of Jesus and think, *I can make him happy if I do this one,* or *He won't be angry or disappointed with me as long as I don't mess up on that command,* then we are not obeying out of love for him. We are simply trying to earn his favor. If you want to conquer sin and obey Jesus, you don't simply try harder to obey. You stoke the flames of your love for him. The antidote for disobedience isn't obedience but love. If you struggle to obey Jesus, then focus on loving him more. Beg God to give you a passion for Jesus. The greater your love grows, the easier obedience becomes.

On the one hand, we can't obey Jesus if we don't love him. On the other hand, we can't love him if we don't obey him. Would you believe someone loved his spouse if he was being unfaithful? No, you wouldn't. What if he repeatedly *said* he loved his spouse while being unfaithful? Would you believe him then? No, you still wouldn't. Why? Because his actions negate his profession. His works trump his words.

When I was in elementary school, my buddy's dad drove the church bus. I loved spending Saturday night at his house and then riding the bus to church on Sunday. They would do all of these silly promotions on the bus routes, and one Sunday everyone who rode the bus was given a cheap, white kite with this written on it in big, red printing: "I ♥ Jesus." Looking back, I can just picture dozens of kids who had no idea who Jesus was flocking to the park and flying their "I ♥ Jesus" kites. How many Christians are like those kids? Over their lives fly "I Love Jesus" kites, but love for him isn't evident in how they live. If we love Jesus, we will live differently (v. 21). We can fly dozens of kites, but it doesn't mean we love Jesus. The only convincing evidence that we do indeed love Jesus is the way we live.

The disciples' love for Jesus will primarily be seen in their obedience to his commands, but Jesus does give them one other way their love for him will be revealed. Their love for Jesus will be revealed by their willingness to sacrifice their immediate comfort and to trust Jesus when he says everything is happening for the Father's glory (v. 28). Jesus promised he would return for them, but his departure is necessary. They struggle to rejoice with him because at this moment their desires are more important than his plan. When we love Jesus, we believe he's in control and whatever he chooses to do is best. We are less concerned with our agendas, our emotions, or our ease, and we focus our energy and attention on what Jesus cares about. Jesus tells his disciples, "If you loved me, you would rejoice that I am going to the Father" (v. 28). Genuine love isn't self-centered. If our love for Jesus is true, it can't be self-centered. If we love him, we will obey him and desire his wishes above our own.

Jesus's Love for His Disciples

Jesus only mentions his love for the disciples once in this passage, but the proof of his love is evident throughout. Not only does he love them, but the Father loves them as well (v. 21). We so casually say, "God loves me." Oh, that the earth-shattering ramifications of God's love for you would bore into the depths of your soul! God—the Creator of the universe, the Holy One who dwells above the heavens—loves you. If you've believed in his Son, he loves you. Though there is no reason for him to love you, he has chosen to love you.

A good friend of mine spent six months in Tanzania, East Africa, building an orphanage. One of the workers sent him a letter describing a recent day at the orphanage:

> Issa arrived close to noon and we walked around the orphanage again and talked for a little while. You could see that he knew something was going on and he was clinging pretty tightly to the ladies who brought him. Amy and I both realized that it was not going to be a simple and smooth good-bye process. I ended up taking him and they hurriedly walked out and drove off. I held Issa inside until I knew they were gone. He was very upset. I tried to comfort him and calm him as best I could.

I can't imagine the fear, anxiety, and uncertainty that comes from losing your parents—the ones who are supposed to love, comfort, and protect you. When Jesus announced he was leaving, the disciples felt as if they were being orphaned. Jesus assures them that they do not need to fear, for they are not being left vulnerable and exposed (v. 18). What a tender statement from the lips of the Lord! He understands what is taking place in the hearts of his disciples. At a moment when they can't adequately capture what they're feeling, he sums it up perfectly and in the same breath gives them three assurances of his love for them.

The Assurance of His Resurrection

The first assurance is right there in verse 18: "I am coming to you." He will return to them. After the resurrection he will not appear to the world—to those who don't believe—but he will appear to his disciples (vv. 19-20). They will see him again and in such a way that they will never doubt Jesus is the Son of God.

This promise of his postresurrection appearance isn't made to us two thousand years removed, but the promise of the resurrection is. That statement tucked right in the middle—"Because I live, you will live too" (v. 19)—*is* true for us. We know of Jesus's love; we are assured of his love because he rose from the dead, conquering death and the grave for us. He went to the cross because he loved us, and he rose triumphantly so we would no longer need to fear death.

The Assurance of His Spirit

Throughout these verses, he assures them that the Father will send his Spirit to indwell them (v. 16). The Father *will* give them another Helper. He calls the Holy Spirit the "Counselor"—the Greek word is *paraclete*. Since it's only used in John, it's tough to nail down a precise definition of this term. It's translated "Helper, Comforter, Advocate." Some translate it literally as the one who "comes alongside." The key to understanding this term is to look at the word Jesus uses right before it. He promises the disciples "another" *paraclete* will come. *Another* means they currently have a *paraclete*. The Holy Spirit will come and fill the role Jesus has been fulfilling with the disciples. He will comfort, strengthen, and teach them, just as Jesus has been doing.

Have you ever wished Jesus was sitting next to you and you could have a face-to-face conversation with him? Have you ever found yourself longing to tell him all about your day and ask him to help you make sense of it all? We have that ability and opportunity because of the Spirit. Just as Jesus could comfort and strengthen his disciples, we can be comforted and strengthened through his Spirit who dwells within us.

Have you really embraced this promise? You may be able to theologically discuss why the coming of the Holy Spirit is a good thing, but can you honestly say his role in your life is similar to the presence of Jesus in the lives of the disciples? We have downplayed this promise from Jesus in our lives and churches. Because of our zeal to defend the sufficiency of Scripture, we have forgotten the significant role the Holy Spirit is to play in the life of every disciple of Jesus Christ. This promise is not given so the disciples can get the answer correct on a theology midterm. Jesus promised them the Holy Spirit so they will know that his love for them will never falter or die but will grow and flourish, even though he's returning to the Father. This promise of the Holy Spirit is their lifeline when the seas get rough over the following days. We can easily take the blessing of the Holy Spirit for granted.

Jesus promises he is going to prepare a home *for them in heaven*, and now he says he's also preparing a home *for himself in them* (v. 17). When the Spirit makes his home in the disciples, he begins his ministry of pointing them to Jesus. Throughout the New Testament we find the Holy Spirit doesn't take the spotlight and shine it on himself; rather, he is the spotlight operator and always focuses the light on Jesus. Even here Jesus promises the disciples the Holy Spirit will come in *his* name and remind them of *his* teaching (v. 26).

The Assurance of His Peace

A common farewell around the time of Jesus was to wish someone "peace." When Jesus wishes them "peace," it's not a superficial good-bye, but a genuine reality (v. 27). He has brought peace with God, and he's giving them a peace the world cannot offer. This peace will soothe their hearts when the world around them is in turmoil. The peace Jesus gives comes through his defeat of mankind's greatest foes: sin, death, and Satan. The cosmic battle is about to begin, but the outcome was decided long ago (v. 30). Satan has nothing to bring against Jesus and will be defeated. Peace for us came through great violence. Peace with God was delivered when Jesus offered up his life to be brutally slaughtered. D. A. Carson reflects on this great irony:

> The pax Romana (peace of Rome) was won and maintained by a brutal sword; not a few Jews thought the Messianic peace would have to be secured by a still mightier sword. Instead, it was secured by an innocent man who suffered and died at the hands of the Romans, of the Jews, and of all of us. And by his death he effected for his own followers peace with God, and therefore "the peace of God, which transcends all understanding." (*John*, 506)

That's the beauty of the gospel. We have peace because Jesus fought a war. He fought our fight, so we could have his peace.

One of the most popular Christian anthems is also the simplest. It says, "Jesus loves me! This I know, for the Bible tells me so" (Anna B. Warner, "Jesus Loves Me").

> At the height of persecution in Communist China, a Christian sent a message to a friend. The message escaped the attention of the censors, because it said simply: "The *this I know* people are well"—but that phrase, the "*this I know* people" clearly

identified the Christian community in China. (Donovan,
"Jesus Loves Me"; emphasis original)

"This I know people." Our confidence is in the love of Jesus. We know
he loves us because we've experienced his love. His love defines us individually and as a community.

Reflect and Discuss

1. How do true disciples reveal their love of Jesus?
2. How does obedience flow out of a heart of love?
3. How can love help you conquer sin in your life?
4. Have you ever prayed for the Holy Spirit to grow your passion for
   Jesus? Take time to do that right now.
5. Now take a moment to contemplate that God himself loves you.
   Pray to grow in your belief of this truth.
6. What three assurances of his love does Jesus give his disciples?
7. How is the resurrection an assurance of Jesus's love for you?
8. Why does Jesus call the Holy Spirit "another Counselor"? What does
   it say about who the Holy Spirit is and what he does?
9. How does the promise of the Holy Spirit display Jesus's concern for
   your ability to live in submission to him?
10. How has Jesus given you peace through belief in him?

Fruit-Producing Faith

JOHN 15:1-17

Main Idea: True disciples of Jesus have a permanent, life-giving, fruit-producing union with Jesus.

I. **True Disciples Bear Spiritual Fruit (15:1-6).**
II. **Identifying Spiritual Fruit in the Life of a Disciple (15:7-17)**
   A. Answered prayer
   B. Obedient love
   C. Inexhaustible joy
   D. Sacrificial love

In John 15 Jesus is preparing his disciples for his upcoming death, resurrection, and ascension to heaven. His final instructions primarily relate to what it means to be his disciple. What does it look like to follow Jesus? How can a person be his disciple after the cross? He uses an illustration based on the fact that we each do what's in our nature. True disciples of Jesus have a permanent, life-giving, fruit-producing union with Jesus. Disciples will bear fruit. It's part of their new nature.

This passage breaks down into two parts. The first part is verses 1-6, the illustration of the vine and the branches. The point of the illustration is simple: being united with Jesus brings life, and life is revealed by fruit. In verses 7-17 we discover what the fruit looks like: answered prayer, obedient love, inexhaustible joy, and sacrificial love.

True Disciples Bear Spiritual Fruit
JOHN 15:1-6

Jesus begins with his seventh and final "I Am" statement in the Gospel of John.

- "I am the bread of life" (6:35).
- "I am the light of the world" (8:12).
- "I am the gate" (10:9).
- "I am the good shepherd" (10:11).

- "I am the resurrection and the life" (11:25).
- "I am the way, the truth, and the life" (14:7).

In each case Jesus is not *a* light, or *a* gate, or *a* truth; he is *the* way, *the* truth, and *the* life. He is unique. The same is true in verse 1. He is *the* vine, *the only* vine, and *the only true* vine. Imagine a rich man dies and leaves a fortune to his heir. News leaks out they're having trouble identifying the person who's the rightful heir. Hundreds come forward claiming to be the heir. The day comes when the judge is going to decide who receives the inheritance. Before he makes his judgment, a solitary figure enters the quiet courtroom and says, "I am the *true* heir." The word *true* means something. It means there are *false* heirs.

When Jesus calls himself the *true* vine, he's indicating the existence of a *false* vine. It's similar to when he said he was the *true* bread that came from heaven. There was other bread that came from heaven, called manna, but it wasn't the *true* bread. Only Jesus was. Can we identify the "false" vine? Multiple times in the Old Testament Israel is called God's vine. In Isaiah 5 a story is told about a vineyard planted with love and tended with care. Instead of growing good grapes, the vineyard grew wild, inedible grapes. In verse 7 the vineyard is identified as the nation of Israel (cf. Ps 80). When Jesus calls himself the *true* vine, he's making a contrast with the nation of Israel. Here's the point: The path to God doesn't go through the nation of Israel; it goes through Jesus. You don't need to become a citizen of Israel to be right with God. You need to become a disciple of Jesus. Don't worry about being in Israel. Instead, focus on being in Jesus. Let's say a person came to the religious leaders in Israel with serious inquiries about how to be made right with God. He would have been instructed to become part of Israel: get circumcised, bring sacrifices to the altar, and celebrate the Jewish festivals and holy days. Jesus essentially says instead, "Becoming an Israelite is unnecessary and ineffective. You need to follow me." Union with Jesus—connection to the true vine—is the only way to please the gardener.

In this illustration the branches are disciples. Jesus mentions two types of disciples—living disciples and dead disciples (v. 2). Jesus came to bring life, and all true disciples are alive. Anyone who's dead is not a true disciple and has never exercised faith. At best such people are like Judas Iscariot. They hang around Jesus without a genuine, life-giving relationship with him. Jesus is divisive. His presence divides true disciples from false disciples. He didn't come to coddle false disciples. He says, "False disciples will be cut away by my Father" (v. 2; my paraphrase). If you don't bear fruit, then you're not connected to Jesus. If your life shows no evidence of Jesus, then you don't belong to him.

If you are connected to the vine, God is going to do whatever it takes to cause you to bear fruit. God will cut you and prune you and trim you and chop you. He is not content to let you stay on the vine bearing little fruit. God is ruthlessly determined to shape you into something much better and more beautiful than you are right now. He is determined to make you more like his Son Jesus. The only way that will happen is through cutting away the parts that are dying so you can grow more and more healthy. God's commitment to your fruit bearing is greater than your commitment to comfort. God will do whatever it takes for you to bear fruit. John Newton, the great eighteenth-century English pastor and songwriter, began a letter this way:

> At length, and without further apology for my silence, I sit down to ask you how you fare. *Afflictions I hear have been your lot; and if I had not heard so, I should have taken it for granted: for I believe the Lord loves you, and as many as He loves He chastens.* I think you can say, afflictions have been good for you, and I doubt not but you have found strength according to your day; so that, though you may have been sharply tried, you have not been overpowered. (Newton, *Amazing Works*, 156–57; emphasis added)

The difficulty you're going through right now may well be an act of kindness on God's part. He loves you, and he is shaping you into something more than you are now. Shaping takes a sharp blade and produces pain, but it's a reminder of God's love and commitment to you. Disciples bear fruit because God will not stop until they do.

The word *remain* or *abide* can confuse us (vv. 4-5). We have a tendency to turn it into an emotion or an experience. Jesus is talking about a fixed reality. He's saying, "True disciples are connected to me. We are united together. Now abide in me. Remain connected to me. Get your life from me. Live your life out of your connection with me." The illustration of the branch helps us understand what it looks like to abide. A branch is only alive if the sap flows from the trunk through the branch. Without sap the branch dies. When people trust Jesus as Lord and Savior, the life of Jesus begins to flow through them like sap through a branch. Jesus has made them alive. His Spirit now indwells them, and he gives them power to serve him and trust him and tell of him and live for him. He promises never to leave them and to sustain them at all times.

The life of Jesus flows through every Christian. Apart from his life, we can accomplish nothing for God; we can do nothing to please God. But because of his life, we now have the ability to deny sin and live for him. The key to the Christian life is Christ's life in the Christian. Because of our connection with him—we are united to him by faith— we have the power to live in a way that pleases him. We need to understand our inability to please God apart from Jesus's power in us. We can do *nothing* apart from him (v. 5). Oh, we can sing in the choir, give an offering, answer questions at small group, hand out bulletins, or go Christmas caroling, but apart from him those things are in our strength and therefore are not pleasing to God. They are the "fruit" of our own effort, the "fruit" of self-righteousness. Our self-righteous fruit does not honor God, does not please God, and does nothing to further the gospel of God.

People who claim to be Christians but do not show evidence of his life flowing through them will be cut off, gathered up, and burned (v. 6). Unless there is fruit of Jesus in you, then you will be cast into the fire. This warning is meant to be taken seriously. Is there clear, unmistakable evidence that the living God resides in you? If he lives in you, he makes his presence known. God does not hide inside his children. I had a conversation with a friend who said he was saved at a young age and then lost that salvation for years as a teenager, college student, and young adult. After years without salvation he was saved again. No. No. I love him but no. God doesn't come and go, and he doesn't hide. If there's no fruit, then God is not present. And if God is not present, then you're not his child, and the fire is waiting for you. Does God live in you? That's what it means to be a Christian.

Your fruit proves you're a disciple, and your lack of fruit also proves something (v. 8). This verse gives the world the right to inspect our fruit. Jesus essentially tells the watching world, "If someone claims to be mine, look at his or her fruit. Fruit will expose the frauds." If you claim to be a Christian, people are always inspecting your fruit, and they have that right. Jesus gave the right to them. Why? Because his followers have nothing to hide. Our fruit testifies to the truth of the gospel. Jesus who died must have risen again because he clearly lives inside us. Because disciples are connected to Jesus like branches to the vine, they will bear fruit. A fruitless disciple is no disciple at all. It does not mean believers won't suffer periods of drought or barren years, but over the course of life, they will see evidence of Jesus's life at work in them.

Identifying Spiritual Fruit in the Life of a Disciple
JOHN 15:7-17

Answered Prayer

If our connection with Jesus is like a branch's connection to the vine, then prayer is like the nutrients flowing back and forth between the branch and the vine. It's natural, due to the connection. We are united with Christ, and that union produces a relationship. Relationships are maintained and strengthened through communication. Jesus communicates with us primarily through his Word ("my words remain in you"), and we respond in prayer (v. 7).

The life of Jesus flows through his followers, and that life blossoms into a vibrant relationship. We receive the Word and respond in prayer. In our illustration of the vine and branches, the gardener (God) wields his word in order to prune and prepare the branches (v. 3). Clean branches sprout fruit, and one type of fruit is prayer. Where there is prayer, there will be answers. God listens to his people. Think about this circle. We receive the words of God (his words inform us, instruct us, and command us). In response to the Word, Scripture, we pray to God (our requests are guided and shaped by the truth of the Word and are therefore in line with God's will). God hears our prayers and joyfully responds to our requests because they were offered up in obedience to his Word. As the Word shapes our desires and the Spirit forms us from the inside out, we will begin to pray for those things that God cares about. God will hear and answer those prayers (cf. 14:13-14). If you aren't seeing answered prayer, are you praying? Is your praying shaped by Scripture, the Word of God? Is your praying a ritual or the overflow of God's life flowing through you?

What does the latter look like? It looks like breathing. You breathe without thinking because blood is pulsing through your veins. When the Holy Spirit is pulsing through you, you pray without thinking. You just talk to God. An e-mail chimes, mention it to God. Someone steps into your office, mention it to God. You can't find your keys, mention it to God. Prayer is as important to the soul as breathing is to the body.

Obedient Love

God loves Jesus, and Jesus in turn loves us with the same type of love (v. 9). In response we love him and demonstrate our love through obedience (v. 10). The way we abide in Jesus is to remain in his love, and the way we remain in his love is through obedience. Jesus isn't saying, "If you want me to love you, you have to obey." He's saying, "If you love me, you demonstrate it through obedience." Obedience doesn't earn love. Obedience is the evidence of love.

How does this text speak to the person who claims to be a Christian but is living in willful, persistent disobedience to Jesus? It says, "You don't love Jesus. You don't bear the fruit of love. Therefore, the life of Jesus is not in you, and you will be cast into the fire and burned." True Christians obey Jesus. Across our country and around the world are people who claim to follow Jesus but don't. It's spiritual insanity to say, "I'm a follower of Jesus, but I don't follow what Jesus says." "I love Jesus, but I don't listen to him." No, you don't. Faith without works is dead! A disciple who doesn't obey is not a disciple; he's a fraud. If Jesus lives in you, you cannot help but produce the fruit of loving obedience. His life in you will cause you to love what he loves, to treasure his words, and to obey, not out of duty but out of joy. You will delight in doing what Jesus wants you to do because he lives in you and is shaping your heart to be like his.

Jesus is the King, and he has the authority to demand our obedience (vv. 14-15), but he doesn't treat us like slaves. Slaves are given commands but no explanations. Jesus invites us into his inner circle as his friends. He doesn't just give us commands; he shares his friendship with us. His friendship makes obedience a delight.

Inexhaustible Joy

Joy is an unmistakable mark of a genuine disciple (v. 11). Christians claim to have the spirit or essence of Jesus taking up residence inside them. Jesus created joy. If you claim the Creator of joy is inside you and you're miserable, then something is wrong. It makes no sense. It's completely illogical. If someone is finding joy in Jesus, then he or she is a disciple of Jesus. Every step we take to help someone find joy in Jesus is a step of obedience to his words. Joy in Jesus is inseparable from knowing and following him. You can't know him and lack joy. You can't follow him and lack joy. You can't be united with him and lack joy. It's a biblical, logical, and theological impossibility. It does not mean every day is easy and filled with laughter, but it does mean your life is ultimately marked by a confidence that Jesus is greater and more satisfying than anything this world has to offer.

Jesus promises joy will flow through him to us like sap through the branches. He says his joy will be in us (v. 11). Joy is not a transaction. Jesus doesn't send a box of joy to be delivered to your doorstep by FedEx. Joy is a relationship. Jesus invites us to his party where we can feast and make merry with him. His joy becomes our joy. He brings us into his joy, and as a result, our joy is filled up to the brim. Jesus takes his Big Gulp of Joy and places our little Dixie Cup right inside. We are not only full of joy, but we are engulfed by joy. Joy above. Joy below. Joy around. Joy under. Joy over. Joy everywhere. Does Jesus have enough joy to weather your circumstances? His storehouse of joy is infinite. His resources are immeasurable. His joy gauge never reaches empty. So if his joy becomes your joy, then your joy can always be full.

The verse about joy (v. 11) follows the verses about obedience (vv. 9-10). We tend to think joy and obedience are mutually exclusive: we have to choose misery and obedience or freedom and joy. That's a lie told from the beginning. Joy comes through obedience.

If the life of Jesus flows through us, then our understanding of this world and our purpose begins to change. Our affections and allegiance change. We start to desire what God made us for. We start to wish and dream for what matters. Our goals start to align with Jesus's calling on our lives. At this point we begin to feel our weakness. Then we cry out for God to help us. As he empowers us to do what he's called us to do, he's empowering us to do what we're beginning to want to do. God's commands and our wants come into line, and for the first time what we want and what we need completely align. Wanting what we need and then accomplishing what we want brings joy. Jesus wants you to live in joy, and if he lives in you, then a steady harvest of joy will appear.

Sacrificial Love

Jesus commands us to love others as he has loved us (v. 12). What an impossible standard for love! I can't do that. How can I possibly obey? The only way I could love like Jesus is if he lived inside me and empowered me to love like that. This is the second time in two chapters Jesus has made love the defining characteristic of his followers. How is this love demonstrated? Through sacrifice (v. 13). Jesus sacrificed for us, and he says the ultimate act of friendship is laying down your life for somebody else. The greatest love is not romantic or erotic; it's sacrificial. Are you laying down your life for others? That's sacrifice—going without something for the good of someone else.

True disciples bear fruit. No fruit, no disciple. If Jesus has taken up residence inside you, you will be different, you will act differently, you will love differently, and you will live differently. The difference is not due to your strength, your effort, or your zeal. The difference is due to the persistent work of Jesus in you. Jesus is alive, powerful, and actively at work in his disciples. An apple tree bears apples, a peach tree bears peaches, and a follower of Jesus Christ loves, prays, and obeys Jesus.

Reflect and Discuss

1. Why does Jesus call himself the vine and his followers branches?
2. What forms do spiritual fruit take in the life of a believer? What fruit is evident in your life?
3. If Jesus is the true vine, what are false vines?
4. How is Jesus divisive?
5. What should followers of Jesus expect if God's commitment to our fruit bearing is greater than our commitment to comfort?
6. How might God's commitment to your fruit bearing change how you respond to different events in your life?
7. How do you "remain" in Jesus?
8. What does your prayer life look like today? Are you praying in confidence of answered prayer? Why or why not?
9. How is prayer a fruit of the Spirit?
10. Describe the difference between obedience to earn love and obedience as evidence of love.

Handling the World's Hatred

JOHN 15:18–16:4

Main Idea: Jesus warns his followers that the world will hate the church, and in their hatred they will lash out at those who follow Jesus.

I. **Why Does the World Hate Christians (15:18-25)?**
   A. The world hates Jesus (15:18).
   B. Jesus has called us out of the world (15:19).
   C. We serve the one the world hates (15:20).
   D. The world is estranged from God (15:21).
   E. Jesus exposed the world's guilt (15:22-25).

II. **How Should Christians Respond to the World's Hatred (15:26–16:4)?**
   A. Don't stop witnessing about Jesus (15:26-27).
   B. Don't fall away, no matter how severe it gets (16:1-4).

Estimates by Christian research groups put the annual number of Christians killed as a direct result of their faith as high as eight thousand (Heneghan, "Christian Persecution"). Another study found 111 countries who either restrict or are hostile to Christianity (ibid.). It's reported that more than one hundred million Christians are suffering persecution around the globe. In North Korea alone, fifty to seventy thousand Christians are being held in detention camps (Zaimov, "Over 100 Million").

Why are Christians subject to such persecution? In John 15 Jesus answers that question. Starting in chapter 13 and going through chapter 17, John records Jesus's instructions to his disciples on the night before his crucifixion. He's been preparing them to follow him and live for him after he returns to heaven. So far Jesus has focused on how he is forming them into a new community called the church. This new community will be recognizable because of the people's deep love for one another, their commitment to obeying Jesus's instructions, and their experience of joy. Now he turns his attention to how the world will view this new community. Jesus tells his disciples about persecution and suffering. He warns them about coming hatred and animosity. The world will hate the church, and in their hatred they will lash out at those who follow Jesus. In this passage we find the words *hate* and *hatred* eight times. Jesus will explain the reasons for the world's hatred and then arm his disciples to face it.

Why Does the World Hate Christians?
JOHN 15:18-25

The World Hates Jesus (15:18)

Jesus begins by saying, "*If* the world hates you" (v. 18; emphasis added), but "if" is not expressing uncertainty. Jesus doesn't say, "In the unlikely event the world hates you." The sense is more "If—and trust me they will." The hatred of the world is a certainty. If you're following Christ, this is a guarantee. If Jesus was hated, so will his followers be. Was Jesus hated? Less than twenty-four hours after he made this statement, he was arrested, tried for crimes he didn't commit, mocked, beaten, whipped, then executed as a criminal. Before being hung on the cross, he was dressed up as a mock king, and while hanging on the cross, he was verbally assaulted before being physically impaled by a spear. Yes, the world hated him.

What does Jesus mean when he uses the word *world?* He's not talking about the planet. He's referring to all those who live in open rebellion to the Creator, which means all people. By virtue of our sin, all people have embraced this anti-God world system. Our sin has ushered us into this rebellious "world" in which we shake our fists at the heavens. Therefore, by definition, the world hates Jesus because it stands opposed to all that God is and is doing.

Jesus Has Called Us Out of the World (15:19)

Jesus chose us "out of" the world (v. 19). When he called us to himself, he called us *from* something. He called us from the ranks of rebellion to become part of his family. This call isn't because we're special. It's a demonstration of his love, and it's due to his unmerited favor. We do nothing to be called, but when people see us leave the fellowship of rebellion to join this new community of brothers and sisters, some will respond in hatred. D. A. Carson wrote, "Former rebels who have by the grace of the king been won back to loving allegiance to their rightful monarch are not likely to prove popular with those who persist in rebellion" (*John*, 525).

When Jesus called us to him, he made us part of a unique people. In 1 Peter 2:9 the church is described as "a chosen race, a royal priesthood, a holy nation, a people for his possession." The King James translated that last phrase, "a peculiar people," but by nature we want to fit in. We want to be loved and respected by the world. The desire for respectability is what has often led to theological liberalism. Christians study with professors and in schools that don't believe the Bible. They're besieged by those who deny the supernatural accounts in Scripture. At some point they've got to make a choice between being accepted by the academics or being shunned for their "simplistic" understanding of Scripture. In other words, deny the Scripture and be accepted, or believe the Scripture and be labeled stupid, silly, and uneducated. Sadly, for many the desire to be accepted by men has caused them to reject Jesus. Beware of wanting to fit in with the world. We don't want to stand out, but Jesus says, "I called you out" (see 1 Pet 2:9). Why? So we could bear fruit so different from what others bear they won't be able to help noticing it (John 15:16). Fitting in with the world is the exact opposite of why Jesus chose us and called us and saved us and sends us. If fitting in with the world were the goal, Jesus wouldn't have to do anything. We fit in with the world perfectly before he called us and rescued us. The purpose of our salvation is wrapped up in living distinctly.

The verse in 1 Peter that calls us "peculiar" (KJV) goes on to say that our uniqueness serves one purpose: "so that you may proclaim the praises of the one who called you out of darkness into his marvelous light" (2:9). Jesus says in effect, "They will hate you because you're different, but you're different because I called you to be different. And your difference is what makes the gospel shine brighter." The difference is not merely external. The Amish are different. That's not what Jesus has called us to do and be. Don't feel guilty using electricity. The difference is much greater. We are different in the kind of fruit our lives produce. The way we're peculiar is that we pray, obey, rejoice, and love in ways that are unnatural to the person who doesn't know Jesus.

We Serve the One the World Hates (15:20)

We follow Jesus. Where did Jesus go? To the cross. You can't follow a crucified Savior and not expect a cross. If our Master (who never sinned) died because of the world's hatred, logic alone tells us we should expect something similar, especially since we *have* sinned. In the face of the world's hatred, it's helpful for us to remember the reason we're hated. It's not personal. People's hatred might be directed at us, but we're not the ultimate target. Jesus is (v. 20). Before the nation of Israel had a king, they were led by the prophet Samuel. One day the people came to Samuel and begged him to ask God for a king on their behalf. Their request greatly troubled Samuel. He had given his life to serve them, and they wanted a king. When Samuel brought the request to God, God encouraged him by saying in effect, "Samuel, don't take it personally. Their problem isn't with you; it's with me" (1 Sam 8:7). When the world hurts and imprisons and kills Christians, it's not about us; it's about Jesus. Their intended target was the King, but they can't reach him, so they settle for taking aim at his followers.

Several apostles were arrested in Jerusalem for preaching about Jesus. When they were brought before the ruling council, they continued to talk about Jesus. The religious leaders wanted to kill them but were talked into letting them go:

> *After they called in the apostles and had them flogged, they ordered them not to speak in the name of Jesus and released them. Then they went out from the presence of the Sanhedrin, rejoicing that they were counted worthy to be treated shamefully on behalf of the Name.* (Acts 5:40-41)

The leaders' problem wasn't the disciples but the disciples' Master. They beat the apostles because they hated Jesus and the disciples served him. The disciples understood what was going on. It's why they rejoiced when they were beaten. They knew the beating wasn't because of them but because of the Name they served, so they felt it was an honor to be beaten for that Name.

Many professing Christians never experience any hatred from the world because they don't serve Jesus. If we wear the uniform with the word "Christian" written on our chests but we go out on the court and help the other team, the other team isn't going to hate us. They'll only hate the ones who actually play for Jesus. In John 15:20 Jesus says all humanity is divided into two camps: those who persecute his disciples and those who listen and obey his word spoken by the disciples. Christians are the point of the spear on which Jesus divides humanity. As we proclaim his words, people will respond one of two ways: they'll receive them or reject them, and with them, the messenger as well.

The World Is Estranged from God (15:21)

Sometimes Christians act surprised by the world's behavior. Too often we expect the world to live in obedience to God. We think a bunch of non-Christians should act like Christians. Jesus reminds us the world is estranged from God (v. 21). The world is living in open rebellion against the Creator. Whenever we're shocked by the world's behavior, it's because we've forgotten the world's condition. The world acting like the world is not shocking, and frankly that in itself is not persecution. But Christians should live differently. Jesus says the world will hate us "on account of [his] name" (v. 21). The hatred of the world comes to those who actually live for Jesus. The world doesn't hate undercover Christians. And we shouldn't make the world's hatred a badge of honor. If we do, it might lead us to act like jerks. Being a jerk doesn't honor God or cause the gospel to shine. We don't actively seek out the world's hatred. We actively seek out Jesus, and the more we do, the more the world will see it and respond negatively.

Jesus Exposed the World's Guilt (15:22-25)

Jesus came to earth and did amazing things. He spoke like no man had ever spoken, and he did works no man had ever done. Yet the people hated him. We normally hate people if they speak and act in a way that is mean, untruthful, or arrogant. Jesus was none of these. Why was he so hated? Jesus entered a world made pitch black by sin, and he shone like the sun at high noon. As a result, all the sin and shame and wickedness around him were seen in the truest and most undeniable light. Jesus made hidden sin visible. He exposed all the ugliness in the hearts of the people. All those who thought they were pretty good saw their sin exposed, and they hated Jesus for it (vv. 22-25).

H. A. Ironside told a story to illustrate this point:

> Years ago, at the time of the opening up of inland Africa by missionaries, the wife of an African chief happened to visit a mission station. The missionary had a little mirror hung up on a tree outside his home, and the woman happened to glance into it. She had come straight out of her pagan environment and had never seen the hideous paintings on her face, or her hardened features. Now, gazing at her own face, she was startled. She asked the missionary, "Who is that horrible-looking person inside the tree?"

"It is not the tree," said the missionary. "The glass is reflecting your own face."

She could not believe it until she was holding the mirror in her hand. When she had understood she said to the missionary, "I must have the glass. How much will you sell it for?"

The missionary did not want to sell his mirror. But she insisted so strongly that in the end he thought it would be better to sell it to her and thus avoid trouble. A price was set, and she took the glass. Fiercely she said, "I will never have it making faces at me again." She threw it down and broke it to pieces. (Quoted in Boice, *John*, 1192–93)

The hatred of the world for Christians is the woman breaking the mirror that shows her true reflection. The world feebly lashes out at Christians due to a guilty conscience. The righteousness of Christ and the presence of his followers remind them of their guilt and shame. Instead of anger Christians have regularly expressed sympathy for their tormentors. We say with Jesus, "Father, forgive them, because they do not know what they are doing" (Luke 23:34). They don't understand that their hatred hides the guilty screams of their tormented consciences. We understand, so we respond with mercy, not anger.

How Should Christians Respond to the World's Hatred?
JOHN 15:26–16:4

Don't Stop Witnessing about Jesus (15:26-27)

Jesus promises to send his Spirit to tell people about him; then he says his disciples will tell people about him (vv. 26-27). We understand these two promises as one promise—the promise his Spirit will empower his disciples to witness about him. The Holy Spirit is called the Counselor and the Spirit of truth (v. 26). He will help the disciples speak the truth about Jesus. The disciples aren't left with this monumental task to accomplish on their own. Jesus promises divine reinforcements. The Spirit of God will be sent from the throne of God to empower the people of God to witness about the Son of God.

The Spirit of God empowers us to tell the truth. To tell the truth, we need to be honest about sin. We face the temptation to minimize sin in order to downplay the difference between Christians and the world. Again this stems from our desire to be loved instead of hated. However, if we're not honest about sin, then we cannot impress upon people the need for a Savior. But honesty about sin begins by being honest about our own sins. It's not always difficult to tell the truth about someone else's sin, but it's far more difficult to be truthful about our own. The Holy Spirit can help witness about our own need of salvation. We must not act as if we have it all together and we've got it figured out. Instead, we must be honest about our own brokenness, weakness, and failure. Then we can talk honestly about our desperate need for Christ, bearing witness about his grace at work in us. If we approach people while unwilling to open up about *our* need for salvation, then our words will seem like nothing more than arrogant, hypocritical condemnation.

There's a danger of redefining sin in order to make the good news easier to hear, but love compels us to be honest: whatever God calls sin, we call sin. We have no authority to call clean what God calls unclean. The Holy Spirit helps us share this truth—difficult truth about sin and judgment—with a humble kindness that is compelling to others. We need to ask God to give us honest words wrapped in warm hospitality. One of the reasons we should try so hard to show hospitality is because we know the message of the gospel is offensive. To present the gospel honestly, we must tell a person that he or she is a sinner who stands guilty before God. But the offense of the gospel is part of a greater message of God's plan to welcome sinners into his family because of the sacrifice of his Son. Hospitality demonstrates the gospel and puts the offense of the gospel in the greater context of God's invitation to be reconciled through Jesus.

To testify about Jesus (v. 27) requires honesty about sin and a willingness to be rejected. No one enjoys rejection. We guard our feelings and friendships to prevent rejection. We'll often cut off a relationship if it seems headed for rejection. When it comes to witnessing about Jesus, we must embrace rejection. In rejection we find fellowship with Jesus. Jesus was rejected, and when his people are rejected on his account, we find unique fellowship and identification with him (Heb 13:12-13). When we fear rejection by the world, we refuse to be identified with Jesus. Rejection by the world means we've joined Jesus outside the camp—where the criminals go, where the despised are sent, where the scum go to die. Whom do we want to be accepted by? Those inside the camp will accept us as long as we're willing to stay silent about Jesus. Or we can speak up, face rejection, and choose to go where Jesus is—outside the wall, outside the circle, outside the city limits. The fear of being hated and rejected by the world often keeps us from speaking about Jesus.

Don't stop witnessing. If you've been silent, start speaking now. Jesus sent the Holy Spirit to help you share the truth about him.

Don't Fall Away, No Matter How Severe It Gets (16:1-4)

Jesus doesn't minimize the severity of persecution (16:1-4). He tells the truth, and the truth protects his disciples from becoming disillusioned. They won't look back and say, "Jesus never told us it would be difficult. He said it would be easy." No, he was honest about the cost of following him. He said they would be cast out of the synagogue and some would be killed (v. 2). To be cast out of the synagogue was a big deal. It meant more than losing your church. It meant being kicked out of your community. Your identity would be erased. Your future plans all shattered. You could not marry a girl from the community. Any children you had would be outcasts. Your family would consider you dead. They would throw a funeral for you and mourn over you. You would be a man without a family or a country. For a Jew, being kicked out of the synagogue would be a fate worse than death. Many would choose death over this dishonor.

It's a far cry from the false promises of the prosperity gospel preached in so many places today. Following Jesus is worth it, and the benefits far outweigh the cost, but there is a cost. Any preacher who tells you following Jesus is the way to good health, riches, or luxury is not following Jesus; he's selling you something.

Following Jesus leads to suffering and persecution. The persecutors will often be driven by religious fervor; they will persecute you as an act of worship to their false God (v. 2). They are misguided but sincere. The reality of persecution should not surprise us. In fact, the lack of persecution we face as American Christians is historically abnormal. The history of Christianity is filled with martyrs. As Tertullian famously said, "The blood of the martyrs is the seed of the church." Our family tree is filled with executions.

There is a price for following Jesus, and Christians through the centuries have been willing to pay the price. Why? The prize is worth the price. Knowing Jesus is worth the cross. In the face of intense persecution, we need to hold on to the truth and cling tightly to Jesus. When living for Jesus and speaking about Jesus brings persecution, don't fall away. Instead, rejoice because God's Spirit will be with you in a unique way as you share in the sufferings of Jesus (cf. 1 Pet 4:12-14).

What's the greatest danger we face in times of persecution? Is it injury? Is it death? No. It's falling away. The greatest danger in persecution is being convinced this temporary life is more valuable than

Jesus. Persecution has a way of sifting the true disciples from the false. Persecution exposes spiritual scavengers—those who circle Christianity, hoping only to get something for themselves. Living for Jesus and telling others about Jesus might cause someone to hate you (cf. Luke 6:22). It may mean you're excluded from someone's circle of friends. You might experience mockery and insults. But don't stop witnessing, and don't stop walking after Jesus. Jesus says in effect, "In the face of persecution, don't fall. Keep walking. Keep trusting. Cling to me."

John Paton was a missionary to the cannibals on the New Hebrides islands in the mid-1800s. He suffered greatly and faced death many times. He described one time when a native tried to kill him with an axe and another man stepped in and saved his life. He wrote,

> Life in such circumstances led me to cling very near to the
> Lord Jesus; I knew not, for one brief hour, when or how attack
> might be made; and yet, with my trembling hand clasped in
> the hand once nailed on Calvary, and now swaying the scepter
> of the universe, calmness and peace and resignation abode in
> my soul. (Quoted in Piper, *Filling Up*, 64)

When you face persecution for following Jesus, whether it comes from a native swinging an axe or a neighbor spreading a lie, cling to the hand once nailed to Calvary and now wielding the scepter of the universe.

Reflect and Discuss

1. How will the world feel toward Christians?
2. How might fear of the world cause one to fall away from Jesus?
3. Why is fitting in with the world in opposition to God's plan to call us out?
4. Why have Christians been called out by Jesus?
5. How might the prophet Samuel's experience help us in enduring the world's hatred?
6. Why was Jesus so hated?
7. What does the Spirit of God empower the people of God to do?
8. Is there a person in your life you haven't shared the gospel with out of fear of rejection? How is the Holy Spirit's help good news for you?
9. What reason do you have to rejoice in the face of persecution?
10. What is the greatest danger we face in persecution? How can we fight this danger?

Life on Mission

JOHN 16:4-15

Main Idea: Jesus calls his disciples to continue his mission by spreading his message.

I. **The Disciples' Mission Is Bigger Than Themselves (16:4b-6).**
II. **The Disciples' Mission Requires Supernatural Help (16:7-15).**
    A. The Holy Spirit will convict the world of sin (16:8-11).
    B. The Holy Spirit will guide the disciples into truth (16:12-15).

A good mission statement shapes the priorities of a company and provides a framework for decision making. If an employee understands the big picture—the mission of the organization—it places his small, daily actions in the context of a grander agenda. A clear mission gives purpose to the mundane. As Christians, what is our mission? Our mission revolves around the gospel. *We have been chosen by Jesus to bear the fruit of the gospel in our lives and share the message of the gospel with our lips.* We are here to continue the mission of Jesus by spreading the message of Jesus.

Though Jesus is leaving, his disciples still have a job to do here on earth. Their job, their mission, is to live together as a new community of faith in such a way that the world will see that the gospel is true and has the power to change lives. They are to serve as witnesses to the gospel. They are to "testify" (15:27) to the unbelieving world about Jesus—who he is and why he came. We must interpret these chapters in light of the mission Jesus gives his disciples. He helps them see that their mission is bigger than themselves (16:4-6) and therefore requires supernatural help (vv. 7-15).

The Disciples' Mission Is Bigger Than Themselves
JOHN 16:4B-6

What Jesus teaches them on the eve of his crucifixion is something they weren't ready to hear earlier. He's waited to tell them "these things" (v. 4) until now. What are "these things"?

First, he has not fully revealed his departure. Throughout the Gospel Jesus speaks of his death, but the disciples don't understand what he's saying. It isn't until after Judas leaves the room that Jesus, carefully and deliberately, helps the disciples understand his coming death, resurrection, and ascension.

Second, he has not fully revealed their mission. Even in this passage we see him unfolding piece by piece his plan for them. They are learning exactly what it will mean to follow him as his disciples after the cross. The cross changes everything. Everything before points to it, and everything after looks back. The cross will become the focal point of the disciples' mission. They will be sent to the nations as messengers of the cross.

Third, he has not fully revealed the world's reaction to the message. If you remember, Jesus has just warned them about the world's hatred (v. 2).

The reason Jesus hadn't told them all of these things is because he was with them. They didn't need to worry about persecution or focusing on a mission; they simply needed to listen to Jesus, follow him, and trust him. But now their role is changing. Jesus is no longer going to be with them physically. He's leaving and entrusting them with the work of calling new disciples.

What would a normal human response be to all that has happened to the disciples this night? Everything they're counting on seems to be torn out from underneath them. I wonder how the disciples felt when Jesus basically said, "I'm leaving. People are going to hate you, but you need to tell them about me." No wonder he follows that news with "Ever since I began to explain this to you, your hearts have been full of grief" (v. 6; my paraphrase). Their response may be natural, but that doesn't mean it's right. In fact, Jesus gives them a mild rebuke in verse 5. From the moment they hear Jesus is leaving, their thoughts are consumed with themselves. All they think about is how this affects *them.* They never once consider what Jesus is thinking or feeling or what his purpose is in all that's taking place. They don't give his wishes or desire a second thought. His concerns are obscured by theirs. They're like the traveler who visits the pyramids in Egypt, turns his camera around to get a picture of himself in front of this wonder of the world, and when he gets home, he realizes all you can see in the picture is his face. He's completely blocked the focal point. The disciples are so focused on themselves they don't even ask Jesus where he's going. The couple of questions they ask him—Peter's in chapter 13 and Thomas's in chapter 14—are not so they can understand what he's doing but to find out how it impacts them.

Why does Jesus rebuke them on an evening when they're already grieving? The reason is not because their grief over his departure is wrong. The reason is because their grief is insignificant compared to what's taking place that next day. Jesus is not demeaning their concern for the future. He's lifting their eyes to look beyond their circumstances to something much greater. What happens on the cross the following day is more important than their health and safety. It's bigger than them. Jesus teaches his disciples to live for something bigger. The mission he gives them as his witnesses is far bigger than their hopes and dreams. The mission is worth giving up conveniences and comforts—like safety, security, stability—to invest in something eternally profitable. What a tragedy to find that what you invested your time, energy, money, influence, and abilities in is gone long before you are. Jesus calls us to invest everything in something bigger than ourselves—his service.

Their Mission Requires Supernatural Help
JOHN 16:7-15

Jesus is leaving, which is good for them. He will go to the cross and then ascend to heaven. Only then will the Spirit be able to come to them (v. 7). The Spirit will be sent *by* Jesus to live in the *disciples* of Jesus as they continue the *mission* of Jesus to call other disciples to *follow* Jesus. We need the Spirit for many reasons, but the context of this promise is our mission as disciples. Jesus doesn't send the Holy Spirit so we can have an invisible butler to bring us cold beverages as we lounge around the pool. He sends the Spirit to empower us to accomplish his mission.

Imagine an ancient king deciding to take a trip to visit one of his cities on the far side of the country. He sends his trusted lieutenant ahead of him to get everything ready for the trip. The day of the trip comes, and his caravan starts out. When he arrives at the city, nothing is prepared for him. No lodging, no food, no meetings, nothing. He calls his lieutenant and asks what happened. His lieutenant says, "I came to help them, and they wouldn't listen to me. I told them what you wanted, and I offered to assist them. I assured them I had the authority and resources to accomplish it, but they ignored me. The few times they spoke to me, it was to ask me to do something for them. It wasn't to do what you asked but to do what they wanted." How would the king respond?

The Holy Spirit wasn't sent to assure us lives of comfort and ease. The Spirit doesn't live in us so we can rest comfortably in our easy chairs doing nothing for the kingdom of God. The Holy Spirit comes to us, disciples of Jesus, to empower us for a mission that cannot be accomplished apart from his supernatural help. Jesus elaborates on the Holy Spirit's role in verses 8-15. He highlights two ways the Holy Spirit advances his mission.

The Holy Spirit Will Convict the World of Sin (16:8-11)

Jesus, the light of the world, exposes sin (cf. 3:19-20). With Jesus's departure, the Holy Spirit will continue to expose sin, but the Spirit will also convict the world of righteousness. How do you convict a person of righteousness? Isn't righteousness a good thing? Throughout the Gospel of John we find two types of righteousness. One type is the righteousness of man *apart from God* (self-righteousness), and the other is the righteousness *of God*. These two types of righteousness regularly came into conflict. For instance, in chapter 9 Jesus healed a blind man on the Sabbath. The Jewish leaders condemned Jesus and characterized themselves as righteous defenders of God's law, but in reality they were more concerned with their own public image than with helping those in need. False righteousness—any attempt to earn God's favor on your own—is always a temptation. When I visited Africa, I was invited to eat at the home of one of the local men. We sat in his backyard and ate a dinner of boiled yams and peanuts. At one point one of his daughters brought out a pitcher of water and began to pour us glasses. He stopped her, took my glass, and poured it out on the ground. She was doing her best to be kind to me, but her best wasn't good enough. He knew if I drank that water, I'd get sick. Her gift of water was a polluted offering. God calls our best efforts to please him "polluted" (Isa 64:6). They're unacceptable. They're tainted by sin and will be poured out as worthless. No one can come to God based on good works.

The Holy Spirit convicts the unbelieving world of sin (v. 9), righteousness (v. 10), and judgment (v. 11). Their judgment about Jesus is wrong. Jesus urged them to "judge according to righteous judgment" (7:24), but they persisted in their unbelief and as a result would face the same condemnation Satan himself faced. The Spirit reveals to the world their sin, self-righteousness, and condemnation in order to call men and women to repentance and faith. The word translated "convict" (v. 8) has the goal of convincing a person to turn from his or her sin. How does the conviction of the Holy Spirit take place? How does he call the unbelieving world to repentance and faith? He speaks through the disciples. The disciples are the agents the Holy Spirit uses to call the world to repentance. Trace the flow of this passage:

- In chapter 15 Jesus calls the disciples to join him in his mission of making more disciples. The chapter ends with the reminder of the Holy Spirit, who will bear witness about Jesus *through the disciples.*
- This chapter reveals their mission will bring suffering and persecution (16:1-4). Then Jesus reminds them of the importance of their mission, which can only be accomplished *by the power of the indwelling Spirit.*

So the Spirit convicts the world by empowering the disciples to bear witness about Jesus. The Spirit brings conviction to the world through the message of the disciples. God blesses this unique combination. His Spirit will take the gospel proclaimed by his disciples and bring conviction to the world. The role of the disciple is to faithfully bear witness to Jesus, and the role of the Holy Spirit is to make that witness spiritually effective. John Calvin wrote,

> How can someone's voice penetrate minds, take root there, and eventually produce fruit making hearts of stone into hearts of flesh and renewing the people themselves unless the Spirit of Christ makes the Word alive? (*John*, 372)

Jesus gives the disciples an impossible task. When they heard, they must have thought, *There's no way we can do that. People won't listen to us. You said yourself they would throw us out of the synagogues. This is crazy! There's no way we can make this work.* They were right. There was no way *they* could make this work, but Jesus, through the Spirit's power, would accomplish everything he promised and commanded. Everything good that has happened in Christianity is the result of the Holy Spirit's power.

Maybe you don't realize the Spirit's power in your life because you aren't busy doing things only he can accomplish.

- Without the Spirit's help you can love people who are like you.
- Without the Spirit's help you can give an hour and a half a week to sit in a service.
- Without the Spirit's help you can attend a Sunday seminar or community group.
- Without the Spirit's help you can put money in the offering plate.
- Without the Spirit's help you can talk about the gospel.

But do you know what you can't do without the Spirit's help?

- Without the Spirit's help you can't love someone who is antagonistic to you and your family.
- Without the Spirit's help you can't be on call 24–7 for a person in need.
- Without the Spirit's help you can't meet weekly with a brother or sister to bear each other's burdens.
- Without the Spirit's help you can't give your hard-earned money when little is left.
- Without the Spirit's help you can't plead with your unbelieving friends and neighbors to repent and believe.
- Without the Spirit's help you can't move your family around the world for the sake of the gospel.

For you to be faithful to the mission to which Jesus has called you, you *need* the Spirit's help.

The Holy Spirit Will Guide the Disciples into Truth (16:12-15)

At this moment the disciples must have questions. Jesus describes a mission that will take an entire lifetime and might require them to give their lives. He unfolds a new community unique in the way it lives together. Their minds must have been buzzing with questions: *How will this look? What should we do? How will we make decisions?* Jesus doesn't answer their questions; he gives them a promise. The Holy Spirit will guide them into all the truth they need to know (vv. 12-15). The answers to their questions will come, but they will come through the ministry of the Holy Spirit. The Spirit of God will indwell them and instruct them as they continue on their mission.

Jesus makes a promise overflowing with kindness and grace. He says the Spirit will "guide" them (v. 13). The only other time that word is found in John's writings is in Revelation 7:

> For the Lamb who is at the center of the throne will shepherd them;
> he will guide *them to springs of the waters of life, and God will wipe away every tear from their eyes.* (v. 17; emphasis added)

The Holy Spirit will guide the disciples to the refreshing springs of truth like a shepherd leading thirsty sheep to a cool, refreshing spring. The Spirit will reiterate and expand the truth taught by Jesus. The Holy Spirit declares the revelation of Jesus Christ to the disciples.

In the following chapter Jesus will talk about those who believe based on the word of the disciples, the Scriptures. This promise of the Holy Spirit's guidance into truth takes a different form for us than it did for the first disciples. They were reminded of what Jesus had taught them personally. We get the teachings of Jesus *through* them. The Twelve chosen by Jesus were used to inscripturate—to put in written form—the truth of Jesus. Now we are brought to the truth by the Holy Spirit as we open up the Word of God. The Spirit works through the Word. The Word is his means of conveying the gospel and bringing conviction of sin. We should never look for spiritual truth apart from his Word.

We receive personal guidance from the Spirit as we read the Word he wrote. I wonder if the reason we don't read the Bible more often is because we don't want to be guided by the Spirit. Too often we want people to agree with us, to rubber-stamp the decisions we've already made. The Holy Spirit is no rubber stamp. He's a sword-wielding, flame-throwing God. We need to come to him humbly and beg him to tell us what to do. Instead we often open our Bibles and treat the Spirit's words like a buffet table, taking what we like and passing by the rest. He promises to guide us, but we must listen to everything he says. The truth can be hard to hear. Sometimes we'd rather be ignorant, even lied to, but the longer we listen to lies, the more painful the truth will be. The Spirit guides us into truth as we listen to him speak through his Word.

Reflect and Discuss

1. What is the mission statement of followers of Jesus?
2. Why hasn't Jesus told the disciples "these things" in verse 4 until now?
3. What questions would you have wanted to ask Jesus if you were with him and his disciples on that night?
4. Why is the mission of God worthy of your sacrifice?
5. Why does Jesus send the Spirit?
6. How will the Holy Spirit convict the world of righteousness?
7. How will the Holy Spirit call them to repentance and faith?
8. What does it reveal about God that he gives his people an impossible task and the means to accomplish it?
9. What are some reasons you might not realize the Spirit's power in your life?
10. How does the Holy Spirit provide personal guidance to Christians?

Liberating and Lasting Joy

JOHN 16:16-33

Main Idea: Regardless of circumstances, a true disciple finds liberating and lasting joy in Jesus as he or she lives out and shares the gospel.

I. **This Joy Is Revealed in a Time of Sorrow (16:20-21).**
II. **This Joy Is Resistant to Every Attack (16:22).**
III. **This Joy Is Refreshed through Answered Prayer (16:23-24).**
    A.   Does this promise mean God has to give me whatever I want?
    B.   How does prayer make our joy overflow?
IV. **This Joy Is Rooted in a Reconciled Relationship (16:33).**

A group of armed guerrillas made an appointment with Pastor Manuel and his family. He thought they were going to authorize him to have an official church, which he had previously discussed with them. One of them went into the house with the pastor's wife, Gloria, and his daughter while the pastor was outside. He was shot five times. The guerrilla who was in the house with the rest of the family yelled, "Make sure that dog stays dead," referring to the pastor. The guerrillas then shot the pastor again, this time in the neck. Following the shooting, Pastor Manuel's wife ran outside and cleaned his face. With the help of her children, she dragged his body under a tree. She ran and got her Bible and, shaking with tears, preached to all those who got near. [Her] ten-year-old son said, "Mum, don't worry, dad died for Christ and now he is with Christ" ("Colombia: Pastor Martyred").

I know intellectually that faithfulness to Jesus could mean suffering, imprisonment, even death, but there's never been a moment where I've felt legitimate fear on account of following Jesus. I've never felt the cold barrel of a gun against my head or the hot breath of soldiers on my neck. What does this type of pressure do to a person? How would you respond if you knew you would face physical attacks for your faith? What would it be like knowing your death would be considered a victory for another religion? This is exactly what the first disciples face. Jesus warns them that from this point forward, persecution and martyrdom are more likely to happen than not (16:2). There will be few if any days when they will feel safe. Any day could be the day they're arrested and killed. History tells us each one of the apostles experienced severe physical persecution, and all but one died as a martyr. Knowing their situation, what would we expect the disciples to be like? The disciples have received their death warrant. It would be natural to assume they're fearful, living out their days in hiding, miserable and unhappy.

That's not what happens, but it would be easier to explain. What actually happens is far more puzzling: this group of men turns the world upside down. They embrace their mission and its consequences. Not only are they faithful, but their joy, peace, and contentment are conspicuous. Even with a death sentence hanging over their heads, they minister and serve with unbridled passion and appear to be profoundly happy.

In the book of Acts, the warning from Jesus comes true. The disciples are kicked out of the synagogue, scorned by the religious elite, and persecuted by the religious establishment. In Acts 5 they're brought before the high priest, questioned about their activities, and rebuked for preaching the gospel—the good news that Jesus Christ died so sinners could be reconciled to God. After being beaten, they leave rejoicing (Acts 5:40-42). The disciples do the exact opposite of what we expect. We expect someone who is tortured to be angry. We wouldn't blame them if they harbored permanent resentment. But they're not angry. They're not unhappy. They leave the beating happier than when they got there.

In our abundance and ease we struggle to find joy, yet they found it in their poverty and affliction. Our circumstances often dictate our emotions and affections. Most of us have reserved seats on an emotional rollercoaster. Someone takes the last doughnut, and we're depressed. Someone gives us a shiny, new toy, and we're filled with joy. Facing torture, prison, and death, how do the disciples experience such profound joy? Regardless of circumstances, a true disciple finds liberating and lasting joy in Jesus as they live out and share the gospel.

Jesus unloads a dump truck of earth-shattering news on the disciples. He tells them about betrayal, crucifixion, and persecution—not just as possibilities but as certainties. Now, as Jesus closes this time of instruction, he tells the disciples he's going to do something in them that will bring a fullness of joy that transcends the darkest, dreariest, most dire and depressing circumstances they will ever face. What does this joy look like? There are four distinctive qualities of this joy.

This Joy Is Revealed in a Time of Sorrow
JOHN 16:20-21

What an inauspicious beginning to the promise of lasting joy (v. 20). If I were instructed to give a pep talk on joy, I'm not sure that would be my opening line. But wait, it gets worse. Not only will they weep and lament, but also the world will rejoice. So those who oppose God and reject Jesus as Messiah will experience joy while the disciples are weeping and lamenting. However, the positions will quickly be reversed. The disciples' sorrow will turn to joy. The sorrow is only for a short time, but the joy will remain.

Sorrow and joy *are* connected. The Pixar movie *Inside Out* is a beautiful parable about the connection between sadness and joy. Our greatest joys often arise out of our deepest moments of sadness. The light shines brightest after the storm. Sorrow and joy are not two random emotions that happen to appear in this order chronologically. The sorrow must take place if the joy is to come. There's no skipping sorrow to get to the joy. Most ladies would love to skip nine months of pregnancy and an excruciating labor and just hold their newborns in their arms (v. 21), but it doesn't work that way. You don't get the newborn without the morning sickness, swollen ankles, and contractions. Jesus tells the disciples they can't get the joy without experiencing the sorrow.

The sorrow is watching Jesus beaten and bruised, hanging lifeless on a cross. It's seeing his disfigured corpse taken down from the cruel tree. The sorrow is watching their Messiah die. They will weep and lament his death while the world rejoices because he's gone. The sorrow of his death is necessary because his death is the only way for mankind to be saved. Without his death, there can be no life. The sorrow of his death is necessary, but it will be short-lived. This conversation begins in verse 16 with the phrase "a little while" and continues because the disciples don't understand what it means: they won't see him for a little while and then after a little while they will see him. The reason the sorrow will only be for a little while is because Jesus will rise from the dead and appear to them. Their sobbing turns to shouting, their crying to cheering, and their mourning to mirth.

After the baby is born, it's not as if the pain of pregnancy is forgotten; it's just that it no longer matters. The nine months of agony become a distant memory after a short time of joy. The disciples' sorrow is real, but it becomes a distant memory the moment Jesus appears to them having conquered death.

This Joy Is Resistant to Every Attack
JOHN 16:22

The joy Jesus gives his disciples can never be taken away from them (v. 22). "No one" will take it. What else carries the same guarantee? Thieves can take possessions away. Disease can take health away. Death can take family away. What about joy? Doesn't it seem people have the power to take joy away? Unkind words, dishonesty, gossip, slander, cruelty, and bullying all seem designed to steal a person's joy, but Jesus guarantees that the disciples' joy cannot be stolen.

Because their joy comes from seeing him again and knowing he's conquered death, no amount of torture or persecution can ever change that. If the disciples' joy is in something else—if they try to find their joy in sex, money, work, or hobbies—then certainly their joy could be taken from them, but since their joy is found in Jesus, his victory over sin and death and the promise of his ongoing relationship with them, then every attack against it will be futile. The devil longs to steal our joy, and it's not usually too hard. Placing our joy in things like relationships, work, events, security, and health is like putting your life savings in a piggy bank, leaving it in a high-crime district at night with a hammer, and adding a note asking people to leave it alone because it's really valuable. You're a fool if you think it will be safe. But if our joy is in Jesus, we trade the piggy bank for Fort Knox, and the devil gets a plastic spoon instead of a hammer. You're a fool if you think he can touch it.

If the disciples' joy comes from a reunion with Jesus, their position in him, and his promises to them, then what weapons could the devil possibly level against their joy? The most powerful weapons are useless. I suppose he could attempt to steal their joy by having them betrayed by a close friend. Or maybe he could try relentless persecution by those who claim to follow God. But the disciples know these assaults will be ineffective. They're going to be ineffective because Jesus already took those attacks and not just defeated them but used them to usher in this joy. Jesus didn't only conquer betrayal and persecution; he turned them into the agents that brought about the disciples' joy. And of course, the ultimate fear, the ultimate weapon, the ultimate joy stealer is death, but Jesus disarmed death. Jesus conquered every enemy! If we find our joy in him, we have nothing to fear. Our joy is impervious to all attacks leveled against it. Jesus's resurrection guarantees he can never die again, and those who follow him will never experience separation from him in death. We may leave our physical bodies, but Jesus will never leave us (cf. 11:25-26).

This Joy Is Refreshed through Answered Prayer
JOHN 16:23-24

The disciples' joy transcends their circumstances and flows from their reunion with Jesus and from confidence they will never experience separation from him again. Their joy in Jesus will serve them like the foundation serves a house: it will be solid and stable, supporting them no matter what kind of storm rages outside. But there will be times when their joy bubbles up and overflows, most often when they experience answered prayer. Joy will flow through them, pulsating through every interaction.

A disciple is like a well drilled deep into an underwater reservoir. No matter what happens on the surface—whether a drought or a natural disaster—the well is always full of water. But once in a while the rain comes, and the well is not simply full of water; it overflows. Cool, clear water gushes out of it, soaking everyone around. As disciples we can always be filled with joy because we are permanently drilled into the joyous reservoir of Jesus Christ, but there are occasions when God will pour down such joyous rain our hearts overflow with joy. These moments come as we press forward in our mission for Jesus Christ, all the while trusting in the power of the Spirit and asking God to do what we cannot.

After the resurrection the first disciples can no longer physically turn to Jesus and ask him to meet a need. Instead, they have the privilege of going directly to the Father and asking him to do whatever they need, and he promises to answer. This promise of answered prayer raises a few questions.

Does This Promise Mean God Has to Give Me Whatever I Want?

The short answer is no. Jesus gives one constraining guideline for this command. In both verse 23 and verse 24 he says we must ask in his name. This immediately rules out the prosperity gospel, name-it-claim-it, best-life-now heresy dominating Christian television. I wonder if we aren't guilty of a related misuse of prayer. Do a mental exercise with me. Think about your recent prayers. Now take out an imaginary sheet of paper and divide it into two columns. Above the column on the left write the word "Comfort," and above the column on the right put the word "Mission." Place your requests in one of the two columns. Here's the criterion: If God answers this request, will it contribute more toward my comfort or my mission? Jesus promises the Father will answer every request made *in his name.* "In Jesus's name" is not a mantra or a tagline. It means we're doing something Jesus commanded to be done! If you define *comfort* in the way it's commonly defined in our society, Jesus doesn't care if you're comfortable. Think about what he tells his disciples. He tells them they're going to be cast out and killed for his sake. The promise of answered prayer is given on the heels of that reality. They aren't to pray for earthly comforts. They're to pray for the kingdom of heaven to advance in this world: "Our Father in heaven, your name be honored as holy. *Your kingdom come.* Your will be done on earth as it is in heaven" (Matt 6:9-11). Jesus taught us to pray for the advancement of his kingdom, not the establishment of our own.

How Does Prayer Make Our Joy Overflow?

Prayer often feels like a duty not a delight, but prayer is how we commune with Jesus, and communion with Jesus is where we'll find joy. The disciples' sorrow turns to joy when they're reunited with Jesus, when they're in his presence again. After his ascension into heaven, prayer is the way to be in his presence. To remain in Jesus happens when his words remain in us and we respond in prayer to him (John 15:7).

The bottom line is this: we need to pray. We must. Not out of duty but out of necessity. Not as a dead requirement but as a desperate plea. We need more of Jesus. We want more joy. Joy comes as we ask Jesus to help us fulfill the mission he gave us. Prayer gives us the power to do what we're called to do. We're called to live holy lives, to be generous, bold, thankful, repentant, and selfless. This only happens as we beg God to work in us. A lack of prayer brings a lack of power, which in turn brings a lack of joy.

Imagine you finally invented the affordable, practical flying car, but you needed just the right wind conditions. You found the perfect spot, gathered your new invention, and headed there. You lined your machine up to fly, but you had to wait for the wind to pick up. Now where you are waiting you can't feel the wind, so you need help. Your friend has joined you just for this. He climbs the nearest hill with phone in hand and waits. You wait in the makeshift cockpit, checking in with him, hoping for the go-ahead. At that moment, is checking in with him a nuisance? Is it drudgery? Or do you wait breathlessly? Asking him over and over, "Is it time?"

When you stand on the precipice, attempting something great, that conversation is not a chore. It's a pleasure. It's filled with breathless anticipation. When we launch out on mission, pleading with God to do something great, prayer is not drudgery. It's breathless anticipation. It's asking God, "Is it time yet? Have you sent the wind? Will we fly now?" Life on mission makes prayer as natural as breathing, as ordinary as our hearts beating.

This Joy Is Rooted in a Reconciled Relationship
JOHN 16:33

In the remaining verses Jesus reminds the disciples they now have access to the Father. In fact, he uses the title *Father* six times in these last few verses. Sin destroyed their relationship with God, but Jesus came and took away the sin of the world. Because of their faith in Jesus and their love for him, they now experience the love of God. The sin-bearing sacrifice of Jesus opened the way to God. They are reconciled to God.

Sin is the root of our unhappiness. We look around and understand something is broken: our relationship with God. The lack of joy in the world can be traced to a lack of peace with God. The only way to have joy is for peace with God to be restored (v. 33). Peace is not a fleeting experience or momentary emotion. It's not a hippie high on drugs flashing a hand sign while living a broken existence. Supernatural peace flowing from a newly restored relationship with God is guaranteed for everyone who follows Jesus, everyone who believes that Jesus is indeed the promised Savior, God's own Son, the only hope for them.

Our responsibility, then, is to believe him. You need to battle the unbelief and doubt that creep into your mind, calling Jesus a liar and undermining your joy. Identify anything that hinders your joy in Jesus. Sometimes it's blatant sin, but often it's misplaced priorities. What hinders our joy is our habit of ingesting so much of the cotton candy of this world that we never get around to feasting on the rich, satisfying joy that is ours in Jesus. We who have believed are "in Jesus." That's how we experience joy in times of trouble and persecution. Though we're still in the world, though we're still engaged in our mission for him, we are *in* Jesus. We're branches connected to the true vine. We receive our strength and nourishment through the vine. We may still have tribulation in the world, but in Jesus we have peace—a peace that fuels a joy that rises above the circumstances of life.

Reflect and Discuss

1. Has God ever brought joy out of your sorrow? When?
2. What are the four distinctive qualities of joy in a believer?
3. Why will the disciples' sorrow only be for a little while? How is this promise still true today?
4. How can Jesus guarantee that the disciples' joy cannot be stolen?
5. What are some ways Satan might attack your joy? How does looking to the cross and empty grave preserve your joy through Satan's attacks?
6. If God were to answer everything from your recent prayers, how many things could be labeled as "comfort" and how many as "mission"?
7. How should the promise of persecution and joy change your prayer life?
8. How does prayer make your joy overflow?
9. Why does mission make prayer a necessity?
10. Think of something in your life right now that is seeking to destroy your joy in Christ. How does the gospel answer its accusations?

Jesus Prays

JOHN 17:1-19

Main Idea: Jesus prays for himself and his disciples on the night before his crucifixion.

I.   **Jesus Prays for the Father to Glorify Him (17:1-5).**
II. **Jesus Prays for the Father to Keep His Disciples (17:6-19).**

Every classic movie adds music to heighten the suspense of the story. Even if you don't know what's happening, you can tell by the crescendo of the soundtrack you've reached the climax. We're getting close to the climax of the Gospel of John. The music is starting to crescendo. In 17:1 Jesus announces, "The hour has come." For the past three years, the disciples have followed Jesus on an expedition. The journey has covered rocky terrain. At times it's been hazardous. Now they're cresting the final rise, and stretched out before them is the summit. Back in chapter 2, when Jesus performed his first miracle, he indicated his hour had not yet come (2:4). In chapters 7 and 8 he twice reiterated his hour had not yet come (7:30; 8:20). Finally, in chapter 12, he indicated the hour was coming (12:27). Here in chapter 17 everything has taken place that's necessary for the hour to come. The hour has finally arrived.

"The hour has come." This is not simply the hour Jesus has been preparing for. It's the hour the entire world has been anticipating. It's the fulfillment of a promise made in the garden that God would send a Rescuer to save humanity from sin. It's the moment when everything will change—when sinful creatures can once again enjoy fellowship with their Creator, when spiritual life triumphs over spiritual death. At the climax of the story, Jesus stops to pray. He pauses at the doorway to the cross to take a moment and cry out for the Father's help.

Jesus Prays for the Father to Glorify Him
JOHN 17:1-5

Jesus begins the prayer with a single request: "Glorify me." Jesus has every right to ask God to glorify him because Jesus is God. He is fully and completely divine. Though he came to earth and took upon himself the form of a servant, he is one with the Father and is worthy to receive mankind's worship, affection, and allegiance. When we talk about the glory of God and glorifying God, we need to remember that we're referring to a noun and a verb. The "glory" of God is a noun and means his majesty or his splendor, his "display of divine goodness" (Carson, *John*, 129). When we talk about God's being glorified (the verb), we mean the appropriate response to his goodness displayed. So the glory of God (noun) is his goodness displayed, and glorifying God (verb) is his goodness celebrated. God is glorious regardless of whether anyone understands who he is, but we glorify God by seeing his goodness and worshiping him for it.

Here when Jesus prays to be glorified, it means his goodness must be *seen* and *celebrated*. For God to answer this request means the greatness of Jesus will need to be *understood* and *acknowledged*. Here's the difficulty: Jesus is about to be cursed. The cross is not only an object of torture but also a sign of God's displeasure (Deut 21:23; Gal 3:13). In order to answer this request, God will have to take someone cursed and rejected and somehow in some way turn the curse into praise and the rejection into applause. God will have to take the disgraceful associations of the cross and make them a badge of honor for his Son. How will he do that?

The answer is found in verse 5. The Father will glorify the Son by restoring him to the position he had with the Father before the foundation of the world. Jesus's divine goodness will be *vindicated* through the resurrection, *displayed* through his exaltation, and one day will be *celebrated* at the consummation. In the scenes of heaven recorded for us in the book of Revelation, we see a day when heaven will cry out with one voice, "Worthy is the Lamb who was slaughtered to receive power and riches and wisdom and strength and honor and glory and blessing!" (Rev 5:12). The Father glorifies Jesus by restoring him to his eternal position of glory in the Father's presence.

Jesus desires to be glorified so he can glorify the Father. Jesus is the Word, the revelation of God's goodness. The author of the book of Hebrews calls Jesus "the radiance of God's glory" (Heb 1:3). To look at Jesus is to see a perfect display of God's goodness. In this prayer Jesus displays God's goodness by securing eternal life for those who belong to him. His willingness to go to the cross, conquering death to gain eternal life for his people, reveals the character of God and ignites praise to God for his goodness. But eternal life is not just everlasting life.

- Eternal life is a relationship with the everlasting God.
- Eternal life is forever delighting in the manifold glories of God.
- Eternal life is seeing God and rejoicing forever in his presence.
- Eternal life is living how we're created to live—in fellowship with our Creator.

Jesus brings God glory by displaying the goodness of God and bringing rebellious creatures into an eternal relationship of delight with this good God. The moment Jesus most reveals the goodness of God is on the cross. Hanging there, suspended between earth and sky, Jesus glorifies God in a way the world has never seen. Never has the holy justice of God and the holy love of God been displayed so powerfully together. We cannot adequately understand how glorious God is without the cross. There we see his holiness and condescension, his wrath and love, and his justice and mercy. All are perfectly displayed through the death of his Son. And in that hour the request of Jesus is answered. In the cross the glorious wrath and love of God are revealed. The Father glorifies the Son, and the Son reveals the unparalleled goodness of the Father to us.

If Jesus's number one priority is to bring glory to the Father, what does that mean for his followers? It can mean nothing less than that the glory of God must be the top priority in your life. Everything you do should have as its purpose the worship of God. Every single detail of your life is intended to reveal and celebrate the goodness of God. The reason we live on mission and share the gospel is so those blinded to God's goodness may see it and worship him. Our goal in sharing the gospel is not to enlist converts but to make worshipers. Do you realize in heaven there'll no longer be evangelism? Evangelism is only necessary where there remain men and women who don't worship God. God's mercy displayed in the death of Jesus Christ fuels our evangelistic fervor. We rejoice in the goodness of God, and we want others to see him and rejoice. Our mission is to help people find joy in Jesus. The clearer they see his goodness and the more his goodness is celebrated in their lives, the more joy they'll find. We drink deeply from the fountain of God's goodness, and we cry out to others, "Taste and see that the LORD *is* good" (Ps 34:8; emphasis added). The recognition of his divine goodness and the call for others to see it and celebrate it *is* our mission.

Jesus Prays for the Father to Keep His Disciples
JOHN 17:6-19

After praying for God to glorify him, Jesus turns the focus of his prayer to the disciples. The disciples were called by the power of God, and now Jesus asks God to keep them from wandering away. Only the power of God at work in them makes it possible for them to follow Jesus, obey his commands, and fulfill his mission. Four times in this chapter and three times in these verses, the disciples are described as those who've been given to Jesus by the Father.

- The end of verse 2—"everyone you have given him."
- Twice in verse 6—"the people you gave me from the world" and "you gave them to me."
- The middle of verse 9—"those you have given me."

We've seen this language used before in the Gospel of John—twice in chapter 6 (vv. 37-39) and once in chapter 10 (v. 29).

Jesus uses the verb "have given," which is in the perfect tense. That means an action happened in the past and has results that continue in the present. In the past God gave Jesus a specific group of people that are his and continue to be his. God chose people, not based on any merit of their own, and gave them as a gift to his Son in eternity past. The apostle Paul told the believers in Ephesus they were chosen in Christ "before the foundation of the world" (Eph 1:4). Prior to salvation we were cold, dead sinners. By nature and choice we were rebels against God. The only way we could ever come to him is if he did a work in our hearts, drawing us to himself. When God does that work, we respond. We see, here in chapter 17, the disciples responded to the work of God.

- They kept the Father's word (v. 6)
- They received it through the teaching of Jesus (v. 8).
- They came to understand and believe what God said (v. 8).

The disciples were responsible to believe, but even their belief was the result of what God said and did.

Let's say you showed up to church one morning with your beautiful, ten-month old baby, dropped him off at the nursery, and headed in to the service. The nursery worker begins to talk to your ten-month-old. "You look so nice. Did you take a bath this morning?" He nods his head yes. "It looks like you're full. Did you eat a yummy breakfast?" Once again, he nods his head yes. "I love your outfit. Did you get dressed in your nice clothes?" Again he answers yes. So he has answered yes to all three questions. He took a bath, he ate breakfast, and he got dressed. But that's not the whole picture. As his parent, you drew the bathwater, lathered him with soap, and rinsed him off. You fixed breakfast, fed it to him, and cleaned up his mess. You washed his clothes, changed his diaper, and then got him dressed. It's true he took a bath, ate breakfast, and got dressed but only because of what you did. You did the work he couldn't do himself. He simply responded. God does the work of calling sinners to salvation. Our responsibility is to *respond* to what God does.

Let's summarize two principles from verses 6-11: **God did the work**. Everything the disciples did was in response to what God had done. The disciples kept the word, but who gave them the word? God. The disciples believed on Jesus, but who sent Jesus? God. And behind all of this was God's choice of them and gift of them to the Son. God not only did the work, but **God used his word**. The way God brought them to faith was through his words. He didn't use visions or apparitions. He didn't open the heavens or rain down fire and brimstone. He created new life in the disciples simply through his words.

What God *has done* for the disciples leads us to what God *will do*. The disciples were saved by the power of God, and the disciples are kept by the power of God (vv. 11-19). Jesus asks the Father to keep the disciples faithful to his word and to his mission (v. 11). Jesus is focused on the disciples' spiritual security. Up to this point he has been protecting them by the Father's name. He has been guarding them from falling away from the truth. Protecting them "by the Father's name" means they will hold to the truth about God. God's *name* refers to his character—all the truth about who God is. Jesus taught the disciples about the character and person of God. They came to know God personally. If the disciples are to faithfully follow Jesus, they must not turn from the truth about who God is.

As the disciples embrace the truth, they're brought into this new community of faith called the church. Entry to this community only comes through believing the Word of God. This church is intended to share an amazing level of unity—a unity that mirrors the unity between the Father and the Son (v. 11). This unity centers on the truth about God revealed in his Word. Truth is the basis of unity. This goes against everything we hear in society. We're told to minimize the truth and focus on what we agree on, ignoring the rest. Genuine unity never comes where truth is discarded because unity is the byproduct of each disciple clinging to the truth about God.

In the sport of rowing, unity is key. Each oar must enter and exit the water at precisely the same time if the boat wants to maintain speed. The way the rowers stay in sync is by listening to the coxswain. The coxswain doesn't row; he sits in the back of the boat and calls out the strokes. The coxswain is the only one who faces forward, so the entire crew must listen to the coxswain's commands and respond. When that happens, the boat flies over the water. Unity doesn't come from everyone rowing their hardest but from everyone submitting to a single voice. As the disciples submit to the voice of God, they grow more and more of the same mind. Their thoughts, desires, and intentions begin to mirror God's, and they experience a unity unfamiliar to the world.

Not only does God's work in them draw them closer to one another, but it also allows them to experience the joy of Jesus (v. 13). What a picture of God's grace! He sends Jesus to reveal the truth about himself and does a work in the disciples' hearts so they embrace the truth. By embracing the truth, they're brought into the joy of Jesus, and now God keeps them from abandoning the truth and guarantees eternally satisfying joy in Jesus. God does the work from start to finish, yet the disciples receive the joy!

The disciples will face real danger. They are targets of a world that hates them and a devil who wants to see them turn away from following Jesus (vv. 14-15). The path of least resistance for the disciples is to turn away. Holding to the truth brings attacks of every kind. Turning from the truth would seem to bring relief. That's quite a temptation. How helpful to know God is keeping them. He is protecting them. Just as he rescued them from the domain of darkness, he will preserve them from every attack. God will keep them faithful to his word and to his mission.

Jesus prays for the Father to sanctify them (vv. 17-18). To "sanctify" is to set something aside for a special use—like fine china reserved for special occasions. The disciples have been set aside for a special use. God chose them to fulfill a specific role in his plan. They serve as his witnesses to the world. The first disciples are the foundation of the church. God has a special role for them to play, and the world is their stage. They fulfill their role as his set-apart witnesses while remaining in the world (v. 15). Their example shows us what it means to be *in the world* but not *of the world*. It would be much easier to be out of the world, but we're not called to monastic living. Kent Hughes observed that for some Christians, "It is possible to go womb to tomb in a hermetically sealed container decorated with fish stickers" (*John*, 402). Christians often take one of three different approaches to dealing with the difficulty of being in the world but not of the world.

Some practice **isolation**, believing the gospel needs to be protected instead of shared. They hear the call to remain faithful to God's Word, and they disengage from all non-Christians. They think, *What better way to keep from falling away than to keep yourself as far as possible from any temptation?* These Christians would love to buy forty acres of land at least fifteen miles outside of town, fashion a compound, and never set foot outside their barbed-wire fence. Their legitimate desire to remain *faithful to God's truth* has caused them to *disregard his mission.*

Some practice **inoculation**, believing the gospel has made them immune to temptation and worldliness. They hear the call to remain faithful to God's mission and immerse themselves fully in the world. They ask, "What better way to reach the world than to blur any possible distinction between a Christian and a non-Christian?" These Christians minimize the biblical teaching on sin and repentance, choosing to live exactly as their non-Christian neighbors. Their legitimate desire to remain *faithful to God's mission* has caused them to *disregard his truth.*

Isolation and inoculation are not the only options. A better perspective is **insulation**, believing a daily focus on the gospel protects us from temptation as we seek to share the gospel with those who don't know Jesus. Insulation means working diligently to balance *faithfulness to the truth* and *faithfulness to our mission.* We recognize Christians should live differently from non-Christians but not by removing ourselves from the world of non-Christians. We live differently *in the midst* of an unbelieving world, and the difference is seen in the unmistakable fruit of Jesus Christ in our lives.

Christian, you need to engage with the world. You may wish all ungodly, corrupting influences were removed from your life and you could forsake the world, leaving it to its own devices, but you've been given a mission to live out and share the gospel in the world.

The disciples will remain faithful because of the work of God. He will keep them faithful to his word and his mission. As they embrace the truth, they will be empowered to accomplish their mission to the world. When the power of God through the instrument of his Word comes to our hearts, it gives us the ability to obey and please him. God works through his Word to empower his people to keep following Jesus, even when following Jesus is tough.

In the mid-1800s John Paton left England on a boat as a missionary to the cannibals in the New Hebrides Islands. God used his Word to keep John Paton faithful to his mission. On one occasion, measles swept through the islands, killing thousands. Paton and some other missionaries were blamed, and their lives were again threatened. Listen to what Paton wrote in his diary:

> Without that abiding consciousness of the presence and power of my dear Lord and Savior, nothing else in all the world could have preserved me from losing my reason and perishing miserably. His Words, "Lo, I am with you always, even unto the end of the world," became to me so real that it would not have startled me to behold him, as Stephen did, gazing down upon the scene. I felt his supporting power. . . . It is the sober truth, and it comes back to me sweetly after 20 years, that I had my nearest and dearest glimpses of the face and smiles of my blessed Lord in those dread moments when musket, club, or spear was being leveled at my life. (Quoted in Piper, *Filling Up*, 81)

Jesus asked the Father to keep his disciples faithful to his words, and the word would keep them faithful to the mission. His prayer has been answered repeatedly over the centuries in the lives of the apostles like Peter and Paul and missionaries like John Paton. And we have confidence his prayer will be answered for us. God will keep us faithful to his Word, and use his Word to strengthen us on our mission to spread the glory of Jesus to the nations.

Reflect and Discuss

1. How can you glorify God?
2. What is Jesus asking for in praying to be glorified?
3. How does God glorify Jesus?
4. Does the cross reveal the goodness of God? How so?
5. Why does Jesus pray for God to keep his disciples?
6. How can the disciples receive joy as a result of God's work?
7. Why does Jesus pray for the Father to sanctify the disciples?
8. How can you be in the world but not of the world?
9. What are some ways you stumble in the command to be in the world but not of it?
10. What would it look like to be in the world but not of it in your neighborhood, job, or school? How would your interactions be different?

A Prayer for the Church

JOHN 17:20-26

Main Idea: Jesus is on his way to the cross to die for us, but before he dies, he stops to pray for us.

I. Jesus Prays That Believers Will Be United in Him.
    A. Unity is not compromising the truth.
    B. Unity is not outlawing any diversity.
    C. Unity is participation in a shared relationship with Jesus.
Excursus: Evidences of a Unified Church
    A. A shared commitment to biblical instruction
    B. A shared understanding of our new identity
    C. A shared pursuit of sacrificial love
    D. A shared discontentment with selfish division
II. Jesus Prays That Believers Will Be Reunited with Him.

In John 17 Jesus is on his way to the cross to die for us, but before he dies, he stops to pray for us. What is important enough to stop and pray for on the way to the cross? Jesus asks the Father to answer two requests.

Jesus Prays That Believers Will Be United in Him

This portion of the prayer has an overarching theme: "May they all be one" (v. 21). Jesus pauses to ask his Father to bring a supernatural unity to his church. While the weight of all the world's sin is being placed on the shoulders of Jesus, our unity is on his mind. What does this unity that's so important to Jesus look like? Let's start with what it's not.

Unity Is Not Compromising the Truth

D. A. Carson wrote,

> [Unity] is not achieved by hunting enthusiastically for the lowest common theological denominator, but by common adherence to the apostolic gospel. (*John*, 568)

Jesus is not praying for unity based on our own personal opinions of who God is but a unity based on who God really is as revealed through his disciples. We are the people who believe on Jesus through the word of his disciples (v. 20). We believe what God has revealed about Jesus in the Bible. Our unity *began* when we heard the truth about God conveyed through the word of the disciples, and our unity *continues* based on that truth (cf. 1 John 1:3).

Every Sunday morning when my church meets, I look around and see scientists and accountants, professors and students, blue-collar workers and management, small business owners and retirees, moms and dads, husbands and wives. There's no reason for them to sit in the same room listening to me unless I am teaching the truth about Jesus revealed in his Word. We didn't go to the same colleges, we don't like the same sports teams, we don't have the same hobbies, but our bond is far stronger than the bond shared by those at the same country club or stadium. All of us know and understand we're sinners deserving of God's punishment and have received God's grace because we believe on Jesus through the word of the apostles. We share something more powerful than a common experience or shared interest. We share Christ, and we don't need to compromise the truth to be unified. Our unity does not come from deemphasizing the truth of God's revelation.

Unity Is Not Outlawing Any Diversity

If you've seen a military documentary, then you can probably picture scenes where battalions of soldiers line up, all wearing matching uniforms, all standing the same way. They are faceless, nameless, and opinionless, but they're uniform. Some believe the church should be a battalion of nondescript soldiers ready to assault the world. This often happens when a leader demands everyone think like he thinks. He often uses the pulpit to bully people into his positions. He's trying to create good soldiers who think, look, and act just like him.

A rigid push for uniformity can actually be one of the most disunifying forces in a church because it denies the reality of the Spirit's unique gifting (cf. 1 Cor 12:4-6). The beauty of diversity is summed up well in the classic quotation: "In essentials, unity. In nonessentials, liberty. In all things, charity." Unity, not uniformity, is what Jesus is praying for.

Unity Is Participation in a Shared Relationship with Jesus

Unity is not compromising the truth or outlawing all diversity. The unity Jesus asks for is a unity of relationship. It's receiving a new identity as one with Christ—being swallowed up in fellowship with God himself, his Son, and his Spirit (vv. 21-23). Christian unity is a result of entering into the deep relationship that exists within the Trinity. Jesus describes the foundational relationship between the Father and the Son (v. 21). The Father is in the Son, and the Son is in the Father. Next he describes the relationship between believers and the Son (vv. 21,23). The Son is in believers, and believers are in the Son. As a result, believers are in the Father (v. 21). Do you see how Christian unity is rooted in our relationship with Jesus?

Our relationship is not exactly the same as the relationship between the Father and the Son. The Father and Son are distinct persons, but they are eternally one in essence. We are brought into relationship with them through faith. We are placed "in Christ," and the Spirit of Christ comes to live in us. By virtue of Jesus's death, burial, and resurrection, we enter into a deep, abiding, never-ending relationship with the Father, Son, and Spirit.

The nature of the church's unity is the unity modeled and enabled by the triune God. Just as the Father and Son are distinguishable yet perfectly unified, so we though different, with different gifts and backgrounds, preferences and appearances, are perfectly united *in* and *through* Christ. If there is a river of love that has eternally flowed between the members of the Trinity, then we find our unity with one another by immersing ourselves completely in it. We get so close to Jesus we become drenched with his love, with the result we cannot help but love one another.

The church in the ancient city of Philippi was experiencing disunity, with disagreements and conflict. Paul writes a letter to help them deal with their conflict:

> *Make my joy complete by thinking the same way, having the same love, united in spirit, intent on one purpose. Do nothing out of selfish ambition or conceit, but in humility consider others as more important than yourselves. Everyone should look out not only for his own interests, but also for the interests of others.* (Phil 2:2-4)

Don't fight and argue, but instead be humble and have unity. How? What's Paul's antidote for disunity in the church? He continues in verse 5: "Adopt the same attitude as that of Christ Jesus." He describes the humiliation of Jesus, how he came as a servant and was put to death as a criminal. What's his point? The only way to draw closer to one another, the only way to grow in unity as Christians, is to become more like Jesus. Our unity is *based in* and *empowered by* Jesus alone.

Christian unity is a unity of relationship, and it's also a unity of mission. The context of this passage is the mission Jesus had given his disciples. As believers discover their unity with one another in their union with Christ, they discover a unity of mission. The Father and the Son are unified in their desire to rescue sinners from the shackles of death (that's why Jesus came), and as each church draws closer to Jesus, their unity will be displayed in a common dedication to the mission of Jesus. Like a nation whose homeland has been attacked by an enemy, the vision of that church will focus more precisely on the mission they've been given. All of the distractions will fade as a common passion develops to see men and women rescued from the horrible clutches of sin. When unity of relationship spills out and overflows into unity of mission, men and women will hear the truth about Jesus from the mouths of disciples of Jesus and will respond in faith to Jesus.

Excursus

Let me fill out this picture of unity by giving four evidences of a unified church.

A Shared Commitment to Biblical Instruction

Unity is not a by-product of discussion and diplomacy; rather, unity flows from a commitment to the Word of God. In John 17:22 Jesus uses the word *glory* in the sense of revelation. The disciples have received the revelation about God through the ministry of Jesus. This glory came not only through his person and works but also through his words. His glory (in v. 22) is parallel to his words (v. 8). We will be one as we continue to hold firmly to the revelation (or glory) of God passed down by the disciples.

When we consider the history of the church, particularly the high-tide moments when the church had the greatest impact on the world, we turn to the book of Acts. In chapter 2 three things merge together—impact on the world, unity of the church, and commitment to the Word.

They devoted themselves to the apostles' teaching, *to the fellowship, to the breaking of bread, and to prayer.*
Everyone was filled with awe, and many wonders and signs were being performed through the apostles. Now all the believers were together and held all things in common. (Acts 2:42-44; emphasis added)

If every member of a church is willing to ask, "What does the Bible say?" and commit to obey it no matter what, that church will experience unity. There will never be unity within a church when the Word of God is neglected. When the good seed of God's Word is no longer spread, you will find the church taken over by the weeds of gossip, selfishness, and conflict. Only the power of God through his Word brings a harvest of peace and righteousness within a fellowship of saints.

A Shared Understanding of Our New Identity

As believers, we are "in Christ." He is the true vine, and at the moment of salvation we are placed in him. Our strength, guidance, and nourishment come solely from that life-giving connection to him. At salvation we are given a new position and identity. Who we are is wrapped up completely in Christ. In *Confessions* by Augustine, the fourth-century bishop of Hippo, he tells about a renowned philosopher who turned to Jesus. At the service when he made a public declaration of faith, because of his new identity in Christ, he wanted a new name. What a compelling picture of a believer's new identity in Christ!

At salvation we receive a new identity in Christ, and we're brought into a community of brothers and sisters whose identity is found in Christ. Our position *in him* allows us to experience unparalleled unity amid incredible diversity. Our new identity in Christ makes us a family. Three times in our text Jesus says the word *Father* (John 17:21,24,25). You and I are brought into the family of God through the work of Jesus Christ. We no longer relate to one another as strangers; we love one another as family members. Christian unity is people from all ethnicities, countries, and social circles becoming family members. It means caring for each man in your church as you would care for your brother and treating each woman with the respect you would your sister.

A Shared Pursuit of Sacrificial Love

We are brought into the love that exists between the Father and the Son. Twice in this passage (vv. 23,26) we are told believers will know and experience that God loves us with the same love he has for the Son. There's no way this understanding of God's supernatural, selfless, sacrificial love can do anything other than overflow into our relationships with others (cf. 13:34). Our love for one another is reflected as we

- bear one another's burdens (Gal 6:1),
- instruct one another (Rom 15:14),
- forgive one another (Eph 4:2),
- pray for one another (Jas 5:16),
- submit to one another (Eph 5:21),
- encourage one another (1 Thess 4:18), and
- provoke one another, not to anger, but to love and good works (Heb 10:24).

Christ is not praying for us to embrace a *concept* but a *conduct*. He wants lives marked by unity—a unity that leads us to walk hand in hand with one another. When one family member hurts, we don't just take note of it; we hurt as well. When a sister feels rejected, we accept her. When a brother begins to stumble, we pick him up. Real unity requires breaking a sweat. Unity takes effort and demands sacrifice.

A Shared Discontentment with Selfish Division

Unity always moves forward, striving for perfection (John 17:23). The word *completely* doesn't mean "spotless" but contains the idea of pursuing the highest degree of unity.

It keeps a target always in front of us. We are never content. We must never say, "We're unified enough." If someone dropped some arsenic in your cup, you wouldn't be satisfied until you were certain every last drop of poison had been removed. Disunity and broken relationships are like poison in the church. We can't be content until every last drop of division is removed—not by getting rid of someone or leaving ourselves but by dealing biblically with division.

There should be no safer place in the entire world for a child of God than in the church. This fellowship should be an attack-free zone. Puritan preacher Thomas Brooks wrote, "Discord and division become no Christian. For wolves to worry the lambs is no wonder, but for one lamb to worry another, this is unnatural and monstrous" ("Legacies"). Do you make your church a safe place? Are you proactively and humbly dealing with differences and disagreements?

Unity in the church is a powerful testimony in the world. Real unity is a *supernatural* work and points to a *supernatural* reason: Jesus lives in us (v. 21). Thomas Manton said, "Divisions in the church breed atheism in the world" (quoted in Hughes, *John*, 411). John MacArthur puts it this way: "The effectiveness of the church's evangelism is devastated by dissension and disputes among its members" (*John 12–21*, 293). Sadly, we can all probably share stories to show that's true. The good news is the reverse is also true. A unified church reveals powerful, life-changing truths to the world. Christian unity reveals Jesus actually did come to the earth, sent by the Father to die on the cross and pay the penalty for our sin (v. 21). The church is the visible display of God's goodness to this world. Each local church is the visible display of God's kindness to its community. We don't have any photographs of Jesus. The church is the photograph. The church is the picture of his love and mercy. There's a picture frame around each church and a sign above us that says, "Come, see what God is like."

When a non-Christian sees a unified church, the only logical conclusion is God loves us just like he loves Jesus (v. 23). A group of believers, spanning generations and ethnicity and gender, all worshiping Christ and ministering to one another, will make the unbelieving stop and say, "God's love is real." A unified church is a billboard declaring Jesus came to earth because the Father loves us with the love reserved for his Son. Could there possibly be a more compelling appeal to a broken world?

Jesus Prays That Believers Will Be Reunited with Him

Christians experience a unique union and fellowship with Jesus right now, but it's only a shadow of what we will experience for all eternity in his presence. In his Father's house we will see his glory (v. 24). We will see the full display of divine goodness. We will experience the presence of Jesus in unveiled splendor. We get a taste of it now—through his Word and by his indwelling Spirit—but in the future we will experience the full delight and joy of unhindered fellowship with our Savior. John Calvin describes the difference:

> At that time they saw Christ's glory as someone shut up in the dark sees a feeble and glimmering light through small cracks. Christ now wants them to go on to enjoy the full brightness of heaven. (*John*, 402–3)

The apostle John said it this way in his first letter:

> *Dear friends, we are God's children now, and what we will be has not yet been revealed. We know that when he appears, we will be like him because we will see him as he is.* (1 John 3:2)

We will see him as he is. We will worship him face-to-face. What a privilege! What a promise! We, who know Jesus and have been received into his family, are going home. We're going to a home unaffected by divorce, unmarked by abuse, and untainted by sin. We're going to a home where we will forever experience perfect and complete harmony. Why? Because we're going to our Father's house.

Joni Eareckson Tada tells a wonderful story about a little boy named Jeff:

> At the end of a five-day retreat for families affected by disabilities, a microphone was passed around so all the participants could share a couple of sentences about how meaningful, how fun the week had been. Little freckle-faced, red-haired Jeff raised his hand. We were so excited to see what Jeff would say, because Jeff had won the hearts of us all at family retreat. Jeff has Down syndrome. He took the microphone, put it right up to his mouth, and said, "Let's go

home." Later, his mother told me, "His dad couldn't come to family retreat because he had to work. Jeff really missed his dad back home." ("Heaven, Our Real Home")

It won't be long until we get to go home. Not much longer and we'll forever enjoy peace and unity in the Father's house. In just a little while we will experience the uninhibited love the Father and Son have shared from before the foundation of the world. But we can begin to experience it here.

The church can be a taste of heaven. When people with different preferences, hobbies, jobs, genders, backgrounds, skin colors, accents, and tastes love one another with a love surpassing all human love, they open a window to heaven, and people begin to feel a breeze from a far-off country and in their souls awaken a long-dormant hope. They want to go to that place and be with those people who know, see, and feel something different, something beyond, something more.

The love of God assures us we have a home and a country on the other side of the sea. This knowledge binds us together and spills out in a love that feels strangely foreign but still familiar. When people see this love displayed in a million little ways, they will hope it's real, and when the hope is confirmed, they will understand the story is true. They will know Jesus lives and Jesus loves.

Reflect and Discuss

1. What does Jesus pray for his followers?
2. What are some things that unity is not?
3. Are there relationships in your life that would not exist apart from the gospel? How has God united you with those people?
4. What passages of Scripture celebrate the diversity of God's people united through the gospel?
5. How can unity with other believers in Christ affect the way you engage in God's mission?
6. List the four evidences of a unified church.
7. To what had the church in Acts 2 devoted themselves? What was the result?
8. How can you pursue sacrificial love in your church?
9. Why is unity in the church a powerful testimony?
10. Does the unity in your church provide a compelling picture of God's intended plan? What steps can you take today to live in unity with other believers?

The Cross: A Sovereign Savior

JOHN 18:1-32

Main Idea: Every step on the way to the cross is planned and controlled by Jesus.

I. **Jesus Was Not a Helpless Victim or a Courageous Martyr but a Sovereign Savior.**

II. **Our Response Should Not Be Pity or Bravery but Faith.**

Like a swelling wave about to crest, John's Gospel arrives at the cross. The "hour" of sacrifice, introduced to us at Jesus's first miracle in Cana, has finally come, but the momentum of this moment had been building long before Jesus's first miracle. It began in a garden at the dawn of history when a promise was made about a Savior. Human history, from its first moments, had been moving toward this point. When it took place, the death of Jesus Christ on a cross became its dividing line. It's no exaggeration to suggest that, even from a secular viewpoint, no event has impacted human history like the crucifixion of Jesus Christ. Everything that took place before looks toward it, and everything that has taken place since looks back. For those of us who claim the title *Christian*, the cross is central to everything we believe, do, and are.

The reason the cross stands as the iconic image of Christianity cannot be traced to first-century marketing savvy. The cross marks the moment God offered his Son as the penalty for our sin, fallen mankind was redeemed, sin and death were defeated, and God extended terms of peace to his enemies at the cost of his Son's life. We cannot overstate the significance of the cross.

Who was responsible for the cross? Who murdered Jesus? *The Romans?* Crucifixion, though probably not a Roman invention, was certainly perfected under their reign. They were the ones in charge when Jesus was crucified. Pilate, a Roman governor, ordered his death. Roman soldiers pounded the nails into his hands and feet. *The Jewish leaders?* They brought Jesus to Pilate and demanded he be killed. When Pilate wanted to release Jesus, the Jewish leaders incited the crowds to chant, "Crucify him!" (Luke 23:21). They were willing to accept responsibility for his death. "His blood be on us and on our children!" they said in Matthew 27:25. *Us?* It wasn't just the sin of the Romans and the Jews that caused him to die. It was your sin and my sin. As the prophet Isaiah said, "We all went astray like sheep; we all have turned to our own way; and the LORD has punished [Jesus] for the iniquity of us all" (Isa 53:6). We're not off the hook. Jesus died because of our sin.

All of these answers are correct in part. However, as John writes his account of the cross, he doesn't focus on human liability. He shows every step on the way to the cross is planned and controlled by Jesus. Jesus said, "I lay down my life so that I may take it up again. No one takes it from me, but I lay it down on my own" (10:17-18). From a human perspective, it seems Jesus is swept to the cross by forces outside his control. Actually, Jesus orchestrates every encounter, and every event reveals his sovereign control. John MacArthur reminds us,

> As God incarnate, Jesus was always in absolute control of all the events of His life. That control extended even to the circumstances surrounding His death. Far from being an accident, Jesus' sacrificial death was the primary reason He took on human life in the first place; it is the pinnacle of redemptive history. (*John 12–21*, 304)

Jesus Was Not a Helpless Victim or a Courageous Martyr but a Sovereign Savior

Jesus doesn't select this garden as a place to hide but as a place to be found (18:2). He chooses a spot well known to Judas, his betrayer, because the time has come for him to lay down his life. Jesus may look like he's being hunted, but he's the one laying an ambush. In chapter 13, when Judas left the upper room to plan his treachery, John ended the account with the sad conclusion, "And it was night" (13:30). Judas left the light of the world to wander in the darkness. Now he returns to Jesus, carrying torches and lanterns (18:3). How tragic to trade the eternal light for a handmade torch.

Jesus takes the initiative (v. 4). He leaves the enclosure of the garden to confront this group that's come to arrest him. He knew they were coming, and he knows what will happen now that they've arrived (13:21-26). Nothing is a surprise. Nothing catches him off guard. After walking out of the garden to confront the soldiers, Jesus asks them a question, not to gather information but to reveal who's really in charge

(vv. 5-6). No other Gospel writer records this exchange. John includes it to show us Jesus is not an actor on stage waiting for direction; he's the one directing every movement. We don't know what exactly makes the soldiers fall to the ground. The point isn't *how* it happens, but *why* it happens. Their collapse reveals Jesus is not arrested in weakness. This brief encounter affirms his control over the events.

Again Jesus issues commands to the soldiers (vv. 7-8). These men who were trained to take orders from their superiors obey the instructions of their captive. They can only do what Jesus allows them to do. Chapter 17 records Jesus's prayer prior to coming to this garden when he prays specifically for the disciples who remain on earth after his departure (17:1-2). Even here, as he's being arrested, Jesus cares for his disciples (18:9). He makes certain the soldiers don't touch them because he's promised to protect and preserve them.

This raises an interesting issue. In 6:37-39; 10:28; and the prayer of chapter 17, Jesus is focused on the disciples' eternal destiny. He will preserve them until the final day when they will join him in heaven. Here in chapter 18 he's simply protecting them from arrest and possible persecution. How does this fulfill the earlier promises of eternal security? Their physical safety illustrates their eternal security. Just as Jesus is in control of every aspect of the physical world—his arrest, betrayal, and crucifixion, including protecting his disciples from persecution—he's also in control of everything in the spiritual realm, including preserving his disciples until that final day. What a wonderful picture of his love and power! What reassurance to his disciples in the coming difficult days. What hope for us. Just as Jesus protects the disciples on that dark day, he will protect and preserve all who follow him.

Peter doesn't understand that Jesus has been headed to this event from the first moment (vv. 10-11). The "cup" is the cup prepared for him by the Father. The cup is full of divine judgment, and Jesus takes it to his lips and drains every last drop on the cross. To Peter the evening's events are spiraling out of control. He thinks Jesus needs protection. He thinks someone needs to stop this arrest from taking place. He thinks someone needs to take charge. Little does he realize Jesus has choreographed every action, and nothing is out of step with his will. Peter's actions to protect Jesus, though understandable, were useless. Indeed, they were a denial of why Jesus came. Jesus was born to die. He was not surprised by the turn of events; he was sovereign over them.

In verse 14 John points us back to Caiaphas's unwitting prophecy about Jesus's death in chapter 11:

He did not say this on his own, but being high priest that year he prophesied that Jesus was going to die for the nation, and not for the nation only, but also to unite the scattered children of God. (11:51-52)

God directed the words of the high priest, so he spoke more than he understood. By John's reminding us of his words, we're assured the injustice Jesus suffers is part of God's plan to rescue humanity from the bondage of sin. John Calvin wrote, "Let us remember that the body of the Son of God was bound in order that our souls might be set free from the bonds of sin" (Calvin, *John*, 410). Jesus is taking deliberate, controlled steps to the cross so we might be set free from sin.

Earlier that evening Peter pledged his devotion to Jesus: "I will lay down my life for you" (John 13:37). Jesus answered, "Will you lay down your life for me? Truly I tell you, a rooster will not crow until you have denied me three times" (v. 38). Peter's actions (18:15-18) begin to fulfill the earlier words of Jesus, providing one more evidence Jesus is aware and in control of every event.

Once again Jesus is the one asking the questions (vv. 19-24). In the first of numerous interrogations, Jesus turns the table on his interrogator:

"Why do you question me? Question those who heard what I told them. . . . If I have spoken wrongly, give evidence about the wrong; but if rightly, why do you hit me?" (vv. 21,23)

Jesus is innocent, but he's not a victim: a victim has no control over his circumstances. He reminds the high priest he taught openly in the synagogue and temple. What did Jesus teach? In the synagogue at Capernaum, he said, "I am the bread of life. No one who comes to me will ever be hungry, and no one who believes in me will ever be thirsty again" (6:35). In the temple he said,

"My sheep hear my voice, I know them, and they follow me. I give them eternal life, and they will never perish. No one will snatch them out of my hand." (10:27-28)

His message was the gospel. He came to die, and through his death he brings salvation to sinners who are cut off from God.

Peter denies Jesus and the rooster crows (18:25-27). Now we have the complete fulfillment of Jesus's words to Peter in chapter 13. Everything Jesus said would happen has come to pass, and everything that's come to pass gives us confidence in the sovereign control of Jesus.

John has been meticulously building the case that Jesus is sovereign over his own betrayal, trial, and death. The final piece of the puzzle is Jesus's death—a topic Jesus addressed many times. Back in chapter 3, at the conclusion of his conversation with Nicodemus, Jesus prophesied his death: "Just as Moses lifted up the snake in the wilderness, so the Son of Man must be lifted up, so that everyone who believes in him may have eternal life" (3:14-15). Jesus makes reference to an account in Israel's history when God sent poisonous serpents to punish the people. God then instructed Moses to craft a bronze serpent, place the serpent on a pole, and lift it up off the ground. Everyone who looked to the bronze serpent would be saved from death. Jesus uses this event as an illustration of his death. There are numerous similarities: people are dying, God intervenes, faith is required. But Jesus highlights another similarity: both means of rescue are "lifted up." Jesus uses the same language in chapter 8. Describing his death, Jesus says, "When you lift up the Son of Man, then you will know that I am he" (8:28). He says it even more explicitly in chapter 12: "'As for me, if I am lifted up from the earth I will draw all people to myself.' He said this to indicate what kind of death he was about to die" (12:32-33). Why are the Romans involved in Jesus's death? Why is Jesus brought before Pilate? Because Jesus chose to die by crucifixion. He prophesied beforehand he would be lifted up in death, and this night he stood before Pilate so that his prophecy would be fulfilled (18:28-32). Every decision had been orchestrated by Jesus, including the choice of a cross. He wrote every note of that evening's symphony and conducted every measure in perfect harmony with his sovereign will.

In 1906, Albert Schweitzer published a book called *The Quest for the Historical Jesus*. In it he wrote,

> There is silence all around. The Baptist appears, and cries:
> "Repent for the Kingdom of Heaven is at hand." Soon after
> that comes Jesus, and in the knowledge that he is the coming
> Son of Man lays hold of the wheel of the world to set it moving
> on the last revolution which is to bring all ordinary history to
> a close. It refuses to turn, and he throws himself upon it. Then
> it does turn; and crushes him. . . . The wheel rolls onward,

and the mangled body of the immeasurably great Man, who was strong enough to think of himself as the spiritual rule of mankind and to bend history to his purpose, is hanging upon it still. (Quoted in Hughes, *John*, 413–14)

Schweitzer viewed Jesus as a victim. Caught up in the swirling political climate, Jesus attempted to make himself great and tragically fell to his death. But on the contrary, in spite of the treachery of Judas, the blasphemy of the Jews, and the brutality of the Romans, Jesus will not allow us to see him as a helpless victim.

There's also been a movement to view Jesus not as a helpless victim but as a courageous martyr. His death serves as a model of selfless love for all mankind and an example we should follow. Yes, Jesus was heroic. Yes, he suffered persecution and death. Yes, his death is an example. But we can't look at him and see a courageous martyr. There's only one proper way to view Jesus. Jesus is the sovereign Savior. His life is not taken from him. He lays it down willingly. We didn't need a victim to die in our place. We didn't need an example to show us how to die. We needed a rescuer who could save us from death. Rulers and authorities didn't overcome Jesus. He voluntarily sacrificed himself to fulfill the eternal plan of God. The power and authority he demonstrated in calming the sea and raising the dead are also revealed in his arrest, trial, and death. At no point did Jesus lose control. Not a breath was taken or a word uttered that did not meet his sovereign approval.

Our Response Should Not Be Pity or Bravery but Faith

When people are abused, we wrap our arms around them and cry. We empathize with their suffering and long for justice. When we think about their pain, our hearts hurt with them. We feel sorry for victims, but we don't put our faith in them for salvation. Had Jesus simply been a victim of senseless violence, then the appropriate response to his story would be compassion, but when we consider the cross of Jesus, compassion isn't enough.

When we hear accounts of great courage, we're inspired to live courageously. The bold faith of martyrs stirs within me a desire to live with greater boldness for the sake of the gospel, but the death of Jesus on the cross should produce more than bravery.

Looking at the cross and seeing in it a call for pity or bravery fails to understand the depth of our problem. If the root of our problem was injustice, then Jesus's dying as a victim could arouse our compassion and motivate us to fight for justice. If the root of our problem was fear, then Jesus's dying as a martyr could inspire us to bravery in sharing the gospel. But the root of our problem is more serious and deadlier: sin has cut us off from God. We've rebelled against our Creator and received a sentence of death. Nothing we do can change our position. No amount of effort can repair our relationship with God. Something radical had to be done for us.

Jesus did just that on the cross. The perfect Son of God was born as a human baby, lived a sinless life, and then took upon himself our punishment. Because of his sacrifice, God has extended terms of peace. If we look at Jesus's sacrifice and pity him or even resolve to die like him, then we call his sacrifice worthless and remain estranged from God. We must respond to his sacrifice by casting ourselves completely on him by taking refuge in him, not our own efforts. The call of the cross is not a call for empathy or bravery but for complete dependence on Jesus Christ.

Reflect and Discuss

1. What does this passage reveal about Jesus that we need to believe?
2. Why is the cross the iconic image of Christianity?
3. Who was ultimately responsible for Jesus going to the cross?
4. What do Jesus's commands to the soldiers reveal about his sovereignty?
5. Read Numbers 21:4-9. When Jesus references this text as a picture of how he will be lifted up, how is he describing the way in which sin is forgiven?
6. Describe the ways this passage shows Jesus is neither victim nor martyr.
7. Why would Jesus go to the cross of his own accord?
8. How is the cross a picture of the seriousness and magnitude of sin in your life?
9. What message about the cross is conveyed when Christians downplay or ignore sin in our own lives?
10. What should be our response to the cross?

The Cross: King of the Jews

JOHN 18:33–19:22

Main Idea: The actions of Pilate, the crowd, and Jesus reveal that Jesus is the long-awaited King of the Jews.

I. The Recognition of the King
II. The Rejection of the King
III. The Response of the King

The United States of America was founded with a unique form of government. The founding fathers fashioned a government without royalty—no king, queen, princes, or lords. Their choice made the United States distinct from the European countries from which it came. In the Old Testament we discover a similar desire in the nation of Israel. Unlike any nation before or since, this nation was distinct. No other nation was chosen and governed directly by God himself. But the desire to be like other nations, particularly to have a king, surfaced repeatedly throughout their history.

In the case of the United States, they didn't *want* a king because they thought they could develop a better type of government. In Israel's case they didn't *need* a king because God led them. They were a theocracy—God governed and defended them—yet they continued to cry out for a human king. Finally, God granted their wish and gave them a king named Saul. Their second king, David, was a great king, but after him the history of Israel is filled with more wicked kings than good kings. After the nation was split in two, both parts were defeated, and the people became captives. Israel's desire to be like the other nations—to have a human king—proved disastrous.

However, that's not the whole story. Long before the people were given a king, God promised to send a King to rule not just over Israel but over all the nations. One of the central themes of the Old Testament is the coming King who will reign over an eternal kingdom. This Old Testament theme sets the stage for what we discover at the end of John. In Genesis 49, before his death Jacob called his sons to circle around him, and he blessed them. His prophetic blessing creates the expectation that a King from Israel will rule a worldwide kingdom (Gen 49:10). This promise is repeated and expanded in Balaam's final prophecy in Numbers 24:17. As we move forward in Israel's history, Moses and Joshua lead the nation into the promised land, but neither of them becomes king. Various judges—like Gideon and Samson—deliver Israel from foreign powers, but they don't become kings. The book of Judges ends this way: "In those days there was no king in Israel" (Judg 21:25).

Eventually Israel gets a king and establishes a monarchy under David. Is David the fulfillment of the promise made in Genesis and Numbers? He's from the tribe of Judah. He has great military success. In 1 Chronicles 17 God makes a covenant with David, and the language he uses answers our question (vv. 11-14). David is not the King, but the King will come from the line of David. He will not only be a son of David but will be a Son of God, and he will rule over an eternal kingdom. After reading these promises, we're left with a question. Who is this King?

In John 1 Nathanael, a devout Jew, calls Jesus of Nazareth "the King of Israel" (v. 49). *Is Jesus the promised King of the Jews?* That's the same question asked by Pontius Pilate, the Roman governor of Israel, in John 18:33. Earlier in chapter 18 Jesus was arrested and turned over to Pilate by the Jewish leaders. Now Pilate interrogates Jesus, which ends in Jesus's being crucified. Is Jesus the King of the Jews? The answer is found in Pilate's actions.

The Recognition of the King

Four times in this account Pilate publicly refers to Jesus as the "King of the Jews." The first time comes after he questions Jesus (18:39). After having Jesus whipped, Pilate brings him out before the Jews and says, "Here is your king!" (19:14). Then he asks, "Should I crucify your king?" (v. 15). Pilate gives in to the people's wishes and orders Jesus's execution but not before having a sign made that calls Jesus the King of the Jews (vv. 19-22).

Why does Pilate continue to use the title "King of the Jews" to describe Jesus? Does Pilate believe Jesus is the prophesied King and this is his response of faith, or is he doing it to mock the Jews for pressuring him to kill a man he wants to release? Ultimately, Pilate's motive doesn't matter. Jesus is publicly identified as the King of the Jews. Not only do the Jewish leaders hear Pilate's repeated pronouncement, but when the sign is tacked up on the cross above Jesus's disfigured face, the whole world sees who is dying there. "The King of the Jews" is written in three languages because this King's death impacts more than one nation. This King brings men from every nation into his kingdom. The pen of Pilate becomes the instrument God uses to announce to the world Jesus is King.

Not only does Pilate call Jesus the King, but his soldiers also dress him up and present him as a king (19:1-5). Pilate mocks Jesus and the Jews. The soldiers who strike Jesus do so to taunt him, but they don't understand that Jesus is a King unlike any king this world has ever seen. He's a King who humbles himself to die so he might deliver those who hate him and rebel against him. The garments they place on him and the horrible crown they force him to wear reveal he is a humble King who rules through his suffering.

The suffering of Jesus reveals the wickedness of our sin, our inability to please God, his grace in saving us, and the certainty of future acceptance. The horrible mistreatment of Jesus gives us confidence in God's promises and reminds us Jesus is our ultimate treasure, for only his death could satisfy the debt of sin we owed. The suffering of Jesus that day so long ago reminds us of truths and realities we easily forget and overlook. Charles Spurgeon once said,

> I received some years ago orders from my Master to stand at
> the foot of the cross until he comes. He has not come yet, but
> I mean to stand there until He does. (Quoted in Mahaney,
> "The Pastor's Priorities," 133)

We stand at the foot of the cross because the cross is the ground of our faith and the foundation of our hope.

The Rejection of the King

The picture we get of Pilate is not particularly flattering. He's not the kind of guy you'd want your daughter to bring home at Thanksgiving. But the true human villains in this account are the Jewish leaders. They deliver Jesus to Pilate (18:35). They choose to pardon Barabbas (a thief, murderer, and thug) (v. 40). With that choice their flimsy shield of spirituality is torn away, and their wicked hearts are exposed. They incite the mob to chant at the top of their lungs, "Crucify!" (19:6). They appeal to God's law as the reason for killing Jesus (v. 7). They threaten to bring questions about Pilate's loyalty before Caesar (v. 12). Finally, they claim Caesar as their only king (v. 15).

What did Jesus do to cause them to respond with this level of hatred? Jesus challenged what they held most precious. Their system of religion was the most important part of their lives. They treasured more than anything the control they wielded over the nation—control through guilt and fear. Jesus came to offer freedom *from* guilt and fear. He taught that their religion wasn't the answer, but the gospel—God's free gift of grace—is what people need.

Why do men and women need the gospel? Because the human heart is like a pigsty. It's dirty and nasty, full of filth. It smells rotten. Mud and waste fill every corner. Religion looks at that pigsty and says, "I can fix it." It gets some wood and builds a nice shed and places it right over the pigsty. It picks out beautiful colors to paint the shed, plants flowers around the outside, and places a hand-carved "Welcome" sign over the door. It looks great at a glance, but when you open the door, the stench of pigs wallowing in their own filth leaks out. Religion only succeeds in changing the appearance, not the heart. Jesus takes a wrecking ball to the shed the religious leaders have built. He exposes their hearts, filthy and defiled. The gospel doesn't deal in cosmetics. It gets dirty. It takes a shovel to the heart's pigsty and starts digging out the muck of sin. It isn't pleasant at first because exposed sin is ugly, but the gospel expels sin and transforms the heart.

We need our hearts changed. We don't need our morals reformed or our behavior modified. If we attempt to change through religion, that is, through what we do—church attendance, charitable giving, disciplined living, strict moralism—we may succeed in putting a fresh coat of paint on our outsides, but inside our hearts will still be pigsties.

The filthy stench of their hearts is exposed in their statement claiming Caesar as their only king (19:15). They're lying—outright, bald-faced lying. Earlier (ch. 8) they told Jesus they were enslaved to no one. They don't view Caesar as their king. They don't have a king! They're more honest than they intend. They have no king because they've rejected the rule of God and the reign of his Son.

Back in chapter 19, verse 7, they said their law was the basis for Jesus's death, but they don't have just any law: they have God's law. What is God's law about? It's about the coming King. It's about Jesus. The law they use to condemn Jesus to death is written about the coming of Jesus. They have the gospel—the life-transforming message is theirs—and they treat it like a code of conduct. "Do this." "Don't do that." "Paint the outside this color." "Plant these flowers." They ignore the life-giving gospel and embrace dead religion. It's their chants of "Crucify! Crucify!" that eventually convince Pilate to deliver Jesus to be crucified (vv. 16-18).

This all takes place during the Passover Festival (v. 14). On the day they celebrate their salvation from the king of Egypt, they kill their own King.

The Response of the King

Three times in this passage Jesus responds to Pilate's questions. His first response is to the question, "Are you the King of the Jews?" (18:33). Jesus is a king, but his kingdom is not a threat to the Roman Empire. His kingdom is different from earthly kingdoms because it's not from this world (18:36). Jesus is not saying his kingdom is disconnected from this world, as if this world doesn't matter. He's saying his kingdom is greater than this world. It's beyond all world powers and includes more than the visible realm.

His kingdom has servants, but his servants operate much differently from the servants of earthly kingdoms. His servants could take up weapons to stop his crucifixion, but those are not his orders. His servants have different goals. Earthly servants seek to protect their king, but Jesus needs no protection. He protects his servants, not the other way around. His servants have different weapons. Earthly servants use swords and shields—in our day, guns and grenades—to do their king's bidding. Jesus's goals are not first physical. They're spiritual. For him earthly weapons serve no purpose. One of the Reformers wrote,

> Christ's "kingdom" is spiritual and must be founded on the teaching and power of the Spirit. It must be built up in the same way, for neither human laws and edicts nor human punishments reach the conscience. . . . However, the depravity of "this world" causes Christ's "kingdom" to be established more by the blood of martyrs than by force of arms. (Calvin, *John*, 418)

Understanding the difference between Jesus's kingdom and earthly kingdoms forces us to look to his Word and not to this world for instructions on how to obey him. If his kingdom was an earthly kingdom, then we could observe other successful earthly kingdoms and operate based on their laws. But the unique nature of his kingdom calls for a unique source of instruction. We get our orders from the Word of the King himself.

Christians often *feel* out of step with the world around us because we *are* out of step with this world. We are citizens of a heavenly kingdom living among citizens of an earthly kingdom. As we follow our King, sometimes we'll feel like we're swimming upstream, against the current of our culture. We can't give up and swim downstream, and we shouldn't make it our goal to change the direction of the current. Instead, we trust God for strength to keep swimming and for opportunities to call others to join us.

Just as his kingdom is a different type of kingdom, Jesus is a different type of king (18:37-38). Jesus's royalty rests in the uniqueness of his authority, as one who bears witness to the truth. The truth Jesus proclaims comes from God (8:40). Often truth is viewed as relative, as something that can be controlled. You can spin the truth to benefit your cause. But truth is fixed. It flows from the lips of God, who himself never changes. Jesus came to reveal God's truth. We can't spin it; we must submit to it. Truth is the instrument God uses to call men and women into his kingdom. Every person is born into slavery, held captive to sin, and deceived by Satan, the father of lies. His lies fill this world. His biggest lie is that we can find happiness apart from God. "If you can win his love, you'll find happiness." "If you're successful at your job, you'll find happiness." "If you buy that boat, you'll find happiness." "If your family's healthy, you'll find happiness." "If you're invited into the inner circle, you'll find happiness." We're like the Olympic sprinter from the movie *Chariots of Fire*. Before running the 100-meter dash, he laments, "Contentment! I'm 24 and I've never known it. I'm forever in pursuit, and I don't even know what it is I'm chasing" (quoted in Keller, *Counterfeit Gods*, 73).

The world feeds us lie after lie, each bigger, bolder, and more outrageous than the last. Jesus speaks the truth. Those who respond to the truth are no longer slaves to the father of lies. Jesus said, "You will know the truth, and the truth will set you free" (8:32). Jesus doesn't spread his kingdom through the sword but through the Word. He brings salvation not through military might but through a message of truth. The gospel message makes kingdom subjects. Christians, as kingdom citizens, serve one another by bringing one another back to the Word of God. We remind one another of what the King said, not common sense or worldly solutions. God promises to transfer rebels from the kingdom of darkness to the kingdom of light through his Word, and through his Word we learn how to live as faithful subjects in his kingdom.

I find great hope in Jesus's final response to Pilate (19:9-11). All human authority is granted by God. Pilate has no authority over this event—the trial and crucifixion—unless God hands it to him. In this moment we see the superiority of Jesus's kingdom. The King of the Jews is about to die, but his kingdom will not be shaken. In human kingdoms, if you take out the king, you create turmoil and the kingdom becomes vulnerable to attack. But Jesus's kingdom is not in danger of being overthrown. He is sovereign over the proceedings. His death will not make his kingdom more vulnerable; it makes his kingdom victorious. His death instituted the spiritual effects of his kingdom. We are liberated from captivity to sin, death, and Satan, and we are citizens in his kingdom. But his kingly reign will someday take a grander form. Jesus will not just rule spiritually; he will bring everything into subjection to himself. He will return and establish a never-ending kingdom governed in perfect righteousness. His kingdom has come but only in part. There will be a day when the King returns and every knee will bow and every tongue confess he is Lord.

The kingdom of Jesus is not a fantasy. It's not a fairy tale. In fact, our fairy tales are human attempts to wrestle with a desire we all feel. We long for a day when a victorious king appears to right all wrongs, defeat our enemies, and dispense justice to the oppressed. Jesus didn't come as a victorious king because we were the enemies. If he had come to dispense justice, we would have been destroyed. The first time he came as a humble King, laying down his life so we could be spared and brought into his kingdom. Next time he will come as the victorious King, establishing his eternal kingdom.

When we comprehend who Jesus is and commit ourselves to Jesus as King, our lives will change. We'll see the world and our role in it differently. Our King has given us a mission, and we'll die trying to accomplish it. We'll live with a wartime mentality, using our time, energy, and resources to serve our King and carry out his orders. There's a big difference between a peacetime and wartime mentality. It might be best illustrated by the ocean liner *Queen Mary*. The *Queen Mary* was built in 1937 to carry passengers between England and the United States. It was a gorgeous ship and featured the best amenities. It was in every sense a luxury liner. But when World War II started, there was little need for a luxury liner. The *Queen Mary* was retrofitted and used as a troop transport. Instead of first-class cabins and luxury staterooms, it now had barracks and a mess hall. Shuffleboard courts were replaced with anti-aircraft guns. The luxury was stripped away because there was a war to be fought. Our King did not come in luxury, and he doesn't call us to luxury. He calls us to carry out his mission. We go to the nations and tell them death is defeated, shame has surrendered, and Jesus is King.

Reflect and Discuss

1. How do we know that David wasn't the King promised throughout the Old Testament?
2. How does God use Pilate to announce Jesus as the prophesied King?
3. Why should the suffering of Jesus give us confidence?
4. How has Jesus given you freedom from guilt and fear?
5. Why does Jesus tell Pilate, "My kingdom is not of this world"?
6. How is Jesus's kingdom different from earthly kingdoms?
7. What lies do you hear about happiness apart from God? How does the gospel respond to those specific lies?
8. Why did Jesus not come as a victorious king the first time?
9. If Jesus had come to dispense justice, what would happen to you?
10. What does this passage reveal about Jesus that you need to believe today?

The Cross: It Is Finished

JOHN 19:23-37

Main Idea: Jesus proves he is the Messiah through the fulfillment of numerous Old Testament prophecies.

I. **Jesus Fulfilled Prophecy.**
    A. The prophecy of the garment
    B. The prophecy of the drink
    C. The prophecy of the bones
    D. The prophecy of the piercing
II. **Jesus Finished Redemption.**

Christopher Hitchens, a self-proclaimed antitheist, was interviewed by a Unitarian minister named Marilyn Sewell. She told him she was a Christian but didn't believe the Bible literally and didn't believe Jesus died for her sins. Hitchens responded,

> I would say that if you don't believe that Jesus of Nazareth was the Christ and Messiah, and that he rose again from the dead and by his sacrifice our sins are forgiven, you're really not in any meaningful sense a Christian. (Sewell, "Hitchens Transcript")

To be a Christian, one must look on the death of Jesus Christ and *believe* on him as the Messiah who takes away the sin of the world. At the heart of Christianity is faith in Jesus Christ, but what is "faith"? Hitchens described his response to someone who claims to have faith. He would say,

> "Wait a minute, you just told me you're prepared to accept an enormous amount on no evidence whatsoever. Why are you thinking that that would impress me?" I have no use for it, when I could be spending time looking through a telescope or into a microscope and finding out the most extraordinary, wonderful things. (Ibid.)

In the first quote Hitchens does an excellent job of describing the heart of Christianity—it is faith in Jesus's death for us. But then he describes faith as accepting an enormous amount on no evidence whatsoever. Is he right? No, biblical faith is not a fool's journey. It's not the search for the fountain of youth. It's not a willingness to shut the brain off and embrace ancient mythology. Faith means you've found the truth and are confident in it. When the darkness of deception parts and the first rays of truth break into our hearts, that's when faith blooms. Faith is the work of God opening our eyes to his truth.

Faith isn't fueled by fantasy. Faith is informed by revelation. We don't believe on Jesus of Nazareth because we're gullible, because we no longer want to think deeply about life, or because we hate the truth. We believe on Jesus because God has revealed himself to us. God has opened our minds to understand the truth. God has delivered us from our gluttonous addiction to lies and given us an insatiable appetite for what is true. The Christian faith is not uninformed or unreasonable. The faith we profess is *informed* by the Word of God, and in his Word we find *reasons* to believe in Jesus. In John 19 we discover two more reasons to believe in Jesus.

Jesus Fulfilled Prophecy

I remember reading an article, written by an ESPN reporter, about a football coach who worked with troubled players. What I found interesting was how much biblical terminology was used in the article. The author mentioned or alluded to redemption, salvation, justice, mercy, and atonement. Could this player be *saved* from his past? Was he *redeemable*? Had he done enough to *atone* for his actions? I don't know if the writer intentionally used Christian terminology, but the terms—and beyond that the concepts—are part of our vocabulary and are hardwired into our DNA. Built into all of us is some understanding that sin must be atoned for. You don't have to take a class in theology to desire justice and believe restitution should be made for wrongdoing.

When we see injustice going unpunished, we can respond one of two ways. We can nod and say, "That's natural selection at work." Or we can cry for justice, for help, for salvation from the wickedness all around us. The Bible informs this innate, human understanding of salvation. It moves salvation beyond the political and physical and anchors it in the spiritual. It tears down the false concept of self-salvation and teaches salvation must come from God. The Old Testament is full of *pleas for salvation* and *promises of salvation*. Mankind has sinned and faces judgment. Evil has oppressed and burdened the people. Where will they find help? God will intervene. He will send salvation. How will God fulfill the promise of salvation? God promised a King who would bring salvation, but he also promised that the King who would rescue the afflicted would himself be afflicted. All of these promises of salvation, deliverance, and justice sound great. The idea of a coming King is exciting. But then Jesus arrives, supposedly as Savior, Deliverer, and Ruler, and ends up executed as a criminal. Is he King? Will he deliver us? If so, then why is he strung up between two criminals to die?

The death of Jesus is the initial fulfillment of the promise. The promises of salvation and justice in the Old Testament include a truth the religious leaders overlooked. The coming King was sovereign and righteous, but he was also afflicted. The prophecy of the coming King could only be fulfilled if the King suffered and died for our sin. John records four different prophecies of the King's suffering and shows how they're fulfilled in the death of Jesus.

The Prophecy of the Garment

After the soldiers gamble for Jesus's garment, John records a quotation from Psalm 22, which is the cry of an afflicted king. This psalm was written by David, who stands as a picture of the Messiah in the Psalter. The Messiah would come from the house of David, be a son of David, and be *like* David. When we read the Psalms, we're instructed to look for a King, righteous and just, and similar to David. David's reign wasn't easy. He had great victories, but he also experienced tremendous affliction. Psalm 22 records some of David's affliction. One particular affliction David suffered reveals what we should expect to happen to the Messiah: "They divided my garments among themselves, and they cast lots for my clothing" (Ps 22:18). At the foot of the cross, four Roman soldiers divide up Jesus's sandals, cloak, and belt. Then they cast lots for his tunic, so that it wouldn't need to be torn in pieces. In their greed and cruelty, they confirm Jesus is the righteous, afflicted King that Psalm 22 prophesied. The apostle John records their actions and then points us to the prophecy to strengthen our faith.

I watched a debate between a Christian pastor and an atheist. When the pastor mentioned fulfilled prophecy as a reason for faith, the atheist scoffed. His comment was that Jesus knew the Old Testament so he intentionally did things to "fulfill" prophecy. "That's not prophecy. That's manipulation," he said. I love R. C. Sproul's response to that suggestion:

John does not say that the Roman soldiers got together and
said, "We should gamble for His garments because it says in
the Jewish Scriptures that someone is going to cast lots for
His clothes and we want to make sure that the Scriptures are
fulfilled down to the last detail." No, this is John's editorial
comment, pointing out that the soldiers, when they went
through this act of gambling for the garments of the Christ,
unknowingly and involuntarily were fulfilling the precise
details of the Old Testament prophesies concerning the death
of the Messiah. John is zealous to help his reader understand
that what happened on the cross was not an accident of
history, but it came to pass through the invisible hand of a
sovereign Providence. (*John*, 367)

If these men are attempting to fulfill Scripture, would they really crucify
the Messiah and then divvy up his belongings right in front of him while
he dies?

The Prophecy of the Drink

Psalm 69, a beautiful psalm of God's salvation and deliverance, includes
these words of affliction from David—words that prepare us for the
Messiah:

> *You know the insults I endure—my shame and disgrace. You are
> aware of all my adversaries. Insults have broken my heart, and I am
> in despair. I waited for sympathy, but there was none; for comforters,
> but found no one. Instead, they gave me gall for my food, and for my
> thirst they gave me vinegar to drink.* (Ps 69:19-21)

John describes the events of the cross in chapter 19, verse 28, and makes
a reference to Jesus's thirst and how the soldiers give him sour wine to
drink—another perfect fulfillment of messianic prophecy from a thousand years earlier.

The Prophecy of the Bones

John writes, "These things happened" (v. 36). He's referring to the
request by the Jewish leaders to break the legs of the three men hanging
on crosses. But when the soldiers get to Jesus, he's already dead, so they
don't break his legs. This fulfills the prophetic words of David in Psalm
34: "One who is righteous has many adversities, but the LORD rescues

him from them all. He protects all his bones; not one of them is broken"
(vv. 19-20). The Messiah—righteous and afflicted—would suffer, but not
one of his bones would be broken. Though the soldier approaches Jesus
with hammer in hand to crush the bones in his legs, the promise of God
is fulfilled. The hammer does not strike; every prophecy comes true.

The Prophecy of the Piercing

The soldiers refrain from breaking Jesus's legs, but one of them takes
a spear and thrusts it into his side. As the soldier pulls the spear back,
blood and water gush out of the wound. The combination of blood
and water has spawned many interpretations, including that it repre-
sents the two ordinances—Communion and baptism. That's reading
too much into John's description. Here's the significance: Jesus is a real
man who dies a real death. Bodily fluids don't come out of a spirit; they
come from a body. Jesus doesn't fake his death. It isn't an act or a hoax.

The piercing also fulfills a prophecy made by Zechariah. The book
of Zechariah is the message that the Messiah is coming, and when he
comes, he will rescue his people from captivity. The Messiah will be both
a priest and a king, and as King he will perfectly obey the will of God.
Near the end of the book, the imagery of the Messiah changes from
the perfect King to the Good Shepherd. God says the people will reject
the Shepherd and follow evil shepherds into destruction. However, God
will still deliver his people through the Messiah, the righteous King and
Good Shepherd, rejected by God's people. God says,

> Then I will pour out a spirit of grace and prayer on the house of David
> and the residents of Jerusalem, and they will look at me whom they
> pierced. They will mourn for him as one mourns for an only child and
> weep bitterly for him as one weeps for a firstborn. (Zech 12:10)

The Messiah, who brings salvation, will be pierced by the nation of
Israel. This is fulfilled when the spear of the Roman, whom the Jews had
employed, penetrates Jesus's side and blood pours out.

These details aren't included to amaze us or disgust us but to help
us believe (John 19:35). The apostle John acts as a witness climbing
into the stand and placing his hand on the Bible. His solemn oath as an
eyewitness is intended to cause belief. "I was there," John says in effect.
"I saw it all with my own eyes—the divided garment, the sour wine, the
unbroken legs, and the pierced side. I saw each one. The reason I'm
telling you is so you'll know the Scripture has been fulfilled and will

believe on Jesus as the Messiah." Each fulfilled prophecy can strengthen our faith in the promise of God to deliver us from death and judgment through his Son.

The cross of Christ cannot simply be a moment in history. Though we study it, we must do so differently from the way we would study medieval architecture. It's fine for a Christian to be bored in a class on British literature, but it's tragic if the cross of Jesus Christ produces nothing more than a yawn and a shrug of the shoulders. The crucifixion of Jesus Christ is a real, historical event, but it can't be consigned to dusty shelves in the back of a library or cobwebbed corners or our minds. Nearly two thousand years after the fact, we read the Gospel accounts of the crucifixion and understand that they were written so we would respond in faith. Matthew, Mark, Luke, and John didn't record this event as a memento for their grandkids. They wrote these Gospel accounts so people would read them and respond by believing in Jesus Christ. We must guard against ever looking at the cross callously or flippantly. Each glance should remind us that God has been faithful to his promises, and it should reinforce our trust in his sovereign grace and his unending mercy.

Jesus Finished Redemption

Something takes place on the cross when Jesus dies. In verse 30 Jesus says, "It is finished" or "It has been accomplished" (v. 30; author's translation). What has been accomplished? The beginning of the answer is found back in chapter 17 when Jesus bows his head and says he has finished the work God gave him to do (v. 4). The work of Jesus on earth, given by the Father, is fully complete. What is that work? That work is bringing salvation to God's people. John the Baptist, whose role was to announce the coming of the Messiah, looked at Jesus and said, "Here is the Lamb of God, who takes away the sin of the world!" (1:29). Jesus's work as sin-bearer and Savior is completed when he lays down his life on the cross. The sacrificial offering of his life completes his divine rescue mission. Jesus offers his life as the Passover Lamb who once and for all brings deliverance and salvation. There's no longer any need for annual sacrifices. The penalty for sin is completely served. The price of redemption is completely paid. The justice of God is completely satisfied. The deliverance of sinners is completely secured.

The writer of Hebrews contrasts the sacrifice of Jesus with the constant sacrifice of lambs in the Jewish temple: "But now he has appeared one time, at the end of the ages, for the removal of sin by the sacrifice of himself" (Heb 9:26-27). When Jesus said, "It is finished," he meant the entire work of salvation was taken care of. Our redemption had been accomplished and applied.

Here lies one of the distinctions between Catholicism and Protestantism. In Roman Catholic theology the death of Jesus Christ isn't a one-time sacrifice. Each week during the observation of the mass, Jesus is being sacrificed again for sin. The elements—wafer and wine—turn into the body and blood of Jesus, and he is once more crucified. In Catholic theology, it is not finished. It has not been completely accomplished. There is more to be done.

Understanding that redemption has been completed motivates faith because it's the only response we have. If redemption isn't finished, then I have to *do something* to earn it or complete it, whether it's taking Communion or being baptized or going on a pilgrimage. When we understand the work of salvation is complete, then we'll also understand we can do nothing—absolutely nothing—to earn it or keep it or maintain it.

- We can only trust in the grace of God to save us.
- We can only believe in his promise of salvation.
- We can only place our faith in his Son, sent to purchase our redemption.

The moment you stop believing Jesus finished salvation is the moment you'll start working for your salvation. You'll wonder what activity you need to do to keep God in your favor. When trials come, you'll wonder if it's because of what you've done. Your relationship to God will become a checklist of dos and don'ts. Do you see how this changes your relationship with God? If he has done everything to secure your salvation, then you will relate to him as the child of a gracious and giving God; but if you need to do something, if his view of you is based on your performance, then that relationship of love and freedom becomes one of guilt and fear. You'll be plagued by worry and doubt about your standing with him. You'll wonder if he's happy with you today. You'll quiver in the corner of the kitchen, wondering what your Father's mood will be when he returns home.

Don't turn God into a vicious and moody Father who demands you act a certain way to earn his love. He is kind. He is loving. He is good, and he has done everything necessary for us to enjoy his love and kindness. As a Christian, your standing before him has been settled by the blood-soaked sacrifice of Jesus. Your hope and confidence must never be in yourself—in what you've accomplished. It must be in Christ and what he accomplished for you on the cross.

Conclusion

Frieda van Hessen was one of Holland's foremost opera singers, but during the Nazi invasion she, as a Jew, was forced into hiding. In the providence of God, her life was spared. After the war someone told her she should convert from Judaism to Christianity, just in case something else was to happen. This suggestion nagged at her until she finally gave in and spoke to a minister. He set up a meeting for her with a Christian lady named Elizabeth who had converted from Judaism. Their Bible study turned into an argument. Frieda just couldn't believe what she was reading from the Gospels. She accused Elizabeth of believing fairy tales. After six weeks of fruitless arguments, they decided the next week would be their last meeting. Elizabeth asked Frieda to read two chapters from the Old Testament before their last meeting—Psalm 22 and Isaiah 53. Frieda writes about that week:

> Six days went by, and I could no longer procrastinate. I went to a small room in the house, closed the door, and opened up the Bible. . . . God, in His wisdom, had said to Elizabeth, "Tell her to read Psalm 22." . . . I found it, and what did I see: "My God, my God, why hast Thou forsaken me?" I . . . remembered that in Bach's "St. Matthew's Passion," the basso, portraying the Lord, sings, "My God, my God, why hast Thou forsaken me?" Still in my rebellion, I said, "What do you know, they stole this from Bach!"
>
> Oh, God is so wise! This finally got my attention. Now I wanted to continue reading to see what else had been "stolen" from Bach! Then I came to verse 16, and read, "They pierced my hands and my feet." Almost in shock, I literally yelled out "That's Jesus!"
>
> . . .
>
> I knew that Jesus died in that devastating way. The Jews stoned people to death but did not crucify them. Crucifixion was a Roman death penalty. Yet David wrote Psalm 22, prophesying this form of death hundreds of years before crucifixion was ever invented and practiced by the Romans.

Then I reread Isaiah 53, and clearly understood that it described the whole crucifixion and resurrection of Jesus. Instantly, God had taken the blinders off my eyes and Satan was defeated! I called Elizabeth, who came over immediately, and together we read Isaiah 53. Then, all of it became very clear to me: how "He was despised and rejected of men," how He was a "man of sorrows and acquainted with grief," how "we hid our faces from Him," how "He had been afflicted and wounded for our transgressions," and how "with His stripes we are healed."

I realized how "all of us, like sheep, have gone astray," and how "He died for our iniquities." Yes, for my sins too.

I reasoned that if David . . . and Isaiah . . . both knew Him, and Paul, a Pharisee, saw Him and knew Him, then I needed no further proof. I accepted Him too, as my Lord and Savior. (Roos-Van Hessen, *Life*, 190–92)

Proof, not speculation, not blind leaps in the dark. God has graciously given us his Word so we might believe on Jesus Christ.

Reflect and Discuss

1. Is faith in Jesus dependent on acceptance without evidence? Why or why not?
2. How does the Bible inform the innate human understanding of salvation and justice?
3. How does Jesus fulfill the prophecy of Psalm 22:18?
4. How does Jesus fulfill the prophecy of Psalm 69:19-21?
5. How does Jesus fulfill the prophecy of Psalm 34:19-20?
6. How does Jesus fulfill the prophecy of Zechariah 12:10?
7. Why does John include the gruesome details about the cross?
8. How should your study of the cross look different from study of other historical events?
9. Why does Jesus say, "It is finished"? How is this good news for you today and not just at the moment you first believed?
10. Does the finished work of Jesus change the way you respond to your own sin? How so?

The Resurrection: An Empty Tomb

JOHN 19:38–20:18

Main Idea: The resurrection of Jesus Christ stands unrivaled as the most radical event in history.

I. **The First Radical Change Is in the Power of Death.**
II. **The Second Radical Change Was in the Position of the Disciples.**

---

*R*adical has a number of meanings, and one is "revolutionary." Or, to be more precise, *radical change* means "an extreme or substantial change in the existing system." A radical event is an event that takes the current system and flips it on its head. Something truly radical changes all we know in an instant. Nothing brought more extreme changes than the resurrection of Jesus Christ. It stands unrivaled as the most radical event in history.

The apostle Paul makes this case in 1 Corinthians 15. Some in the Corinthian church were saying there was no resurrection of the dead. They claimed Jesus didn't rise from the dead, and it didn't really matter. "Not so fast," Paul says in effect. "If Christ has not been raised, . . . your faith is worthless; you are still in your sins" (1 Cor 15:14,17). That's how radical the resurrection is. If it didn't happen, we would still be in sin, and everything we believe about God, Jesus, and salvation would be empty and meaningless. The resurrection brought profound changes in our faith, purpose, and standing before God.

In John 19:38-39 we get the first clue this passage is about change. John includes a detail about each man that reveals a change in his attitude. Joseph of Arimathea had been a secret disciple but was now publicly identifying himself with Jesus. Nicodemus, who had secretly come to Jesus at night when no one would see him (ch. 3), also comes out of the dark and identifies himself as a follower of Jesus. It doesn't take much imagination to understand the potential danger in identifying with one who was just executed for sedition and blasphemy. If Joseph's and Nicodemus's lives weren't in danger, their reputations certainly were. What change took place in these men? What prompted such courage? In the same chapter where John documents secret disciples who were afraid to follow Jesus, he also records this statement made by Jesus: "Truly I tell you, unless a grain of wheat falls to the ground and dies, it remains by itself. But if it dies, it produces much fruit" (12:24). Like the first flowers blooming in the spring, these two men are the firstfruits of the great harvest that will come from Jesus's death. They also serve as a signal to readers of the Gospel that changes are coming, and the most radical one is near.

Consider a second change in this passage. Once Jesus laid down his life, the persecution and affliction were over. He had paid our debt to sin. He had fully received the righteous wrath of God. His suffering was complete. Now his body is treated differently. He is no longer abused as the sacrificial Lamb. He is treated with respect as the only begotten Son of God, the true King of Israel (19:40-42).

Mary assumes that the body of Jesus has been stolen by grave robbers or moved by the authorities (20:2). She doesn't consider the possibility of resurrection. Peter and John—the beloved disciple—enter the tomb, and John deliberately calls our attention to the grave clothes (v. 7). This is actually the second time grave clothes are mentioned in John's Gospel; the first was at the tomb of Lazarus (11:43-44). When Jesus raised Lazarus from the dead, Lazarus came out of the tomb still wrapped in the linen cloths. Jesus's resurrection is different from the resurrection of Lazarus. We aren't given many details but enough to understand Lazarus will die again; he will need his grave clothes one more time. Jesus will never need his own. He will not see death again. Something happened when Jesus rose from the dead that did *not* happen when Lazarus was resurrected.

What does John believe when he enters the tomb? He believes Jesus rose from the dead (20:8-10). He doesn't completely *understand* it—all of the puzzle pieces won't fit together until later—but he *believes*. The appearance of angels confirms what John believes (vv. 11-13). Jesus's missing body is not due to grave robbers but to the all-powerful hands of God. I wonder if the angels' question to Mary isn't a slight rebuke. At this point she still hasn't considered the possibility Jesus is alive. All she can think about is where his *body* is, not where *he* is.

Jesus is the good shepherd, and when he calls his sheep by name, they respond (cf. John 10:3-4). When Mary hears the voice of her shepherd, who calls her by name, she understands it's him (20:14-16). She wants to hold on to Jesus lest he leave again. He tells her, "Don't worry

Mary. Don't hold on to me. I'm not leaving for good. I have not yet
ascended to my rightful spot at my Father's side" (v. 17; my paraphrase).
He charges her to go and tell his disciples he's alive and will soon be
returning to his heavenly position.

This passage is all about change:

- the change in Joseph and Nicodemus from secret disciples to
  open followers,
- the change in the treatment of Jesus from affliction to affection
  and adoration,
- the change in the grave from full to empty,
- the change in John as he looks and believes in the resurrection,
  and
- the change in Mary from weeping to rejoicing.

These are small changes; they're the aftershocks. The earthshaking
change is the resurrection. When Jesus rises from the dead, the existing
system is irrevocably altered. It will never be the same.

The First Radical Change Is in the Power of Death

Birth and death are the common human experiences. They're simply
unavoidable. Human life—that short span of time between womb and
tomb—is described by God as a vapor (Ps 39:5). Your life lasts no longer
than the steam from your morning shower. We're like the grass in our
backyards: green, lush, and healthy one day, withered and dying the next.
This is Mary's mind-set when Jesus dies. She goes looking for his body,
the part of him that's left when his life is extinguished. Upon finding the
body gone, her report to the disciples is essentially, "I didn't see his body"
(John 20:2). But look at what she says in verse 18. She doesn't say, "I have
seen the Lord's body." She says, "I have seen the Lord!" Jesus conquered
death. He stared into death's cold, cruel eyes, and with infinite power he
defeated death, rendering death impotent. Prior to the resurrection of
Jesus, every person walked this earth with an executioner's blade above
his neck, never sure when death would strike, but Jesus disarmed death—
he showed us what awaits those who are his once they pass from this life.

The writer of Hebrews said that through his death Jesus destroyed
the one who has the power of death, the devil, and delivered all those
"who were held in slavery all their lives by the fear of death" (Heb 2:15).
The fear of death causes us to try to minimize the effects of aging. We're
told, "Be younger, eat healthier, color your hair, and remove wrinkles."

We don't want to face the truth. We're aging, and every day brings us closer to the grave. We try to cosmetically push death further into the future. If we ignore death, maybe death will ignore us. The fear of death chains our hopes and dreams to the earthly, transient desires of this life. If Jesus hadn't conquered death, we might as well spend all of our energy eating, drinking, and being merry, for tomorrow we might die, but because Jesus conquered death, we can live for the next life, the eternal life, not this temporary one. We are participants in Jesus's resurrection, and our priorities should reflect that truth (cf. Col 3:1-2).

Here is why materialism and Christianity cannot peacefully coexist. Materialism is pursuing happiness by accumulating stuff in this life. Christianity is giving up stuff in this life to pursue happiness in Jesus. Materialism is the binding death uses to chain us to this world. We try to insulate ourselves from eternity by mounding up more and more treasures around us. We're like children building a pillow fort of cars and cash, hoping it will stop death's progress. It's a silly and sad way to live. For us as Christians, the resurrection of Jesus brings a revolutionary change in our perspective. We don't live for the seen but the unseen. Because Jesus conquered death and lives forevermore, death no longer has a claim on us, and we're free to live for what lasts. We're able to live with open hands, giving up everything in this life because we're guaranteed another, greater, eternal life with Jesus.

The Second Radical Change Was in the Position of the Disciples

One hundred eight times in the Gospel of John, Jesus refers to God as "Father." Twenty-seven times he says "my Father." Seventy-one times he says "the Father," and only one time does he refer to God as the disciples' Father. He does that here in verse 17, as he passes the message to the disciples through Mary. He tells her to say he is ascending to "my Father and your Father." It's also the only time in John's Gospel he calls the disciples his "brothers." When Jesus rises from the dead, the position of his disciples is radically altered. They're no longer cut off from God, enemies, dead in trespasses and sins. They're family members. The sacrifice of Jesus Christ for their sin, and the divine acceptance of that sacrifice demonstrated in the resurrection, ushers them into a new family with God as their Father and Jesus as their brother.

Only when God does a work in our hearts, granting us the gift of faith, do we become his children (1:12-13). From our perspective we must believe on Jesus Christ to become part of God's family. But that's not all that needed to happen. Jesus had to do something. He had to pay for our sin so we could be declared righteous. His sacrifice had to be accepted by God so we could be forgiven. That's why, after he rose from the dead, his first words to the disciples, through the lips of Mary, were that they were now, by faith, part of God's family—sons of God and brothers of Jesus.

Many wonderful promises become ours because of our position as children of God.

The promise of inheritance: the immeasurable riches of God are eternally ours. This promise helps us move beyond the flat-screen TVs and new cars that occupy so many people's dreams. We should be willing to die penniless if that's what God desires, knowing an eternal treasure chest awaits us upon our entrance into the Father's house.

The promise of love: we are now God's children. No matter what kind of earthly father you had, you now have a perfect Father. His love for you will not ebb and flow based on his emotions. His treatment of you won't be affected by your performance. He will love you enough to chasten you when you sin, not because he's vindictive but because you're his child and he wants what is best for you.

The promise of acceptance: Jesus's ascension to the right hand of the Father brings assurance we will be accepted into the Father's house. We didn't become God's children because of what we did but because of what Jesus accomplished. So our confidence in our standing before God doesn't rest in what we do but in what Jesus has done on our behalf. As long as Jesus stands at the right hand of God, all who follow him will be welcomed into God's presence. If God accepted Jesus, then he has accepted you.

Who the disciples are is bound up totally in who they have become in Christ. No longer are they merely sons of Adam; they are now sons of God. Their validation won't come from other people but has come from what Jesus revealed to them about their new position, their new identity. A new identity in Christ, as members of God's family, radically changes every area of life. For instance, we call one another "Brother" and "Sister" because we relate to one another as members of God's family. This relationship affects our prayer lives, how we give, and how we care for others.

The resurrection of Jesus Christ is not trivial. The resurrection is central to our faith. Marcus Borg wrote,

For me it is irrelevant whether or not the tomb was empty. Whether Easter involved something remarkable happening to the physical body of Jesus is irrelevant. My argument is not that we know the tomb was not empty or that nothing happened to the body, but simply that it doesn't matter. (Borg and Wright, *Meaning*, 131)

The apostle Paul would disagree: we must believe the tomb was empty because Jesus rose from the dead, was vindicated by the Father, secured our salvation, and brought us into the family of God. He told the Romans, "If you confess with your mouth, 'Jesus is Lord,' and believe in your heart that *God raised him from the dead*, you will be saved" (Rom 10:9; emphasis added). Without the resurrection, there's no gospel. The gospel is the good news, and the best part of the good news is that Jesus won. Death was defeated and eternal life is ours through him.

Reflect and Discuss

1. If the resurrection is true, where should it be on the list of important events in history? Why?
2. How has your life changed through belief in the resurrection?
3. How do your Sunday gatherings celebrate and remind you of the resurrection?
4. Why does John mention the grave clothes left in the tomb?
5. How does the resurrection free us from the fear of death in day-to-day life?
6. What impact does freedom from fear of death have on the way you spend your money and use your free time?
7. How can you approach God in prayer as his child?
8. What has God promised to his children?
9. How would your daily life change if the resurrection was on the forefront of your mind each day?
10. If the resurrection had never happened, would your life be any different? Explain.

The Resurrection: My Lord and My God

JOHN 20:19-31

Main Idea: John reveals that the most moral, religious, pious person is dead in sin, but the one who trusts Jesus and commits to following him has been given life.

I. **How Do We Obtain Life?**
   A. Confess Christ is Lord.
   B. Commit to following Christ as Lord.
II. **Once We Obtain Life, How Will We Live?**
   A. We will live in relationship with Jesus.
   B. We will live on mission for Jesus.
   C. We will live in the blessing of Jesus.

John writes this Gospel to every person who is spiritually dead, trapped in sins, and awaiting God's judgment. In other words he writes it to every person, including you and me. By describing the condition of man as dead and offering man eternal life through faith in Jesus, John reveals a line that divides mankind into two categories, dead and alive. Then he extends the offer of life to each one of us. This issue is bigger than physical life and physical death; it extends beyond the seventy or eighty years you may have on this earth. The matter at stake is *eternal* life and *eternal* death.

How Do We Obtain Life?

Spiritual life comes through belief (v. 31). We must believe that Jesus is the promised Messiah, the Son of God, and upon believing we become recipients of eternal life. But what does it mean to believe? Genuine belief includes both confession and commitment.

Confess Christ Is Lord

"Confess" here does not mean an admittance of guilt but the declaration of certain propositional truths. There are certain statements we must testify to as being true. We must confess that Jesus is the Messiah; he is the promised Savior of the Old Testament. The promises of God to send salvation are kept in the person of Jesus. We must confess that Jesus is the Son of God. We can't overlook, undermine, or deny his deity and still call ourselves Christians. We must confess that Jesus rose from the dead (v. 27). If we deny the resurrection, then we do not truly believe.

How do we know what we should believe? It is not through sight: Jesus tells Thomas the following generations would need to believe without seeing him (v. 29). We understand what to believe based on the truths revealed in God's Word. Unlike Thomas we believe based on the testimony of the disciples. Through their divinely inspired words we understand who Jesus is, and we learn to confess the truths that bring salvation.

Commit to Following Christ as Lord

We must hold to certain truths, but belief is not a mere intellectual exercise. Belief involves a person's committing himself to embrace these truths personally. Belief has a relational element: it is a commitment from one person to another person. Belief also has a volitional element: it is a decision to embrace truth. These two aspects of belief are perfectly demonstrated in Thomas's response to the appearance of Jesus: he confesses Jesus is his Lord and his God (v. 28). His confession is clear: Jesus is God. This is the only time in the Gospel that someone speaking to Jesus addresses him as God, and it echoes the first verse: "In the beginning was the Word, and the Word was with God, and the Word was God" (1:1).

His confession is interlaced with commitment. He calls Jesus "Lord." The word can mean "sir" or simply be a synonym for God, but it can also be used for "Master." That's the way Thomas uses it here. He stands before the risen Christ and understands that this one who has power over life and death has the right to rule his life. Thomas willingly submits himself to the control of Jesus. This commitment is personal. Thomas doesn't utter these words with cold detachment. He personalizes them. "Jesus is," Thomas says, "*my* Lord and *my* God."

Further, belief in Jesus can't happen at the point of a sword because it is not about the words you say but a personal decision to commit yourself to Jesus as your Lord. Here lies one of the hidden dangers of something like the Sinner's Prayer. Many well-intentioned believers have encouraged someone to repeat certain words after them in order to be saved. Those words may have a clear confession of faith, but there is no guarantee that the person making the confession is willing to make a commitment to Jesus. Confession without commitment only serves to soothe a person's conscience on the way to hell. Churches are full of men and women who can draw a map of the Romans Road but have never turned from their sin to walk the way of Jesus Christ.

Many professing Christians view their commitment to Christ as more of an affiliation. When it's beneficial to them, they'll talk about personal commitment to following Christ, but the moment things change—life gets difficult, love grows a little cold, and faith seems harder—they will demonstrate that their confession was empty. They simply parroted the truths of Christianity without ever making a commitment to following Christ. Faith must include certain truths about Jesus—his deity, death, and resurrection—but the truths must travel along the road of commitment accompanied by a willingness to follow Christ and to persist in obedience. It's not enough to *say* that Jesus is the great treasure buried in the field. We must sell all that we have to *purchase* the field. We must confess *and* commit.

Once We Obtain Life, How Will We Live?

Just as the disciples illustrate what it means to believe, they also give us an example of what it means to live as one who has been made alive in Jesus Christ.

We Will Live in Relationship with Jesus

It is no accident that John declares his purpose for this book—that his readers might have life—immediately after he records the resurrection. Jesus's victory over the grave is our confidence in eternal life. The promised life comes only through connection with him. When we placed our faith in Jesus Christ, we were placed *in* Christ. Eternal life became ours because the life of Christ now courses through our spiritual veins. Like the adopted child welcomed into a new family, we have been welcomed into an intimate, eternal relationship with the triune God. Just as that child's existence is now completely swallowed up in the experiences of life in this new family, our existence is to be completely swallowed up in our relationship with Christ. We are to move, laugh, serve, love—everything—in him.

We Will Live on Mission for Jesus

The new life Jesus gives begins in this life and extends eternally. Only a small portion of it is lived in our current earthly existence. Jesus calls us to use this brief time for a grand and glorious purpose. He commissions us to take the message of the gospel to those who have not heard it so they can believe, receive forgiveness of sin, and find life in him. He sends his disciples in the same way in which he was sent (vv. 21-23): in obedience to the Father, empowered by the Spirit, to proclaim the message of salvation. That is our pattern for ministry. The significance of this work demands a supernatural commission and supernatural empowerment.

There is no greater joy than to serve the Father. And to think that he placed us in a body of like-minded believers so that we could band together in our service for him! Each church is uniquely commissioned by God to take his message to the world. We have the privilege of proclaiming the wonders of God's salvation to those who are desperately in need of it. Don't miss out on the great honor God has given you as his ambassador, and don't minimize the role of the church in God's great plan. We were saved into the greatest institution the world has ever known so that we could declare the greatest message the world has ever heard.

We are sent by Jesus in the same way that he was sent by the Father. Don't forget that Jesus came to us. He didn't wait for us to come to him. He descended from heaven, took on the form of a man, and ministered in the villages and towns where men lived. Jesus took the initiative. He sacrificed comfort. He went out to us where we were. Too many Christians shout advice to drowning men from the safety of the shore, but that's not what Jesus did. He dove in and swam out to rescue us. It's easy to view evangelism the same way a doctor might view a deadly outbreak. We make sure we've got our hazmat suits on, and then we'll stand outside the quarantined area and offer suggestions to anyone who comes to ask. Maybe we'll even train the workers who go in to help. But we don't learn that model from Jesus. He sprinted into the middle of the outbreak and rescued those who had been infected. He willingly sacrificed his life so they might be saved.

We Will Live in the Blessing of Jesus

When Jesus miraculously enters the room where the disciples are hiding, he discovers a group of men trembling in fear, but once they see him, the fear melts and "the disciples rejoiced when they saw the Lord" (v. 20). Their fear turned to gladness, and their sorrow turned to joy, exactly as Jesus had told them (16:20). The presence of Jesus transformed their attitude from sadness to gladness.

In this text Jesus repeats the greeting, "Peace be with you," three different times (vv. 19,21,26). It's been suggested that this is nothing more than a standard greeting, the Hebrew equivalent of "hello." If so, then why does John record it three times in seven verses? It's because Jesus is reminding them of an earlier promise: "Peace I leave with you. My peace I give to you. I do not give to you as the world gives. Don't let your heart be troubled or fearful" (14:27). The presence of Jesus transformed their attitude from anxiety to peace. Then Jesus promises that everyone who trusts him will be blessed (20:29). *Blessed* doesn't simply mean happy. It means a person is accepted by God. They have, through faith, become recipients of all God's blessings. God's favor is permanently placed on them through the person of Jesus Christ.

Jesus repeatedly told the disciples, "Come to me and you will receive eternal life, real peace, lasting joy, and divine acceptance." God wants us to be happy. He wants to bless us. He created us to pursue joy in him through Jesus. But we don't take his offer seriously. Instead of pursuing these blessings he promises, we settle for empty substitutes around us. Few people have taught this as clearly as C. S. Lewis:

> If we consider the unblushing promises of reward and the staggering nature of the rewards promised in the Gospels, it would seem that our Lord finds our desires, not too strong, but too weak. We are half-hearted creatures, fooling about with drink and sex and ambition when infinite joy is offered us, like an ignorant child who wants to go on making mud pies in a slum because he cannot imagine what is meant by the offer of a holiday at the sea. We are far too easily pleased. ("The Weight of Glory," 26)

The Gospel of John was written to help us understand that there is a greater pleasure than the mud pies of this world. Jesus offers us the ultimate treasure: eternity with him. Here is where all of these truths merge. Eternal life—ours through faith in Jesus Christ—brings us into relationship with God. In relationship with God we discover immeasurable blessings. These blessings that flow to us from the person of God motivate our mission. We want to bring others into the infinite joy of relationship with God.

Reflect and Discuss

1. What does John want us to believe from this passage?
2. How does someone obtain eternal life through Jesus?
3. What two things does genuine belief include?
4. How does a person confess Christ as Lord?
5. How does the relational element of belief alter how you think about obedience?
6. Once someone obtains eternal life through Jesus, how will they live in the present?
7. Describe the difference between those committed to following Jesus and those who want simply to affiliate themselves with Jesus.
8. How does the way Jesus was sent provide us with our own pattern for ministry?
9. Do you spend time pursuing those who don't know Jesus? What might look different if you modeled your evangelism after Jesus?
10. Do you believe God wants to bless your life through Jesus? In what areas is this hardest to believe?

Follow Me!

JOHN 21

Main Idea: Jesus gives us a clear picture of what it looks like to live as his disciple.

I. **Our Confidence Will Not Be in Our Own Strength but in the Sovereignty of Christ.**

II. **Our Comfort Will Not Be in Our Own Morality but in the Mercy of Christ.**

III. **Our Concern Will Not Be for Our Own Priorities but for the People of Christ.**

IV. **Our Commitment Will Not Be to Our Own Comfort but to the Cross of Christ.**

Myth 1: For a mature believer suffering is easy.

Myth 2: The amount we suffer is based on our behavior.

Myth 3: God isn't in control of suffering.

Jesus calls us to follow him. As we journey through life, we can either chart our own course or follow the path of Jesus. Twice in this final chapter Jesus says, "Follow me" (vv. 19,22). That sums up the message of the Gospel of John. Jesus is the promised Savior who calls us away from the path of destruction to follow him into eternal life. Each reader is left with a question: Will I follow Jesus? This final chapter gives us a clear picture of what it looks like to live as a follower of Jesus Christ.

Our Confidence Will Not Be in Our Own Strength but in the Sovereignty of Christ

What's the point of including the fishing story right here? Consider the last few chapters. Chapters 13–17 describe the night preceding Jesus's death and focus on his final instructions to the disciples. Chapters 18–19 chronicle the arrest, betrayal, and crucifixion. Chapter 20 declares the wonderful truth of the resurrection. Now chapter 21 begins with a story about fishing.

This story paints a portrait. The disciples were not hobby fishermen; they were experts. Prior to Jesus's call as disciples, they had made their living on the sea. They hop into the boat to catch some fish but have no luck—all night long but not a single fish. Can you imagine the frustration? It's no big deal for an amateur to come up dry, but a group of professional fishermen working all night and not catching a thing? That doesn't happen. They must have been tired and cranky. The sun's starting to rise, and they hear a voice from the shore call out a prodding question: "You don't have any fish, do you?" It gets worse. "Cast the net on the right side of the boat and you'll find some." They decide to listen and catch 153 fish in one net—so many fish that John realizes it is Jesus. This was a miraculous catch. Only Jesus could have done it.

It's a great story, and it's a great picture of following Jesus. We can't do it on our own. Regardless of our gifts and abilities, our experience or our strengths, we are unable to follow Jesus apart from his work in our lives. Jesus told the disciples that apart from him they could do nothing (15:5). Any effort to serve him in our strength will be as effective as the disciples' fishing. "Serving Christ in our own strength, trying to do it our own way, is like going after Moby Dick with a pickle fork" (Hughes, *John*, 455–56). You can become an expert in selfish living on your own. If you make instant gratification your ultimate goal, you can succeed in your own strength. No one can stop you from earning a gold medal in self-promotion. On the other hand, if you want to give up your personal comfort for someone else's eternal good, your effort is not enough. If you want to be a godly wife and a contented mother, you will fail in your own strength. If you desire victory over that area of sin that constantly plagues you, your best intentions will fall short. All the good you do will be empty and short-lived apart from the effective power of Jesus Christ working in and through you. That's why this fish story is so encouraging. If we follow Christ, we don't need to rely on our own strength. He will provide exactly *what* we need exactly *when* we need it.

There's a reason they didn't catch any fish. They caught nothing so Jesus's power could be demonstrated. But did they realize that in the moment when the net kept coming up empty? We may experience seasons of frustration that serve a purpose we can't see. As we follow Jesus, there may be days, weeks, months, even years when it feels as if we are failing. We may be following Jesus, doing what he says, and yet feel as if everything is going wrong. And to make it worse, we may not be able to see the purpose in it. It may not be until much later, if ever, that we discover the reason. In those times the object of our trust will be revealed.

What made it worse was that the disciples' area of failure was the area they had the most confidence in. They were professional fishermen! If there was anything they excelled at, it was fishing. Jesus used this area to teach the disciples a vital lesson: following him meant their confidence couldn't be in their own strength but must be in his sovereignty.

Our Comfort Will Not Be in Our Own Morality, but in the Mercy of Christ

No disciple took greater comfort in his own work, effort, and moral standing than Peter. Nothing he said lacked confidence. There was little doubt in his mind he could do whatever he set his mind to. It didn't seem to register he was imperfect, he had faults and failures, and he was a sinner. On the night that Jesus was arrested, Peter pledged undying devotion to him. He went as far as to claim that he would lay down his life for Jesus. Jesus responded by predicting Peter's betrayal (13:38). Peter's denial of Jesus—just as Jesus predicted—shattered his false veneer of morality. Like pulling the final Jenga piece from the bottom of the tower, it caused his self-righteousness to come crashing down. That's an experience we all need to have. We must come to the point where we realize that no lasting comfort can be found in our morality.

Peter needed to be broken, but he also needed to be restored. That's exactly what Jesus does. In many ways he recreates the scene of Peter's denial to remind Peter that his life can't be built on human morality; it must be founded on divine mercy. Only twice in John's Gospel do we read about a charcoal fire, here (in verse 9) and in 18:18. The first is when Peter denies Jesus three times, and the second when Jesus restores Peter three times. The smell of charcoal burning—a reminder of Peter's greatest failure—would become a soothing aroma as Peter is forgiven.

Jesus's first question was, "Simon, son of John, do you love me more than these?" (v. 15). That is, "Do you love me more than these other men love me?" This is exactly what Peter had based his comfort on. "I love Jesus more than other people do!" How could he who denied Jesus three times claim to love Jesus more than someone else? The foundation of his self-righteous morality had eroded, and he was forced to confront the reality he wasn't good enough. His effort wasn't enough. Twice more Jesus asked Peter if he loved him (vv. 16,17). All three times Peter responded yes. This is the mercy of Jesus at work. For so long Peter was like a lame man, dragging himself around on a pair of crutches. When he denied Jesus, the crutches splintered. He could no longer lean on his own self-righteousness. But Jesus didn't leave him helpless. With great mercy he restored Peter. In mercy he lifted him up and healed him. No longer was Peter the one doing something. Now it was Jesus. Peter didn't have to do anything. He didn't do penance. He wasn't baptized. He did nothing to atone for his failure. Jesus atoned for Peter's failure. Peter did nothing but receive mercy.

The street sign hanging over the path Jesus calls us to walk does not say "Morality." It says "Mercy." His mercy is our comfort. When we fail—and we will fail—his mercy will restore us. Remember what the old Puritan preacher Richard Sibbes said: "There is more mercy in Christ than sin in us" ("The Bruised Reed").

Our Concern Will Not Be for Our Own Priorities but for the People of Christ

Not only does Jesus restore Peter, but he also commissions him. He instructs Peter to feed his sheep. We know from chapter 10 that Jesus's sheep are those who will believe in him. When we place our faith in Jesus Christ, we are united to him and to all who believe in him. He ushers us into a new community of faith. We are naturally selfish people. Never in Scripture are we told to love ourselves, but on more than one occasion we're told to love people just like we love ourselves. It is assumed we love ourselves. If we aren't following Jesus, we are living for ourselves. That doesn't mean each person who doesn't follow Christ is an outright hedonist, but it does mean we ultimately make our decisions based on the good we feel it will bring to us. Not every decision and not every area of life, but the ultimate trajectory of our lives will be what we perceive as our own good.

Following Jesus means our priorities will be radically altered. Instead of serving ourselves, we will serve those who are part of the church—his sheep. Our focus will not be internal but external. The way of Jesus is filled with opportunities to serve our brothers and sisters. There is so much a church can mine from Jesus's instructions to Peter.

The sheep are Jesus's sheep, not Peter's. The head of the church is Jesus, not a man. He is the one we are to follow. His instructions guide us. The faithfulness of a shepherd is measured in only one way: how faithful he is to the Word of God.

The sheep need to be on a strict diet of Scripture. No substitute will do. Only God's Word will nourish the sheep and bring growth. Peter figured this out. That's why he wrote, "Like newborn infants, desire the pure milk of the word, so that you may grow up into your salvation, if you have tasted that the Lord is good" (1 Pet 2:2-3).

Those who shepherd must know God's Word. The word *pastor* literally means "shepherd." A pastor's role is to feed the flock the food of the Word. That's why all pastors/elders need to be men skilled in handling Scripture. They are men who, when you meet with them, make God's Word more clear to you.

A shepherd's first priority is to feed the sheep. Jesus didn't tell Peter to build his church. In fact, Jesus says that he would take care of building the church (Matt 16:18). Peter was to feed the sheep. A shepherd's number-one duty is the ministry of the Word.

Shepherds must be motivated by love for God. Jesus asked Peter if he loved him. Then in response to Peter's declaration of love, Jesus said, "Feed my sheep" (John 21:17). Love for God must motivate those who lead the church. If anything else becomes the motivating factor, then they open themselves up to serious dangers. Doctrinal aberration, personal agendas, soapbox issues, confused priorities, and personal kingdom building are all the result of loving something else more than God.

Sheep meet together to feed on God's Word. We gather corporately to feast on the Word of God. Consuming his Word causes us to grow, mature, and obtain the strength to go out and serve God.

Sheep should be growing. If you are being fed the Word of God by a shepherd, you should see effects from that diet. A baby eats and becomes an adult. An adult eats and gets stronger. Are you eating the food of God's Word? It's possible to come to dinner every week and have the food spread before you but not consume any. If you stop eating, there will be noticeable signs. Over time your appetite will start to falter; you'll no longer crave the food you once loved. Over time your strength will fail; you'll lack the energy and vitality you once had.

Peter could minister the gospel of grace to others because he had experienced it. When Jesus restored Peter, Peter gained firsthand knowledge of the mercy of Christ. You can't effectively teach people about God's mercy unless you've experienced it yourself. Ministry that flows from a need to compensate for guilt is destructive. If we try to help others to earn or keep God's favor, we will do far more harm than good. Effective ministry is from one imperfect, broken sinner to another imperfect, broken sinner. As recipients of God's mercy, we remind one another of the grace found in Jesus Christ, we walk arm in arm to Jesus for healing, and we feast together on the good food of the Word of God.

Our Commitment Will Not Be to Our Own Comfort but to the Cross of Christ

Where did Jesus go? He went to the cross. It should come as no surprise to us that following a crucified Savior may mean there is a cross for us. That's what Jesus was telling Peter (vv. 18-19). A time was coming when he would be bound, taken against his wishes, and killed. We need to be prepared to suffer for the sake of the gospel. Not all of us will suffer in the same way, but if we are faithful to follow Christ, there will be suffering of some type. The only way we can prepare for suffering is by learning to view it from God's perspective. That's tough: we've all heard false perspectives on suffering that cloud our ability to see suffering through God's eyes. This passage clears up our vision by debunking three common myths about suffering.

Myth 1: For a Mature Believer, Suffering Is Easy

As an old man Peter would be carried where he didn't want to go (v. 18). Writing to suffering Christians, Peter cautioned them not to be surprised at their "fiery ordeal" (1 Pet 4:12). If suffering were easy or light, would Peter have described it with those words? Only pseudo-spirituality pretends suffering is easy. The gospel doesn't minimize suffering; it helps us see its ultimate purpose and gives us strength to endure.

Myth 2: The Amount We Suffer Is Based on Our Behavior

When Peter heard about his own suffering, his first response was, "What about [John]?" (v. 21). That's what we often do when suffering comes. We look at those who don't appear to be suffering and ask, "What about them?" We do that because we look at suffering through the lens of legalism: "Because of my sin, I have to suffer some, but I shouldn't have to go through more than that guy. Look at his sin." We often act as if we only receive the suffering we deserve and that we really don't deserve for it to last long. "So take it away, Lord, and give it to someone else." We say suffering isn't fair, but when we think clearly, we don't want fair. Fair is eternal suffering in hell. God may have you suffer greatly but give little suffering to a brother or sister. The difference doesn't depend on you; it depends of God's gracious, sovereign plan.

Myth 3: God Isn't in Control of Suffering

Of all the myths about suffering, this one is most prevalent and most dangerous. The logic goes like this: suffering is the result of sin. God doesn't sin. Therefore, suffering is outside of God's control. That logic will not hold up under the scrutiny of Scripture. Even here it fails. What would happen to John was determined by what Jesus's will for John was (v. 22). So that means what would happen to Peter—suffering and death—was determined by Jesus's will for Peter. God has a purpose for your suffering. Your suffering is not meaningless. It is not random. It is God's will for you. We may not understand the full scope of his purposes in sending suffering, but we should never doubt that he does have a purpose. Listen to an older and wiser Peter as he instructs the sheep:

> *Dear friends, don't be surprised when the fiery ordeal comes among you to test you as if something unusual were happening to you. Instead, rejoice as you share in the sufferings of Christ, so that you may also rejoice with great joy when his glory is revealed. . . .*
> *So then, let those who suffer according to God's will entrust themselves to a faithful Creator while doing what is good.* (1 Pet 4:12-13,19)

Peter did entrust his soul to a faithful Creator. History records that Jesus's prophecy came true, and Peter was martyred for his faith when he was an old man. That means that for more than thirty years he faithfully followed Christ, aware that he was going to die the painful death of a martyr. In his example we see someone whose commitment was not to his own comfort but to the cross of Christ.

Conclusion

The Christian life is in one sense difficult, but in another sense it is simple. It is difficult because we are sinners who live in a cursed world, but it is simple because Jesus boils down the Christian life to two words: "Follow me." That's it—follow Christ. Sometimes he will lead us to the mountaintop and sometimes through the valley. Will we follow him?

At my house we've been reading John Bunyan's classic allegory on the Christian life, *Pilgrim's Progress*, together as a family. The story is about Christian, who leaves the City of Destruction to journey to the Celestial City. As he journeys, he faces many difficult situations: the Slough of Despond, the Valley of Humiliation, the Giant Despair, Doubting Castle.

He suffers at the hands of the wicked prince's servants and watches his traveling companion, Faithful, get killed by the mob in Vanity Fair. Each character and situation brings to life truths from Scripture. But the greatest thing about *Pilgrim's Progress* is its simplicity. Each morning as we read the next chapter around the breakfast table, I'm reminded the question I will face that day is, Will I follow Christ? Will I stay on the King's path that leads to the Celestial City? Some days I will be tempted to turn back to the City of Destruction. Some days I'll be sidetracked at Doubting Castle. There may also be some day when I'll be attacked by the citizens of Vanity Fair. But, like Christian, I need to continue to travel the King's path where my confidence is in Christ's sovereignty, not my strength. My comfort is in his mercy, not my morality. My concern is for fellow pilgrims, not my own plans. And by his grace, my commitment is to his cross, not my comfort.

Reflect and Discuss

1. Why is the story of the disciples fishing good news for tired Christians?
2. Describe a time in your life when you felt like everything was going wrong. How do these times reveal the object of your trust?
3. What is Jesus showing the disciples by allowing them to fail at fishing?
4. Why is it good news for Christians that our comfort is the mercy of Christ rather than our morality?
5. Do you believe Christ's mercy has covered your sins? How does your answer affect your daily life?
6. How has following Jesus changed your priorities?
7. How has experiencing the mercy of Christ prepared you for proclaiming it? What specific examples from your own life display Christ's mercy?
8. What are three common myths about suffering? Which myth are you most likely to believe?
9. Why is it good news that God is in control over suffering in your life?
10. How has the cross made it possible for Christians to endure suffering?

WORKS CITED

Aitken, Jonathan. *John Newton: From Disgrace to Amazing Grace*. Wheaton, IL: Crossway, 2007.

Alcorn, Randy. *In Light of Eternity*. Colorado Springs, CO: Water Brook, 1999.

Anderson, Leith. "Valley of Death's Shadow." *Preaching Today*. Tape No. 131.

Augustine, Aurelius. *Confessions*. Translated by R. S. Pine-Coffin. New York, NY: Penguin Books, 1961.

Bacon, Francis. *The Essays or Counsels, Civil and Moral (1625)*. Pages 341–56 in *Francis Bacon: The Major Works*. Edited by Brian Vickers. Oxford World's Classics. Oxford: Oxford University Press, 1996.

Barclay, William. *The Gospel of John*. The New Daily Study Bible. Louisville, KY: Westminster John Knox, 2001.

Biesecker, Michael. "Tape Shows Progress of a Death." *The News and Observer*. Accessed November 21, 2008. http://www.newsobserver.com/2771/story/1300808.html.

Boice, James Montgomery. *The Gospel of John*. 4 vols. Grand Rapids, MI: Baker, 2007.

Borchert, Gerald L. *John 1–11*. NAC 25A. Nashville, TN: B&H, 1996.

Borg, M. J., and N. T. Wright. *The Meaning of Jesus: Two Visions*. San Francisco, CA: Harper, 1998.

Brooks, Thomas. "Legacies." *Puritansermons.com*. Accessed February 24, 2017. http://www.puritansermons.com/sermons/brooks1.htm.

Bunyan, John. *The Works of John Bunyan*. 3 vols. Edinburgh: Banner of Truth, 1991.

Calvin, *John*. Crossway Classic Commentaries. Wheaton, IL: Crossway, 1994.

Carson, D. A. *The Gospel According to John*. PNTC. Grand Rapids, MI: Eerdmans, 1991.

Chan, Francis. *Crazy Love: Overwhelmed by a Relentless God*. Colorado Springs, CO: David C. Cook, 2008.

Chopra, Deepak. "Dalai Lama." *Time*. May 12, 2008.

"Columbia: Pastor Martyred." *The Voice of the Martyrs.* October 12, 2009. Accessed at http://www.persecution.com/public/newsroom.aspx ?story_ID=MTky, on 10/16/09.

Davey, Steven. *The Hush of Heaven.* Raleigh, NC: Wisdom for the Heart, 2008.

———. *Nehemiah: Memoirs of An Ordinary Man.* Greenville, SC: Ambassador, 2001.

———. "Sovereignty . . . in the Nursery." Unpublished sermon.

———. *When Heaven Came Down . . .* 3 vols. Raleigh, NC: Wisdom for the Heart, 2001–2003.

Dever, Mark. *The Message of the New Testament: Promises Kept.* Wheaton, IL: Crossway, 2005.

———. *The Message of the Old Testament: Promises Made.* Wheaton, IL: Crossway, 2006.

Donovan, Richard Neill. "Jesus Loves Me." *Sermon Writer: Making Preaching More of a Joy!* Accessed November 19, 2015. http://www .lectionary.org/HymnStories/Jesus%20Loves%20Me.htm.

Edwards, Jonathan. "God Glorified in the Work of Redemption, by the Greatness of Man's Dependence upon Him, in the Whole of It (1731)." Pages 66–82 in *The Sermons of Jonathan Edwards: A Reader.* Edited by Wilson H. Kimnach, Kenneth P. Minkema, and Douglas A. Sweeney. New Haven, CT: Yale University Press, 1999.

Elson, John T. "Toward a Hidden God." *Time.* April 8, 1966.

Ferguson, Sinclair. *Grow in Grace.* Carlisle, PA: Banner of Truth, 1989.

Gibbs, Nancy. "Baby, It's You! And You, and You…" *Time.* February 21, 2001. Accessed July 14, 2017. http://www.time.com/time/world/article /0,8599,99079-2,00.html.

Grudem, Wayne. *Systematic Theology.* Grand Rapids: Zondervan, 1994.

Harvey, Dave. *When Sinners Say I Do.* Wapwallopen, PA: Shepherd Press, 2007.

Heneghan, Tom. "Christian Persecution Doubled in 2013, Reports Annual Survey by Open Doors." *Huffington Post.* January 9, 2014. Accessed July 14, 2017. http://www.huffingtonpost.com/2014 /01/09/christian-persecution_n_4568286.html.

Hughes, Kent. *John.* Preaching the Word. Wheaton, IL: Crossway, 1999.

Isaacson, Walter. *Benjamin Franklin: An American Life.* New York, NY: Simon & Schuster, 2003.

Keller, Timothy. *Counterfeit Gods: The Empty Promises of Money, Sex, and Power, and the Only Hope that Matters.* New York, NY: Dutton, 2009.

The Kingsmen Quartet. "Excuses." *Born Again.* Arden, NC: Crossroads Entertainment, 2004.

Lewis, C. S. "Is Theology Poetry?" Pages 116–41 in *The Weight of Glory*. HarperCollins revised edition. New York, NY: HarperOne, 2000.

———. *The Lion, the Witch and the Wardrobe*. New York, NY: HarperCollins, 1950.

———. *Mere Christianity*. Revised and enlarged edition. New York, NY: HarperOne, 2015.

———. *The Screwtape Letters*. New York, NY: HarperOne, 2015.

Lieber, Jill. "He Wants to Save the World." *USA Today*. February 17, 2000.

Lloyd-Jones, Sally. *The Jesus Storybook Bible: Every Story Whispers His Name*. Grand Rapids, MI: Zonderkidz, 2007.

Louw, J. P., and Eugene A. Nida. *Greek-English Lexicon of the New Testament: Based on Semantic Domains*. New York, NY: United Bible Societies. Logos.

MacArthur, John. "Foreword." Pages 7–20 in *Foundations of Grace: 1400 BC–AD 100*. Edited by Steven J. Lawson. A Long Line of Godly Men. Sanford, FL: Reformation Trust, 2006.

———. *John 1–11*. The MacArthur NT Commentary. Chicago, IL: Moody, 2006.

———. *Why One Way?* Nashville, TN: Word, 2002.

Mahaney, C. J. *Living the Cross-Centered Life: Keeping the Gospel the Main Thing*. Portland, OR: Multnomah, 2006.

———. "The Pastor's Priorities: Watch Your Life and Doctrine." Pages 117–36 in *Preaching the Cross*. Edited by Mark Dever, Ligon Duncan III, R. Albert Mohler Jr., and C. J. Mahaney. Wheaton, IL: Crossway, 2007.

Mcdougall, Christopher. "The Hidden Cost of Heroism." *Men's Health*. November 26, 2007. Accessed July 14, 2017. http://www.nbcnews.com/id/21902983/ns/health-behavior/t/hidden-cost-heroism/#.WP-obGnyvIV.

Morris, Leon. *The Gospel According to John*. NICNT. Grand Rapids, MI: Eerdmans, 1979.

Murray, John. *Redemption Accomplished and Applied*. Grand Rapids, MI: Eerdmans, 1955.

Newton, John. *The Amazing Works of John Newton*. Alachua, FL: Bridge-Logos, 2009.

Ostling, Richard N. "Who Was Jesus?" *Time*. August 15, 1988. Accessed July 14, 2017. http://www.time.com/time/magazine/article/0,9171,968139,00.html.

Oldenburg, Ann. "The Divine Miss Winfrey?" *USA Today*. May 11, 2006. Accessed July 14, 2017. http://usatoday30.usatoday.com/life/people/2006-05-10-oprah_x.htm.

Packer, J. I. *Knowing God*. Downers Grove, IL: InterVarsity, 1973.

Piper, Don. *90 Minutes in Heaven*. Grand Rapids, MI: Revell, 2004.

Piper, John. *Desiring God: Meditations of a Christian Hedonist*. Portland, OR: Multnomah, 2003.

———. *Filling Up the Afflictions of Christ: The Cost of Bringing the Gospel to the Nations in the Lives of William Tyndale, Adoniram Judson, and John Paton*. Wheaton, IL: Crossway, 2009.

———. "Foreword." Pages 13–16 in *Pierced for Our Transgressions: Rediscovering the Glory of Penal Substitution*. Edited by Steve Jeffery, Michael Ovey, and Andrew Sach. Wheaton, IL: Crossway, 2007.

———. *God Is the Gospel*. Wheaton, IL: Crossway, 2005.

———. "I Have Authority to Lay It Down and I Have Authority to Take It Up Again." *Desiring God*. April 11, 1993. Accessed July 14, 2017. http://www.desiringgod.org/messages/i-have-authority-to-lay-it-down-and-i-have-authority-to-take-it-up-again.

———. "'I Will Not Be a Velvet-Mouthed Preacher!' The Life and Ministry of George Whitefield: Living and Preaching as though God Were Real (Because He Is)." Desiring God 2009 Conference for Pastors. February 3, 2009.

———. *The Legacy of Sovereign Joy*. Wheaton, IL: Crossway, 2000.

———. *The Pleasures of God*. Portland, OR: Multnomah, 1991.

———. *Seeing and Savouring Jesus Christ*. Wheaton, IL: Crossway, 2004.

———. "Where I Am There Will My Servant Be: A Call to Treasure Christ Together." *Desiring God*. September 3, 2006. Accessed July 14, 2017. http://www.desiringgod.org/messages/where-i-am-there-will-my-servant-be-a-call-to-treasure-christ-together.

Pink, A. W. *Exposition of the Gospel of John*. Grand Rapids, MI: Zondervan, 1975.

Pollock, John. *Amazing Grace: John Newton's Story*. San Francisco, CA: Harper & Row, 1981.

Ridderbos, Herman. *The Gospel of John: A Theological Commentary*. Grand Rapids, MI: Eerdmans, 1997.

Roos-Van Hessen, Frieda E. *Life in the Shadow of the Swastika*. Charlotte, NC: Ahavah, 2006.

Sewell, Marilyn. "The Hitchens Transcript." *Portland Monthly*. December 17, 2009. Accessed July 14, 2017. http://www.portlandmonthlymag

.com/arts-and-entertainment/category/books-and-talks/articles
/christopher-hitchens.

Sibbes, Richard. "The Bruised Reed." Accessed April 25, 2017. Accessed July 14, 2017. https://www.monergism.com/thethreshold/sdg/bruisedreed.html.

Sproul, R. C. *John*. St. Andrew's Expositional Commentary. Lake Mary, FL: Reformation Trust, 2009.

Spurgeon, Charles H. "Sermon #1795." *Metropolitan Tabernacle Pulpit*. Pasadena, TX: Pilgrim, 1974.

Stedman, Chris. "What Oprah Gets Wrong about Atheism." *CNN*. October 16, 2013. Accessed July 14, 2017. http://religion.blogs.cnn.com/2013/10/16/what-oprah-gets-wrong-about-atheism/comment-page-20.

Swanson, James L. *Manhunt: The 12-Day Chase for Lincoln's Killer*. New York, NY: HarperCollins, 2006.

Tada, Joni Eareckson. "Heaven, Our Real Home." *Preaching Today*. Tape No. 157.

Time. "The Moon Landings Were Fake." *Conspiracy Theories. Time*. Accessed May 21, 2015. http://content.time.com/time/specials/packages/article/0,28804,1860871_1860876_1860992,00.html.

Townsend, James. "C. S. Lewis' Theology: Somewhere between Ransom and Reepicheep." *Faith Alone*. Accessed January 8, 2009. http://www.faithalone.org/journal/2000i/townsend2000e.htm.

Van Biema, David, and Jeff Chu. "Does God Want You to Be Rich?" *Time*. September 18, 2006. Accessed May 8, 2017. http://content.time.com/time/magazine/article/0,9171,1533448,00.html.

Voice of the Martyrs. "Colombia: Pastor Martyred." Accessed October 16, 2009. http://www.persecution.com/public/newsroom.aspx?story_ID=MTky.

Wheatley, Phyllis. "To the University of Cambridge, in New England." Accessed April 25, 2017. http://www.mhhe.com/socscience/english/hudson/poetry/works/wheatley.html.

Wittmer, Mike. *The Last Enemy: Preparing to Win the Fight of Your Life*. Grand Rapids, MI: Discovery House, 2012.

Zaimov, Stoyan. "Over 100 Million Christians Are Being Persecuted for Their Faith in Jesus Christ, Says Christian Charity Report." *Christian Post*. July 31, 2015. Accessed July 14, 2017. http://www.christianpost.com/news/over-100-million-christians-are-being-persecuted-for-their-faith-in-jesus-christ-says-christian-charity-report-142144.

SCRIPTURE INDEX